Pierre Louÿs

Photograph of Pierre Louÿs probably taken in the 1890s, and published
in the magazine *Le Capitole* not long after Louÿs's death in 1925.

PIERRE LOUŸS
(1870–1925)

A Biography

H. P. CLIVE

1478
1978

Clarendon Press · Oxford

Oxford University Press, Walton Street, Oxford OX2 6DP

OXFORD LONDON GLASGOW NEW YORK
TORONTO MELBOURNE WELLINGTON CAPE TOWN
IBADAN NAIROBI DAR ES SALAAM LUSAKA
KUALA LUMPUR SINGAPORE JAKARTA HONG KONG TOKYO
DELHI BOMBAY CALCUTTA MADRAS KARACHI

© *Oxford University Press 1978*

British Library Cataloging in Publication Data

Clive, Harry Peter
    Pierre Louÿs (1870–1925).
    1. Louÿs, Pierre—Biography   2. Authors, French—19th century—Biography
    848'.8'09   PQ2623.08Z/   77-30282

    ISBN 0-19-815751-7

*Printed in Great Britain by
Cox & Wyman Ltd.,
London, Fakenham and Reading*

Preface

A BIOGRAPHER of Pierre Louÿs is faced with serious problems of balance, as far as the over-all presentation of the life and literary career of his subject is concerned. Fernand Gregh summed up this career in a terse statement: 'Dix ans, puis le silence pendant vingt ans, puis la mort.'[1] In other words, the span of Louÿs's productiveness was extremely brief, especially when measured against the length of the silence, or near-silence, which followed it. During the latter period, moreover, Louÿs led a life of increasing isolation, marked by ill health, material difficulties, and great personal unhappiness. It has therefore seemed appropriate to concentrate, in this biographical study, on the period extending from the year 1890, which saw Louÿs's entry into literary society and the first appearance of one of his poems in a 'serious' review, to the year 1901, in which the definitive version of his last completed novel, *Les Aventures du roi Pausole*, was issued in book form. The main part of the book is accordingly devoted to this period. It is preceded by a short section dealing with Louÿs's early years, and followed by a summary account of his activities during the remaining twenty-four years of his life.

I wish to record my gratitude to Mme A. Pierre Louÿs, Mme S. Louÿs, and Mme C. M. Louÿs for kindly authorizing me to examine and quote from letters by Pierre Louÿs preserved at the Bibliothèque Jacques Doucet in Paris; and to Mme Catherine Gide and members of the Comité Gide for similar permission with regard to the letters from André Gide to Pierre Louÿs which can be consulted in the same library in a transcription made by A. Naville. Many of the extracts I reproduce have not been published before. I should like to thank M. Jacques Naville for the kindness he showed me on several occasions, and M. François Chapon, the librarian of the Bibliothèque Doucet, for his unfailing helpfulness. I also wish to pay tribute to the generosity of Dr Robert Fleury who is ever ready to open the treasures of his splendid collection of Louÿsiana to other scholars. My indebtedness to his book *Pierre Louÿs et Gilbert de Voisins: une curieuse amitié* (Paris, 1973) will be evident from my repeated references to documents quoted therein (at the same time, my research has enabled me to modify some of the dates assigned by him to certain events, especially in Louÿs's youth).

I am grateful to the following publishers for permission to quote extensively from the works indicated: J. Corti: *Correspondance de Claude Debussy et Pierre Louÿs (1893–1904)*, ed. H. Borgeaud; Éditions Gallimard: *André Gide-Paul Valéry. Correspondance 1890–1942*, ed. R. Mallet; André Gide, *Si le grain ne meurt*; Jean Delay, *La Jeunesse d'André Gide*; Éditions Aubier Montaigne: *Pierre Louÿs. Œuvres complètes*; A. Blaizot: *Éditions originales romantiques et modernes, importants autographes de . . . Pierre Louÿs, Paul Valéry . . . provenant des collections de M. Victor Sanson. Vente du 25 juin 1937.*

I wish to thank the Canada Council for awarding me various grants which have enabled me to carry out research in France, and Carleton University for placing at my disposal certain sums of money to cover typing and photocopying charges.

Finally, I am indebted to several colleagues and friends for their assistance and advice, and particularly to Charles Hérisson and Armand Roth who read an early version of the book and to Albert Halsall who generously shared with me the task of proofreading. My wife provided invaluable help.

H.P.C

Contents

List of Abbreviations

The following abbreviations are commonly used in the course of this book:

Biblis A: Importante correspondance autographe inédite de Pierre Louÿs à son frère (1890–1915), Librairie Biblis, Paris, 1936.

Biblis B: Importante correspondance autographe inédite de Pierre Louÿs à son frère (1890–1915). Seconde et dernière partie, Librairie Biblis, Paris, 1937.

OC: P. Louÿs, *Œuvres complètes*, 13 vols., Éditions Montaigne, Paris, 1929–31.

Such other abbreviations as are used will be self-explanatory.

Prelude: 1870–1889

PIERRE-FÉLIX Louis, who was to achieve literary fame under the name 'Pierre Louÿs'—by which he will be designated throughout this book—was born at Ghent on 10 December 1870. His father, Pierre-Philippe Louis, was then fifty-eight years old.[1] He had married twice: on 10 October 1842 Jeanne-Constance-Aimée Blanchin,[2] who bore him two children, Lucie Aimée[3] and Georges;[4] and on 3 December 1855, some three years after Jeanne's death, Claire Céline Maldan[5] by whom he had two sons, Paul Raphaël Armand[6] and Pierre-Félix. Claire was twenty years younger than himself.

Pierre-Philippe Louis practised as a lawyer in Épernay. He lived with his wife and Paul in the rue Nationale in nearby Dizy-Magenta. However, the outbreak of the Franco-Prussian War caused them to leave Champagne which lay uncomfortably close to the battlefields of Alsace and Lorraine and was indeed in the direct path of the German army advancing on Paris. For a time they stayed at Sainte-Adresse, a seaside resort near Le Havre, together with Lucie and her husband Edmond Chardon. When the latter returned to his administrative post in Paris on 11 September, the others remained in Sainte-Adresse. On 26 September, by which time the capital was under siege, they fled northwards, first to Lille where they lodged at the Hôtel de la Gare, and on 29 September to Ghent, where they put up at the Hôtel du Lion d'Or.[7] On 5 October they took up more permanent residence at 22 rue Basse in the same town. It was in this house that Pierre Louÿs was born at ten o'clock on the morning of 10 December.

The Louis family returned to Dizy on 19 March 1871. Pierre was baptized there on 18 September of that year. His god-parents were his step-brother Georges Louis and his cousin Elisabeth Mougeot, the daughter of Dr. Félix Mougeot who was to become deputy for the Haute-Marne and President of the Conseil général of that department.[8]

Pierre Louÿs's family was not lacking in distinction. His paternal ancestors included Baron Louis, a Minister of Finance

under Louis XVIII, while his mother counted among her fore-
bears two well-known figures of the Napoleonic era: Raphaël
Sabatier, a consultant surgeon to the Emperor and a founder
member of the Institut de France; and General Andoche Junot,
Duc d'Abrantès, Governor of Portugal and Illyria, whose wife
Laure achieved renown in her own right as the author of celebrated *Mémoires* of the Revolution and Restoration. The Duke's
sister, Louise Junot, was Pierre's great-grandmother.

Louÿs later took great interest in his ancestry and assembled a
considerable amount of genealogical information, going back as
far as the early seventeenth century. He planned to publish this
material, but unfortunately never did.[9]

Pierre Louÿs appears to have had a singularly unhappy childhood. His mother, a person of some culture and a talented amateur
painter, died in 1879 when he was only nine. Five years later he
lost his brother Paul to whom he was deeply attached. More than
one entry in his early diary testifies to the profound and enduring
grief which their deaths caused him. Thus, reading *Les Misérables*
several years later, in 1887, he was greatly moved by Jean Valjean's farewell speech to Cosette and especially by his references
to the suffering experienced by her mother, Fantine:

Enfin, quand j'ai lu ces adieux sublimes de Jean Valjean . . . j'ai pleuré,
pleuré, pleuré comme un enfant, songeant à Paul et à bien des choses.
Je ne pleure plus jamais; je n'avais pas pleuré ainsi depuis un an peut-
être. Ayant fini le volume, je l'ai refermé et je suis remonté dans ma
chambre où j'ai sangloté dans mon édredon, la tête dans mes mains, à
genoux, heureux de pouvoir pleurer en pensant à mon pauvre frère et
à ma pauvre maman.

'Elle s'appelait Fantine. Rappelle-toi ce nom: Fantine. Mets-toi à
genoux toutes les fois que tu le prononceras. Elle a bien souffert. Et
t'a bien aimée.'

Oh! maman, maman! ma pauvre maman! Tout cela s'appliquait si
bien à elle! Elle a bien souffert. Et t'a bien aimé. Tu me l'as dit tant de
fois . . .

Pauvre frère! Il nous aimait tant! Et moi! Je l'idolâtrais . . . Mon
Dieu! faites que je meure comme lui![10]

His brother's death from tuberculosis had a particular poig-
nancy for Pierre, for he believed himself condemned to succumb
to the same disease. At the same time, he felt the loss of his

brother and his mother all the more keenly, since he received
scant affection from his father. One can only guess at the causes of
this coldness. An age gap of almost sixty years might be considered sufficient reason in itself, but there could be a different
explanation. Thirteen years separated Paul's birth from that of
Pierre. It has been suggested—notably by Claude Farrère in his
book *Mon ami Pierre Louÿs*—that Pierre-Philippe Louis was perhaps Pierre's father in name only, and that the real father may have
been none other than his step-brother Georges, who was then
twenty-three years old. All this is, of course, mere speculation.
What is clear from Pierre's diary is that he was disconcerted and
frightened by his father's harshness, and that he looked increasingly for love and guidance to Georges, whom he believed to be
endowed with moral and intellectual qualities vastly superior to
his own. The most striking early evidence of his feelings towards
his brother is to be found in a diary entry dated 23 September
1887, prompted by Georges's arrival at Dizy where Pierre was
spending his school holidays:

Dès qu'il est là, je suis tout autre. Ma gaieté, ma paresse, mes plaisanteries, tout cela s'en va pour faire place à une perpétuelle admiration.

Quand je le vois, il me semble que la suprême distinction, la suprême
intelligence, et la suprême bonté (pour moi) soient devant mes yeux . . .

Je l'aime beaucoup, mon frère. Je puis même dire que c'est la
personne que j'aime le plus au monde, en ce moment. Et pourtant . . .
je ne l'aime pas comme j'aimais Paul. Je ne l'aime pas comme on aime
son frère: je le sens trop au-dessus de moi. Je l'aime énormément, mais
comme une personne à qui l'on doit tout et dont on se sent adoré.[11]

In view of the important place Georges occupied in Pierre's
life, it may be opportune at this point to present a brief account
of his distinguished career in the French civil and diplomatic
service. Pierre's high opinion of his qualities was evidently shared
by many influential persons. After serving in the Ministry of
Justice for three years, Georges was transferred in 1880 to the
Ministry of External Affairs, in which he held various senior
appointments before being posted to Cairo in 1893 as Minister
Plenipotentiary and French Superintendent of the *Caisse de la dette
publique*, which was jointly administered by France and England.
He remained in Cairo until 1902, when he was recalled to France
to serve first as Director of the consular and commercial sections

and, from 1904 onwards, as Director of Political Affairs at the Quai d'Orsay. Finally, in 1909, he became Ambassador to Russia, a position he occupied for the following four years. His ultimate recall was due to a fundamental disagreement in policy between himself and the Prime Minister Raymond Poincaré, one of whose first acts on being elected President in 1913 was to relieve Louis of his ambassadorship. This dismissal was later portrayed as an event of disastrous consequences by certain political observers—such as F. Gouttenoire de Toury in *Poincaré a-t-il voulu la guerre? Poincaré—avec Iswolsky—contre Georges Louis*[12]— who claim that the circumspect diplomatic course steered by Louis might have prevented the outbreak of the First World War, if his efforts had not been deliberately torpedoed by his own superiors.

It was to Georges, then, that Pierre turned for counsel, encouragement, and affection. With increasing maturity he was to feel the difference in their ages less acutely and achieve a greater intimacy in his relations with his brother. Yet the sentiments he analysed so perceptively at sixteen remained essentially unchanged: at no time did he lose either his admiration or his gratitude—if anything, both gained in intensity. For him, Georges stood for ever on a pedestal which set him high above most men, and especially above himself.

Two large collections of letters addressed by Pierre Louÿs to Georges Louis were sold by the Librairie Biblis, Paris, in 1936 and 1937. The two catalogues prepared on those occasions (hereafter designated *Biblis A* and *Biblis B*) reproduce many interesting passages which reflect the significant role played by Georges in the formative phases of his brother's life. They also cast a revealing light on numerous incidents in Pierre's youth, as well as on his literary aspirations.

Our knowledge of Pierre Louÿs's early life is mainly limited to whatever information may be gleaned from the posthumously published *Journal intime* which covers the following four periods: 7–13 January 1882, 1 January–19 April 1885, 24 June 1887–16 May 1888, 14 April 1890–1 March 1891. In 1882 he enrolled as a pupil at the École alsacienne in Paris, at the junction of Montparnasse and the Latin Quarter. There he remained until the summer of 1888 when he transferred for the final *année de philosophie* to the

Lycée Janson-de-Sailly in Passy. From March 1885 onwards he shared Georges's apartment, first at 105 rue Notre-Dame-des-Champs, almost next door to the École alsacienne, and from the spring of 1888 at 49 rue Vineuse, close to the Trocadéro. Georges thus assumed responsibility for his younger brother, at least during school terms, from the time he was about fourteen years old.

Pierre's earliest ambition was to become a diplomat, a choice clearly determined by his feelings for Georges. At the same time, he developed an ever greater interest in literature during his later teens, and his excellent performance in French composition, for which he was regularly awarded the highest marks, encouraged him to think that if he were to devote his leisure hours to writing he might one day achieve some success as an author. The idea is first formulated in a diary entry dated 5 January 1888.[13] Ten years later Louÿs observed: 'Il faut noter cette date qui ouvre ma vie actuelle.'[14]

Subsequent entries testify to his growing preoccupation with literary matters. His favourite writers at this time included Musset, Gautier, Sully-Prudhomme, Flaubert, Loti, and Renan. He also particularly admired Leconte de Lisle, whose French versions of the classics were largely responsible for kindling his enthusiasm for Greek literature. Indeed, his first literary efforts were considerably influenced by the Parnassian poet, as he rue-fully acknowledged to Léon Blum in December 1889: 'jusqu'à présent je fais à satiété du faux Leconte de Lisle sans pouvoir m'ar-racher à cette influence qui m'enlève toute originalité'.[15] Among the poets of earlier centuries, he felt an especial affinity with Ronsard and Chénier. But the achievements of all these writers paled, in Louÿs's view, before the titanic genius of Victor Hugo, 'le plus grand écrivain de tous les temps et de tous les pays'.[16] His purchase in June 1887 of the complete edition of *La Légende des siècles* proved a highly significant event in his life; thirty years later he still remembered the impact made by that first reading: 'Mon "besoin féroce" d'écrire—et ma vocation—datent de là.'[17] His personal Trinity, he proclaimed in January 1888, was composed of 'Le Père, le Fils et Victor Hugo'.[18] The diary is full of such eulogistic references to Hugo, nor did Louÿs ever abjure his cult for this particular idol. Thus, when invited by a magazine in 1901 to name his favourite poet, he replied firmly: 'Aujourd'hui 14

décembre 1901, à 9 heures du soir, après avoir lu très attentive-
ment votre questionnaire, je vote sans la moindre hésitation pour
Victor Hugo.'[19] And in 1917 one of his first questions to the
young Cardinne-Petit whom he was interviewing for the post of
private secretary was 'Aimez-vous Victor Hugo?'[20]

It was during his final year at the École alsacienne (1887–8) that
Pierre Louÿs formed a friendship with André Gide which, notwithstanding frequent bitter quarrels, was to last seven years.
Gide, who had been forced to withdraw from the school in 1878
because of his 'mauvaises mœurs', returned there for the year
1883–4, during which he was placed in the same form as Louÿs.
The following summer he was once more removed from the
school, this time for a period of three years. The two boys had
thus already met prior to the *année de rhétorique*, but it was only
now that their relations became more intimate. Gide has given a
detailed account of their first contacts in *Si le grain ne meurt*, the
memoirs of his early life. Attracted by Louÿs's intellectual
brilliance, he longed to strike up a closer acquaintance, but was
restrained by shyness. The initial approach was eventually made
by Louÿs, after Gide had one day ousted him from his customary
position as the star pupil in French composition—an incident that
could well have aroused Louÿs's hostility, but which instead,
characteristically, awakened his curiosity and made him eager to
get to know his rival. This first conversation, which must have
taken place in February or March 1888, was succeeded by almost
daily meetings after school. The earliest extended reference to his
new friend in Louÿs's diary, on 6 May, is not devoid of a certain
unwitting irony: 'c'est le seul de la classe qui ait des goûts littéraires, le seul qui s'enthousiasme comme moi, le seul à qui on
puisse parler d'autre chose que des p'tites femmes . . .'[21] In addition to discussing their literary preferences, they explored fresh
territory together, struggling, dictionary in hand, through Keats's
Hyperion, or reading *Faust*, which so moved Louÿs that he paid its
author the highest and sincerest tribute at his command: 'Ce
Gœthe est admirable, unique, hugolesque!'[22]

The frequency of their meetings in no way diminished when,
having passed the first part of the *baccalauréat*, both left the École
alsacienne in the summer of 1888, Gide for the Lycée Henri IV,
Louÿs for the Lycée Janson-de-Sailly. In fact, their friendship

assumed an even greater intimacy during the following year, especially after the death of Louÿs's father on 14 April 1889. 'Nous voilà orphelins tous les deux . . .', Louÿs wrote to Gide. 'Je n'ai plus personne de ceux qui m'ont connu enfant: je sens combien tu me plains. Aime-moi plus encore: il ne me reste que mon frère et toi.'[23]

At the same time, if Gide remained his closest friend, Louÿs found among his new fellow students three particularly congenial companions: the intellectually brilliant Marcel Drouin, Gide's future brother-in-law; Maurice Étienne Legrand who, under the name 'Franc-Nohain', later became a popular poet and dramatist, much acclaimed for his wit and versatility; and Maurice Quillot who was likewise to try his hand at writing—his best-known book, *La Fille de l'homme*, appeared in 1914, with a preface by Louÿs—before abandoning all thoughts of a full-time literary career in order to devote himself to managing his family's dairy business in Burgundy. Together with them and Gide, Louÿs founded in 1889 a fortnightly magazine disarmingly entitled *Potache-revue*. It was printed at Nevers whence Legrand hailed, and edited by 'Arsène Reynaud' who was none other than Quillot. The other collaborators also wrote under assumed names: Drouin as 'Stello', Legrand as 'Claudius Ocella', Gide as 'Zan-bal-Dar', Louÿs himself as 'Fernand Tellore'. The initial number featured a 'Présentation au lecteur' in which Louÿs, proclaiming that the magazine constituted 'le journal des jeunes', declared war on Parnassian aesthetics and condemned especially theoreticians such as Théodore de Banville and Grammont who sought to impose rules and restrictions on poetry: 'Mort aux Parnassiens', / Le vers, libre! Notre *Potache* / A pris sa hache / Et plus de roi!' In addition to this somewhat bombastic manifesto, Louÿs contributed pastiches of Sully-Prudhomme and Verlaine to *Potache-revue*. The magazine proved a short-lived venture, running to only three issues (dated 3 February, 15 February, and 3 March 1889).

Another equally naïve but touching proof of Louÿs's literary aspirations is furnished by a poem he addressed to Gide in July 1889, after passing the second part of the *baccalauréat*:

Hier soir j'ai fini ma dernière journée
De Lycée, et ma vie est désormais tournée
Vers le but invisible où nous marchons tous deux,
Vers l'énigme en travail sous les horizons bleus,

D'où l'on verra sortir l'aurore surgissante . . .
Bien que je la désire et que je la pressente,
Combien elle est douteuse encor! Pour moi du moins.
Serons-nous les acteurs? Serons-nous les témoins
De cette éblouissante et pompeuse féerie?
Serons-nous les premiers? Clorons-nous la série?
Et verra-t-on sortir les grands rayons tremblants
De nos jeunes cheveux ou de nos cheveux blancs?
Ou du front d'un autre homme?
                                    O Gide quand j'y pense
J'ai parfois des moments de sombre défaillance.
'A quoi bon?' et je prends ma tête dans mes mains
Tant nos rêves géants me semblent surhumains.
Mais ce n'est qu'un éclair, crois-moi. Je veux te suivre
Ou marcher avec toi, ou devant toi, mais vivre
Des longs enchantements de ceux qui font des vers.
J'irai vers le bonheur, vers les frissons et vers
La gloire . . . Et si parfois l'un de nous cède et tremble
Nous nous consolerons en travaillant ensemble
Sans envier personne et sans demander rien
Car la vie est à nous et nous nous aimons bien.[24]

Further evidence of Louÿs's affection for Gide is provided by the
letters he wrote that summer during a journey which took him
first to Chaumont, in the Haute-Marne, where he stayed with Dr.
Félix Mougeot, and later to Switzerland and Italy in Georges's
company. Characteristic of his feelings is his reply to a note
received from Gide after a lengthy period of silence, during which
he had been unable to communicate with him for lack of an
address:

Je rageais de ne pouvoir écrire, de ne pouvoir penser avec toi . . .
mais si tu m'avais vu ce matin trembler des mains quand j'ai reconnu
ton écriture, tu comprendrais pourquoi je n'ai plus le courage de te
gronder . . . Si j'ai été si fâché, vois-tu, c'est parce que je ne t'ai jamais
tant désiré que depuis le commencement du mois [August 1889].
J'avais toujours à te parler, toujours des confessions prêtes à partir,
des épanchements prêts à couler et des enthousiasmes auxquels il ne
manquait que d'être éprouvés à deux. Je suis si heureux de causer avec
toi, maintenant![25]

In the same letter Louÿs discussed a subject which was much on
his mind in those days, namely the joy of literary creation:

Ecrire! écrire! Passer la nuit devant ces instruments de sacerdoce: la plume, le papier, l'encrier, la table, et se mettre en travail seul! Se féconder soi-même, loin des autres, par la seule puissance que donne le beau à ceux qui en sont fous; réaliser l'idéal; exprimer l'inexprimable; lutter avec ce qu'on sent; écraser la pensée sous le mot et la montrer vaincue, vivante, dévoilée, pure de tout nuage, figée éternellement, c'est là qu'est tout, Gide! C'est le but de la vie, c'est le devoir pour ceux qui peuvent, c'est le bonheur, la félicité pour la vie entière, et la joie énorme pour quelques heures, aux heures d'accouchement.

In Louÿs's eyes no other experience offered such exquisite rewards. The die was cast: he would be a writer. Although he enrolled at the Sorbonne that autumn, his heart was never in his studies. He applied himself only intermittently to them, and then mainly in obedience to his brother's admonitions. His time and energy were increasingly occupied by literary projects, when they were not simply devoted to the task of making his life as agreeable as possible.

Louÿs's lack of enthusiasm for his studies may well have been influenced by Gide's reluctance to pursue a formal education, once he had obtained his *baccalauréat* in October 1889. With his mother's approval, further instruction was confined to private twice-weekly lessons in French composition. One day that autumn the two friends climbed to the sixth floor of a house in the rue Monsieur le Prince, in the Latin Quarter, in search of a room suitable for meetings of the *cénacle* they proposed to establish. The window overlooked the roofs of the École de médicine, behind which they could see the Seine and the spires of Notre-Dame and, in the far distance, Montmartre. Contemplating the city spread out before their eyes, they echoed Rastignac's famous challenge to Paris: 'Et maintenant. . . . à nous deux!' Unlike Balzac's hero, however, it was not for social or financial success that they longed, but for artistic fulfilment: 'Et nous rêvons tous deux la vie d'étudiant pauvre dans une telle chambre, avec la seule fortune qui assure le travail libre ... Et s'enfermer là, avec le rêve de son œuvre, et n'en sortir qu'avec elle achevée.'[26]

Already Louÿs's aesthetic ideas were clearly formulated. 'La mort peut disperser les univers tremblants, mais la Beauté flamboie et tout renaît en elle', Leconte de Lisle wrote in 'Hypathie', one of his *Poèmes antiques*. For Pierre Louÿs, Beauty constituted the supreme artistic ideal, one infinitely more significant than

Morality or Truth. This Beauty, he maintained, revealed itself essentially through form, which must accordingly take precedence at all times over intellectual content. 'La pensée cherche le vrai; oh! que c'est peu intéressant!' he wrote to Gide while the latter was working on *Les Cahiers d'André Walter*. 'La forme s'illumine du beau, que veux-tu de plus? Que rêves-tu de mieux?'[27] Unlike Louÿs, Gide was, from the outset, primarily concerned with the exposition of ideas. For that purpose he deliberately chose an extremely sober language, devoid of stylistic embellishments, in the belief that 'l'ornement n'a raison d'être que pour cacher quelque défaut et ... seule la pensée non suffisamment belle doit craindre la parfaite nudité.'[28] Louÿs deplored the 'anti-literary' nature of such an attitude and vainly sought to divert his friend from the course he was pursuing.

Since he regarded music as the perfect vehicle for artistic expression, Louÿs attached the greatest importance to musical quality in verse and consequently rejected elaborately ordered rhyming schemes in favour of rhythm: 'Je veux faire de la poésie essentiellement musicale, c'est-à-dire du *Rythme*, et non de la Rime,' he affirmed in December 1889.[29] The aim should be rhythmic perfection, not simply within the over-all structure of a particular stanza, but in each individual line. The ideal poem would thus consist of a series of *vers libres*—blank verse, akin to a poetic prose. This conception of poetry led Louÿs to view the composition of verse as very useful training for the kind of prose he aspired to write eventually, 'la prose idéale, rythmée comme la poésie, la prose que Flaubert avait prédite, "où l'on entendrait les vibrations des violoncelles"'.[30] Accordingly, he wrote nothing but poetry for several years, until he believed himself qualified to tackle prose.

Louÿs's objections to the Parnassians' preoccupation with rhyme in no way implied a rejection of other prominent features of their poetry. Indeed, his own early verse displayed several of these, notably the element of impersonality which characterizes so much of their work. It need hardly be added that he warmly approved of the emphasis they placed on formal beauty. Gide had no doubt about the true nature of his friend's artistic affinities. In 1892 he wrote to his mother: 'Tu commets la plus fâcheuse erreur quand, lisant les vers de Louÿs, tu parles à son sujet d'école moderne—Louÿs est aussi peu moderne que possible (j'exagère un peu), pas symboliste du tout, mais encore de l'école précédente du Parnasse: de Gautier, Banville, Hugo, Heredia . . .'[31] Louÿs was, in fact, known among his friends as 'le Parnassien'; Gide, on the other hand, was called 'le Symboliste'.[32]

The Young Pierre Louÿs

THE FOLLOWING passages, chosen mainly from later recollections by Louÿs's friends, but including also several contemporary documents, give some indications of his appearance and personality in his early twenties. They may serve as an introduction to the detailed account of the years from 1890 to 1901 which constitute the most productive period of his literary career.

Son aspect extérieur n'était pas moins séduisant que la nature de son esprit. Un beau visage un peu pâle, à la fine moustache naissante, deux grands yeux charmés, chargés d'une douce ironie tempérée de sérénité, une régularité de traits encadrés par la courbe double de sa chevelure en bandeaux, vers les oreilles; des lèvres admirablement dessinées, point trop larges, glissant mollement aux commissures; un nez très net, aux narines un peu sensuelles; un menton de volontaire. Ce beau visage d'éphèbe pensif, à peine mélancolique ou parfois illuminé d'un éclat de gaieté juvénile, surmontait un corps de grandeur moyenne, flexible, onduleux, pur, aux membres bien proportionnés, avec des mains longues et délicates, fort soignées . . .

La simplicité des ses vêtements, beaucoup plus soignés qu'il ne nous était en général habituel, était d'un goût toujours parfait. Même dans quelques circonstances où elle ne manqua point d'apparaître recherchée, elle était encore si bien calculée et si conforme à ce qui le plus harmonieusement convenait à son apparence, qu'on ne lui eût pu reprocher rien de théâtral ni de déplaisant.

A une époque où les vernissages des Salons de Peinture constituaient un événement mondain capital, il apparut une fois, pantalon gris, redingote de coupe désuète, cravate de soie noire nouée d'un triple tour, gants clairs, badine à la main, et chapeau de très haute forme, non point l'image ressurgie d'un dandy de 1835, mais comme s'il eût été Alfred de Musset lui-même, et, tout naturellement, le *lion* de la saison. Pourtant il ne jouait pas un rôle, il n'affectait point une attitude; il était si bien lui qu'on n'aurait pas cru possible qu'il fût autrement. On le vit, on l'admira; et cependant, selon le vœu ou la prescription de Brummel, il était si suprêmement élégant qu'on aurait fort bien pu ne pas le distinguer, ne pas s'en apercevoir.

André Fontainas, 'Pierre Louÿs—un peu de sa figure', *Mercure de Flandre*, March 1928

Louÿs ne reculait d'ailleurs devant aucun des inconvénients du dandysme, et je le trouvai, un jour de vernissage du Salon, presque gêné, tant la foule faisait haie sur son passage, revêtu qu'il était d'une redingote de coupe merveilleuse, et la nuque cerclée dans un collet si haut qu'on l'aurait pris pour un proconsul de la Convention ; sans doute pour se soustraire au murmure d'admiration qui le suivait, il vint à moi, pauvre pardessus vulgaire, comme à un sauveur et nous déambulâmes dans le jardin des sculptures, lui alors plus à l'aise, et moi plein d'orgueil à me mouvoir près d'un astre traînant comme une comète, une queue brouhahante de populaire.

Henri Mazel, *Aux beaux temps du symbolisme, 1890–1895*, Paris, 1943, p. 129

Un jour j'y [à la Librairie de l'art indépendant] rencontrai un jeune homme aux cheveux magnifiques qui fumait un bon cigare, serré dans une longue redingote, son chapeau haut de forme sur ses genoux ; une jeune femme brune, aux beaux yeux noirs et aux fortes lèvres, appuyait les mains sur sa chaise ; elle riait de plaisir, charmante, en le regardant. Il semblait heureux en même temps que pressé de vivre ; je le reconnus pour l'avoir rencontré dans l'atelier de Jacques-Émile Blanche, qui faisait alors son portrait. C'était Pierre Louÿs.

André Lebey, *Jean de Tinan, Souvenirs et Correspondance*, Paris, 1922,. p. 8

Louÿs était d'une rare élégance de gestes, de silhouette, d'allure, mais gardait un air maladif. Il était mou, comme en guimauve ; sa main fondait dans celle qu'on lui tendait. Une sorte de génie respirait sur son front et dans ses regards, rachetant ce qu'il avait d'un peu bellâtre. Il bégayait à la moindre émotion, c'est-à-dire souvent, en ébullition pour un rien et calme seulement à ses moments perdus.

André Gide, *Journal 1939–1949. Souvenirs*, Paris, 1966, p. 136

Quel être délicieux, alors !

Prodigue, ingénieux à satisfaire les désirs de ses amis, il leur faisait de délicates surprises ; on ne savait d'où venaient certains présents que l'on trouvait en rentrant chez soi, qu'il déposait sans laisser son nom : un livre rare, des fleurs, une cravate (les hommes en portaient de somptueuses, alors), des gants ou un parfum nouveau . . .

Violent, jaloux de son indépendance, susceptible et pointilleux presque autant que Marcel Proust, mais beaucoup moins prêt que Proust à vous excuser et à se noircir lui-même . . . Il eût été aussi bien musicographe qu'entomologiste, que biologiste, il avait l'œil d'un martin-pêcheur, porta longtemps une loupe dans sa poche. Il se tenait au courant de tout . . . Vous pouviez l'interroger sur n'importe quel objet: s'il n'était pas muni pour vous la rendre sur-le-champ, vous auriez bientôt la réponse désirée. Ainsi lancé par quelqu'un ou quelque chose sur une piste à laquelle il n'avait point encore songé, ses recherches et ses musardines l'aiguillaient vers une autre . . .

L'influence de Pierre Louÿs, personne n'aurait pu s'y soustraire. Dès le matin, je songeais au moment où, avant dîner, je sonnerais à sa porte. Il vous accueillait avec sa charmante [politesse] cérémonieuse, vous contait sa dernière découverte . . .

Jacques-Émile Blanche, 'La Jeunesse de Pierre Louÿs. Gide et Louÿs à l'École alsacienne. Louÿs et Claude Debussy', *Les Nouvelles littéraires*, 13 June 1925

Je pense qu'il n'y a que vous qui puissiez être l'auteur du délicat envoi des *Fugues de Bach*, rien n'aurait pu autant toucher mon cœur de musicien—soyez donc infiniment remercié . . .

Letter from Debussy (probably October 1893) *Correspondance de Claude Debussy et Pierre Louÿs (1893–1904)*, ed. H. Borgeaud, Paris, 1945, p. 28

Il était, en ce temps-là, le plus timide, le plus impérieux, le plus délicat et le plus entêté des jeunes hommes, d'une séduction et d'une élégance que je n'ai vues qu'à lui. Il se montrait d'abord plein de réserve, et même d'un mystère quasi diplomatique, exquis dans les manières, infiniment attentif à toutes les formes et aux nuances, balbutiant d'une voix très basse et très douce les paroles gracieuses qui nous gardent et qui ne mènent à rien les indiscrets. Mais la confiance créée, paraissait le véritable Pierre. Ses grands dons, ses curiosités si nombreuses, sa culture vaste, surprenante et toujours entretenue, ses enthousiasmes parfois montés jusqu'à la violence, ses caprices foudroyants et irrésistibles, les surprises charmantes qu'il savait faire, et tous les traits d'un caractère absolu dans l'amitié, dans l'admiration, dans leurs contraires, dominé par cet attachement invariable, inconditionnel, véritablement mystique qu'il ressentait pour la perfection de notre art, se manifestaient si vivement qu'il nous semblait auprès de lui être toujours à quelque degré moins jeunes, moins ardents, moins volontaires, moins variables; et nous nous sentions à la merci de cette flamme. Tyran délicieux, soi-même esclave de ce qu'il trouvait de plus beau dans les œuvres et dans les choses, il imposait merveilleusement ses dieux et ses idoles.

Paul Valéry, 'Pierre Louÿs (1870–1925)', *Les Nouvelles littéraires*, 13 June 1925

Ce Louÿs est le charme même . . .

Entry in Jean de Tinan's diary, soon after he had made Louÿs's acquaintance (quoted by Auriant, 'Petite histoire littéraire et anecdotes', *Mercure de France*, 15 June 1939)

Si je sais ce que peut être l'Amitié, c'est à la sienne que je le dois . . .
Naturellement aimable et bienveillant, il se réservait assez longtemps,
distant et proche, ouvert et fermé à la fois; mais, quand il était certain
d'un accord total, il se donnait tant qu'il ne savait plus ce qui était à lui,
ce qui était à vous . . . Ses fournisseurs, ses relieurs. . ., ses libraires
devenaient les nôtres et, parfois, les factures en retard,—même d'édition,—étaient soldées en secret, sans qu'il prît la peine de vous avertir.

Qui ne l'a connu que dans ses dernières années ne peut se faire
une idée de sa jeunesse et de son rayonnement. Il était magnifique,
animait et recréait tout autour de lui, sans même y penser, spontané-
ment . . .

Autour de lui, sans fin, éternellement, l'encens des cigarettes. Il ne
cessait de fumer. Environ deux ou trois paquets par jour.
André Lebey, *Disques et pellicules*, Paris, 1929, pp. 211, 214–16

Je vois assez fréquemment votre ami Louÿs qui m'a parlé de vous ces
temps-ci. Je l'aime vraiment beaucoup. Il a une sorte de fougue nerveuse qui se retient et qui plaît.
Henri de Régnier, *Lettres à André Gide (1891–1911)*, ed. D. J. Niederauer, Geneva, 1972, p. 25 (extract from letter dated June 1891)

Il [Louÿs] s'est conduit avec moi de façon à me faire rougir de gé-
nérosité.
André Gide–Paul Valéry. Correspondance 1890–1942, ed. R. Mallet,
Paris, 1955, p. 209 (letter from Valéry to Gide dated 14 July 1894)

Qui n'a pas connu Pierre Louÿs lors de sa vingtième année, n'a pas
contemplé dans leur rayonnement, la fière noblesse du corps et l'ardeur,
jamais contentée, de l'intelligence. La liberté enivrée de ses propos, sa
merveilleuse culture si profondément assimilée que, citant des pages et
des poèmes ignorés, il oubliait parfois le nom de leurs auteurs, je ne
sais quoi de très rare et très simple, de très affable ou de très distant,
selon les minutes ou les personnes, l'élégance involontaire du geste et,
jusque dans la rêverie, une politesse toujours présente, tout en lui se
dépêchait, dès l'abord, de conquérir les esprits et les cœurs; tout en lui
était offrande et lumière.
Robert de Flers, 'Aphrodite est en deuil: Pierre Louÿs est mort hier',
Le Figaro, 5 June 1925

Years of Promise: 1890–1895

1890

AT THE beginning of this year, Louÿs's relations with Gide were still very close. 'Tous les succès que je te souhaite ce sera du bonheur pour moi', he assured his friend in a New Year's message.[1] Later that same month he accompanied Gide to the funeral of one of his aunts. 'Sa pensée est douce, que je comprends, de vouloir notre amitié sereine et forte dans les tristesses', Gide wrote in his diary.[2]

The two friends also made a joint literary pilgrimage on 8 January to the Hôpital Broussais to see Paul Verlaine. The purpose of the visit, undertaken at Louÿs's suggestion, was to seek advice concerning the literary magazine they proposed to found. Notwithstanding the shabby and dismal surroundings in which the interview took place, they were overawed by the presence of the celebrated poet. Verlaine talked to them about Mallarmé and Rimbaud, informed them of the completion of *Bonheur* ('C'est un bonheur qui ne paraîtra pas heureux'), and discussed prosody ('Il y a là comme un travail de menuiserie, de charcuterie plutôt. Il faut arrondir le vers comme un boudin'). Louÿs published an interesting account of the visit, under the title 'Paroles de Verlaine', in the review *Vers et prose* in September 1910. Some months after their first conversation he met Verlaine once more, under still more pathetic circumstances. Wandering along the rue Montmartre one afternoon, he caught sight of the poet who was half-drunk. He was also penniless. Louÿs, his respect for Verlaine in no way diminished by the latter's pitiable appearance, arranged to take him to a photographer the following day.[3] It is not known whether Verlaine kept the appointment.

The preparations for the launching of the review, to be called *Journal des inconnus*, progressed as far as the drawing-up of 'Statutes' by the prospective editorial board which, in addition to Louÿs and Gide, was to include Léon Blum, Marcel Drouin, and Gide's friend and distant relative André Walckenaer. According to these Statutes, the purpose of the review was to have been 'de préciser les tendances de la nouvelle école et de créer un lien entre les jeunes'. It was to present poems and stories, as well as criticism, and to accept contributions only from persons under twenty-five years of age.[4] The project was eventually abandoned.

Despite the divergent views they held regarding the function of literature, Louÿs and Gide felt genuine admiration for each other's talents. Gide recognized the merit of Louÿs's poems, while Louÿs had an especially high regard for Gide's prose style. 'De tous nos camarades ... c'est celui qui a le plus d'avenir et de beaucoup', he wrote to Jean Naville in February 1890. 'Si j'ai jamais connu un type épatant c'est bien lui. Je t'assure que je voudrais bien avoir un jour la prose qu'il a aujourd'hui.'[5] Yet it was during this period that their relations first showed signs of serious strain. That this initial estrangement should have coincided with the composition of the *Cahiers d'André Walter* is, of course, far from accidental; nor should it cause any surprise that it was Gide who first overtly expressed irritation. From the outset Louÿs had assumed the dominant role in their friendship. Endowed with a vast curiosity and, in particular, with a passionate interest in literature, music, and fine art, Louÿs lived almost permanently in a state of feverish intellectual excitement. He was himself amused by his propensity to 'catch fire': 'Décidément, je m'emballe trop', he admitted in a diary entry in 1888, adding, however: 'Mais c'est bien bon tout de même, ces enthousiasmes-là!'[6] His eagerness to share his excitement with his friends made him appear domineering at times, so anxious was he to elicit from them a response as deeply felt as his own. Thus the imperiousness he displayed on such occasions reflected probably more his seemingly inexhaustible capacity for being intellectually stimulated than a strong desire to impose his tastes on others. As a rule, the evident pleasure his aesthetic experiences and 'discoveries' gave him in such full measure readily communicated itself to his intimates who, captivated by his personality, were quite willing to accept his ascendancy over them. Gide, whose feelings were initially close to hero-worship, was no exception. Yet gradually he began to react against Louÿs's domination. His efforts to attain intellectual independence became more determined and deliberate as he grew preoccupied with his first literary ventures.

The year 1890 was thus of critical importance in their relations, for Gide's attempts to shake himself free from Louÿs's influence led him to adopt an uncompromising attitude which made any meaningful and mutually profitable exchange of ideas increasingly more difficult. Louÿs was forced to the conclusion that Gide not only did not understand him, but did not wish to understand him. It was unfortunate in the circumstances that Louÿs continued to offer gratuitous and occasionally tactless advice, and, moreover, that he did so at times in dogmatic accents which must have driven Gide even further into his shell of self-protective intransigence. Louÿs evidently failed for a long time to perceive the true reason for Gide's changed manner, and when he was openly accused by Gide of being overbearing, he dismissed the reproach as comically exaggerated. A notable instance of his no doubt well-intentioned but blatantly insensitive behaviour during this crucial period in their relations can be found in his letter of 27 March 1890 which, in Jean Delay's view, 'marque une date et peut-être un tournant dans l'histoire de leur amitié'.[7] In this letter quoted in *Les Débuts d 'André Gide vus par Pierre Louÿs* by Paul Iseler, Louÿs enjoins Gide to read Paul Bourget's novel *Cruelle énigme* in which he has detected parallels with Gide's own subject, and cautions him against providing his readers with grounds for charges of imitation; expresses exceptionally warm feelings for Gide's book, while making it clear that these are prompted by his personal affection for the author rather than by any objective admiration for a work so essentially 'anti-literary' in character; announces his desire to contribute a brief passage—'oh! presque rien, une demi-page'—to the book, 'comme les petites filles qui fourrent des fleurs coupées dans les bras de leur Vierge, à l'église, pour l'aimer plus quand elle sera un peu faite par elles'; and, finally, declares his great pleasure at having re-established a certain intimacy with Gide during their conversation the previous evening ('Je me suis revu ou plutôt je t'ai revu comme l'année dernière et je suis redevenu calme').[8] How is one to account for this juxtaposition of affectionate remarks and of statements likely to trouble and vex his correspondent? Was Louÿs simply guilty of insensitiveness or was he motivated by malice? Delay plumps for the latter explanation, whereas Iseler cites the letter among those which furnish proof of friendship. Iseler's interpretation appears closer to the truth, especially in the light of a significant passage in another letter dating from the same period:

Adieu, mon bon, mon cher, mon excellent, . . . sache voir sous tous mes reproches, un cri de sympathie, qui ne peut pas toujours se manifester par des louanges parce que les louanges ont toujours un air peu sincère,—et qui se fait jour comme il peut.

Rappelle-toi qu'Alceste n'est jamais si amoureux que le jour où il injurie Célimène.[9]

Gide left Paris in May in search of the solitude he considered essential for his writing. At first he chose Lac Pierrefonds, near Compiègne, as his retreat, but when Louÿs paid him an un-announced visit on his second day there he realized that he would not find the desired tranquillity so close to the capital. He there-upon stayed for several weeks in Dauphiné, before spending July and August as usual on the family estate at La Roque in Nor-mandy. In his eagerness to devote all his time to the *Cahiers d'André Walter* he refused an invitation from his uncle Charles Gide to attend the sexcentenary celebrations of the founding of the University of Montpellier in late May, an event which attracted delegates from many countries.

Louÿs attended as a member of the Sorbonne contingent. He welcomed the journey, for it fitted in well with his plans. In April, at the wedding of his sister Lucie's son Jacques Chardon, he had made the acquaintance of a young cousin by marriage, Marie Chardon, with whom he had fallen head over heels in love: 'Depuis trois ans, depuis trois ans j'appelle celle qui doit venir! . . . Elle est venue', he wrote exultantly in his diary on 2 May,[10] and several other ecstatic entries testify to the emo-tional impact made on him by their first meeting. The trip to Montpellier offered an opportunity to visit Marie at Cholet, the small town thirty miles south-west of Angers where she lived with her parents. He also planned a short 'pilgrimage' to various places associated with Ronsard in the Vendôme, during his return journey.

His desire to see Marie again made Louÿs contemplate the ceremonies at Montpellier with some impatience. 'Je voudrais déjà être là-bas,' he wrote peevishly in his diary on 20 May, shortly before leaving Paris, 'et en avoir fini avec ces fêtes absurdes de Montpellier, qui vont m'ennuyer, je le devine, au delà de toute mesure.'[11] To ward off the anticipated boredom, he took on his journey a selection of books which, he drily noted, should not prove 'monotonous': Homer, Sophocles, Ausonius, Tibullus,

Ronsard, Baïf, Heine, Hugo, Mistral, and the Bible. He further-more added to his travelling equipment the two special nibs without which he felt himself incapable of composing a single line of poetry ('je compte en faire si l'on me fiche la paix à Montpellier'), as well as a generous supply of elegant writing-paper. The Sym-bolists had a mania for handsome paper, splendidly coloured inks and waxes, and exquisite handwriting. Louÿs delighted in such refinements. His script was generally acknowledged to be the most beautifully 'medieval' of all. Unlike Laurent Tailhade who wrote his letters in white ink on black notepaper, Louÿs favoured the combination of white paper and purple ink.

Contrary to his gloomy forebodings, Louÿs enjoyed himself enormously at Montpellier. 'Je chercherais vainement dans ma vie entière quinze jours plus complètement heureux que ceux que je viens de passer', he wrote to Gide on 4 June. He particularly welcomed the opportunities which the festivities offered for con-tacts with foreign visitors and greatly appreciated the warm comradeship which sprang up spontaneously among the students, in complete disregard of their different national background. 'Jamais, jamais tu ne te feras une idée de l'enthousiasme *anti*-patriotique des délégués les uns pour les autres, et du bonheur intense, délirant, qui nous a tous envahis pendant les fêtes de Montpellier. C'était un débordement d'amour insensé, irraisonné, une suite d'accolades, un tutoiement spontané, une fraternité irrésistible. On se recherchait, on allait les uns vers les autres non pas *malgré* les frontières, mais *à cause* des frontières mêmes.'[12] In this atmosphere of happy conviviality and general friendliness new attachments were quickly forged. Louÿs was especially attracted to two students from Geneva, Bérard and Barbier; to another from Lausanne, named Berdez; and to 'un petit Montpelliérain qui m'a parlé de la *Tentation* [i.e. *La Tentation de Saint Antoine* by Flaubert] et de Huysmans, de Verlaine et de Mallarmé en des termes . . . tu sais, celui-là je te le recommande'. The name of the young man thus recommended was Paul Valéry.

The official ceremonies began on 23 May with the reception by the Mayor and the Rector of the distinguished delegates sent by numerous European universities as well as by academic institu-tions from as far away as North and South America. The festivities reached their climax on Saturday, 24 May, when President Sadi Carnot honoured them with his presence, and they terminated upon his departure early the following morning. Sunday and Monday belonged to the several hundred student delegates from France and abroad. They met on the Sunday to convey greetings from their various associations to their colleagues at Montpellier and, on the same day, presented a historical pageant in the streets of the town, in which pride of place was naturally accorded to the University's most famous alumnus, François Rabelais. The highlight of the final day, 26 May, was formed by a banquet held at the Mediterranean resort of Palavas. Many years later Paul Valéry recalled the circumstances in which he had made Louÿs's acquaintance on that occasion:

Tout s'achevait par un banquet à Palavas. Sur le bord de la mer, avant l'heure de ce festin suprême, je me vois au milieu d'un groupe d'étudiants de Lausanne. C'étaient de charmants compagnons. Une autre compagnie de jeunes Suisses survint, qui nous entraîna vers la terrasse d'un café. Quelqu'un qui n'était ni blond ni Suisse s'assit auprès de moi. Le destin avait pris les traits de ce voisin délicieux. Nous échangeâmes quelques mots. Il venait de Paris. Les noms de Hugo, de Baudelaire, de Verlaine, de Wagner, ayant passé dans la conversation, nous nous sommes levés et nous prenant par le bras, marchant comme dans un monde lyrique, nous composâmes à grands pas une intimité instantanée. Pendant cinq minutes nous nous sommes communiqué nos idées essentielles du moment, avec un feu et une sympathie qui ne laissaient pas d'étonner nos camarades suisses. Ce jeune homme me donna sa carte: '*Pierre Louis*' . . . puis nous nous perdîmes dans la foule . . .[13]

On parting from his new friends, Louÿs promised to send Bérard a volume of Ronsard, Berdez a copy of Barrès's *Un Homme libre*, and Valéry the collection of his own poems which he hoped to publish shortly. 'Gradation descendante', he ironically commented to Gide; nevertheless, he added, 'de tous les trois c'est encore Valéry qui m'intéresse le plus'.[14] And it was with Valéry that he immediately commenced an intensive correspondence about literature. Thus began a friendship which was to continue until his death.

His relations with Gide deteriorated rapidly during the following weeks. Jealous of the contacts Louÿs had made at Montpellier, Gide accused him of unfaithfulness. Louÿs had evidently anticipated Gide's reaction, for in his letter of 4 June he had been at pains to reassure him: 'lorsque je valéryse et que je m'emberdèze, je ne dégide pas, au contraire.' By the end of June, Gide's suspicions extended to Louÿs's activities in Paris. This time he received a more teasingly ambiguous reply: 'Pourquoi doutez-vous, homme de peu de foi? Pourquoi ces craintes, ces jalousies? Est-ce que tu vas me faire des scènes? Tu deviens honteusement immoral, mon Alain. Oui, j'ai un amant, monsieur mon mari. J'en ai même plusieurs qui me consolent en ton absence. Et je trouve d'une exquise naïveté que tu me demandes leurs adresses.'[15] The banter conveys, nevertheless, an impression of genuine affection and the general tone of the letter is conciliatory. When, however, Gide self-righteously contrasted his own ascetic existence, entirely devoted to the pursuit of literary perfection, with what he castigated as Louÿs's life of pleasure and debauchery, and went on to draw conclusions, highly flattering to himself, regarding the excellence of their respective moral and literary ideals, Louÿs struck back angrily:

Quant à être différents, nos rêves, parbleu c'est bien certain. Mais inférieurs l'un à l'autre, c'est enfantin que de le soutenir—toi tu veux sentir, sentir n'importe quoi. Moi je veux exprimer, exprimer la seule beauté. Nomme ton rêve comme tu le voudras, le mien est purement littéraire. Il n'est pas ascétique *volontairement* . . . je trouve l'ascétisme stérile; mais il sera peut-être austère par sa nature même et sans nul orgueil ni vanité de moine . . . Si je te disais de mon côté que ce rêve est le plus élevé des deux, qu'il a un but vraiment grand—ne s'occu-pant que de l'âme, tandis que le tien est petit et borné, souillant sa force à contraindre le corps—j'aurais peut-être raison, et cependant tu hausserais les épaules, te sentant grand malgré tout. Mais sois donc aussi impartial que moi, et veuille donc me comprendre! Je me donne bien la peine de t'interpréter, tu pourrais me le rendre, il me semble![16]

The passage shows that Louÿs was adopting a less dogmatic attitude than Gide, and it explains why he should have laughed away incredulously Gide's protestations that he was 'like wax' in Louÿs's hands and forced to counter-attack in order to protect his own integrity. In reality, Louÿs pointed out bitterly, Gide clung unyieldingly to his ideas: '*Jamais* tu ne m'as dit par exemple: "tu crois?—ou: oui, c'est possible—ou: tu as peut-être raison, etc. . . ." Tu n'as que deux mots à mon égard: "C'est absurde" ou "c'est évident".'[17]

Thus the tensions which had gradually built up over the previous months suddenly intensified until they reached breaking-point. By mid-July Louÿs's exasperation at the impossibility of discussing any subject with Gide in an objective manner had become so acute that he proposed a temporary cessation of their correspondence. Following the exchange of a few more letters of little significance, contact between them was interrupted until September.

In the meantime Louÿs had found a more congenial correspondent in Valéry to whom he had sent a characteristically impetuous letter from Marseille, dated '29 mai 1890 minuit':

Il faut absolument que je vous écrive ce soir, mon cher ami, bien que je n'aie aucun prétexte et que je ne sache pas le moins du monde ce que je vais vous dire. Comme je ne vous connais pas le moins du monde, je ne puis vous parler de vous. Je suis donc forcé de vous parler de moi, —ou de mes goûts personnels, ce qui est la même chose. Si vous saviez comme je suis embarrassé! Je suis une machine à théories; c'est là mon caractère principal . . .[18]

There followed a lengthy exposition of Louÿs's theories on art. Valéry promptly responded with an outline of his own views. During the following months the two new friends regularly exchanged ideas and frequently sent one another their latest poems. That they derived considerable pleasure from this contact is evident from the tone of the letters as well as their frequency, for by the end of the year each had written on at least twenty-four different occasions.

To Valéry, 'un jeune homme perdu au fond de la province',[19] his new friend represented the sophisticated and cultured life of the capital 'où ni les livres, ni les Cluny, et les Louvre ne font défaut',[20] where one could converse with 'Mallarmé l'Enchanteur'[21] and meet Paul Verlaine, 'Que j'aime vos lettres!' he wrote to Louÿs on 13 July. 'Vous ne pouvez guère comprendre, heureux poète! ce que disent quelques pages pleines d'art tombées de Paris, du Paris vivant et intelligent, dans la cervelle du malheureux qui vient passer deux heures chez lui, le soir, après la journée de caserne.'[22] Valéry quickly discerned in Louÿs a kindred spirit, dedicated to the pursuit of Beauty and adopting towards art and the artist a quasi-mystical attitude closely akin to his own. On 2 June he wrote, in reply to Louÿs's first letter: 'Ainsi vous êtes aussi, vous, un réfugié dans son Rêve, un reclus dans son cerveau, un amoureux du pays divin—n'importe où hors du monde!'[23] And

on 15 June: 'vos théories me plaisent,—non qu'elles soient entière-
ment semblables aux miennes—mais parce que chez vous comme
chez moi est inébranlablement fondé le culte du Beau et le mépris
du reste!'[24] For his part, Louÿs was from the outset captivated by
Valéry's intelligence and refined taste.

Louÿs's impact on Valéry's thought was negligible: despite his
youth, the 'petit Montpelliérain' had already evolved a clear-cut
aesthetic theory of his own, and he possessed too independent a
mind to be easily swayed. On the other hand, Louÿs exercised a
significant influence on his early literary activity, as Valéry later
readily acknowledged:

L'amitié de Pierre Louÿs fut une circonstance capitale de ma vie. Un
hasard d'entre les hasards me le fit connaître, et cette vie fut toute
changée. Que de fois nous avons parlé de notre rencontre! Sa consé-
quence fut pour moi d'être presque aussitôt contraint à écrire. Mon
nouvel ami exigeait que je me fisse un devoir, et comme une pratique
vertueuse, de ce plaisir que j'avais pris quelquefois sans le pousser
jusqu'à la peine. La plupart de mes premiers vers ne furent faits que
pour être échangés contre les siens, ou bien pour nourrir la petite
revue qu'il avait fondée et qui ne s'alimentait que de poèmes.[25]

It is greatly to Louÿs's credit that he should so quickly have
recognized Valéry's talent and offered him such constant encouragement and generous praise. The first time Valéry sent him
some of his poems ('Pour la nuit', 'Élévation de la lune', 'Les
Chats blancs'), Louÿs declared: 'Une chose est certaine, c'est que
ces trois sonnets contiennent les plus beaux vers inédits que j'aie
eu encore le bonheur de lire.'[26] In another letter he wrote: 'Si
vous croyez mon cher ami que des vers comme les vôtres m'en-
gagent à vous montrer les miens! Mais je n'ai rien, moi, que des
essais, des tâtonnements, des ébauches ... Non seulement vous
avez des théories mais vous pouvez déjà les appliquer. Quel âge
avez-vous donc?'[27] Upon receiving further poems from Valéry
('Le Divin adultère', 'Viol') he affirmed: 'Dès aujourd'hui, entendez-
le bien, vous êtes sûr de votre avenir prochain, et dès que vous
viendrez à Paris vous serez reconnu comme un des dix ou douze
jeunes qui savent et qui sont de vrais poètes. Vous êtes, je le crois,
beaucoup plus mûr que moi, quoique un peu plus jeune et j'ai
confiance que vous arriverez plus vite.'[28]

On several occasions he urged Valéry to persist with the composition of 'difficult' poems. Thus, when Valéry sent him five

lines of a sonnet entitled 'Narcisse parle', adding that he had
abandoned it 'désespérant de faire entrer tout ce que je songeais
là-dedans',[29] Louÿs admonished him: 'Votre sonnet? Vous
n'avez pas le droit de le laisser inachevé. J'entrevois quelque
chose d'admirable sous vos doigts. Les cinq vers que vous me
citez sont parmi les meilleurs que je connais de vous; je veux les
autres . . .'[30] Three weeks later he reminded Valéry: 'Et le "Narcisse"? vous savez que je le *veux*.'[31] Valéry eventually published an
extended version of the projected sonnet in *La Conque*.

Louÿs also advised Valéry to which reviews he should offer his
poems—*Les Écrits pour l'art* and the *Revue indépendante*—and
which he ought to avoid (on *La Plume*: 'Vous ne savez donc pas
que c'est une collection de ratés qui a fondé cette revue imbécile,
et que c'est même la seule raison de son petit succès?'[32]). He even
tried to get some of Valéry's poems accepted by the *Revue
d'aujourd'hui* which had been the first serious magazine to print
one of his own ('L'Effloraison', on 25 July 1890), but found to his
dismay that it had folded in the meantime.[33] He furthermore
urged Valéry to bring out a volume of poetry in the autumn and
suggested possible publishers.[34] Finally, he seized every opportunity to read Valéry's pieces to poets of his acquaintance, such
as Régnier, and delightedly reported their favourable comments.

In view of the important services rendered to him by Louÿs
during this early period in his literary career, it is understandable
that Valéry should have considered their friendship 'une circonstance capitale de ma vie'. When Louÿs chided him for
submitting his poems to *La Plume* rather than to other reviews,
Valéry expressed complete confidence in his judgement: 'Faites
de moi ce que voudrez. Dans la galère je ramerai, vous, soyez la
vigie. Prenez mes vers et agissez à votre guise; sachez que je ne
désapprouverai *rien*. Vous êtes l'ami, l'ami lumineux et qu'il faut
suivre et qui est nécessaire à l'être hésitant, ignorant que je suis.'[35]
He gratefully acknowledged Louÿs's frequent acts of kindness and
generosity: 'Quel homme! Quel ami vous faites!'[36]

Louÿs always retained an admiration for Valéry's poetry and
later continued to do his best to promote his friend's interests.
Thus Paul Léautaud has stated that the inclusion of the then almost
unknown Valéry in the *Poètes d'aujourd'hui* published by himself
and Adolphe van Bever in 1900 was due entirely to Louÿs's
insistence.[37] A further striking instance of Louÿs's generosity

towards Valéry occurred on the occasion of the composition of 'La Jeune Parque'.[38]

Like Gide, though with less diligence, Pierre Louÿs busied himself during the year 1890 with plans for launching his literary career. He intended to publish a small volume of poetry, under the title *Choses murmurées*, before his twentieth birthday in December, 'uniquement pour faire date'.[39] In this connection he was proposing to follow the example of certain Symbolist poets who delighted in issuing their compositions in slim but elegantly produced *plaquettes*, in editions usually limited to some one hundred copies and bearing the proud announcement that they would not be reprinted—in which respect, Camille Mauclair remarked ironically, the poet 'était bien sûr de ne pas mentir'.[40] The very idea of a popular success was abhorrent to them, for they considered public acclaim to be all too often founded on ignorance and false artistic values. The only recompense to which they aspired was to gain the esteem of a select group of 'true' artists. For these writers, to quote Mauclair once more, 'la "tour d'ivoire" était vraiment . . . une réalité habitable'.[41] Some even earnestly took precautions to guard against the risk, however slight it must have appeared, of achieving fame among a wider circle of less refined readers. Louÿs fell into this latter category. Thus he wrote in his diary on 15 April 1890:

Très probablement je changerai de pseudonyme à chaque ouvrage pour dérouter encore plus ce vulgaire profane pour qui j'ai de la pitié comme homme, de la pitié religieuse, mais du mépris comme poète, du mépris souverain . . . je veux rester célèbre au milieu d'un petit groupe d'amis, je veux être aimé de vingt personnes et encore est-ce beaucoup.[42]

And on 24 July 1890:

C'est la horde des poètes qu'il faut, au haut des vers, conquérir,—et non cette infâme et infime tourbe populaire qui grouille dans les salons illettrés sous la livrée des habits noirs. Oh! l'horrible peuple! la hideuse engeance. Non! ils ne les liront pas, mes vers, même pas ils ne baveront dessus, de haine et d'admiration; non. J'ai assez de dix poètes, non de mille bourgeois . . .[43]

In pursuit of his desire to win the friendship and ultimately the professional esteem of the writers he most admired, Louÿs deliberately set about cultivating the acquaintance of some of the leading figures of Parisian literary society. In the course of the year 1890 he collected several notable 'scalps'; most important of all, he succeeded in establishing personal relations with Stéphane Mallarmé and José-Maria de Heredia, both of whom played a significant, if essentially different role in his life and career.

Mallarmé occupied a unique position among the writers and artists of the day, especially those belonging to the younger generation who were attracted to his modest apartment at 89 rue de Rome as worshippers are drawn to a temple. He was the high priest, and the divinity at whose altar he officiated was called Pure Art. Even more than his poetry, it was his remarkable personality which inspired the veneration in which he was universally held, a veneration so profound that thirty-eight years after his death André Fontainas could still declare: 'Son nom, je ne l'ai jamais lu, je ne l'entends pas sans frémir'.[44]

Countless tributes have been paid to Mallarmé's delightful character, to his innate kindliness, his lucid intellect and refined taste. He had, moreover, a beautifully modulated voice which added considerably to the charm of his conversation: Gide described it as 'une voix douce, musicale, inoubliable'.[45] The visitor, leaving behind him the discordant sounds of the outside, materialistic world, was met at the door by Mallarmé himself who ushered him into the small dining-room which constituted, as it were, the sanctuary—'un foyer de lucidité inaltérable'[46]— where the mysteries of the cult were celebrated amidst a haze of curling tobacco smoke. Standing in his customary place before the stove and with the perennial pipe in his hand, Mallarmé would launch into a long monologue to which the visitors listened in reverent silence, fascinated by his views, enchanted by the delicate and poetic manner in which he developed his ideas, dazzled by his intellectual brilliance and felicitous language. He gave his listeners the privileged feeling of hearing an exceptionally gifted artist *thinking aloud*, and therein lay perhaps the paramount fascination of those evenings. None, with the occasional exception of Henri de Régnier and later of Paul Valéry, dared interrupt the master of the house. They sat silent, overawed by the skill and splendour of the improvisation. It was not that Mallarmé sought in any way to dominate his audience or to impose his opinions on others, in fact he rather regretted the timid acquiescence with which they were received; but, Fontainas remarks, 'Nous nous taisions. Qu'eussions-nous dit?'[47]

At the same time, his young admirers saw in Mallarmé much more than a poet of distinction and a man of impeccable judgement: in their eyes, he represented the incarnation of an ideal:

Pour la première fois, près de lui, on sentait, on touchait la réalité de la pensée: ce que nous cherchions, ce que nous voulions, ce que nous adorions dans la vie, existait; un homme, ici, avait tout sacrifié à *cela*. Pour Mallarmé, la littérature était le but, oui, la fin même de la vie; on la sentait ici, authentique et réelle. Pour y sacrifier tout comme il fit, il fallait bien y croire uniquement. Je ne pense pas qu'il y ait, dans notre histoire littéraire, exemple de plus intransigeante conviction.[48]

Mallarmé's influence thus transcended the sphere of poetry and even the larger field of aesthetics. The acknowledged Master of Symbolism, he became himself a symbol for the younger generation: to quote Paul Fort, 'il est l'image de l'art pur, s'isolant de tout élément étranger et s'enfermant jalousement en lui-même, dans l'immuable et solitaire sérénité, comme dans un temple clos aux profanes'.[49] Moreover, Mallarmé's utter disinterestedness, his complete disregard for financial reward, for mundane success or public honours made an indelible impression upon the aspiring young writers who came into contact with him; hence the Symbolists' distaste, indeed horror, at the thought of writing for gain. 'Nous qui vivions dans l'entourage de Mallarmé, l'idée seule que la littérature pût nous "rapporter" nous faisait honte', affirmed André Gide. 'Se faire payer, pour nous, c'était "se vendre" dans la pire acception du mot. Nous n'étions pas à acheter.'[50] As Camille Mauclair observed, 'Dans l'entourage de Verlaine et de Mallarmé, le sale argent n'a hanté personne.'[51] Quite the contrary: never has the expression 'filthy lucre' seemed more apposite than when applied to the Symbolists' attitude towards money: to rely for one's livelihood on income derived from literature was to compromise one's artistic integrity. It was therefore generally understood that Mallarmé's purpose in retaining his teaching post at the Lycée Condorcet, rather than make his living with his pen, was to ensure that his literary activities would not be subject to any pressures or constraints. The artist was regarded as a being set apart by his genius from the rest of mankind. In his tribute to Louÿs in *Les Nouvelles littéraires* on 13 June 1925, Paul Valéry recalled: '*Artiste*, il y a trente ans, signifiait pour nous un être séparé, consacré, à la fois victime et lévite, un être choisi par ses dons, et de qui les mérites et les fautes n'étaient point ceux des autres hommes.' Mallarmé was the artist *par excellence*. Indeed, to his disciples he seemed to fulfil brilliantly all the requisite conditions for canonization in the religion of Pure Art; not for nothing did they refer to him as 'Saint Mallarmé'.

Pierre Louÿs, who fervently subscribed to Mallarmé's ideas before he had even met him and remained under their influence all his life, made the poet's acquaintance in June 1890, shortly after his return to Paris. From Montpellier he had gone to Marseille for a few days before travelling north by way of Toulouse, Bordeaux, and La Rochelle which he reached on 4 June. Two days later he was at Cholet, but the meeting with Marie Chardon left him despondent, as he was still uncertain of her feelings towards him. As a result, he was plunged into a deep mental depression throughout his 'Pèlerinage en l'honneur de Ronsard'— the title inscribed by him on a sketch-book containing seventeen pen-drawings he made of Bourgueil, Blois, Vendôme, and Chinon, among other towns, and which figured in the posthumous sale of his manuscripts. 'Depuis mon départ de X . . . [Cholet] jusqu'à mon arrivée à Paris j'ai été triste comme jamais je ne l'avais été', he confessed to Gide.[52] He was back in the capital by 17 June at the latest, and straightaway turned his attention again to literary projects, foremost among which was now the publication of an anthology of contemporary poetry. It was in this connection that he wished to enlist Mallarmé's support. Louÿs accordingly called on Mallarmé on 19 June, and was received with characteristic generosity. On 26 June he reported cryptically to Gide: 'A l'occasion d'un vaste projet dont tu ne sauras rien avant son exécution, saint Mallarmé me disait la semaine dernière ces propres paroles: "Mais, Monsieur, non seulement je vous approuve et vous soutiens, mais je vous promets l'appui de tous mes amis".'[53] The anthology was eventually to take the form of the review *La Conque*.

Charmed by Mallarmé's great cordiality, Louÿs eagerly accepted his invitation to attend the usual Tuesday evening reception the following week. On that occasion he felt, however, disconcerted by Mallarmé's manner which struck him as excessively oracular. 'Mallarmé pontifie d'une façon insupportable', he noted in his diary that evening (24 June).[54] And on 16 July he wrote to Valéry: 'Savez-vous que certains, à commencer par Mallarmé, pontifient d'une façon absolument insupportable et pionesque? Et ils sont d'une ignorance! Ainsi l'autre jour en parlant de Ruskin chez Mallarmé, pas un, pas même le chef, n'avait lu une ligne de Ruskin ... Et Mallarmé est professeur d'anglais à Condorcet ... J'étais renversé.'[55]

This unfavourable reaction in no way affected his admiration for Mallarmé's poetry. In July he spent many hours at the Bibliothèque nationale copying the edition of Mallarmé's poems—a photolithographic reproduction of the poet's own handwriting— which the *Revue indépendante* had brought out in 1887. And when Valéry complained on 14 September that he had been trying unsuccessfully for two years to obtain the text of Mallarmé's 'Hérodiade' and despaired of ever laying hands on it,[56] Louÿs promptly copied some thirty lines of the poem and dispatched them to Montpellier with the comment: 'Si je commençais toutes mes lettres par de pareils vers, je pense que vous me pardonneriez, mon cher ami, de ne point répondre à vos sonnets par mes ennéades, et par mes rythmes à vos teintes.'[57]

Of the persons Louÿs saw that first evening in Mallarmé's apartment, only Rodolphe Darzens found favour in his eyes: 'il me ravissait, celui-là ...', Louÿs wrote in his diary. 'Il a une chic tête et une bonne voix. Je ne le lâche pas.'[58] Born in Moscow in 1865, Darzens, whose parents were French, had left Russia at the age of twelve and completed his schooling at the Lycée Condorcet in Paris, where his fellow pupils included André Fontainas, René Ghil, Éphraïm Mikhael, Stuart Merrill, and Pierre Quillard. In addition to some volumes of poetry (*La Nuit*, 1884; *Le Psautier de l'amie*, 1886; *Strophes artificielles*, 1888), he published *Pages en prose* in 1887, and attracted wider attention with a playlet, *L'Amante du Christ,* which was performed at the Théâtre libre (of which he was secretary-general) on 19 October 1888 and printed with a curious frontispiece, by Félicien Rops, of Christ possessing the author's features. A French translation by Darzens of Ibsen's *Ghosts* was given by the Théâtre libre on 29 and 30 May 1890. In addition, he was responsible for the publication of *Le Théâtre libre illustré* which appeared in 1889 and 1890.

He was, furthermore, closely associated with the literary review *La Pléiade* which was the forerunner of the *Mercure de France*. At the time Louÿs became friendly with him, Darzens was joint editor with Tola Dorian of yet another magazine, the *Revue d'aujourd'hui,* founded the previous year. It published, among other notable items, several poems from Verlaine's *Bonheur,* as well as his *Critique des 'Poèmes saturniens'*; Villiers de l'Isle-Adam's story *L'Amour sublime*; and Mallarmé's celebrated lecture on Villiers de l'Isle-Adam.

The *Revue d'aujourd'hui* deserves a place of honour in any biography of Pierre Louÿs, for it was the first 'serious' literary magazine—*Potache-revue* could hardly lay claim to that epithet—to print his work. Following their initial meeting on 24 June, Louÿs twice called on Darzens at the offices of the review, located in the rue des Martyrs. On the second occasion he showed Darzens, not without trepidation, one of his 'ennéades', a poem he had sent to Valéry in June with the indication that it had been composed on 11 May and which had earned Valéry's warm praise ('C'est tout simplement beau, d'une beauté de rêve'[59]). The poem, originally entitled 'L'Éclosion de l'idole', was now called 'L'Effloraison'. To Louÿs's amazement, Darzens at once accepted it for publication in the review. Louÿs left the rue des Martyrs, on that Thursday, 17 July 1890, with feelings of elation tinged with a certain melancholy: 'Je songeais que c'était mon début, que, pour la première fois, des vers de moi, dans une revue sérieuse, seraient imprimés, et je ne sais quelle tristesse me prenait, comme d'une défloraison.'[60] 'L'Effloraison' was printed in the *Revue d'aujourd'hui* the following week, on 25 July, in what unexpectedly turned out to be the final issue of the magazine. The poet's name appeared as 'Pierre Louys'. The modified form of the surname had occurred in the diary as early as 3 February 1888, below a newly composed poem. The middle name 'Félix' (and the corresponding initial) had also been discarded in due course, but the diaeresis was to be a later refinement. 'Ce n'est pas seulement l'y grec, c'est le tréma maintenant', Louÿs announced to Gide on 16 September 1890. 'Un de ces jours je supprimerai l'O. Peut-être l'U aussi. Mais je laisserai le tréma. Ça sera tout de même mon nom à peu de chose près!'[61] The final 's' was sounded.

Louÿs was to retain his regard for Darzens, even though by December of that same year he felt dismayed that he had preferred his poetry to that of Henri de Régnier. Yet in 1918 he still believed that his original favourable impression had been justified: 'Je ne m'étais nullement trompé, c'est Darzens qui ne s'est pas connu. Il y avait en lui un germe de grand poète et il ne s'en est pas vanté.'[62] Certainly Darzens did not fully live up to the promise he had given in his youth. During the 1890s he published two novels of no particular distinction, *Ukko'Till* (1891) and *Le Roman d'un clown* (1898), after which he appears to have faded almost completely from the literary scene. In 1901 he devised the scenario for a ballet in three scenes, *Lorenza*, for which the music was composed by the same Franco Alfano who, some twenty years later, was to complete *Turandot* after Puccini's death. Rodolphe Darzens died in Paris in December 1938.

As Louÿs prepared to leave Paris for a holiday at the beginning of August 1890, he could look back with some satisfaction on the progress he had made during the past months towards his chosen goal. He was beginning to move in literary circles; he had met some of the luminaries, notably Mallarmé and Verlaine, and had attended his first literary banquet—the one held on 22 July to celebrate the award of the Legion of Honour to Léon Dierx. Moreover, if his friendship with André Gide had cooled off for the time being, he derived much pleasure from the stimulating correspondence with Paul Valéry for whose poetic talent he felt increasing admiration. On the day of the dinner given in Dierx's honour he received two new sonnets from Valéry, one of which, 'Le Jeune Prêtre', especially delighted him. 'Quel talent il a, celui-là; c'est un vrai', he wrote in his diary that evening, on his return from the dinner. 'S'il continue, il arrivera plus loin qu'aucun de ceux que j'ai vus aujourd'hui.'[63]

Finally, Louÿs could take some pride in the fact that one of his poems had appeared in a respected review. If this may seem a rather modest achievement, it must be remembered that he was, after all, only nineteen. He had every justification for viewing his prospects with excitement: 'La vie est belle; la vie est rouge; la jeunesse est vigoureuse, musclée, toute-puissante, et la route s'ouvre . . .' But he could not refrain from adding the faintly disturbing question: 'Vers quel but?'[64]

Louÿs left Paris on 1 August for Geneva where he renewed contact with several Swiss students he had met at Montpellier. Afterwards he travelled for some time in Savoy. He is known to have been at Saint-Gervais on 7 August. His letters to his brother indicate that by 17 August he had arrived at Annecy, and that on

20 August he was at Aix-les-Bains where he remained until 23 August. His travels reached their climax with his arrival, in the late evening of 25 August, at the famous monastery of the Grande Chartreuse where, he had enigmatically informed Valéry before his departure from Paris, 'je fais une retraite dans un but que j'ignore jusqu'à ce qu'il me soit révélé'.[65] The monastery, set amidst spectacular mountain scenery, is the mother house of the Carthusian order founded by St. Bruno in 1084; the rule of the order prescribes prayer, silence, and extreme austerity.

During his stay in Dauphiné a few weeks earlier Gide had been so 'hallucinated' by the sight of the Grande Chartreuse that he had toyed for a long time with the idea of visiting it and perhaps even staying there. Finally, after much wavering, he had left the region early in July without having set foot inside the monastery. On 17 July, from Cambremer in Normandy, he sent the following explanation to Louÿs:

Cette année j'ai désiré la solitude pour y écrire *Alain*—j'ai voulu la chartreuse, la Grande! mais quand j'ai compris sa suprême splendeur et que la vie de là-haut était sublime à ce point qu'elle écraserait toute autre pensée que celle de la perfection—je m'en suis détourné dans la crainte de perdre mon livre et de déflorer ce rêve si longtemps caressé en apportant dans cette retraite la moindre pensée profane. Plus tard![66]

Louÿs was dismayed to learn that Gide might visit the Grande Chartreuse. 'Pourquoi me voles-tu mes idées?' he wrote querulously on 15 June. 'C'est moi qui voulais non seulement aller à la Gde Chartreuse mais me faire chartreux pour un temps.'[67] Impressed by Gide's description of the monastery, he then became all the more eager to carry out his intention at the earliest opportunity.

Despite his mystifying statement to Valéry that the purpose of his visit had not yet been revealed to him, Louÿs had three definite aims in mind in planning his stay: reading, meditation, and writing. He brought with him a varied collection of books: the Bible; *The Imitation of Christ* (in Latin); the *Spiritual Exercises* of St. Ignatius of Loyola; two volumes of Ronsard's poems; Pascal, *Pensées*; Flaubert, *La Tentation de Saint Antoine*; Baudelaire, *Les Fleurs du mal*; Verlaine, *Sagesse*; Huysmans, *A Rebours*; Henri de Régnier, *Poèmes anciens*; Renan, *Pages choisies*; Villiers de l'Isle-Adam, *Akédysséril*; Hugo, *La Légende des siècles*; Goethe, *Faust* (in both French and German); Wagner, *Parsifal*; and a *Lexique des termes d'art*. On his first morning at the monastery, seated in his small cell, Louÿs contemplated this carefully chosen selection with satisfaction: 'Avec ces dix-huit volumes, *seul* avec eux, je suis heureux. Les religieux ne sont pas à plaindre ... Moi qui ai dit tant de mal de l'ascétisme quand je croyais que c'était une lutte, que de bien n'en dirai-je pas désormais, sachant que c'est une joie profonde, un raffinement de volupté.' Yet the solitude he so ardently desired appeared threatened that first day by the attentions of the Father Coadjutor who interviewed him: 'Il ne comprenait rien; il me parlait comme à un élève de la rue des Postes; il voulait me faire confesser après-demain! C'est aujourd'hui le jour de la sortie des pères; il doit m'emmener avec lui; j'essaierai de me faire comprendre; ce que je veux avant tout, c'est qu'il me laisse la paix; je suis venu ici pour être seul et je veux l'être.' He looked forward to a period of undisturbed work: 'Mes livres m'attendent et le papier blanc m'attire ...'[68]

If the Bible and the *Imitation of Christ* furnished him with much matter for meditation, it was to the *Spiritual Exercises* of St. Ignatius of Loyola that Louÿs turned for the techniques of contemplation. In this choice he was directly influenced by Maurice Barrès's novel *Un Homme libre* which, on its publication the previous year, had brought its author instant fame. The hero of the book seeks, as an essential step towards the complete realization of his 'moi', to analyse and 'catalogue' different emotional responses and he trains his mind and sensibility in such a way that he may become capable of evoking a specific emotion at will. In order to achieve this aim, he has recourse to the method elaborated by that 'prince des psychologues', St. Ignatius of Loyola, who, with its aid, 'obtint, sur les âmes les plus superbes, de prodigieux résultats'.[69] In other words, he puts the *Spiritual Exercises* to a very precise mechanistic use which is, in truth, very far removed from the pious purpose envisaged by the founder of the Society of Jesus. Louÿs grew increasingly aware of this fact, the more he studied the techniques prescribed by St. Ignatius and applied himself to putting them into practice. 'Vous avez lu Barrès je crois,' he wrote to Valéry after his return to Paris, 'et vous n'avez sans doute jamais lu Saint-Ignace, c'est-à-dire que vous vous faites une idée radicalement fausse des *Exercices spirituels*. La "Méthode" de Loyola est tout entière un procédé de contemplation destiné à intensifier jusqu'aux limites de la folie l'hallucination volontaire. Barrès en a fait un procédé d'analyse! C'est à le jeter par la fenêtre.'[70] Not that Louÿs himself remained faithful to St. Ignatius's intentions; on the contrary, his own 'exercises' differed from the latter in another sense, inasmuch as their nature was aesthetic rather than religious.

Louÿs began by sketching out plans for three books which, he thought, could be composed on the model of the Bible, the *Imitation of Christ*, and the *Spiritual Exercises* respectively.[71] All three appear to have had as a common principle the replacement of the Christian religion by a Cult of Beauty, and the substitution of a God of Beauty for the Christian God. For this purpose, Louÿs used certain significant passages from the original texts, either unchanged or suitably modified to fit the new context. In the first book, he proposed to depict a Christ 'qui serait à la fois prêtre du Beau et incarnation de l'Amour du Beau, partie intégrante de la Beauté' and whose mission on earth would be to redeem mankind by purging its anti-aesthetic blasphemies and to announce to man that 'Dieu a mis au cœur de ses élus le sentiment palpitant de l'émotion artistique vers un idéal qu'ils soupçonnent sans le voir, et qu'ils n'osaient encore appeler Dieu.' Some of the pronouncements of this new Christ recall, and at times indeed reproduce, certain verses of the Sermon on the Mount. Furthermore, adapting Christ's exhortation that the true believer should avoid the ways of the hypocrites who pray in public where they are most likely to be seen, and should instead retire to the privacy of his own dwelling, there to pray in secret (Matt. 6: 5–6), Louÿs would have his Christ enjoin the true aesthete not to imitate the hypocrites who 'sans rien aimer ni sentir, entassent leurs médiocrités au pied des montagnes à la mode et sur les plages courues du monde', but to seek out pure emotions far from the multitude, 'car la beauté se réfugie dans la solitude silencieuse; et la retraite est favorable aux émotions prolongées'. The new religion would have for its doctrine: 'Aimez la Beauté'.

The central character of the second book was to be a religious, and, more precisely, a poet whose life had been broken by love and who was turning to contemplation for his only solace. Like the author of the *Imitation*, Louÿs imagined mystical dialogues between the monk and his 'ideal'. But whilst in the *Imitation* a Faithful Soul converses with Christ, Louÿs proposed to have the poet seek guidance from his Muse, 'incarnation du Beau, ou de l'aspiration au Beau'. As before, Louÿs made use of various appropriate quotations, transposing them from a purely religious context to one more closely related to aesthetic appreciation and artistic creation. However, the outline of this plan is considerably more sketchy than that of the first book. It concludes with the Muse's pronouncement that the ideal human life is one spent far from the madding crowd.

 The third volume was to consist of spiritual exercises designed to increase each day 'l'*intensité* et la *continuité* de l'émotion artistique'. Once more Louÿs substituted 'Beauty' for 'God', so that St. Ignatius's *Principle* and *Foundation* now read: 'L'homme est créé pour louer, honorer et servir la Beauté divine. Et les autres choses qui sont sur la terre sont créées à cause de l'homme et pour l'aider dans la poursuite de sa fin idéale . . .' The Exercises themselves would be based on the principle 'que la vie de l'homme doit être consacrée au Beau, et que toute pensée bourgeoise, tout désir grossier, toute admiration indigne, est un péché' and they would be arranged in accordance with the 'admirable' method and plan devised by the Spanish saint.

Following this lengthy preamble, Louÿs proceeded to the first of his two *Méditations*. Barrès had inserted meditations on Benjamin Constant and Sainte-Beuve into *Un Homme libre*. Louÿs chose for his subjects the orchestral prelude to *Parsifal* and Victor Hugo's *La Légende des siècles*. The two meditations are separated by a *Colloque* which forms by far the longest and most personal portion of the section in the *Journal intime* dealing with Louÿs's stay at the Grande Chartreuse. It is evidently modelled on the third book of the *Imitation of Christ* which features a dialogue between Christ and the Faithful Soul (*Anima fidelis*). For his colloquy Louÿs retained the latter interlocutor, who represents himself, but, characteristically, he replaced Christ by 'La Grâce', the incarnation of artistic inspiration, corresponding to the Muse of classical antiquity. 'C'était bien la grâce qui me parlait,' he later assured Valéry. 'qui répondait avec calme à mes questions désordonnées et terminait sur des paroles de paix. C'est du moins ce que j'aime à inventer, et le rêve est loisible à tous.'[72]

The Colloquy falls into two distinct parts. The first was written immediately after the meditation on *Parsifal*, in the course of that long night of 27 August when, during eight hours, Louÿs was gripped by an intense exaltation which he strove to maintain at fever pitch with the aid of generous doses of tobacco and green liqueur. It is a moving document: the *cri du cœur* of a young poet, filled with dreams of glory, but uncertain of his gifts. The Faithful Soul inquires sadly why so few men who have been endowed by the Muse with a profound love of Beauty possess also the ability to achieve it. The Muse reproaches the poet for his lack of faith and taxes him with ingratitude: has he not felt her presence, however fleetingly, on more than one occasion? He should there-fore realize that he has already been set apart from the common multitude of men. 'Tu m'invoques, tu sais donc que j'existe; . . . sur tant d'hommes que tu connais, combien m'ont sentie comme toi, combien m'ont recherchée, combien m'ont aimée? Deux ou trois?' Instead of complaining, the poet ought to be infinitely grateful to the Muse for allowing him a glimpse of that supreme happiness which millions will never know. Even should the Muse decide not to give herself fully to him, he owes her 'une perpétuelle reconnaissance pour avoir été, ne fût-ce qu'une heure, privilégié'. He must never forget that he has been touched by grace. The poet protests, however, that it would have been kinder to leave him ignorant of Beauty than to initiate him into its cult and then condemn him to everlasting anguish and regret at the thought of his unfulfilled aspirations: 'Je me serais cru heureux, ne sachant pas le bonheur. La lumière divine ne m'aurait pas brûlé les yeux.' In reply, the Muse reminds the poet of his youth: 'Compte les années, compte-les, et réponds toi-même. Parmi ceux que tu envies, parmi ceux même que tu n'oses envier, com-bien, à dix-neuf ans, m'avaient connue plus que toi?' At that age no one knows himself or is capable of foreseeing his eventual development; there is no cause as yet for either pride or despair. Not until much later will the poet be in a position to decide whether his Muse deserves to be cursed or blessed. Until then, 'Aime-moi, car tu m'as connue, et ceux qui m'ont sentie en eux ont le devoir de se mettre à la tâche, et peut-être un peu le droit d'attendre!'

The first part of the Colloquy concludes with a reaffirmation of Louÿs's belief in the primacy of Beauty: 'la Beauté seule est vraie, et le reste ne vaudrait pas la peine de vivre'. The artist must devote all his efforts to the pursuit of this ideal, even though he cannot know whether they will ultimately lead to success or failure.

In the second part of the Colloquy,[73] written on the following evening, the poet beseeches the Muse to set at rest his 'heretical' doubts about the continuing survival of Beauty. He points out that in *La Légende des siècles*, which represents 'la perfection faite humaine', Hugo celebrated man's progress towards moral Good and towards Truth, but did not speak of his progress towards Beauty; yet the latter stands as high above Truth as the soul stands above the body, the dream above reality, and the senses above reason. Should Hugo's silence be taken as an indication that man is no longer capable of reaching out towards Beauty? and consequently, towards God, since God is Beauty? No mortal being, the Muse replies, may presume to interpret the Eternal Will, for it is inscrutable. Long ago it directed her to provide inspiration, not merely for individual artists, but for an entire nation—the Athenians. The eclipse of the Greek nation does not, however, signify the disappearance of Beauty itself. The Muse has merely, over the centuries, become less prodigal and more selective: whereas she once offered herself munificently to an entire people, she now chooses her favourites with greater circumspection; but those whose minds she touches remain her devotees for ever. The poet should therefore take courage: 'Le progrès vers le Beau existe.' The Colloquy, which might justly be called a Hymn to Beauty, thus ends on a note of hope.

In a letter to his brother Louÿs set out his 'timetable':

lever: 6h.; 7h.: messe; 8h.: déjeuner; 9h.: Loyola; 10h.: *Imitation*; 11h.: dîner; midi à 2h.: sortie, promenade dans les bois; 2h.: poésies philosophiques; 3h.: Loyola (no. 2); 4h.: profondes réflexions; 5h.: poésies purement de forme; 6h.: souper; 7.: sortie pour excit. préalable; 7h. 1/2: au travail; de 9 à 11h.: coucher. En résumé, je ne fais des vers que le soir, et je m'y prépare toute la journée.[74]

The frequent periods of meditation put Louÿs into a state of high spiritual exaltation. Moreover, the lonely walks in the magnificent mountain forests near the monastery, the eremitic life he led, the solemn religious ceremonies he attended amidst the white-robed monks, all these experiences had the effect of heightening the excitement produced by the long hours of solitary reading and contemplation. Nor did the latter activities cease at eleven o'clock in the evening, as he prudently led his brother to believe. He prolonged them until four and five o'clock in the morning, interrupting them only to repair to the chapel for the midnight service. Furthermore, he carefully shut all daylight out of his cell, in eager obedience to St. Ignatius's precept that the retreatant should deprive himself of all light by closing the shutters and doors while in his room, unless he needed the light to say his prayers, to read or to eat. As a result, Louÿs's mode of life engendered a hallucinatory feeling of timelessness which intensified still further the extraordinary elation he felt:

C'est aux lueurs des hauts cierges blancs que je lisais Huysmans entre le livre de Job et le livre de Jésus, sans me soucier du soleil ni des choses, et *Sagesse* entre Baudelaire et le *De Imitatione Christi*, pris parfois moi-même (telle est la contagion des esprits) d'une telle ferveur religieuse indépendante de la foi, que je jetais tous les livres profanes fussent-ils littérairement mystiques, pour ne garder devant moi que les actes de foi sincère . . .[75]

Louÿs found effective aids to stimulate his imagination still further: 'pour m'énerver davantage encore je buvais de la chartreuse verte par gorgées en fumant d'âcres cigares choisis pour la nuit.'[76] Only opium appears to have been neglected; perhaps the monks would not have tolerated it.

Not surprisingly, Louÿs's never very strong constitution proved unequal to the strain to which it was so dramatically subjected. Already on 28 August he noted in his diary: 'la veille et le jeûne, c'est plus qu'il n'en faut pour me fatiguer'. With characteristic heedlessness he ignored the warning signs and continued to draw excessively upon his physical resources. The result was that he lost twelve pounds in five days, fell ill, and was promptly sent home by the reverend fathers. 'Plaignez-moi, mon ami,' he wrote dolefully to Valéry on 9 September, 'car je m'étais promis de longues semaines de silence et de solitude. Huit jours auraient suffi, je pense, ou dix peut-être pour achever la préparation religieuse et j'aurais fait alors en cellule ce que j'étais venu y faire: mon premier volume de vers.'[77] As it turned out, he was back at Dizy by 2 September.

Notwithstanding its tragicomic conclusion, the retreat at the Grande Chartreuse remained for Louÿs one of the most cherished memories of his youth. Valéry relates[78] that during his later years of silence and isolation Louÿs, dismayed and grieved by what he considered ill-founded interpretations of his work, contemplated writing a book about the formative stages of his career, to be entitled *A dix-neuf ans*. In it he proposed to describe the aesthetic criteria and exalted artistic aspirations he had formulated at that time, and to demonstrate that his entire literary output had remained faithful to those ideals. The Grande Chartreuse episode would certainly have been accorded pride of place in such an *apologia de operibus suis*.

Finally, the visit was significant in one other respect. On 28 August Louÿs wrote in his diary: 'Quelle joie, quelle jouissance intérieure dans cette retraite! Quel contentement de ne plus parler et de retourner les yeux à l'intérieur dans la solitude de la cellule ... Jamais je n'ai si bien vu qu'aujourd'hui que de temps on perd à vivre dans le monde; depuis hier j'ai plus lu, j'ai plus réfléchi, j'ai plus vécu que je n'aurais fait en une semaine à Paris.'[79] Although he continued to frequent society for several more years, these reflections help to explain in part the future course of his life. Twenty years later he virtually turned his study into the monastic cell whose stillness he had found so marvellously conducive to intellectual concentration, and there, remote from the tumult of the metropolis, he spent the long silent hours of the night in solitary meditation and, as he once remarked, in conversation with his books. His recollections of the profound exaltation he had experienced during his retreat at the Grande Chartreuse may be regarded as one of the factors responsible for the noctiphilia which increasingly determined the pattern of his life.

On 9 September Louÿs resumed his correspondence with André Gide. The letter opened on an affectionate note: 'Tant de choses, tant de choses j'aurais à te dire, ami, que depuis huit jours je recule à l'idée de commencer; et aujourd'hui que je me décide enfin à rompre notre mutuel silence, c'est pour te demander quelque chose de toi, ton écriture, tes idées, et la nouvelle tant attendue de l'achèvement du cahier.'[80] The remainder of the letter is taken up with a long and enthusiastic account of his days at the Grande Chartreuse. When, shortly afterwards, Louÿs learned that Gide had indeed finished his novel, he expressed his pleasure at the news ('Ah! mon ami, mon ami! cette fois-ci c'est de la vraie joie. *Alain* achevé, cela me soulage comme si je l'avais fait moi-même') but his congratulations were tinged with a certain irony,

owing perhaps to his mortification—which he freely acknowledged—that Gide had outstripped him: 'Seulement je t'en veux
d'avoir fini avant moi. Il est vrai que tu fais de la prose très
vulgaire. Tandis que moi je me vautre dans l'éthéré. Tu alignes des
mots sans mesure et sans rythme . . . Tu fais de la pâture d'âme,
ha! ha! Et l'art? tu t'en fiches un peu? Enfin nous verrons ce que
ce sera. Il serait pourtant possible que ce soit (et non pas fût)
passable? hé? vieux?'[81] These remarks augured badly for any
resumption of intimate relations between the two friends. It will
be readily understood that Gide felt in no hurry to submit his
manuscript to Louÿs's mocking appraisal.

Gide had, in fact, already turned elsewhere for advice. He had
come up to Paris from La Roque at the end of August in order to
show the completed first version of the book to his cousin Albert
Démarest, with whom he had always been on excellent terms and
of whom he speaks frequently and with great affection in his
memoirs. Since Démarest 'fut consterné par l'intempérance de
mon piétisme et par l'abondance des citations de l'Écriture',
Gide reworked the text and suppressed some two-thirds of the
biblical references.[82] This revision occupied several weeks.
However, on Sunday, 19 October, he was able to inform his
mother that he was about to read the new version to Démarest
and that he intended to take it to the publisher Perrin on the
following day (Perrin agreed shortly afterwards to publish the
book at the author's expense).[83]

It was not until later that same week that Gide read the *Cahiers
d'André Walter* to Pierre Louÿs. It is interesting that Gide not only
turned to someone else for advice on the book, but that he did
not even allow Louÿs to hear the text until he had submitted it to
a publisher (who may have already accepted it). Nothing could
more forcefully demonstrate Gide's determination to escape
completely from the ascendancy Louÿs had formerly had over
him. In the circumstances it is greatly to Louÿs's credit that his
reactions should have been so favourable. That his pleasure at
Gide's achievement was genuine is clear from his diary: 'Début
merveilleusement étrange. Décidément, c'est bien. Dieu! que je
suis heureux! . . . C'est superbe. Je le dis sans faux enthousiasme,
sans emballement aveugle, en pleine sûreté d'idée et de jugement;
c'est un chef-d'œuvre . . . Je suis bien heureux, heureux comme
pour moi.'[84]

Gide was naturally pleased by the admiration Louÿs so openly expressed for his book. Yet it was not long before their relations became once more strained, then downright hostile. This is hardly surprising, in view of Gide's firm resolve to keep Louÿs at a distance. It does not appear to have occurred to Louÿs, however, that he might himself have been in some measure responsible for his friend's reserve. 'Gide change beaucoup', he noted on 12 November 1890. 'Change-t-il réellement? Ou me suis-je mépris autrefois? Je ne sais. Mais je l'ai bien mal connu s'il était ainsi. Depuis un an je n'ai pas passé un quart d'heure avec lui sans qu'il m'ait dit une chose blessante . . .' After a reference to the interruption of their correspondence during the summer, Louÿs continued: 'Nous nous sommes revus. Et dès le premier jour, je crois, il a repris pour me parler le même ton d'hypocrisie dédaigneuse qui m'avait révolté l'hiver dernier. Jamais de laisser-aller, jamais d'oubli, jamais d'amitié. Seul avec moi, il ne parlait plus qu'avec les réserves et les poses d'un journaliste célèbre qui se sent écouté dans un salon par quarante reporters prêts à noter ses mots. Quand il me demandait mon avis, c'était pour me prendre en faute, et relever mes théories avec un sourire en dessous.' The only occasion, he noted, on which Gide had shown him any real cordiality was when he had expressed his admiration for *André Walter*. From this he concluded that the dominant trait of Gide's character was his egoism: 'Lui, rien que lui. Tout ce qui ne se rapportait pas à lui était indifférent. Je n'avais pas souvenir d'un service rendu par lui dans le seul but de m'être utile, ni d'une attention à mon égard dans le seul but de me faire plaisir. Je me disais que si je n'étais rien, si je n'avais pas eu l'ombre d'avenir, il m'aurait regardé quelque temps, puis il aurait passé . . . comme il a fait pour d'autres.'[85]

It might be added that others who knew Gide during those early years have also mentioned his rather stilted manner which often suggested a carefully assumed pose. Thus Maurice Barrès recalled that Gide 'se fabriquait un personnage littératuture, grelottant, guindé, enfantin, un peu fol, très cultivé, et d'ailleurs charmant',[86] while Henri de Régnier, himself not the most easygoing of men, wrote less charitably: 'Il était bien prétentieux et guindé. On avait envie constamment de lui demander:—Gide, qu'avez-vous? Gide, que vous est-il arrivé? Tout semblait aménagé en lui pour le comble de l'antinaturel.'[87]

Surprisingly, on the day following Louÿs's long diatribe against Gide, a reconciliation took place. 'Quand on est très heureux,' he wrote on 13 November, 'on n'a envie de rien écrire. Le malentendu est dissipé. Nous sommes amis, plus amis qu'avant, plus amis que jamais . . .'[88] Nevertheless, even if Louÿs and Gide once again agreed to 'bury the hatchet', it is clear that the fresh crisis added further material to the store of mutual resentment they had built up during the preceding year and upon which they would continue to draw, with increasingly destructive effect, at each future clash. Indeed, a letter written by Gide to his cousin Jeanne Rondeaux little over a week after the reconciliation demonstrates that it was much more superficial than Louÿs imagined. Describing how he had spent his twenty-first birthday, on 22 November, Gide related that, feeling depressed and lonely, he had called on Louÿs in the afternoon. However, the visit did not cheer him as he had hoped, for Louÿs's conversation 'est merveilleusement apte à refouler au plus fin fond de soi-même toutes les intimités qui voudraient s'épancher'.[89]

The reconciliation produced one immediate result: the partial realization of a project formed that spring. It will be remembered that Louÿs had made the charming, if not entirely practical, suggestion that he should contribute a short passage to Gide's book.[90] It was then decided that each would leave one page blank in his first work, to be completed by the other. It soon dawned upon the two friends, however, that Louÿs was as incapable of writing a page of *André Walter* as Gide was of composing one of Louÿs's sonnets.[91] A compromise was therefore adopted: Louÿs would contribute a preface. Subsequently, exasperated by Gide's behaviour, Louÿs lost all interest in the idea, but he now took it up once more, and when *Les Cahiers d'André Walter* appeared in early January 1891 the book contained an introduction by 'Pierre Chrysis' which served the purpose of stressing the posthumous nature of the publication. This introduction was omitted by Gide from later editions. The proposal that he should himself make some contribution to Louÿs's first volume appears to have been quietly dropped.

Anxious to make greater progress with his university studies, Louÿs restricted his literary activities that autumn to the evening hours. 'De 9h à 2h du matin si tu savais quel geindre c'est que

mon bureau!' he wrote to Gide on 19 September. 'Quel merveilleux métier tout de même: on est toujours heureux, même
quand on ne trouve pas. Et quand on trouve! Ah! quand on
trouve!'[92] Louÿs was once again concentrating his efforts on the
volume of poetry he was still hoping to publish before his
twentieth birthday. The original title *Choses murmurées* had by now
been replaced by that of *La Vierge*, which suggested a thematically
linked series of poems. He later described himself as having been
'hanté par la *Vierge*' during his travels that summer,[93] and he had
worked on the volume during his short stay at the Grande
Chartreuse. By 16 September he had made good progress with
seven of the thirteen poems which were to make up the *plaquette*.
Three days later he reported to Gide: 'Ma grossesse se poursuit
sans encombre. La *Vierge* est aujourd'hui un bel embryon, bien
sain, et je compte être délivré vers la fin d'octobre.'[94] It was to be
many more months, however, before the volume was published,
in an extended form, and under its ultimate title *Astarté* (in the
meantime some of the poems were printed in *La Conque*).

Another project with which Louÿs briefly flirted at this time
was a verse play on the story of Joseph and Potiphar's wife. He
proposed it to Rodolphe Darzens when the latter invited him in
September to write something for the Théâtre libre which needed
fresh material. Darzens was doubtful about the suitability of the
subject, but Louÿs decided to go ahead none the less: 'Il a peur du
ridicule. Le ferai-je quand même? Mais oui, je le ferai! et raison
de plus.'[95] A month later, his imagination stirred by a theatrical
performance he had attended at the Théâtre Beaumarchais, he
wrote in his diary: 'Dire quelle exaltation j'ai eue jusqu'au soir, et
quelle envie de brocher en quinze jours la légende de Joseph! Ah!
tous les vers chantaient dans mon oreille, des scènes s'ébauchaient,
des actes s'éclairaient davantage . . .'[96] Only a very short fragment
has survived.[97] It is not known why Louÿs abandoned the play,
which was to present 'la lutte de la femme contre l'IDÉE. Et le
triomphe de l'idée!' Louÿs's choice of subject is of some interest,
since it indicates his early preoccupation with a theme which was
to attain its most successful formulation in the novel *Aphrodite*:
the opposition between imagination and reality.

Despite the abandonment of this project, Louÿs soon had the
pleasure of seeing more of his work in print, for an article he had
composed on 'Le Naturalisme survivant' was published in the

magazine *Art et critique* on 1 November. He chose for this occasion the pseudonym 'Claude Moreau', perhaps as a tribute to the painters Claude Monet and Gustave Moreau who were greatly admired by the Symbolists. Furthermore, three of his poems collectively entitled 'Emaux sur or et sur argent' appeared in the December 1890–January 1891 issue of *La Wallonie*, a review published in Liège by Albert Mockel which, as Louÿs informed Paul Valéry, was 'une revue très française bien que ou plutôt parce que publiée à Liège; les Liégeois, comme vous le savez . . . considérant le mot *belge* comme une injure et un mensonge'.[98] The poems had been accepted for publication by Henri de Régnier, who was a member of the editorial board of *La Wallonie* and, incidentally, Louÿs's future brother-in-law.

During the final months of 1890 Louÿs continued to extend his contacts within the literary circles of the capital. Among other regular cultural gatherings, he frequented those organized by Léon Deschamps, who had founded the review *La Plume* in the spring of 1889 and, in the autumn of that year, had inaugurated a series of Saturday evening meetings. These were at first held at the Café Fleurus, but before long they were moved to the basement of the Soleil d'Or in the place Saint-Michel, where the large numbers of persons attracted by these events could be better accommodated. There, according to a note printed in *La Plume*, 'tous les artistes se donnent rendez-vous pour dire ou entendre des vers, faire de la musique ou deviser d'Art'. In the autumn of 1890 the meetings began at 9 o'clock on the first and third Saturday of each month, the opening event taking place on 18 October. Ernest Raynaud gives an amusing account of these gatherings in his recollections of the Symbolist movement.[99] As already indicated, Louÿs did not think highly of the review; he remained equally unimpressed by the meetings. That of 18 October, for instance, he found 'tellement nul' that he left it precipitately to return to the Opéra-Comique where he had spent the earlier part of the evening. These occasions were none the less useful for the opportunities they afforded for making the acquaintance of other writers.

Louÿs also returned to the rue de Rome and this time quickly fell under Mallarmé's spell. 'Mallarmé est un homme charmant . . .', he noted in his diary on 16 October. 'Il a un charme presque féminin, silencieux, isolé. Il parle bas, dit peu de mots, mais fait un sort à toutes ses phrases.'[100] Louÿs had written to Mallarmé on 11 October, requesting permission to call upon him in order to seek his opinion on certain poems. Invited to present himself on the following Tuesday evening,[101] Louÿs took with him some of his own pieces, but the main purpose of his visit was to show Valéry's sonnet 'Pour la nuit' to Mallarmé.[102] The next day he was able to announce to Valéry: 'Mon ami, vous êtes sacré.' Mallarmé had thought very highly of the poem: 'Il l'a lu avec lenteur, relu, mesuré, et il a dit, bas: "Ah! c'est très bien." Et, comme je le faisais parler, il a repris: "C'est un poète, il n'y a pas l'ombre d'un doute." Puis, se parlant à lui-même: "Grande subtilité musicale." Et, se tournant vers moi: "En avez-vous d'autres?" Je n'avais que celui-là et j'ai bien fait, je crois. Vous lui en enverrez d'autres ... vous-même.'[103] Valéry acted upon the advice and wrote to Mallarmé, enclosing two sonnets, 'Le Jeune Prêtre' and 'La Suave Agonie' (the former was dedicated to Pierre Louÿs). Mallarmé promptly sent an encouraging reply. This exchange of letters marks the beginning of the friendship between Mallarmé and Valéry. They did not meet until the following autumn when Louÿs accompanied Valéry to the rue de Rome. Louÿs himself, during subsequent years, frequently attended the Tuesday evening receptions and sometimes visited Mallarmé at Valvins. On more than one occasion he gratefully acknowledged the debt his generation owed to Mallarmé. Thus he wrote on 26 December 1894, with reference to a publication by Mallarmé; 'Tout m'y rappelle votre esprit et vos causeries du Mardi soir, ce cours plus que supérieur où depuis dix années notre génération s'est formée.'[104] Later he greatly regretted that he had never made a note of Mallarmé's remarks.[105] His admiration for Mallarmé survived the passage of time. R. Cardinne-Petit, his secretary in 1917, relates that Louÿs sent him out one day to buy Nadar's celebrated photograph showing the poet of 'Hérodiade' seated at his table, with the famous Scottish plaid draped around his shoulders; and that he subsequently displayed the portrait prominently on one of his bookcases.[106]

Finally, the last weeks of the year 1890 were memorable for the friendly contacts Louÿs established with two poets he particularly admired, and with whom his personal life was to be closely associated: Henri de Régnier and José-Maria de Heredia. Although

Régnier was six years older than Louÿs and had already published several volumes of poetry—*Lendemains* (1885), *Apaisement* (1886), *Épisodes* (1888), *Poèmes anciens et romanesques* (1890)—he was still largely unknown. Once again Louÿs's artistic intuition enabled him to recognize talent where others saw relatively little as yet. 'Je goûte depuis peu la jouissance exquise d'être presque seul à le juger à son rang', he wrote in his diary on 28 December. 'Nul ne le connaît; nul ne l'aime. Voici dix mois déjà que les *Poèmes anciens* sont parus, et la foule ignore son nom comme s'il n'était pas né, et les gens de lettres n'ont pas lu plus de vers de lui que de moi . . . J'assiste seul à l'éclosion d'un génie qui feint de s'ignorer, et qui a une telle modestie, avec une telle horreur de la réclame, qu'il se nomme encore disciple, alors que de longue date il est maître.'[107] Régnier's modesty was not quite as apparent to everyone. 'Sous des allures d'une cordialité charmante, encore qu'un peu hautaine, il cachait le sentiment constant, mais discret de sa supériorité', Gide recalled.[108]

Louÿs's first impressions of Régnier had been none too favourable. 'Régnier était là, et quelques autres . . .', he recorded in his diary after attending his first Tuesday meeting in Mallarmé's apartment in June 1890. 'Régnier a une tête en mâchoire de cheval. Tous me déplaisaient.'[109] In fact, as his portraits show, Régnier looked distinguished rather than handsome. He was also something of a 'cold fish', as Paul Reboux recalls in his memoirs: 'Henri de Régnier était un haut gentilhomme, aux minces moustaches tombantes à la chinoise, aux longues mains, au long nez, au long menton, qui avait l'air de tellement s'ennuyer, et qui était si froid derrière son monocle, qu'auprès de lui on avait envie de se mettre un chapeau pour ne pas attraper un rhume. Mais comment se couvrir devant un homme aussi correct et aussi courtois? Et on s'en allait en éternuant et se mouchant.'[110] Yet Régnier possessed a discreet charm and Gide discovered that while he was often taciturn in public, his conversation in private could be delightful.[111]

Louÿs felt increasing admiration for Régnier's poems, as is evident from the fact that he took the trouble to copy several for Valéry's benefit. By the end of the year his enthusiasm knew no bounds: 'Henri de Régnier est non seulement un grand poète, mais—et de jour en jour je le vois davantage,—c'est évidemment le poète attendu.'[112] And Louÿs did not hesitate to include

Régnier among the distinguished poets—such as Leconte de Lisle, Heredia, Mallarmé, Verlaine, and various well-established younger writers—whose contributions opened the different issues of *La Conque*. Indeed, the name of the review itself and the quotation appearing on its title-page—'*La Conque* "où je souffle un appel à quelque dieu qui passe . . ."'—were taken from the poem 'Ariane' which Régnier had published in *Épisodes*.

In November 1890 Louÿs sent to Régnier the aforementioned three poems which subsequently appeared in *La Wallonie*.[113] In accepting them, Régnier warmly congratulated the author on their excellence. His kindness and generosity further increased Louÿs's admiration: 'J'ai lu, relu, appris ses quatre pages, les premiers éloges vrais que j'aie reçus d'un vrai poète. Si je deviens jamais ce qu'il est, je serai comme lui indulgent aux jeunes. Des lettres comme celle-là ne coûtent guère et ce sont de vraies joies pour ceux qui les ouvrent.'[114] A friendship soon developed between the two young men. Jacques-Émile Blanche painted their joint portrait in 1892.

The other new contact Louÿs made towards the end of that year was of even greater significance, since it admitted him to one of the most brilliant literary salons of the day and, at the same time, led to his introduction to the two women who were to play the most prominent roles in his life. On 9 December 1890, the day preceding his twentieth birthday, Louÿs wrote exultantly in his diary:

Le dernier jour de mes dix-neuf ans aura eu une joie: Heredia m'écrit, et m'envoie en autographe le sonnet sur les *Amours* de Ronsard. J'ai d'abord eu Mallarmé, puis Darzens, puis Régnier; cette fois, c'est Heredia. Cette année peut-être je connaîtrai Leconte de Lisle. Le reste viendra comme il pourra, sans que je m'en inquiète. Et ma vie sera bien ainsi. Puis viendront les peintres, Rops, Moreau, Rodin; les musiciens, Massenet, Reyer, et le jeune que j'attends. Que m'importeraient les autres? Oh! la vie dans un très petit cercle de grands hommes.[115]

Heredia's note was a belated acknowledgement of a letter Louÿs had addressed to him on 12 May, signed with the pseudonym 'Chrysis' (this name, which he also used for the preface to *Les Cahiers d'André Walter* and as the title of more than one poem, was taken from Victor Hugo's sonnet 'Le Satyre': its reappearance as the heroine's name in *Aphrodite*, on the other hand, owes less to Hugo than to Lucian, who bestowed it on one of the courtesans in the *Dialogi meretricii*). In the letter, 'Chrysis' drew Heredia's attention to two rhymes in Ronsard's 'Élégie à M. A. de Muret'— 'Thermodontée/domptée' and 'Phorce/force'—which, he suggested, would be most suitable for a poem in the 'Hercules' section of *Les Trophées*. Louÿs followed this intriguing missive with a flattering postcard from Bourgueil on 8 June: 'Je viens de Surgères,' he informed Heredia, 'je vais à St.-Cosme, à Vendôme, à Gâtine, à la Poissonnière . . . vous me pardonnerez si je ne puis penser à Ronsard sans songer à vous . . .'[116] Finally, he wrote once more in the autumn to express the hope that Heredia had been able to make use of the rhymes.[117] Soon afterwards Heredia succeeded in discovering the identity of his mysterious correspondent and, at the same time as he sent him the autograph of his sonnet 'Sur le Livre des Amours de Pierre de Ronsard', he invited Louÿs to call. On 12 December, the latter reported to Valéry that he had visited the poet who had read to him sketches for three splendid sonnets on the theme of Hercules and the Amazons.[118] It should be added that Louÿs was genuinely attracted by Heredia's poetry which left its mark on some of his own early sonnets. Indeed, as Y.-G. Le Dantec drily remarks, this influence 'lui aurait peut-être été *fatale* si Mallarmé n'avait pas existé . . . et si la sensibilité de l'auteur de *Bilitis* n'eût pas dû *fatalement* l'affranchir des trucs de son futur beau-père'.[119]

On 13 December Louÿs accompanied Henri de Régnier to one of the receptions which Heredia regularly held on Saturday afternoons in his apartment at 11 bis rue Balzac. There was a striking contrast between these gatherings, at which the visitor was greeted by sounds of noisily cheerful conversation, and the Tuesday evenings in the rue de Rome where the neophyte's first impression on entering the sanctuary was one of utter tranquility. Yet quite a few persons who went to listen to Mallarmé met again at Heredia's on the following Saturday. This was true, in particular, of most of the younger Symbolist writers.

On arrival at the rue Balzac, the visitor was ushered into a small room, from which a door led on the right to the large drawing-room where the ladies were assembled, while another door, to the left, gave access to the poet's own study:

La porte s'ouvrait sur un nuage épais de fumée dans lequel flottaient quelques apparences d'écrivains. Au milieu, une pipe à fin tuyau en main, Heredia recevait, levant sur un corps un peu trapu sa belle tête à barbe grisonnante, à cheveux en brosse, avec cette particularité: un œil bleu, un œil noir ... Il offrait à tout venant des cigares ... et à quelques heureux il découvrait la cachette des purs havanes qui lui venaient tout droit de son pays natal, et dont s'embaumait dans un nuage bleuté cet olympe de poètes.[120]

Heredia was admired for his poetry, he was widely respected for his opinions and literary judgements which reflected a cultured and discerning mind free of the prejudices and the pretentiousness so frequently encountered in a person of his distinction, and, above all, he was loved for his delightful personal qualities. 'Heredia,' wrote Régnier, 'exerçait une sorte de fascination. Elle résidait dans sa personne même. On aimait en lui un homme généreux, serviable et bon. Il dégageait une influence de joie, de sécurité, d'énergie. Son assurance en face de la vie et de l'art était un spectacle réconfortant.'[121] Similar tributes occur in countless memoirs of the period, Gide being almost alone in striking a discordant note in the general chorus of praise.[122] The deep affection which Heredia inspired in his younger acquaintances was movingly expressed by André Fontainas: 'De combien de mes aînés— fort peu!—eussé-je assuré: "Celui-là, tout entier, j'aurais accepté de l'être?" Heredia, oui! la souriante certitude, la plénitude de son talent, surtout la beauté forte de son âme, loyauté du poète et de l'homme fraternel.'[123] The welcome he extended to Pierre Louÿs was characteristically warm and generous:

Heredia m'a reçu comme Jupiter aurait reçu Ganymède si Ganymède avait été Orphée, ou comme le Christ a dû accueillir St. Jean la première fois qu'ils se sont rencontrés. C'était à croire que c'était moi l'aède, et lui le petit jeune ... il ne s'occupait que de moi, il ne parlait qu'à moi, il me demandait mon avis sur tout, il voulait absolument me faire dire des vers: 'Quand les gens sont sympathiques, on aime bien savoir ce qu'ils font.' ... Il m'a serré la main en me disant que j'étais son ami, qu'il fallait que je revienne régulièrement le samedi, et que 'j'allais être l'enfant de la maison' puisque j'étais le plus jeune...[124]

One can understand why Heredia's daughter Marie, who later wrote under the name 'Gérard d'Houville', gave the title *Le Séducteur* to a novel inspired by her father.

The beautiful Marie and her two equally delightful sisters formed an added attraction of these receptions. All three were to take writers for their husbands. The eldest, Hélène, 'beauté sévère aux noirs cheveux plaqués sur un front de marbre',[125] married the novelist and scientist Maurice Maindron, a man of vast erudition and considerable eccentricity. His interest in warfare led him to collect early armour, and he was reported to dress himself on occasion, when at home, in cuirass, arm-guards and thigh-pieces 'pour imiter . . . les reîtres violant les nonnes'.[126] After his death, Hélène became the wife of the literary critic René Doumic. Marie, the second daughter, was described by Fernand Gregh as 'une ravissante jeune fille dont les grands yeux noirs semblaient des fleurs' and as 'grande, mince, souple, vive, rieuse, avec des douceurs soudaines de la voix et un arrière-fond de mélancolie'.[127] Photographs taken in her youth show her to have been strikingly beautiful. In her honour was formed the Club des canaques, over which she ruled with the title of Reine Marie Ire. Among its members, apart from Louÿs, were Gregh, Léon Blum, Henri de Régnier, and Marcel Proust. Louise, the youngest of the three sisters, known to her intimates as 'Loulouse', was likewise very attractive. 'Tout d'elle était parfait,' Gregh recalled, 'la coupe du visage, les beaux yeux vifs, le nez à la fois noble et spirituel, le corps souple dans sa verdeur fringante.'[128] Over the years, Louÿs was to grow attached to all three girls. He eventually married Louise, but it was for Marie that he conceived the deepest love.

For the time being, however, his primary attachment was still to Marie Chardon. In December his sister Lucie made, on his behalf, a formal request for Marie's hand.[129] The request was not refused outright, but it would appear that one of the conditions imposed by Marie's father for giving serious consideration to his suit was that Louÿs should first obtain his *licence*.

It was in mid-December that André Gide made the acquaintance of Paul Valéry. On 14 October 1890 Louÿs had written to Valéry: 'Mon ami Gide, dont la famille habite Montpellier, ira vous voir, si vous le permettez, vers la fin du mois; je vous le recommande, bien que ce soit très inutile. Mais ne me délaissez pas trop pour lui! Ce sera, pour vous, je le devine, un des "quelques amis"; le numéro 3.'[130] Louÿs had often spoken warmly of Gide in his letters to Valéry, who now expressed his pleasure at the forthcoming meeting, while affectionately reassuring Louÿs: 'Je suis bien heureux de voir arriver votre légat Gide . . . Ne craignez pas qu'il vous fasse oublier—rien ne vous ferait oublier!'[131] In fact, Gide did not visit Montpellier until December, when he travelled south to spend the last fortnight of the year with his uncle Charles Gide who taught political economy at the University of Montpellier. He and Valéry were instantly attracted to each other. Valéry expressed his delight in a letter to Louÿs on 18 December: 'Je suis, mon cher, dans l'extase et le ravissement de votre ami Gide. Quel exquis et rare esprit, quel enthousiasme des belles rimes et des pures idées! Nous parlons beaucoup de vous et de Paris . . . Une seule chose m'attriste, ne pas vous avoir avec nous sur les hautes terrasses ensoleillées et tièdes du Peyrou . . .'[132] At the same time, Valéry became rapidly aware of the fundamental difference in the character of his two Parisian friends. 'Votre amitié semble confirmer cette opinion qui place la cause des affections dans une certaine dissemblance', he wrote on 21 December.[133] If Valéry had asked Gide's views concerning the moral problem on which he had only recently sought Louÿs's advice, he would have discovered that they were even more dissimilar than he had thought. In his letter to Louÿs on 9 December Valéry had broached what he described as 'une question si intime, si secrète, si environnée de langes sacrés que ma plume hésite à tracer de vagues phrases et des interrogations ardentes':

Mon ami, vous avez vingt ans. Pouvez-vous me confier (et comme un conseil) si vous avez résolu le triste problème de la chair? . . . Je m'entends. Quelle est votre attitude vis-à-vis de ce mal quasi inévitable et que croyez-vous qu'il soit beau et bon de faire? Ceci me tourmente cruellement. Se livrer totalement à son instinct c'est subir une *maxima capitis diminutio* intolérable à celui qui, le moindrement, a vu l'art. S'abstenir, c'est s'interdire non seulement une chose mais l'autre, c'est troubler sans cesse le cours limpide et conscient de son travail par des fièvres inesthétiques . . .[134]

Unlike Gide who had not yet overcome the inhibitions produced by his puritanical education,[135] Louÿs had indeed resolved the 'sad problem of the flesh' to his satisfaction. He had already stated his attitude in a curious diary entry addressed to his father on the first anniversary of the latter's death.[136] Asceticism, he argued, was both useless and childish: it was only right that man should satisfy his natural appetites. Moreover, by allowing the body to have its due, he would be freeing the soul for higher pursuits:

Père, j'ai fait deux parts dans ma vie, pour la plus grande pureté de mon être. J'ai délivré l'Ame dès sa jeunesse, et elle plane. Le Corps, ai-je pensé, ne vaut pas la peine qu'on cherche à le sauver; pourquoi donner à l'âme un but inférieur à elle-même? pourquoi la souiller toute la vie dans une lutte honteuse et stérile . . . L'essentiel c'est que l'Ame ne se commette pas avec le Corps, c'est qu'au spectacle des Désirs elle évite de ternir les Pensées . . . Puisque je ne veux pas avoir conscience de mon corps, mon âme tend avec liberté vers un but inflexible: L'Idéal du Beau . . .

Suiting practice to theory, Louÿs had his first sexual experiences with Parisian prostitutes long before his twentieth birthday.[137] He now expounded these views to Valéry, summing them up with the reflection: 'Et qu'importe ce que fait le corps, tant que l'âme n'en est pas sa dupe.'[138] Valéry was impressed: 'J'admire par-dessus tout en vous cette haute et claire foi littéraire qui n'hésite plus, qui de toutes pièces a créé dans votre âme une morale pratique si enviable et si nette.'[139]

1891

ON HIS excursions into literary society Louÿs soon had a companion whose timidity contrasted strikingly with his own growing self-assurance. The completion of *Les Cahiers d'André Walter* and, still more, the disappointment occasioned by Madeleine Rondeaux's refusal to marry him—he had hoped that the book would persuade her into a favourable decision—made Gide eager to abandon his self-imposed seclusion and led him to seek distraction in the discovery of Paris and its cultural life. In Pierre Louÿs he found a willing guide. Moreover, Louÿs's easy manner and spontaneous gaiety helped him to overcome to some extent his paralysing shyness. 'Je crois bien que, sans Pierre Louis, j'aurais continué de vivre à l'écart, en sauvage', Gide later admitted.[1]

Louÿs urged Gide to call on Heredia and present a copy of his book to him: 'Je lui ai parlé de toi. Il t'attend, me répétait-il.'[2] Gide hesitated. Henri de Régnier, whose acquaintance he made at a banquet in honour of Jean Moréas on 2 February, then showed the novel to Heredia and invited Gide to accompany him to the latter's receptions. On 7 March Gide allowed himself to be led by Louÿs and Régnier to the rue Balzac. His first impressions of the literary world were decidedly unfavourable: 'J'étais vraiment terrifié de cette féroce curée que c'est—le "monde des lettres"? On s'entremange furieusement ...', he reported to Valéry. 'Tout y devient matière à journalisme et à lançage—le salon de Heredia ressemble à une agence de réclames—et c'est pour ça que Louis et Régnier m'y ont mené—mais j'en ai eu assez d'aujourd'hui ...'[3] Nor was Gide greatly impressed by his host, about whom he was to write later that 'son cerveau était un peu moins ouvert que ses bras'.[4] Gide none the less returned to Heredia's receptions Saturday after Saturday. Perhaps he was not quite as disinterested as he pretended. To Valéry, however, he expressed ironic admiration for Louÿs 'qui ne quitte une réunion que pour une autre et compte à la fin de la journée le nombre de mains serrées'.[5] No doubt Gide reacted equally tartly to the 'règles de l'autolançage' evolved by the practically minded Louÿs and communicated to him 'for his benefit':

1. Ne jamais *demander* quoi que soit à personne.
2. Faire croire qu'on n'a besoin de personne.
3. Laisser entendre qu'on a le grand honneur d'être accueilli avec bienveillance par d'autres.
4. Parler peu; être toujours modéré et silencieux sur soi-même.
5. N'être jamais collant afin de se faire désirer, mais répondre à toutes les invitations pour faire connaître sa tête.
6. Enfin, sans faire jamais de requête, provoquer des obligeances spontanées . . .[6]

It should again be stressed that Louÿs's object was not to obtain financial gain or popular acclaim, but to establish contact with certain prominent men of letters and, if possible, to win their esteem. Gide may have shared these aims, but he quickly grew dismayed at the self-advertisement their achievement entailed. Despising what he regarded as the 'commercial' aspect of most literary salons, he appreciated all the more the disinterested and idealistic spirit manifested by Mallarmé, to whom he was introduced at the Moréas banquet by Maurice Barrès. He attended one of Mallarmé's receptions for the first time on 10 February. A cold prevented him from being present a fortnight later when Oscar Wilde paid his first visit to the rue de Rome.[7] If Louÿs was there, he doubtless remained quietly in the background, as befitted his youth. It was not until the end of that year that he and Gide became acquainted with Wilde.

Shyness does not necessarily imply excessive modesty or morbid self-doubt. Despite his 'invincible timidité', Gide took a confident view of his own gifts and thought himself capable of making a significant contribution to the literature of the period. On 26 January 1891 he wrote to Valéry: 'Mallarmé pour la poésie, Maeterlinck pour le drame—et quoique auprès d'eux deux, je me sente bien un peu gringalet, j'ajoute Moi pour le roman. Puis viennent les autres et que les "genres" nouveaux trouvent des voix nouvelles, qui seront aussi hautes encore que Mallarmé, que Maeterlinck . . . et que moi-même si la réalité ne prosterne mon rêve.'[8] Louÿs does not appear to have seen himself in a similar light, as a pioneer of a new literary movement. In any case, his leanings towards Parnassianism made him somewhat less susceptible to the attractions of Symbolism, although certain of his early poems were clearly at least partly influenced by the latter. His main preoccupation during 1891 was the preparation of the poetry magazine he had been planning for some time. It was only natural that it should contain many Symbolist poems, for its purpose was to present the work of the younger poets; but it was not conceived as a manifesto for the movement.

Each number of *La Conque* was to open with a previously unpublished piece by 'un des poètes les plus justement admirés de ce temps' (to quote from the note on the inside cover of the first issue). Accordingly, while collecting material from young and unknown writers, Louÿs was also soliciting contributions from the established poets he most esteemed. On 7 February 1891 he once again turned to Mallarmé who, the year before, had so readily pledged his own and his friends' support: 'Quelques amis s'unissent à moi pour publier une revue de vers, dont j'ose croire que l'apparence vous plaira. Tirée à *cent exemplaires* sur papier de Hollande, elle sera rédigée uniquement par de jeunes poètes inédits lesquels se réservent le seul plaisir d'en faire le service à ceux de qui l'avis leur est cher ou de qui, en écoliers très inexpérimentés, ils recevront d'utiles critiques avec reconnaissance . . .' In this connection, Louÿs explained, they had thought of approaching Verlaine, Heredia, Dierx, and Régnier, and were requesting from each of them a sonnet or other short poem to serve as a frontispiece for the different numbers of the review. And he added: 'Ai-je besoin de vous dire, maître, que votre concours me sera plus que tout autre précieux et que j'attends de vous le plus grand honneur que notre *Conque* puisse recevoir . . .'[9] Mallarmé complied with the request, as did the others. Louÿs was particularly pleased by Heredia's generous response: 'Quelle crème que cet homme', he commented delightedly, in communicating the good news to Gide.[10]

The first number of *La Conque* was dated 15 March 1891. A note indicated that publication would be limited to twelve issues of 100 copies each, printed on *de luxe* paper. In actual fact, only eleven appeared, dated 15 March, 1 April, and then monthly until 1 December, with the final number being put out undated. In addition to Leconte de Lisle, whose poem 'Soleils! Poussière d'or . . .' opened the series, the following 'most justly admired' poets contributed to the magazine: Léon Dierx, 'L'Odeur sacrée'; Heredia, 'Le Tombeau du conquérant'; Mallarmé, 'Éventail'; Swinburne, 'The Ballad of Melicertes—In Memory of

Théodore de Banville', 'La Ballade de Mélicerte—A la mémoire de Théodore de Banville'; Judith Gautier, 'L'Amrita des dieux'; Verlaine, 'Chanson'; Jean Moréas, 'Le Retour'; Charles Morice, 'Vers'; Maurice Maeterlinck, 'Lied'; and Henri de Régnier, 'Heure'. Furthermore, a note in the ninth and tenth issues announced a future contribution from Oscar Wilde, which would presumably have opened the proposed twelfth number (the latter was also to contain an original etching by Félicien Rops).

The inclusion of Swinburne in this list may appear surprising—that of Wilde can be explained by Louÿs's introduction to him in late 1891—but like Dante Gabriel Rossetti and other Pre-Raphaelite poets he enjoyed a considerable reputation in France. He maintained, moreover, personal contacts with several French writers, including Mallarmé, and it may well have been at the latter's suggestion that Louÿs approached him. Louÿs himself seems to have known his work well, and the admiration Swinburne expressed for Victor Hugo no doubt increased the esteem in which he already held the English poet. 'Je voudrais que tu l'entendisses,' he wrote to Gide on 4 February 1890, 'lui l'esthète, lui le lyriste exquis, aussi ennemi de la rhétorique que de la déclamation, je voudrais que tu l'entendisses parler d'Hugo.'[11]

Louÿs retained his enthusiasm for Swinburne's poetry in later life. Robert Harborough Sherard, the friend and biographer of Oscar Wilde, relates that a group of French writers headed by Louÿs at one time resolved to publish a volume entitled *Vers offerts à Monsieur Swinburne*, in protest against the bourgeois moral prejudice which, in their view, had deprived the poet of the award of the Nobel prize for Literature he so clearly deserved. Swinburne died, however, before the project could be carried into effect. Louÿs thereupon wrote to Sherard: 'You have had an immense loss in England this year [i.e. 1909]—Swinburne. He was the greatest living poet. When I think that he used to write to me when I was nineteen years old, that he contributed to my first review, and that during twenty years I have been allowing him to die without going to see him I cannot console myself.'[12]

Louÿs himself published seventeen poems in *La Conque*, ten under his own name or initials, and seven under the pseudonym 'Claude Moreau' which had already done service for the article 'Le Naturalisme survivant'. All were reprinted in *Astarté*, often considerably revised and with different titles. After Louÿs, the most prolific contributors to *La Conque* were Valéry and Léon Blum. The latter, who was two years younger than Louÿs, was to achieve a brilliant reputation as a literary and dramatic critic before turning to politics and becoming France's first socialist Prime Minister. Another future politician often encountered in the pages of the review is Henri Bérenger (he was, in 1925–6, French Ambassador to the United States). Other frequent contributors were Edmond Fazy, Eugène Hollande, and, from the fifth issue onwards, Camille Mauclair. Gide had pieces in three numbers: two long poems, 'Nuit d'Idumée' and 'La Promenade' in nos. 2 and 10 respectively, and eight shorter poems signed 'André Walter' in the final issue.[13]

The appearance of the new magazine did not pass unnoticed; in particular, it gave rise to an interesting and not unsympathetic article in the austere *Journal des débats* on 7 April 1891, in which the critic Henri Chantavoine (who signed himself 'S') addressed some pertinent remarks to the young poets of *La Conque*. While commending them somewhat ironically on their originality, Chantavoine sounded a not untimely warning against preciosity and the temptations of excessive obscurity:

Presque tous ces jeunes ménétriers sont des impressionnistes plus ou moins hardis qui sont, je pense, ravis d'exprimer des nuances d'idées ou de sentiments très délicates dans une langue plus précieuse qu'ingénue, à l'aide d'une prosodie subtile—ou négligée comme il vous plaira. Ils sont tous originaux . . . Peut-être ne se rendent-ils pas assez compte qu'il est plus facile d'être singulier que d'être personnel—et leur dédain de se trouver compris tout de suite par tout le monde les conduit-il sans qu'ils s'en aperçoivent ou qu'ils s'en soucient, à devenir élégamment inintelligibles.

He then singled out Valéry's 'Narcisse parle' (printed in the first number of *La Conque*) for favourable comment, though not without once again tempering his praise with a note of caution:

Ce Narcisse qui parle et qui pleure, n'est-ce pas,—à mon goût du moins—, de l'Ovide mélangé avec du Verlaine, c'est-à-dire du paganisme un peu défraîchi mélangé de mysticisme un peu étrange?

O divine simplicité! sauve-les, ces jeunes modernistes,—sauve-nous tous tant que nous sommes, de la tentation d'être compliqués, pour amuser les artistes, et pour étonner les bourgeois!

It is, in retrospect, amusing to find this warning addressed to the poet who, many years later, was to compose in 'La Jeune Parque' a work which, on his own admission, 'passe pour un des plus obscurs de la langue française'.[14] Louÿs himself had no doubts about Valéry's talent. On 2 May he wrote to his former teacher Th. Cart: 'Je vous supplie de relire le 'Narcisse' et de retenir le nom de son auteur. Valéry est de tous les collaborateurs de *la Conque* celui en qui j'espère le plus.'[15]

Shortly before the publication of the first number of *La Conque*, an incident occurred which, in view of its dramatic impact on Louÿs's outlook and comportment, must be counted among the most significant in his life. It determined in large measure his conduct during the following years and imprinted upon his character certain traits which it would never shed.

Ever since his brother Paul had died from tuberculosis in 1884, at the age of twenty-seven, Louÿs had been obsessed with the idea that he, too, would be carried off in his youth by the same disease. On 27 June 1887 he wrote in his diary, in a reference to Marie Bashkirtseff:

La pauvre fille est morte poitrinaire, et Dieu lui a refusé la suprême consolation qu'il donne aux phtisiques: l'ignorance de leur mal et l'espérance de leur guérison. Et moi aussi je mourrai poitrinaire, et, comme elle, je l'aurai su avant même que la maladie n'éclate, quand mes poumons ne la contenaient qu'en germe. Oui, je mourrai de cela, peut-être cette année, peut-être dans deux ans, peut-être beaucoup plus tard, à vingt-cinq ou trente ans, mais j'en mourrai, je le sais, c'est une maladie qui ne pardonne pas. Je mourrai en pleine jeunesse . . .[16]

Another entry, dated 5 January 1888, reads:

Pourquoi faut-il que dans tous mes projets, dans tous les rêves d'avenir de mon imagination de dix-sept ans, je voie se dresser devant moi, hideuse, menaçante, la terrible phtisie pulmonaire? Pourquoi faut-il que, au moment où je suis si heureux de me dire 'A vingt-cinq ans je serai peut-être célèbre', une voix que je ne veux pas entendre, que je repousse épouvanté, me crie à l'oreille incessamment: 'A vingt-cinq ans, tu seras pourri'? Oh! mon Dieu, mon Dieu, plus que sept ans à vivre . . .[17]

If before he had had a premonition of his early death, an instinctive awareness of the presence of the still dormant disease, his fears received what appeared to be clear confirmation early in 1891. He recorded the event in his diary on 1 March:

Cette fois, l'heure est venue. C'est la phtisie. Depuis cinq ans je l'attendais. Serait-ce à dix-huit ans, à vingt-sept, à trente-deux? C'est à vingt. Vraiment, c'est trop tôt. Sans plaintes stupides, sans puérils regrets, j'ai le droit de le dire. C'est trop tôt. J'ai si peu vécu! si peu, si peu, si peu! Tant de choses encore que je ne connais pas! que je n'aurai jamais connues. Et surtout mourir sans avoir rien fait. Mourir sans pouvoir se dire à soi-même qu'on a eu un moment d'orgueil légitime. Et sans avoir rien commencé dans la belle vie espérée. C'était bien la peine 'd'avoir quelque chose là'![18]

Several years later Louÿs explained to Georges how he had obtained this confirmation of his fears. Returning 'très faible, pâle et toussant' from a consultation with Louis Landouzy, the well-known specialist for pulmonary diseases, he discovered that the latter had prescribed 'pilules de créosote' and 'frictions au gant de crin' (absorption of beechwood creosote and rubbing with a friction-glove were two methods then widely used in the treatment of tuberculosis, which was, however, commonly regarded at that time as a fatal illness). Accordingly, on reading the prescription, he felt like a man 'qui s'entend condamner à mort'.

When the infection subsequently cleared up, Louÿs considered that he had been only temporarily reprieved, and that it was merely a question of time before the bacillus would strike again and carry him off. This conviction that he was living on borrowed time accounts for both the restlessness which characterized his existence during the following years, and his feverish pursuit of pleasure. He felt as if he had to cram the experiences of a lifetime into the space of a few years, a few months, a few weeks . . .

Quand j'ai vu que ce n'était que partie remise, le souvenir de cette journée où j'avais regretté toute la vie que je ne connaissais pas, m'a tout à fait dérangé l'esprit. J'ai voulu faire en trois semaines ce qu'on fait en trente ans. Mais quand le pli a été pris, je n'ai pas pu me rattraper et j'ai continué avec la même hâte à tout connaître et à tout avoir. J'achetais vint-cinq volumes par semaine; je suis resté une fois quatre nuits dehors à la suite . . . Ma collection de gravures qui aurait dû se faire en dix ans a été achevée en moins d'un mois. Quand j'ai voulu voir Amsterdam, j'ai pris le train quatre heures après en avoir eu la première idée. Pour tout ainsi . . .[19]

Viewed in the light of these remarks, much that might otherwise seem puzzling in Louÿs's activities and conduct during the years following his illness in March 1891 becomes comprehensible. It is hardly surprising that, constantly haunted by the thought of the sword of Damocles he imagined to be hanging over his head, he should have yielded increasingly to self-indulgence which, in turn, led to ever greater moral instability. This self-indulgence found expression in a certain capriciousness, as well as in an excessive touchiness: independent, and determined to preserve his independence, he became highly sensitive to real or imagined slights. At the same time, he grew increasingly extravagant in the expenditure of money and in the use of his physical and emotional resources. He generously offered presents to his friends, for no other reason than that they were his friends and that it delighted him to give them pleasure. With equal lavishness he gratified his own taste for beautiful things, especially for handsomely bound books and *objets d'art*, with which he filled his rooms. His spending became particularly reckless after he had received a sizeable legacy out of his father's estate on his twenty-first birthday. Within three years he had squandered all of it. Financial difficulties form a recurrent theme of his letters to Georges who frequently supplied him with funds. Yet despite the fits of depression into which these anxieties plunged him with distressing frequency, he does not appear to have made more than a half-hearted attempt to find the steady employment that would have provided him with a regular source of income. Such projects form another recurrent topic of this correspondence. There are numerous references to the possibility of Louÿs entering the government service or joining the staff of some newspaper. Nothing ever came of these plans. To make matters worse, there were prolonged periods when he could make little progress with his literary work. Louÿs was himself painfully aware of his moral instability, exemplified further by the frequency with which he fell in love and became involved in *affaires*. Georges's departure for Cairo in 1893 deprived him of an important restraining influence. 'Je n'ai pas de force de caractère et j'en souffre plus que de tout', he wrote to Georges on 7 June 1895, adding pathetically: 'Je crois qu'il est grand temps que tu reviennes et que tu me dictes ma vie.'[20]

Even his closest intimates do not appear to have suspected this darker side of Louÿs's life. It is remarkable that, throughout many periods of acute unhappiness, the charm of his personality remained unimpaired, so that his friends could still recall it with delight thirty years later.

The circle of Louÿs's literary acquaintances continued to extend steadily, partly through the various receptions and gatherings he attended, and partly as a result of the contacts he made, both among younger and older writers, in connection with the publication of *La Conque*. At the same time, the review was indirectly the cause of a fresh quarrel between Gide and Louÿs. 'Louis m'a meurtri cruellement hier', Gide announced dramatically to Valéry on 17 June 1891.[21] After spending several weeks at Uzès, where his grandmother lived, he had travelled to Paris in mid-June to deliver to Louÿs a poem he had composed for *La Conque*. Eager for an early reunion, he had written to invite Louÿs to dinner on the day of his return. However, on arrival, he found a letter which abruptly cooled his excitement: 'Dans l'impossibilité absolue où nous sommes mon frère et moi de comprendre ta carte,' Louÿs wrote, 'il n'est guère possible de se concerter. Est-ce ta pièce, ou toi, ou l'un portant l'autre qui arrive, arrives, ou arrivez? Dans le cas où ce serait toi je le regretterais parce que je dîne en ville. Et dans la suite ma soirée est prise jusqu'à huit heures du matin. Du reste, ne viens pas m'embêter en ce moment; je suis en pleine licence, et on ne me voit qu'à la Sorbonne.'[22]

Gide was greatly distressed: 'Je n'en ai pu dormir de la nuit; de telles choses me font du mal, comme d'une amante', he informed Valéry.[23] Nevertheless he called early the following morning on Louÿs, who welcomed him with his customary disarming smile, scolded him for taking his letter too seriously, added that he could not spare him more than a few moments as he had to leave almost immediately for the Sorbonne, and then spent the next ninety minutes showing him various newly acquired treasures. He also, rather tactlessly, told Gide that his poem could not appear in the forthcoming issue of the review as planned, as he intended to insert instead a poem by Camille Mauclair (whom Louÿs had recently met at the Sorbonne). Gide's mortification was thus rendered more acute by jealousy. Louÿs, he observed peevishly to Valéry, 'est emballé maintenant pour le jeune Camille Mauclair qu'il a *découvert* ces derniers temps . . . il est évident que nous pâlissons.'[24]

The fresh quarrel—followed by a partial reconciliation—reopened earlier wounds. Gide assessed, in somewhat extravagant terms, the effect of this latest incident on their relations:

Malgré tout cela, j'aime Louis comme je ne saurais m'empêcher d'aimer un avec qui j'ai fait tous les premiers rêves vierges. Je sens que j'ai pour lui cette tendresse encore—faiblesse peut-être, et que je reste toujours son ami, mais lui ne peut plus être le mien; de son côté mon cœur n'est plus que douloureuse blessure. Il m'a parlé déjà plusieurs fois comme une mauvaise maîtresse et la meurtrissure d'harsoir est tombée là où déjà il y avait des cicatrices à peine. Je n'attends de lui plus aucune joie; je n'ai plus de lui que de l'ennui.[25]

Gide's increasing awareness of the incompatibility of their temperaments led him to draw the logical conclusion: he should see less of Louÿs. At the same time, Louÿs's manifest failure to realize that their relations had entered a new critical phase appeared to Gide further evidence of his superficial character: 'il croit que tout est resté de même, il ne *regarde* jamais'.[26] From Montpellier, Valéry addressed soothing words of comfort to the 'cher cœur meurtri, comme un oiseau saignant et ivre' and did his best to pour oil upon the troubled Parisian waters: 'Louis est un enfant, vous êtes deux enfants, aimez-le comme il est, avec sa fougue excellente et sa volonté qui veut violer la Gloire. Tout ce qui vous a froissé vient chez lui d'un ordre supérieur. Endormez sa fièvre par la magie de vos sourires et de vos caresses. Qu'il soit calme entre vos paroles.'[27] However, tranquillity was not easily re-established, for Gide's exasperation was such that he no longer felt any inclination to revive their former association. 'J'ai revu Louis', he wrote in his diary on 25 June. 'Miséricorde! Est-ce que nous allons nous réconcilier? ... Déjà trois fois nous avons eu de grandes explications; nous avons déjà fait cette douloureuse expérience; nous ne pouvons pas nous "entendre"; dès lors, l'intimité est impossible. Alors pourquoi recommencer encore?'[28] They continued to see one another, none the less, and resumed to some extent their earlier relationship; but Gide, at any rate, was convinced that, in view of the disparity of their characters, they ought not to aspire to be more than 'd'excellents camarades, ou des amis sans profondeur'.[29]

Gide was not only exasperated by Louÿs's frequent flippancy, he had also become bored—the word recurs in his references to

Louÿs during this period—by the kind of literary discussion in which Louÿs took much pleasure and which he himself increasingly abhorred, as being excessively analytical and essentially destructive in its critical approach: 'je n'ai plus, de ses discussions verveuses et paradoxales, que de la fatigue et de l'ennui . . . oh, de l'ennui'.[30] And to Valéry he asserted: 'Louis m'a donné l'horreur des livres.'[31]

Another source of irritation to Gide was Louÿs's addiction to practical jokes. Some of these were intended to make fun of Gide's moral rigidity. Thus on one occasion Gide, on answering the door, found himself confronted by a naked young woman, while Louÿs and some friends gleefully watched the encounter from the floor below. Another time, on the pretext that a sick friend wished to see him, Louÿs sent the unsuspecting Gide to an apartment where he was warmly welcomed by a lady of easy virtue who promptly attempted to initiate him into the mysteries of love. Another, more harmless, prank took the form of a letter supposedly written by a female admirer of the *Cahiers d'André Walter* who professed her eagerness to make the author's acquaintance.[32] Other jokes were of a more childish nature, such as the letter sent in an elegant long envelope addressed to 'Mademoiselle Andrée Gide' and bearing a large green seal on which the initials 'P.L.' were decorously intertwined. The message inside consisted of the statement 'I love you' expressed in a variety of languages.[33]

In addition to pursuing his university studies which now occupied a major part of his day, if his statements to Gide are to be believed, Louÿs was endeavouring that spring to improve his financial situation. 'J'ai cru que j'aurais une bonne nouvelle à t'annoncer à ton arrivée,' he wrote to Georges on 17 June, on the latter's return to France after a prolonged absence abroad, 'que je gagnais ma vie maintenant tout seul.'[34] He was, in fact, negotiating a contract with the daily newspaper *Le Gaulois* which, under the forceful and imaginative editorship of Arthur Meyer, had attained a position of exceptional prestige. It was somewhat incongruously proposed that he should contribute a children's story each week, for which he was to receive a regular fee of 100 francs, giving him an income of 5,200 francs over the whole year. This sum, together with a further 1,200 francs which he hoped to obtain from another journal, would have been sufficient to secure for him a certain measure of financial independence. Quite apart from the money, a contract with *Le Gaulois* would have been a feather in any young writer's cap. An added attraction was the possibility of subsequently publishing the stories in book form. However, nothing came of the project.

For Louÿs the summer of 1891 was filled with the music of Richard Wagner. Though his knowledge of the operas was sketchy, he was already an enthusiastic admirer of the German composer who enjoyed a considerable vogue among the Symbolists. It is significant that one of the subjects he had selected for 'meditation' during his retreat at the Grande Chartreuse should have been the Prelude to *Parsifal*. A quotation in German from the same opera appeared at the head of 'L'Effloraison', the poem printed by Darzens in the *Revue d'aujourd'hui*. Now Louÿs was able to pay his first visit to Bayreuth, where he hoped to combine pleasure with study, for ostensibly the principal purpose of the journey was to improve his knowledge of German in preparation for the *licence* examination the following year ('je parle allemand comme un enfant de huitième', he was forced to recognize with some mortification on his arrival in Germany[35]).

At Karlsruhe Louÿs met A.-Ferdinand Hérold who travelled with him to Bavaria. Hérold was to be his companion on several other journeys. Gide described him as 'le meilleur des camarades, le plus fidèle des amis'.[36] Five years older than Louÿs, he was already a familiar figure in all the literary salons. A person of learning and refinement, Hérold was also a poet and playwright who had already published several works (*L'Exil de Harini*, 1888; *La Légende de Sainte Liberata*, 1889; *Les Pæans et les Thrènes*, 1890; *La Joie de Maguelonne*, 1891). He was for many years the dramatic critic of the *Mercure de France*.

The two friends reached Bayreuth on 1 or 2 August. On the latter day Louÿs attended his first performance of *Parsifal*. At that time the Festspielhaus still held the exclusive rights to the staging of the opera which was not presented elsewhere, other than in concert form, until its production at the Metropolitan Opera House, New York, on 24 December 1903. Although Louÿs had heard much of the music and prepared himself conscientiously for the experience—'Ce soir donc, je serai à point, grâce à cette espèce de retraite comme pour une première communion,' he wrote to Georges on 2 August[37]—he quickly realized how superficial and incomplete his knowledge had been. His admiration for the work increased with each hearing. Between 2 and 6 August he attended no fewer than three performances of *Parsifal*, the third of which was memorable also for another reason: Téodor de Wyzewa, one of the guiding spirits of the influential *Revue wagnérienne*, arranged for him to be seated in Cosima's box and introduced him to her family.[38] He also heard a performance of *Tristan and Isolde*. Needless to say, he did not meet the composer himself, despite Robert Cardinne-Petit's circumstantial account of a supposed encounter, for Wagner had then been dead for over eight years.[39]

Louÿs's ecstatic descriptions of his impressions alarmed Georges who feared that all this excitement might place an excessive strain on his brother's already weak constitution. As a result, Louÿs received a letter enjoining him to leave Bayreuth forthwith. In his reply, on 7 August, he pleaded to be allowed to stay a little longer:

Je suis consterné de ta lettre et depuis une demi-heure je me promène de long en large dans ma chambre sans me décider ni à partir quand tout me retient ni à rester contre ton gré.—D'abord rien (à part *Tristan*, mais c'est fini) ne me surexcite ni me fatigue. L'émotion que *Parsifal* me donne est une extase continuellement douce et bienfaisante. Tu sais que, chez moi, même ces émotions-là se transforment en enthousiasme la première fois. Mais à présent je suis tout à fait calmé et je me laisse envahir doucement par la joie la plus pure et la plus absolue que j'aie jamais eue. Je suis selig [i.e. 'intensely happy'].

And he continued reassuringly: 'Une des choses que je projette le plus souvent depuis que je suis ici c'est de te donner à lire le texte de *Parsifal* quand nous serons ensemble. Tu verras alors s'il y a quoi que ce soit de dangereux pour un pauvre jeune homme qui a besoin de repos.'[40]

Louÿs remained at Bayreuth for a further week, during which he heard his fourth performance of *Parsifal*. It was not until 13 August that he left the intoxicating atmosphere of the Bavarian Festspielstadt for the more restful and relaxing air of Thuringia, though even then he regretted missing the final performances of the opera ('cette étrange pièce est devenue pour moi, à un tel point le But, que je demande par quelle folie je m'en vais ailleurs quand il y en a deux encore où je pourrais être'[41]). After spending the night at Meiningen, he arrived on the following day in the little town of Eisenach which, owing to its beautiful surroundings, attracted many summer visitors, as it still does to this day. There Louÿs lodged during the following two weeks at the Hotel Elisabethenruhe, whose name, with its associations with *Tannhäuser*, was bound to please so ardent a Wagnerite. The famous song contest which provided the subject for the opera had been held in the year 1207 at the Wartburg, the ancient castle built by the Landgraves of Thuringia on a hill near the town.

By 29 August Louÿs had returned to Paris. Gide was still at La Roque, writing the *Traité du Narcisse*. They had not met for several weeks, but had corresponded fairly regularly. Freed from the friction provoked by personal contact, their relations had regained the warmth of earlier days. 'Tu es décidément le seul', Louÿs assured Gide in August. 'Je ne sais pas du tout pourquoi, mais tu es le seul.'[42] In September Gide wrote: 'Toi dans les vers, moi dans la prose. Nous comprendrons peu à peu que nous sommes *les deux seuls*. C'est pourquoi je t'aime aussi, grand compagnon des nobles routes, et voici pourquoi il nous faut décidément vivre ensemble.'[43]

A curious feature of their correspondence is the occasional use of a sexually equivocal vocabulary. Thus, in a letter sent from Amsterdam on 15 July, Gide signed himself 'Ta légitime'.[44] On 29 July he informed Maurice Quillot, in a letter addressed jointly to him and to Louÿs, and therefore evidently intended also for the latter's eyes: 'Louÿs est mon mari légitime; vous êtes mon grâcieux adultère . . . Depuis longtemps déjà je cherchais quelque chose à cacher à mon vieux cocu, parce que ça me vexait d'être sans mystère.'[45] Another letter to Louÿs, on 31 August, is headed 'Mon mari'.[46] Entering into the spirit of the pleasantry, Louÿs replied on 1 September: 'Je trouve que pour une femme légitime tu m'es bigrement infidèle. Et tu me trompes avec *mes* amis, Druyn [*sic*], Quyllot [*sic*], et ceteris. Et nous ne *pouvons* pas divorcer! C'est ça le diable.'[47]

The bantering tone of these letters suggests that this was no more than an innocent game which may well, as Jean Delay observes, have contained an element of literary preciosity.[48] A passage in Gide's letter of 18 September (addressed to 'Ma petite évaporée') lends substance to this conjecture: 'Nous sommes comme deux amies, car si peu hommes vraiment. Tu m'accom pagnes en mes rêves esthétiques. Nous sommes comme Alcée et Sappho.'[49] The practice becomes more intriguing when carried on at an emotionally highly charged pitch, as when Gide, complaining to Valéry about Louÿs's hurtful flippancy, declares: 'de telles choses me font du mal, comme d'une amante'.[50] Prevented by his inhibitions from enjoying normal relations with the opposite sex, Gide was indeed, to some extent, using friendship as an emotional substitute. That he was by no means unaware of this is proved by a revealing passage in a letter to Valéry in November 1891: 'J'ai voulu jusqu'alors *faire l'amitié*, comme on "fait l'amour". C'est ridicule. Cela vient de ce que je ne veux pas faire l'amour.'[51] Gide invested his friendship with other young men with an emotional intensity which frequently led him into displays of possessiveness and jealousy. He could not bear the thought that any of his friends might have a more intimate confidant than himself; to each of them, he later recalled, 'je m'offrais . . . aussi complètement que j'exigeais que chacun se donnât à moi'.[52]

On 19 September Valéry arrived in Paris with his mother for a month's stay. He had not informed Louÿs of the precise date of his arrival, certain that he would find him at the rue Vineuse. He was to be disappointed, for Louÿs was spending a week in Brittany.[53] They did not meet until the following Saturday, 26 September. In October Louÿs arranged Valéry's introduction to Mallarmé. He wrote to the latter on 7 October:

Mon ami Paul Valéry, que vous connaissez de nom, je crois, est à Paris et rêve de vous voir. Voulez-vous me permettre de le présenter à vous, et quel jour? Si je n'avais craint de distraire inutilement votre solitude, il y a deux mois, je vous aurais écrit de Bayreuth, où nous avions si souvent, Hérold et moi, le souvenir des idées remuées quelque mardi pour nous. Vraiment quelque chose nous manquait dans la salle et nous sentions au milieu une place vide, à votre nom . . .[54]

Mallarmé replied by return, proposing the Saturday evening of the same week, and thus it was on 10 October that took place what Henri Mondor has called 'l'heureuse rencontre de Valéry et Mallarmé'.[55] Valéry afterwards set down an account of the conversation. which was published by J.-P. Monod in his book *Regard sur Valéry*,[56]

Louÿs saw little of Gide during the early part of that autumn, for except for a brief visit to Paris in October to meet Valéry, Gide remained at La Roque. Not until he had finished *Le Traité du Narcisse*, at the beginning of November, did he return to live in Paris. Louÿs's opinions apparently still carried some weight with him, for he explained to Valéry that 'Louis . . . est si content [du *Traité du Narcisse*] que j'ose te le dédier'.[57] His relations with Louÿs had, in fact, remained remarkably untroubled during their separation. 'J'en suis heureux,' he observed to Valéry, 'car nous ne pouvons être qu'au mieux ou qu'au plus mal.'[58] On the white cover of the first edition of the book, the words *Traité du* appeared above an elegant narcissus drawn by Louÿs.

Louÿs himself, in addition to editing and publishing *La Conque*, was still engaged in the preparation of the *plaquette* of poems. His interest in Greek literature also led him to undertake the first of his translations from that language. Although *Les Poésies de Méléagre* were not published until two years later, the original edition bears, on its final page, the note: 'Traduit en novembre 1891 et achevé d'imprimer le 29 juin 1893'. A manuscript sold after Louÿs's death assigns the translation more specifically to the period between 27 October and 13 November.[59] This initial version underwent some changes before it was printed.

The choice of Meleager is a clear indication of Louÿs's strong predilection for the Hellenistic age. Meleager of Gadara, who lived in the first century B.C., is known and admired as a poet of short elegiacs on love. Both the erotic subject-matter and its extremely delicate treatment were likely to appeal to Louÿs. Meleager also compiled a 'garland' of epigrams drawn from his own compositions as well as from those of a number of contemporary and earlier writers. This collection served subsequently as the basis for the famous *Greek Anthology*. Meleager's amatory pieces were widely imitated by the poets of the French Renaissance, notably Ronsard, for whose lyric verses Louÿs felt such profound admiration. Moreover, among the later poets who adapted Meleager's epigrams were two who particularly appealed to him: André Chénier and Heredia, himself an enthusiastic student of the Pléiade. Louÿs's interest in Meleager may thus have been awakened in the first place by these precursors, or he may have encountered Meleager's poems directly in the *Greek Anthology* which became one of his favourite books. When, during his stay in London in the following summer, he sought a subject for the play he wished to write for Sarah Bernhardt, it was to the *Anthology* that he first turned for inspiration.

The inclusion, among works 'en préparation' listed in the December issue of *La Conque*, of 'Sainte Marie de Magdala' indicates that Louÿs was also contemplating at this time the resumption of an earlier project. He had been fascinated by the story of Mary Magdalene for several years. In a questionnaire reproduced in his diary on 26 October 1887, he entered her name in answer to the question 'Dans l'histoire tout entière, quelle est la femme que vous admirez le plus?'[60] His interest in the subject was further stimulated by a performance of Massenet's oratorio *Marie Magdeleine* which he heard at a concert of the Colonne Orchestra on 18 December 1887. The music made a great impression on him: 'Je n'ai qu'un mot à dire: c'est sublime.'[61] On 6 May 1888 he wrote in his diary:

Je ferai une *Marie-Madeleine*. C'est un sujet qui m'a toujours tenté . . . C'est une légende, traitons-la en légende et arrangeons-la à notre bon plaisir. Je mettrais Massenet en prose, pour tout dire en un mot . . . Un premier contraste entre sa vie de famille et la vie de plaisir qu'elle mène plus tard, un second contraste entre sa vie écœurante et son amour pour le Christ me paraissent intéressants. Il y aurait même là matière à un grand roman, comme *Salammbô*. C'est à voir.[62]

The published diary contains no further reference to the project, but a long fragment of a poem about Mary Magdalene was found among Louÿs's papers after his death. At least a part of that fragment had been completed by August 1888.[63] The heroine's name appears as 'Méryem', which was the form used by Massenet. Louÿs's interest in the story may have been further increased by Rodolphe Darzens's playlet *L'Amante du Christ* which was staged at the Théâtre libre in October 1888 and published that same year by Lemerre. Despite the fact that the resumption of the project in 1891 proved ephemeral, the subject continued to haunt Louÿs. This is evident from the note he added in 1918 to the diary entry on the concert performance of *Marie Magdeleine* in 1887: 'Voilà qui est très intéressant. C'est pour la première fois le sujet d'*Aphrodite*: préférer l'idée à la réalité.'[64] It was, incidentally, Louÿs's early ambition to become in literature what Massenet was in music—a desire which, in 1897, prompted the wry remark: 'C'est bien à peu près ce que je suis devenu,—hélas!'[65]

On 3 November, the very day on which Gide informed Valéry of the completion of the *Traité du Narcisse*, a person renowned for his own particular brand of narcissism and who was to play a significant role in Gide's life visited Mallarmé. Oscar Wilde had made Mallarmé's acquaintance in February 1891. He signalled his return to Paris in late October by sending Mallarmé a copy of *The Picture of Dorian Gray* which had appeared in the interval. In an accompanying note he announced his intention of calling on Mallarmé on the following Tuesday. Louÿs may well have been present on that occasion. In any case, there must have been many opportunities for them to meet, for Wilde became 'le "great event" des salons littéraires' of that season.[66] Wilde is mentioned as a future contributor in the ninth and tenth issues of *La Conque*. The ninth issue is dated '1er novembre', but it cannot be concluded from this that Louÿs had made his acquaintance prior to that date, since the later numbers of the review were published with some delay. The earliest evidence of a personal contact is provided by an exchange of letters at the end of November. On 28 November Wilde wrote to Louÿs:

Cher Monsieur Louÿs, J'accepte avec le plus vif plaisir la gracieuse et charmante invitation que vous et M. Gide ont eu la bonté de m'adresser. Vous m'indiquerez, n'est-ce pas, l'endroit et l'heure.

Je garde un souvenir délicieux de notre petit déjeuner de l'autre jour, et de l'accueil sympathique que vous m'avez fait.

J'espère que les jeunes poètes de France m'aimeront un jour, comme moi à ce moment je les aime.

La poésie française a toujours été parmi mes maîtresses les plus adorées, et je serai très content de croire que parmi les poètes de France je trouverai de véritables amis.

Veuillez présenter à M. Gide l'assurance de mes sentiments les plus distingués. Veuillez, cher Monsieur Louÿs, l'agréer'.[67]

While the wording of this letter does not rule out the possibility that Gide had been present at the 'petit déjeuner', this seems unlikely in view of Gide's own account of his first meeting with Wilde: 'Je souhaitai le connaître, tout en n'espérant pas y arriver. Un hasard heureux, ou plutôt un ami, me servit, à qui j'avais dit mon désir. On invita Wilde à dîner. Ce fut au restaurant. Nous étions quatre, mais Wilde fut le seul qui parla.'[68] The friend in question was evidently Pierre Louÿs who replied to Wilde on 29 November, proposing that they should meet at the Café d'Harcourt, in the place de la Sorbonne, at eight o'clock—presumably that same evening (a *petit bleu* would have reached Wilde very quickly).[69] The fourth member of the dinner-party may have been Stuart Merrill.[70]

We know from Gide's engagement-book that he saw Wilde almost daily during the following fortnight,[71] and his correspondence makes it clear that Louÿs was present at many of these meetings. Thus Gide refers, in a letter to Valéry, to 'Wilde qui cause . . . à la fin de repas où il m'a fait boire, des repas qui durent trois heures, avec Merrill et P.L. ou bien à Montmartre chez Aristide Bruant . . .'[72] And in another letter to Valéry he gives a somewhat breathless account of his unusually active social life: 'Quelques lignes de quelqu'un d'abruti, qui ne lit plus, qui n'écrit plus, qui ne dort plus, ni ne mange, ni ne pense—mais court avec ou sans Louÿs dans les cafés ou les salons serrer des mains et faire des sourires. Heredia, Régnier, Merrill, l'esthète Oscar Wilde, ô admirable, admirable celui-là . . .'[73]

Wilde, whose character contained a strong element of the tempter and corrupter, appears to have quickly divined the fundamental insecurity of Gide's introspective nature and to have taken a perverse pleasure in challenging his moral principles and aesthetic ideals. Jean Delay has rightly stressed that Gide's meetings with Wilde during this initial period of their acquaintance constituted an important stage in his 'de-Christianization'.[74] As might be expected, Louÿs's relations with Wilde were of a very different kind. Since he was not, like Gide, full of religious scruples or plagued by sexual inhibitions, Louÿs was not similarly vulnerable to the morally disruptive effect of Wilde's apologues and paradoxes. Despite the disparity in age and literary achievement, their initial contacts quickly developed into a friendship between near-equals. Moreover, while Wilde never felt any particular affection for Gide, he was attracted to Louÿs and soon conceived 'une particulière tendresse' for him.[75] He presented him with a copy of the recently published *A House of Pomegranates*, inscribed:

> Au jeune homme qui adore la Beauté
> Au jeune homme que la Beauté adore
> Au jeune homme que j'adore.[76]

Wilde was not only won over by Louÿs's personality; he also quickly formed a high opinion of his intelligence and literary talent. Shortly after their first meeting he sent him the manuscript of *Salomé* for his comments. This is the latest of the three extant manuscripts, all of them in French, written wholly or largely during Wilde's stay in Paris in November and December 1891. Although Wilde seemed to regard this version at the time as little more than a working draft—'Ce n'est pas encore fini ou même corrigé, mais ça donne l'idée de la *construction*, du motif et du mouvement dramatique', he informed Louÿs[77]—the text is virtually identical with the published version. The manuscript, which is now in the Rosenbach Museum at Philadelphia, contains interlinear observations and suggested improvements in Louÿs's handwriting, but Wilde took note, for the most part, only of the remarks bearing on points of French grammar (although often credited with an excellent command of the French language, he could be guilty of the crassest of howlers: he once concluded a story with the statement 'A ce moment, la reine, il est mouru!'[78]). It is true that Louÿs was not the first person to be shown Wilde's play: both Stuart Merrill and Adolphe Retté had already proposed certain corrections. Nevertheless, the fact that Wilde should have turned for advice to this almost unknown young poet whose acquaintance he had only recently made clearly reflects the highly favourable impression he had formed of Louÿs. The publication of the play in February 1893 was to furnish further proof of Wilde's affection, for *Salomé* was dedicated to Pierre Louÿs.

In December 1891 Louÿs came into the money left to him by his father, some one hundred thousand francs. He was now financially independent, but the correspondence with Georges suggests that the latter continued to exercise some control over the use which Louÿs made of the inheritance. At any rate, Louÿs felt obliged, on occasion, to account to him for his expenditure.

1892

THE YEAR 1892 occupies an important place in Louÿs's life for
several reasons. He visited London and there was introduced to
Sarah Bernhardt who was indirectly responsible for his writing
Aphrodite; he had his portrait painted for the first time; his hopes
for marriage to Marie Chardon collapsed; he was drafted into the
army; and his volume of poetry, which he had been preparing for
such a long time, was finally published. Although the title-page
bears the date 1891, a note on the final page indicates that printing
was not completed until 24 April 1892. The volume was published
on 21 May, under the title *Astarté*. Louÿs had decided on the
change from *La Vierge* towards the end of the preceding year: the
new title is mentioned in the tenth issue of *La Conque* (dated 1
December 1891, but probably published later) among the forthcoming works of contributors to the review.

Louÿs first approached the well-known Brussels publisher
Edmond Deman who had brought out Mallarmé's *Pages* in 1891.
Louÿs wrote to him on 27 January 1892:

Je serais heureux de publier sous votre marque mon premier volume
de vers. J'en réunis les éléments et je peux avoir terminé à la fin de la
semaine. Ce sera un court recueil de vingt pièces pour la plupart parues
dans *La Conque*, et de peu d'étendue. Quarante-huit pages suffiront,
titres et tables compris.

Le volume s'éditera à mes frais ou aux vôtres, dans le format et avec
les caractères employés pour *Pages*. Au cas où vous ne vous chargeriez
pas des frais, veuillez me dire quelles sont les plus basses conditions que
vous puissiez me proposer, pour un tirage à cent exemplaires (75
hollande et 25 Japon).[1]

Characteristically, Louÿs was thus from the outset planning a
limited edition on luxury paper. Presumably Deman's proposal
exceeded his means, for *Astarté* was eventually published by the
Librairie de l'art indépendant in Paris and printed by J. Royer of
Annonay, the same firm which had printed *La Conque*. The
edition consisted of one hundred numbered copies: 4 on China,
9 on Whatman, 12 on Japanese, and 75 on Holland paper.
Edmond Bailly, the owner of the Librairie de l'art indépendant,

was well known to the young Symbolists who were grateful for the encouragement he offered them and still more for his readiness to publish their works. He was, for instance, responsible for the first editions of nearly all of André Gide's early works. His trade mark was an oval medallion enframing a siren drawn by Félicien Rops, with the motto: *Non hic piscis omnium*. His bookshop at no. 11 chaussée d'Antin was a popular meeting-place for the younger generation of writers and musicians, for Bailly was also interested in music (in 1893 he brought out a splendid edition of Debussy's cantata *La Damoiselle élue*) and he even dabbled in composition. His other great passion was occultism, which led him to edit an esoteric review called *Haute Science* and to offer for sale collapsible 'turning tables'. Sometimes his wife obliged a visitor by evoking her faithful spirit Bakoun who, after predicting literary success for the anxious inquirer, would discreetly counsel him to purchase a book from the shelves lining the walls. It was to this sanctuary of the arts, both black and white, that Louÿs, balked in his desire to tread in Mallarmé's footsteps in Brussels, now turned.

For his very first volume Louÿs managed to secure the collaboration of one of his favourite painters, Albert Besnard. The latter, now largely neglected, was among the most celebrated and versatile artists of the age.[2] Louÿs's admiration for him dated back at least to 1887, when he ranked Besnard's *Le Soir de la vie* among the eight best pictures exhibited in that year's Salon.[3] In March 1888, intrigued by an enthusiastic report from Georges, he visited an art-gallery in the rue de Sèze, where he saw two 'superb' water-colours by Besnard, one of them depicting 'une "nuit" qui souffle dans sa main pour en faire jaillir toutes les étoiles qui illuminent une à une le ciel'.[4] Since the picture had already been sold, Georges subsequently commissioned the artist to paint a copy which he hung in their apartment. A visit to an exhibition of pastel drawings on 19 April 1888 afforded Louÿs a further opportunity to appreciate the artist's skill and rendered him 'de plus en plus fou de Besnard'.[5] The latter was showing some ten pictures 'dont deux admirables, trois ou quatre très beaux et deux incompréhensibles'. Louÿs described some of them in detail in his diary, notably two called *Le Matin* ('mi-japonisme, mi XVIIIe siècle') and *Fleur d'eau*. The latter inspired Louÿs's unfinished poem of the same title, which Le Dantec tentatively ascribes to the year 1890,[6] but which may well have been written earlier. The composition of two further incomplete poems printed by Le Dantec[7] was prompted by another of Besnard's pictures, *Sirène*, which, Louÿs claimed, surpassed in excellence even *Le Matin* and *Fleur d'eau*. The poem 'La Femme aux paons' in *Astarté* was inspired by one of Besnard's water-colours. Another poem, entitled 'Glaucé', a piece remarkable for its evocation of striking colours and its pervasive atmosphere of sensuality, is dedicated to Besnard who acknowledged the tribute somewhat wrily: 'Quand plus tard on lira *Glaucé*, on dira: ce Besnard devait être bien sensuel pour qu'on lui dédiât une semblable poésie, mais on pensera que j'étais un coloriste bien subtil pour vous avoir inspiré des notes d'une si sensible harmonie.'[8] For *Astarté* Besnard designed a lemon-tinted cover displaying a multicoloured drawing of a nymph emerging from a spring, surrounded by lilies. The title as well as the artist's initials appear on the cover.

The combination of brilliant colour-scheme and profound sensuality which characterizes many of the poems in *Astarté* is reminiscent not only of Besnard's pictures, but also of the Pre-Raphaelite movement which enjoyed such a high reputation in France during the final decades of the nineteenth century. Public interest had been awakened, in particular, by Émile Blémont's articles in the review *Renaissance artistique et littéraire* (founded by him in 1871), and by Gabriel Sarrazin's study *Poètes modernes de l'Angleterre*, published in 1885. In his reply to Jules Huret's *Enquête sur l'évolution littéraire*, Maeterlinck named Rossetti and William Morris among his favourite poets (*Écho de Paris*, 15 June 1891). Louÿs himself, when listing his literary and artistic preferences in his first letter to Valéry on 29 May 1890, cited Rossetti among the poets he most admired.[9] Indeed, his earliest surviving verse includes translations of some lines from 'The Blessed Damozel' and of a short piece, 'Song and Music', both dating from not later than 1889.[10] Several years later Louÿs rendered into French at least three of the four sonnets making up the 'Willowwood' section of Rossetti's 'The House of Life'.[11] This version was prepared at the request of Claude Debussy who wished to make an arrangement of the text for tenor or high baritone.[12] However, the musical setting does not appear to have been completed, although Debussy was still working on it in 1900.[13] There is no record of any performance, and no score was ever published.

Astarté opens with the poem 'A Paul Ambroise Valéry'. This serves as a preface to the volume proper, which is composed of twenty-five pieces: 'Une Allégorie: Glaucé', described as a 'frontispiece'; twenty-three poems divided into three series introduced by different quotations; and a concluding poem, 'Le Symbole', dated 'Grande Chartreuse, Bayreuth, Eisenach, Passy, 1890–1891'. The quotations are taken, respectively, from the stanzas on love composed by the seventh-century Sanskrit poet Bhartrihari, from a life of the fourteenth-century Dutch mystic Jan van Ruysbroek, and from Oscar Wilde's *The Young King*, one of the stories in *The House of Pomegranates*. Almost every poem is dedicated to a friend or acquaintance. If many of them are fundamentally akin to the Symbolist literature of the period, others, particularly in the final section, are closer to the Parnassian aesthetic. It is probably no coincidence that among the latter figure the poems dedicated to Heredia, Leconte de Lisle, and André de Guerne (who was known as 'le Vicomte de Lisle'). Both the distinctive literary trends which influenced Louÿs's early work are thus represented in the volume, occasionally even in the same poem. Several of the most successful pieces in the collection result, indeed, from the fusion of these two contrasting styles.

The other dedicatees include Oscar Wilde; Jules Maciet, a well-known art collector, a lifelong friend of Albert Besnard and an intimate of Georges Louis; and Judith Gautier, the daughter of Théophile Gautier and one of the most colourful literary figures of the day, whom Louÿs had invited to contribute to *La Conque*. The remainder belonged to Louÿs's own generation: Gide, Valéry, Drouin, Mauclair, Hérold, Quillot, André Walckenaer, Albert Mockel, Bernard Lazare, and Paul-Albert Laurens who had been a fellow pupil of Gide and Louÿs at the École alsacienne and was later to draw illustrations for several of Louÿs's books. Louÿs had met Lazare and André de Guerne the previous spring when, together with Régnier, Hérold, Pierre Quillard, and Robert de Bonnières, they had founded a dining-club under the name of Les Sept sages.

The birth of *Astarté* coincided with the demise of *La Conque*. It is not certain why the planned twelfth number was never published. Louÿs himself later gave as the reason that Félicien Rops had failed to complete the fronstispiece he had promised.[14]

Perhaps Louÿs was also running out of suitable material. Already on 21 February 1891, when the first number was still in the press, he had noted in his diary: 'Le seul point noir, ce sont les vrais rédacteurs, les jeunes, qui manquent un peu. J'espère qu'ils viendront.'[15] Very few came forward, and of those only Mauclair contributed fairly regularly to the later numbers. The bulk of the contents continued to be furnished by the poets who had already filled the earlier issues. The eleventh number was, incidentally, the only one not carrying a date. It should normally have been published on 1 January 1892, but probably did not appear until May. Apart from the opening poem by Régnier, it consisted solely of pieces by Valéry, Gide, and Louÿs. A further puzzling aspect is that plans were even made for a thirteenth, 'secret' issue. However, like no. XII, this seems to have remained an unrealized project.[16]

In May Louÿs had his portrait painted by Jacques-Émile Blanche, together with Henri de Régnier. Actually, Gide was also to be in the picture, but as he was spending the three months from March to May in Munich, the sittings began in his absence. Louÿs dispatched progress reports to Bavaria. On 15 May: 'Trois poses déjà avec Régnier chez Blanche. Le tableau sera très probablement terminé avant ton retour, et on te remplace avantageusement par une fleur japonaise.'[17] On 17 May: 'Le tableau de Blanche avance beaucoup. Régnier est assis de profil et tient sa main comme une main de justice; moi, je suis vautré sur un divan comme une femme; la fleur japonaise est commenceé, on essaiera qu'elle te ressemble . . . Cela marche à merveille. Ne reviens pas, il faudrait tout changer.'[18] Not for the first time, Gide took Louÿs's facetiousness too seriously, and had to be pacified and reassured. 'Mais qu'est-ce qu'il y a donc dans l'air de Munich pour que tu ne saches plus lire mes lettres?' Louÿs inquired on 20 May. 'Non seulement tu es sur le tableau de Blanche, mais ton absence le gêne tout à fait, et comme il nous demandait par quel moyen on pourrait t'arracher à Wagner, Régnier et moi avons dit en chœur: "Pour le décider à revenir il faut lui écrire de rester."'[19] And Régnier wrote solicitously the next day: 'Qu'a pu vous écrire ce monstre de Pierre Louÿs? Mais vous êtes indispensable à Paris et il y faut revenir au plus tôt. Votre place est vacante sur le canapé bleu de Jacques-Émile et personne n'est en droit ni en passe de l'occuper.'[20]

In the end, however, notwithstanding Gide's return to Paris at the end of May, he was not included in the joint portrait. Instead, Blanche painted him separately. 'Tous les matins à Auteuil chez Jacques Blanche: il vient de finir mon portrait', he was able to report to Valéry on 12 July.[21]

In June 1892 Pierre Louÿs paid his first visit to London. The purpose of the journey was to improve his knowledge of English, in preparation for the *licence* examination he was due to take in July. Although he had been learning the language for several years, his command of it clearly still left much to be desired, for a few days after his arrival he informed Georges in some disgust that he had been obliged to resort to sign language when buying handkerchiefs. He added that, on being presented by Oscar Wilde to the actress Marion Terry, who was playing the part of Mrs. Erlynne in *Lady Windermere's Fan* at the St. James's Theatre, he had conversed with her 'dans un dreadful english qu'elle a fait semblant de comprendre'. In short, he acknowledged ruefully, he lacked any competence in the spoken language: 'Au commencement, tout me manquait à la fois: les mots, la grammaire, la prononciation surtout . . .'[22] By 8 July, however, he was able to assure Georges that 'mon anglais va mieux',[23] and the following year Wilde did not hesitate to describe him as a 'perfect English scholar'.[24]

Louÿs probably reached London on 12 or 13 June, in the company of a young girl named Lucile Delormel.[25] He found rooms at 301 King's Road, in Chelsea, for 20 francs a week.[26] During the first three weeks of his stay he saw Oscar Wilde almost daily and was frequently wined and dined by him. In consequence, he soon found himself in financial difficulties, for, as he pointed out to Georges, 'je suis presque ici au compte d'Oscar Wilde, et je suis obligé, par politesse élémentaire, de lui rendre tous les jours (à lui ou à ses amis) les repas qu'il m'offre. J'en ai pour une guinée toutes les fois, une guinée ou plus.'[27] In another letter he stressed that he had not incurred needless expenses ('Je t'assure que j'ai été très raisonnable et que je n'ai pas gaspillé mon argent . . .') but that the cost of living was very high in London.[28] Within a fortnight of his arrival he was forced to ask Georges to send more money. Although he had so carefully prepared the ground, he dreaded Georges's reaction, especially as his attitude to money had already aroused his brother's displeasure during the preceding weeks. The following letter, written perhaps a day or two after his request for further funds, reflects his anxiety:

Ah! une vraie lettre enfin! J'aurais voulu que tu me voies l'ouvrir et la lire et pleurer comme avec toi, les jours où nos brouilles cessent. C'est la meilleure lettre que tu m'aies écrite depuis deux ans. Comme il faudrait peu de choses pour que tout cela s'éclaircisse; un peu de parchemin avec un titre de licence ... Et peut-être que ce matin tu regrettes cette lettre parce que tu en as reçu une seconde où je te dis que mardi sans doute je n'aurai plus d'argent ... Et puis je veux surtout te rappeler que je t'ai demandé un jour dans ma chambre, il y a un mois, de ne jamais te fâcher vraiment de mes dépenses. Cela a une petite importance pour moi, c'est vrai, et je comprends bien que tu t'en inquiètes, mais les questions d'argent ne sont rien et il ne faut pas que cela nous sépare. Tu m'as compris et tu m'as dit que tu me demandais surtout de travailler. Eh bien je travaille.[29]

Georges's reaction to the request for more money was as unsympathetic as Louÿs had feared. He sent a cheque for twelve pounds, but expressed his anger in an accompanying note. 'Ta lettre m'a fait beaucoup de peine,' Louÿs replied, 'et je désespère tout à fait de comprendre ce qui se passe entre nous ... Moi je ne peux plus vivre comme cela.' He had earlier suggested that Georges should visit him in London, but now the proposal was curtly dismissed: 'Je t'ai demandé de venir à Londres et tu le peux ... Maintenant tu refuses de me voir ... je n'ai vraiment rien fait pour mériter cela.'[30] A week later, he entreated Georges: 'Ecris-moi un peu, mon cher Georges, et ne me fais pas trop sévère mine.'[31] These passages provide striking evidence of Louÿs's moral and emotional dependence on his older brother. Unfortunately, relations between them were soon to grow worse.

On this first visit to London, Louÿs was delighted by the refined manner of Wilde's friends. Gide has described his impressions in *Si le grain ne meurt*:

Ce n'est pas du tout ce qu'on croit ici, me disait-il. Ces jeunes gens sont des plus charmants ... Tu ne t'imagines pas l'élégance de leurs manières. Ainsi tiens! pour t'en donner une idée: le premier jour où je fus introduit près d'eux, X. à qui je venais d'être présenté, m'a offert une cigarette; mais, au lieu de me l'offrir simplement comme nous aurions fait, il a commencé par l'allumer lui-même et ne me l'a tendue qu'après en avoir tiré une première bouffée. N'est-ce pas exquis? Et tout est comme cela. Ils savent tout envelopper de poésie. Ils m'ont raconté que quelques jours auparavant, ils avaient décidé un mariage, un vrai mariage entre deux d'entre eux, avec échange d'anneaux. Non, je te dis, nous ne pouvons imaginer cela; nous n'avons aucune idée de ce que c'est.[32]

It was not until his second visit, in 1893, that Louÿs criticized the behaviour of some members of Wilde's circle. In June 1892 he established a particularly close friendship with one of Wilde's protégés, John Gray, whom he had previously met in Paris. Their relations attained a high degree of intimacy, as is shown by Louÿs's farewell letter before returning to France: 'I know you are quite a *friend*, such a terrible word! how many have you? how many have I? Do we know? You shall go in [*sic*] Paris. We will meet again and often. I wish now one thing: to be for you what you have been for me during that short month. Give me your hand.' They corresponded over several years.[33]

It was through Oscar Wilde that Louÿs met Sarah Bernhardt. The celebrated actress was then appearing in a season of French plays at the Royal English Opera House; she was, in addition, taking part in rehearsals of *Salomé*, which Wilde was planning to put on at the Palace Theatre. 'Vous savez les nouvelles, n'est-ce pas?' he wrote to Louÿs in great elation in mid-June. 'Sarah va jouer *Salomé*!!'[34] The Lord Chamberlain refused, however, to licence the production, on the grounds that biblical characters must not be portrayed on the stage. The venture thus fell through, and Wilde gave vent to his frustration and anger in a series of interviews, in one of which—to the Parisian daily *Le Gaulois*—he even announced his intention of permanently settling in France. When he left London on 3 July it was, however, not for Paris that he headed but for Bad Homburg, where, in a spirit of considerable self-pity, he proceeded to take the waters.

For Louÿs, his introduction to Sarah Bernhardt was an event of momentous importance. He had worshipped her ever since seeing her in Sardou's *La Tosca* in January 1888. The occasion had inspired a long ecstatic entry in his diary, beginning: 'Oh! Sarah! Sarah! Sarah la grâce! Sarah la jeunesse! Sarah la beauté! Sarah la divine! Je suis fou, je suis hors de moi, je ne sais plus ce que je fais, je ne pense plus à rien, j'ai vu Sarah Bernhardt hier soir . . .'[35] He had even written to tell her of his fervent admiration: 'Depuis que je vous ai vue je ne dors plus.'[36] His excitement on being presented to her in London can therefore be imagined. R. Cardinne-Petit has related Louÿs's own account of the meeting:

Elle me sourit. Son sourire me donna de l'assurance. J'osai l'admirer tout haut. Elle me demanda, de sa voix dorée, ce que je faisais.
— Je suis poète, Madame, lui répondis-je, pourpre.
— Poète!... Je l'aurais deviné.
— Pourquoi, Madame?
— N'avez-vous pas rougi tout à l'heure?... C'est charmant!...
Vous êtes poète!... Alors, faites-moi une pièce, me dit-elle, cependant que j'effleurais sa belle main de mes lèvres éblouies.[37]

Louÿs took Sarah Bernhardt at her word, and in a state of feverish excitement he sketched the plan for a three-act play in prose and verse. So closely did he identify his heroine Chrysis with the actress who would portray her on the stage that the scenario ends with the indication 'Mort de Sarah'. The manuscript which, in addition to the outline, contains a partial first draft of the play, is headed 'Londres. 28 juin 92'. It constitutes the first version of what, after many changes and revisions, eventually became the novel *Aphrodite*.

In a letter which, from internal evidence, must have been written on 11 July, Louÿs informed John Gray of his intention to leave London on the following Thursday (14 July). He had, in any case, returned to France by 17 July, for Gide broke his journey from Montigny-sur-Vingeanne in Burgundy (where he had been staying with Maurice Quillot) to the family home at La Roque in Normandy, in order to spend that and the following evening with Louÿs in Paris. The reunion gave rise to a letter from Gide, composed immediately after his arrival at La Roque on 19 July, which throws further revealing light on his conception of friendship. In it Gide again employed the extravagant language he had already used to characterize his relations with Louÿs and other intimates in his correspondence the previous year.[38]
A few days earlier he had written to Louÿs from Montigny: 'Plus je vois Maurice, plus je t'aime. Ne pouvant être auprès de toi, je suis venu à Montigny pour parler de toi. Je te détestais en arrivant ici, mais Maurice t'aime tant que j'ai compris qu'il me fallait t'aimer encore plus ... Le souvenir de toi m'enfièvre ... Ici Maurice me fait fumer, je deviens atroce et passionné.'[39] He

left Quillot precipitately because, he later confided to Valéry, 'tous deux absolument seuls dans la maison de campagne, nous devenions libidineux, et mon ami provocant. Le soir de mon départ, je suis arrivé chez Pierre Louÿs que j'ai trouvé pire.'[40] Yet after receiving an apologetic letter from Quillot, he wrote to Louÿs: 'Ne me connaît-il pas assez pour savoir que je souhaite, que j'aime l'inquiétude; pourquoi me demander comme pardon de m'avoir inquiété?'[41]

The language used in his letter to Louÿs on 19 July is no less ambiguous (although there is no doubt about his renewed irritation with their 'discussions'):

Plus on est amants, moins on est amis. Après une amitié comme celle du 17 avec l'amante, on est embêté de retrouver l'ami raisonneur dans la nuit du 18; on pense que les femmes sont insupportables et sottes quand elles discutent—ou, si c'est l'ami qui parlait, on trouve qu'il compromet fort l'échange des idées avec cette façon de 'ne pas aimer les choses' qui consiste à les nier, de sorte que l'autre est forcé nécessairement d'être muet, brutal ou non sincère ... Un rôle insoutenable d'amant autorise toutes inconstances: prends garde de n'avoir été pour moi qu'une maîtresse. Quant à Maurice, c'est une petite garce raccoleuse, un petit péché plus ou moins perpétuel ... Je me remets au travail qu'on se repent toujours d'avoir quitté—et croyant me serrer contre toi, malgré moi, j'ai fait tes bras se refermer sur du vide.[42]

A letter couched in similar language reached Louÿs from Quillot. This time he expressed his distaste for such terminology in a letter to Gide on 23 July: 'J'ai reçu une lettre de [Quillot], il est charmant. Mais je t'en supplie, et je t'en supplie, usez d'un autre vocabulaire quand vous m'écrirez. Si vous devenez Goethe et Shakespeare comme je n'en doute pas, je serai obligé de publier vos lettres et la postérité croira que nous avons eu des mœurs infâmes. Il faut la détromper dès maintenant, d'abord parce que ce n'est pas vrai ...'[43] Gide replied: 'On ne nous accusera pas de mauvaises mœurs, car si nous en avions nous les cacherions, or nous ne les cachons pas (je trouve ce syllogisme d'un beau comique).'[44] In a letter to a friend in 1894 Gide firmly refuted any suggestion that his early friendships might have contained an element of sensuality: 'Aucune de mes amitiés jusqu'à présent n'a été mêlée d'aucun charme ou trouble sensuel. Toutes ont été si exemptes d'ambiguïté, que Quillot, Pierre Louÿs et moi avons pu jouer là-dessus et parfois la simuler plaisamment sans crainte.'[45]

Certainly, as far as Pierre Louÿs is concerned, everything points to the conclusion that his leanings were at all times solely towards heterosexual love. Thus he broke with Oscar Wilde because of the latter's relations with Lord Alfred Douglas, and Claude Farrère has described an incident in Louÿs's later life which similarly illustrates his abhorrence of male homosexuality:

Je me souviens que, dans une soirée prétendue poétique, il s'écarta tout à coup de moi, parce que j'avais enveloppé de mon bras un jeune poète, ou soi-disant tel, qui était Jean-Jean de Lavallière, alors supposée fille, car les chirurgiens ne s'étaient pas encore occupés d'elle pour en faire un garçon. Jean-Jean portait une défroque masculine. Pour rasséréner Pierre, je dus lui engager ma parole que ce mousse de la flotte était une fille. Tout le monde alors, comme moi-même, en était persuadé. Louÿs ayant compris, me serra fortement la main.[46]

Louÿs had decided to take the *licence* examination in Paris. 'Si j'ai renoncé à passer en province, c'est que je serais tellement honteux si par malheur j'échouais', he explained to Georges. 'J'aime encore mieux tenter Paris et ne pas avoir l'air de me cacher. Si je suis reçu, comme je l'espère, j'en serai bien plus content.'[47] He faced the ordeal with optimism: 'Je crois bien être sûr d'être reçu à l'écrit,' he wrote to Georges from London on 8 July, 'et je suis aussi plus confiant pour l'oral'.[48] He knew that much depended on a successful result: his professional prospects; his future relations with Georges; even his marriage to Marie Chardon. Unfortunately, he failed the examination, and all his hopes for a serene future collapsed. Already before the examination he had wondered whether it might not be more advisable to postpone the marriage until he had completed the year's military service he was due to commence in November. Now he realized that his failure would signify even longer delays—assuming that M. Chardon was, indeed, still willing to consider his suit, which was far from certain. In a fit of despondency, he concluded that there was little point in pursuing the matter further and he asked his sister Lucie to inform Marie's parents of his decision:

J'espère que tu comprendras, ma sœur, combien c'est dur pour moi de renoncer maintenant à un rêve de deux ans sans savoir si je ne passe pas à côté du bonheur, et si elle ou moi ne regretterons pas, plus tard, la décision que je prends seul . . . Maintenant mon examen vient d'élever un nouvel obstacle, plus grand que les autres peut-être; et je pense, comme toi, que je ne suis plus dans les conditions nécessaires pour maintenir ma demande. Toi qui as su toutes mes émotions à ce sujet, tu peux juger de celle que j'ai à t'écrire ceci; je suis sûr que tu l'annonceras à Mme Chardon de façon à ce que sa fille n'en soit ni triste ni blessée...[49]

While the collapse of his plans affected Louÿs deeply, his depression was rendered more intense still by Georges's reproving attitude. He expressed his unhappiness in one of the most moving of the nearly five hundred letters listed in the *Biblis* catalogues:

Je crois qu'il vaut mieux que je parte encore. Tu parais avoir si peu de plaisir à vivre avec moi que je vais continuer à t'épargner ma présence le plus que je pourrai. En mai, j'ai pris presque tous mes repas au restaurant; en juin et juillet, j'ai été en Angleterre et ensuite viendra mon année de service. Tu ne me verras plus beaucoup ... Comme vraiment tu ne comprends guère ce que je pense ni ce que je sens, tu dois croire que tout cela m'est égal comme le bonheur de Marie. J'espère que tu sauras un jour que je ne peux pas vivre en guerre contre toi. Je suis terrifié de ce que j'écris. Comprendras-tu cela?... Je ne sais comment tu entendras cette lettre, ni si tu la liras autrement que moi. Je veux te dire que je suis seulement affreusement triste et tremblant.[50]

This letter marks the lowest point in Louÿs's relations with his brother.

As he had proposed in his letter to Georges, Louÿs set out almost immediately on another journey. The frequency with which he corresponded with Georges during his renewed absence from Paris and the lack of any evidence of estrangement in his letters (or, at any rate, in the extracts reproduced in the *Biblis* catalogues) suggest, however, that his brother had relented towards him. Only occasionally does one find reminders of recent tensions, as in the letter of 22 August, in which Louÿs complains of being left without news: 'Si tu es fâché je te supplie de me dire de quoi, et si tu ne l'es pas, ce n'est guère gentil de me le laisser croire ... Écris-moi quelques mots, je t'en conjure.'[51] The same letter contains an interesting reference to Louÿs's financial situation. After requesting Georges to send some money, he adds: 'Je règlerai tout au moment de partir pour le régiment, mais j'ai peur que mes économies forcées de l'année prochaine ne suffisent qu'à peine à rétablir l'équilibre.' It would thus appear that he had agreed not to spend more than a certain amount during any one period and that he had already exceeded the current limit to such extent that not even the reduction in his personal expenses during his year's military service was likely to restore the balance. In that case, his early discharge from the army must very seriously have aggravated the position.

Louÿs stayed during the month of August and the first part of September in Bayreuth and its vicinity. Oscar Wilde, whom he visited at Bad Homburg, was to join him in Bayreuth, but failed to keep the appointment. Louÿs attended several more performances of *Parsifal*. He stayed that year at the Hotel Fantaisie, in the small village of Donnedorf to the south-west of the town, and it was in the park of the nearby Château de la Fantaisie that he whiled away many hours translating some of Lucian's dialogues about the lives of courtesans. He hoped to publish these translations at the same time as his French versions of Meleager's poems. By 1 September he had completed three-quarters of the text and, he informed Georges, he hoped to finish the remainder before his departure.[52] He arrived back in France on 12 September, clutching some unexpected additions to his luggage: 'Je suis amoureux encore une fois, c'est stupide. Je voyage avec une botte de roses et trois photographies de la même jeune fille, deux mois après avoir failli en épouser une autre. Je l'ai fait un peu exprès, mais je me suis laissé prendre plus que je ne voulais.'[53] The lady's name was Marie Wittmann. Louÿs was disconcerted by his emotional instability: 'Je suis "dispersé"', he admitted, thereby ruefully acknowledging at least the partial truth of Régnier's recent accusation that he was 'paresseux, dispersé et fêteur'.[54]

After the calm spring and summer days Louÿs's friendship with Gide ran into a heavy storm that autumn. It all began with one of Louÿs's more imaginative jokes. One day in September Gide, while still at La Roque, received a postcard showing a view of Nicaragua and bearing a message purportedly sent by Louÿs from Managua where, he explained, his brother had unexpectedly been appointed Minister Plenipotentiary.[55] Despite the French stamp and the Parisian postmark, Gide apparently fell into the trap and duly wrote several letters to the address in Nicaragua mentioned on the card. After Louÿs had owned up to the hoax, he proposed on 2 October that whenever, in future, either of them intended to tell the truth and nothing but the truth, he should mark his letter with a special sign in the form of a circle surmounted by a cross.[56] Gide did not relish such childish games: 'Je ne sais pas ce qui dans quelques années pourra rester de cette amitié si nous continuons à jouer avec toutes ces clowneries de haute école.'[57]

Moreover, Gide's irritation at Louÿs's pranks was fanned into violent anger by his lurid accounts of the life he was leading in Paris. Louÿs's letter of 2 October contains a particularly colourful passage: 'L'éreintement s'étale sur ma face et la gueule de bois altère ma voix. J'ai passé la nuit et l'aube dans tous les bouges des Halles avec Robert Shérard, l'ami de Wilde, et tous les jeunes macs du quartier. Nous avons bu du rhum, de la bière, du vin, nous avons mangé du lard dans la rue et des huîtres avec deux petites putains de seize ans qui avaient des choux-fleurs syphilitiques suppurants, et gros comme des noix.' This dramatic report was followed four days later by an appeal to Gide to return to Paris forthwith if he wished to find his friend still alive: 'Je viens de rester vingt-deux heures sans dormir, à errer jour et nuit dans Paris, et je me suis même compromis hier d'une façon très exagérée. Je suis un peu honteux de ce que je fais et pour la première fois de ma vie je me dégoûte ce matin affreusement. Reviens vite me dire que tu m'estimes . . .'[58] In reply, Louÿs received a violent diatribe against his wickedness:

Tes honteuses défaites, dans ces nuits de Paris dont tu parles, sont bien de toutes tes plaisanteries, les plus lugubres. Ah! puissent-elles n'être que contées! Mon amitié c'est quelque chose d'autre . . . Crois-tu qu'elle va t'accompagner dans des chutes? . . . crois-tue que je puisse sentir autre chose que du mépris, sinon de la pitié peut-être? Je n'aime pas te chercher *en bas*; et quand je veux voir un ami, c'est devant moi que je regarde. Vah! tu ne te méprises pas assez . . . tu n'aurais pas écrit sinon ceci, dont tu ne t'es pas aperçu: 'Je me suis même compromis d'une façon exagérée.' Alors pour toi, c'est là le pire; tout se maintient à peu près tant qu'*on ne le sait pas* encore; ce que tu es, il faut que tu le caches, et tu ne sauvegardes ta fierté que par mensonge. J'ai l'air furieux, je suis surtout triste . . . Je te l'ai dit, mon amitié ne t'accompagne pas dans ces hontes et quand tu t'en vas, je la pleure . . .[59]

The exceptionally sharp tone of Gide's condemnation may be partly attributable to the fact that he was in the middle of a grave emotional crisis, for his attempts to persuade Madeleine

Rondeaux, who was visiting La Roque, to marry him were again meeting with refusal. It is understandable that he was in no mood to be amused by Louÿs's antics. Surprisingly enough, his attack drew only relatively mild return fire. 'Tu me dégoûtes profondément avec tes pruderies de vieille femme', Louÿs responded, but the general tone of his reply was essentially good- humoured.[60]

It was almost certainly that autumn that Louÿs made the acquaintance of Claude Debussy. The composer's numerous biographers have been unable to determine the circumstances or even the approximate date, but Louÿs himself ascribed his 'discovery' of Debussy to the year 1892.[61] Suggestions as to the place of their original meeting include the tavern Auberge du clou in the avenue Trudaine, and Edmond Bailly's bookshop. It might even have been Mallarmé's apartment in the rue de Rome, for Debussy frequently attended the Tuesday receptions by this time. There is likewise much disagreement about the role Louÿs played in the development of Debussy's career. That he provided considerable moral support and practical help during several crucial periods over the next ten years is beyond doubt and amply documented in the published correspondence. Views differ, however, concerning the 'educational' influence Louÿs may have exercised on his older friend (Debussy was thirty in 1892). According to Valéry, the composer 'trouva dans Pierre Louÿs un appui, des conseils, même un enseignement ou des clartés essentielles sur les lettres, et en somme le plus précieux soutien de sa carrière, sous toutes les formes, dans tous les moments et dans toutes les difficultés, jusqu'à la gloire'.[62] Jacques-Émile Blanche, who likewise knew both extremely well, was no less emphatic: 'Claude était fort peu cultivé, presque illettré. Louÿs dirigea ses lectures, fit de son élève l'étonnant délicat au jugement si sûr qu'il devint ensuite.'[63] On the other hand, some writers, such as Debussy's friend and biographer René Peter, and Henri Borgeaud, the editor of his correspondence with Louÿs, have dismissed as ridiculous the idea that Debussy still had need of a 'literary adviser'. Edward Lockspeiser, however, in his excellent book on 'Claude de France', rejects the suggestion that Valéry 'had exaggerated the benevolent rôle played by Louÿs in Debussy's life' and concluded that 'his assessment of Louÿs's influence on Debussy was the simple truth'.[64]

Louÿs saw the year out in military uniform. Like Gide, he commenced his one-year military service in November 1892. Gide was discharged almost as soon as he reported at Nancy, the medical review board pronouncing him to be '[un] homme instruit, au front bombé, pouvant se rendre utile à la patrie plutôt par ses études que par son service militaire',[65] which was a polite way of saying that it considered him to be suffering from tuberculosis. Louÿs's military career, if slightly longer, was scarcely more spectacular. Soon after his arrival at the Courbet Depot at Abbeville, on 12 November, he was confined to the infirmary on account of a bout of bronchitis, whereupon his early enthusiasm for army life quickly waned. By the end of the year he had grown weary of barrack life, was speculating on his chances of a medical discharge, and appealing to Georges to pull a few strings with a view to shortening the odds.

1893

RELEASE DID not come to Louÿs until 4 February, when the review board pronounced him unfit for military service. While he was naturally delighted at the prospect of leaving Abbeville, the decision had the depressing effect of lending substance to the fears he had entertained for some years regarding his precarious health: the army doctors apparently agreed with the civilian specialists that he was doomed.

In January, in anticipation of an early discharge, he had proposed to Gide that they should travel abroad together in the spring, either to Spain and Carthage or to Asia Minor. Though tempted, Gide hesitated. 'Je connais le désir du voyage, et du voyage même avec toi', he replied on 4 February. 'Le premier, j'ai rêvé celui-ci comme une chose délicieuse. J'en suis aujourd'hui terrifié; je pressens si bien et si vite toutes nos exaspérations réciproques. A la première femme accostée tu ne te soucieras plus de moi.'[1] Gide then persuaded his mother to accompany him on a journey to Spain and, in informing Louÿs of his travel plans on 3 March, suggested that they might meet there after his mother's return to France: 'Je voudrais là-bas, sitôt seul, ou mieux encore sitôt ensemble, ouvrir à tous événements toutes les portes.'[2] This arrangement failed to please Louÿs, whose rejection must have been in particularly offensive terms, if one is to judge by Gide's reply of 10 March: 'Ta lettre, pauvre Louÿs, est d'un puant imbécile et ton méchant crachat, d'une injustice toute petite . . . Tu ne viendras pas en Espagne!!! Tant pis. Après quelque lettre charmante peut-être l'eussé-je regretté—mais après cette cramoisie . . . Et puis zut. Adieu saligaud.'[3]

Further meetings between Louÿs and Gide can be counted in days rather than weeks: a period in May 1893; a very brief reunion in Paris in late September or early October 1893, preceding Gide's departure for Africa; a few days at Champel in July 1894; a very short spell in Paris in December of the same year; and the few days in Algiers in March 1895. Several of these occasions were marred by bitter quarrels. Had it not been for

Gide's lengthy absences from Paris, their friendship would no doubt have ended even earlier.

Gide was not the only person with whom Louÿs quarrelled that year, for in the spring he broke with Oscar Wilde. Their relations, though never close, had until then remained extremely cordial, as is shown by Wilde's request to Edmond Bailly, in December 1892, to send the proofs of *Salomé* to Louÿs for correction,[4] and still more conclusively by the fact that when the play, in its original French version, was published simultaneously in Paris (by the Librairie de l'art indépendant) and in London (by Elkin Mathews and John Lane) on 22 February 1893, it was dedicated 'A mon ami Pierre Louÿs.' Ironically, this token of affection led to a momentary strain, for Wilde felt hurt by the unduly flippant cable Louÿs sent in acknowledgement. 'Is the enclosed really all that you have to say to me in return for my choosing you out of all my friends to whom to dedicate *Salomé*?', Wilde complained. 'I don't understand what your telegram means; some trivial jest I suppose; a drop of froth without wine. How you disappoint me!'[5] Wilde's irritation was, however, short lived and a few weeks later Louÿs travelled to London for the express purpose of attending the first night of *A Woman of No Importance* at the Haymarket Theatre on 19 April.

The few days Louÿs spent in London on that occasion were of decisive importance for his future relations with Wilde. Only now did he realize that not all the actions performed by Wilde and his friends were as refined and poetic as those he had witnessed with admiration on his previous visit. He no longer felt at ease in their presence. 'Londres est charmant,' he informed Georges, 'mais je suis dans une société qui me gêne un peu.'[6] And on 22 April, shortly before leaving, he wrote: 'Oscar Wilde a été charmant pour moi, j'ai déjeuné presque tous les jours avec lui, mais j'aurais préféré qu'il me donnât d'autres convives.'[7] The truth is that Wilde had become less discreet about his sexual activities; in particular, he made no secret of his affair with Lord Alfred Douglas. Highly damaging testimony was to be offered at Wilde's trials two years later by employees of the Savoy Hotel, concerning his conduct while staying there with Douglas in March 1893. It is clear that Louÿs became aware of their association. In this connection there is a significant entry in the

Goncourts' diary on 30 April, describing a conversation between Edmond de Goncourt and Henri de Régnier:

Sur le nom d'Oscar Wilde, Henri de Régnier, qui est chez moi, se met à sourire. J'interroge ce sourire: 'Ah! vous ne savez pas? . . . Du reste, il ne s'en cache pas. Oui, il s'avoue pédéraste . . . C'est lui qui a dit un jour: "J'ai fait trois mariages dans ma vie, un avec une femme et deux avec des hommes!" . . . Vous ne savez pas qu'à la suite du succès de sa pièce, à Londres, il a quitté sa femme et ses trois enfants[8] et s'est établi dans un hôtel à Londres, où il vit matériellement avec un jeune lord anglais. Un de mes amis qui a été le voir m'a décrit la chambre, où il n'y a qu'un seul lit avec deux oreillers, et quand il est là, est arrivée en pleurant sa femme, qui lui apporte tous les matins son courrier.'[9]

The friend in question was almost certainly Pierre Louÿs who had returned to Paris only a few days earlier.

Although in his letters to his brother Louÿs expressed distaste for Wilde's intimates rather than for Wilde himself, his attitude towards the latter inevitably underwent a change. Moreover, with the Parisian salons he frequented buzzing with titillating rumours about the sexual tastes of 'l'esthète Wilde', he felt increasingly embarrassed by his association with the subject of the scandal. According to R. H. Sherard, Georges advised him 'to cease an acquaintance which might injure his social prospects'.[10] Louÿs resolved to break with Wilde, and at their next meeting he provoked a quarrel which terminated their friendship. Louÿs later told Gide that Wilde had said to him: 'Vous pensiez que j'avais des amis. Je n'ai que des amants. Adieu.'[11] Wilde, in discussing the incident with Gide in Algeria in 1895, denied, however, ever having made such a remark and gave a different account:

Il a commencé, dans la chambre d'hôtel où nous étions, par me dire des choses affreuses, par m'accuser; parce que je n'ai voulu lui donner aucune explication de ma conduite; et je lui ai dit que je ne lui reconnaissais pas le droit de me juger; mais qu'il n'avait, si cela lui plaisait, qu'à croire tout ce qu'il entendait raconter sur moi; que tout cela m'était égal. Alors Louis m'a dit que, dans ce cas, il ne lui restait plus qu'à me quitter. Et moi je l'ai regardé tristement, parce que j'aimais beaucoup Pierre Louis, et c'est pour cela, pour cela seulement, que ses reproches me faisaient tellement de peine. Mais comme je sentais que tout était fini entre nous, je lui ai dit: 'Adieu, Pierre Louis. *Je voulais avoir un ami; je n'aurai plus que des amants.*' C'est là-dessus qu'il est parti . . .[12]

In a letter to More Adey in September 1896 Wilde gave a more succinct account of his quarrel with Louÿs: 'Three years ago he told me I would have to choose between his friendship and my fatal connection with A.D. [Lord Alfred Douglas]. I need hardly say that I chose at once the meaner nature and the baser mind.'[13] Evidently Louÿs was not simply asking Wilde to choose between two friends: he made it clear that he intended to break with Wilde unless the latter ceased his homosexual relationships with Douglas, which is a choice of a very different kind.

Different suggestions have been made regarding the date and place of the quarrel. Guillot de Saix argued that there had been an initial altercation at 'Hambourg'—doubtless a mistake for 'Bad Hombourg'—in 1892, followed by a partial reconciliation, and by the final break in 1894.[14] Claude Farrère ascribed the quarrel to the period immediately following Wilde's release from prison in 1897—and asserted that until that time Louÿs had believed him to have been the victim of trumped-up charges![15] As for Gide, his account in *Si le grain ne meurt*, while offering a plausible over-all sequence of events (though without mention of Louÿs's second visit to London), is too vague to permit an exact determination of the relevant date; nor is he much more precise regarding the place, which he tentatively identifies as 'Baden, je crois'. It can now be stated with certainty that the quarrel took place in Wilde's room at the Hôtel des Deux-Mondes in the avenue de l'Opéra in Paris, shortly before 25 May 1893. On that day Louÿs sent a letter to Wilde, at that address, in which he coldly reproved him for seeking to involve a mutual acquaintance (Léon Daudet) in their recent dispute: 'En ce qui vous regarde, je n'ai rien à ajouter à ce que je vous ai dit l'autre jour, sinon que je m'étonne de votre insistance et du bruit que vous semblez vouloir faire autour d'un incident dont je ne m'attendais pas à vous voir abuser ...'[16] In June Louÿs wrote to John Gray: 'Tu sais que je suis complètement brouillé avec Mr. Wilde et que je ne peux plus le rencontrer nulle part.'[17]

Unable to worship at the Wagnerian shrine at Bayreuth, where the Festspielhaus remained closed that summer, Louÿs was fortunate to be invited to spend several weeks in a setting in which the memory of the composer was sure to be frequently evoked. The second of the four manuscripts of *Aphrodite* offered for sale in 1926 carries a note added by the author in 1896, which indicates that the major portion had been written at Le Pré des Oiseaux, Judith Gautier's property at Saint-Énogat in Brittany, between 18 and 31 July 1893.[18] He probably stayed there until at least the middle of August. Judith Gautier's association with Wagner, and especially their brief but passionate love affair in the summer of 1876, are too well known to need retailing here. As a result, she enjoyed considerable prestige among the French Wagnerites. She had also published a book on *Richard Wagner et son œuvre poétique*. Le Pré des Oiseaux was, of course, named after Walther von der Vogelweide whose praises are sung by Walter von Stolzing in *Die Meistersinger von Nürnberg*. According to Judith Gautier's biographer Dita Camacho, the land and house at Saint-Énogat had been given to her by the publisher Lacroix in compensation for the loss of a manuscript. She had a small cottage constructed at the far end of the garden, in which she used to receive her friends. It was there that Louÿs worked on his novel.[19]

In August, Georges Louis was posted to Cairo as Minister Plenipotentiary and French Superintendent of the Caisse de la dette publique. Louÿs's first reaction to the news of Georges's appointment was to beg his brother to allow him to accompany him: 'Je n'habiterai même pas chez toi, mais je serai dans la même ville et c'est tout ce que je veux te demander.'[20] Georges apparently refused his consent. Louÿs hastily returned to Paris where he arrived by 26 August at the latest.[21]

After his brother's departure Louÿs left the rue Vineuse and moved into a small apartment at 8 rue Rembrandt, near the Parc Monceau. It was soon furnished with numerous treasures, as André Lebey later recalled:

Il habitait alors un rez-de-chaussée étroit, de deux pièces parallèles, ouaté d'étoffes orientales, plaqué de livres et de gravures, rue Rembrandt. Dès la porte fermée, la ville et la vie moderne disparaissaient; on passait le seuil de quelque mille et unième nuit. Tout apparaissait nouveau pour moi, du petit bureau blanc de Maple où deux lynx bleus de Deck veillaient l'encrier de Delaherche, hérissé de gros porteplumes, à un lavabo japonais fabuleux, à la cheminée de bois aux deux colonnes où la vitrine centrale, en demi-cercle, laissait voir une Astarté verte modelée par Judith Gautier. L'odeur du tabac blond épaississait l'atmosphère en la parfumant, et il y avait toujours, à portée de la main, d'innombrables boîtes de cigarettes et de cigares près des divans, de même que, sur le bureau, de nombreuses bouteilles d'encre recherchée, de plusieurs couleurs.[22] Louÿs celebrated his newly acquired independence by offering lavish entertainment to his friends. He even engaged a professional bartender for his receptions, 'un vrai chimiste arrivé à mêler aux œufs le champagne et la muscade', as Valéry admiringly reported to Gide, 'ou finalement à présenter cet inouï Last Drink—fait de toutes les liqueurs imaginables—et qui a le goût d'eau claire—et qui assomme'.[23] Valéry, who was again temporarily residing in Paris, was seeing a good deal of Louÿs, and their frequent meetings made him forcefully aware of the exceptional fascination of his friend's personality: 'Louis a sur moi une manière d'ascendant—un extraordinaire pouvoir d'irrésistibilité, moitié celui de femme, qui dure avec sa présence—et suffisamment quand il n'est pas là pour que je ne *désire* même pas alors exercer sur ce rapport et ce don n'importe quelle méthode d'arrangements, de permutations ou d'analyse—ce qui est bien le plus étonnant.'[24]

Gide's feelings towards Louÿs were markedly less warm. He had not written to Louÿs for some time, he informed Valéry, and since he had fallen silent Louÿs had taken to sending him the most charming letters: 'Je les lis plus ou moins suivant les jours, suivant son style, mais je n'en suis plus agité'.[25] Gide himself returned to Paris briefly in late September or early October, before setting out on a journey to North Africa with Paul Laurens. It is not known whether he met Louÿs at this time, though this seems likely. If he did, Louÿs may well have become aware of a change in his outlook, for Gide had undergone a profound moral transformation during the summer which caused him to reject the Christian religion and its puritanical ethic. In this connection, he hoped that the journey to Africa would provide him with an opportunity to achieve a well-balanced life in which normal sexuality occupied an important place. Instead, the homosexual experience with the boy Ali at Sousse revealed to him the true nature of his tendencies.

In November Louÿs accompanied Claude Debussy on a momentous journey to Ghent, the city of his birth. The expedition was undertaken for the purpose of persuading Maurice Maeterlinck to authorize Debussy to set *Pelléas et Mélisande* to music. The play, published in Brussels the previous year, had been well received at its first performance at the Théâtre des Bouffes-Parisiens, on 17 May 1893, by an audience which included Mallarmé, Whistler, Régnier, Blanche, Clémenceau, Barrès, Debussy, and probably Louÿs himself. Debussy at once began working on the score, while Régnier and Camille Mauclair approached the author on his behalf, thus paving the way for the journey in November. Debussy informed Ernest Chausson of the success of the meeting: 'J'ai vu Maeterlinck avec qui j'ai passé une journée à Gand; d'abord il a eu des allures de jeune fille à qui on présente un futur mari, puis il s'est dégelé et est devenu charmant . . .'[26] According to Louÿs, Debussy had been scarcely less shy: 'C'est moi qui ai parlé pour lui, parce qu'il était trop timide pour s'exprimer lui-même; et comme Maeterlinck était encore plus timide que lui et ne répondait rien du tout, j'ai répondu aussi pour Maeterlinck. Je n'oublierai jamais cette scène . . .'[27]

During the autumn of 1893 relations between Debussy and Louÿs became increasingly intimate. 'Depuis deux mois nous ne nous quittons pas,' Louÿs wrote to his brother on 25 November, 'et je le trouve jusqu'à présent d'une fréquentation très agréable.'[28] Accordingly, when he decided in November to move from the rue Rembrandt—because, he later told Farrère, he could no longer bear the noise made by the iron gates of the nearby Parc Monceau when they were closed at night[29]—he searched for an apartment at Neuilly which he could share with Debussy. Eventually they abandoned the idea, because 'les meilleures amitiés résistent rarement à l'obligation de vivre en commun'.[30] Instead, Louÿs took an apartment at 1 rue Grétry, close to the Opéra-Comique, which was then under reconstruction, the previous building having been destroyed by fire in 1887 (the new theatre did not open until December 1898).

Towards the end of the year 1893 Jacques-Émile Blanche painted a second portrait of Louÿs (it was later owned by Mr Ronald Davis and displayed at his bookshop in Paris). One day, in Blanche's studio, Louÿs was introduced to a young man of seventeen, André Lebey, who was then still a pupil at the Lycée Michelet.[31] Shortly afterwards they met once more at the Librairie de l'art indépendant.[32] André Lebey was invited to the rue Rembrandt and soon became a regular visitor and an intimate friend. Apart from Valéry, Lebey was the only companion of his youth with whom Louÿs was to maintain a warm personal relationship until his death. Lebey shared his interest in literature and himself became a prolific writer, best remembered for his historical studies such as the *Essai sur Laurent de Médicis, Le Connétable de Bourbon*, and *Louis-Napoléon et la Révolution de 1848*, but he was also a poet and novelist.[33]

A few days after speaking to Louÿs in the Librairie de l'art indépendant, Lebey was presented by Edmond Bailly to another writer on the threshold of a promising career.[34] Jean Le Barbier de Tinan was then nineteen years of age; Bailly would shortly publish his first book, *Un Document sur l'impuissance d'aimer*. Rachilde, who knew him well, for he became a regular contributor to the *Mercure de France* (edited by her husband, Alfred Vallette) and a popular figure at the weekly receptions held in the offices of the review in the rue de l'Échaudé-Saint-Germain, called him 'le beau ténébreux'.[35] With his good looks, refined manners, and exuberant spirits, Tinan was, in Camille Mauclair's phrase, 'l'image même de l'adolescence fine, rieuse et charmante'.[36] His dress was no less striking, for he favoured black velvet waistcoats resplendent with rows of silver buttons, and liked to wear, draped over his shoulder, the kind of satin-lined cape associated with the heyday of French Romanticism. The over-all effect was sometimes further enhanced by a small bunch of violets carried in a pocket over his heart.[37] Tinan was, Mauclair remarked, a young man 'né pour l'amour donné et reçu, pour tout ce qui dore la vie'.[38] He was forever falling in and out of love, with all the profound joy and anguish one was entitled to expect from a person of his sensibility. Nor was he at all averse to allowing his friends to perceive the extent of his sufferings, as Francis Jammes recalled in his memoirs: '[Tinan] avait l'air d'une longue jeune fille délicate, ce qui ne l'avait point empêché d'être cruellement blessé d'amour, un peu comme un héros de Musset. Il m'en fit une allusion discrète et voulut que je me rendisse compte de l'extraordinaire état de palpitations dont il souffrait. Ayant appuyé un instant ma main sur son gilet, j'enregistrai des chocs si précipités et si violents que jamais oiseau poursuivi par un épervier n'en dut ressentir de semblables.'[39]

Louÿs, Lebey, and Tinan soon took to spending almost all their evenings together in the Latin Quarter. For several years they formed an inseparable trinity.

It was in 1893 that Louÿs began his association with the *Mercure de France* which was to prove so important for his literary career. His first contribution appeared in the September number. It consisted of the French translation of ten epigrams by Meleager, together with a short life of the poet. This life also appeared in *Les Poésies de Méléagre* which the Librairie de l'art indépendant published the following month. As already noted, the translation dated back to the autumn of 1891, but the text had been revised since then. The life was not completed until 26 February 1893, according to the date printed beneath it. The volume was dedicated on the title-page 'à un poète lyrique', who was identified on a later page as José-Maria de Heredia.

In December the Librairie de l'art indépendant brought out *Lêda ou la louange des bienheureuses ténèbres*, the first of the seven stories Louÿs planned to write on ancient subjects. He finished only four others, which were published during the following three years: *Ariane ou le chemin de la paix éternelle, La Maison sur le Nil ou les apparences de la vertu, Danaë ou le malheur, Byblis ou l'enchantement des larmes*. Of the remaining two, *La Sirène* and *L'Amour et la mort d'Hermaphrodite*, only fragments survive.[40] Louÿs initially proposed giving the over-all title *L'Heptaméron d'Amaryllis* to the collection, subsequently considered *Les Sept douleurs*, and eventually chose *Le Crépuscule des nymphes*. Under this title the five completed stories were printed together in 1925, in what was most probably the last publishing venture negotiated by Louÿs.

Finally, mention should be made of a slim *plaquette* entitled *Chrysis ou la cérémonie matinale*, which was likewise published by the Librairie de l'art indépendant in 1893. This short text, previously printed in *La Wallonie* in 1892, was to become the opening chapter of *Aphrodite*.

1894

IN JANUARY 1894 Louÿs moved into his new apartment in the rue Grétry. Here he continued to entertain his friends, especially at the Wednesday receptions which were attended by Gustave Kahn, Henri Albert, Francis Vielé-Griffin, Robert de Bonnières, Pierre Quillard, the Natanson brothers, even Heredia, besides such regulars as Régnier, Valéry, Hérold, Tinan, and Lebey. On several occasions Debussy, accompanying himself on his host's harmonium, sang the music he was composing for *Pelléas et Mélisande*. 'Les réceptions de la rue Grétry étaient délicieuses, uniques. Je n'en ai jamais trouvé de pareilles', Lebey later recalled.[1]

The early part of 1894 was, however, an unhappy period for Louÿs. 'J'ai eu un mois malheureux et j'étais peu en train de faire quoi que ce fût', he complained to Georges on 15 February. 'Ennuis de santé, d'argent, d'amitié . . .'[2] A month later he was still suffering from ill health.[3] In fact, hardly a winter passed that did not provide Louÿs with cause to deplore the Parisian climate and its deleterious effect on his health. He seems to have been particularly prone to recurrent bouts of bronchitis. For this reason he longed increasingly for warmer countries and, during the following years, took to spending most of his winters in either Spain or North Africa. Perhaps his weak constitution was one of the factors which led him to regard warm and even torrid climates as the only atmosphere in which his imagination could flourish freely; they were at the same time the inspirational sources of the literature he most admired. In 1912 he wrote: 'Les écrivains que j'admire le plus, voici leurs noms, et une adresse: Chateaubriand—Louisiane. André Chénier—Constantinople. Leconte de Lisle—"L'Isle" Bourbon. Flaubert—Nubie. Renan—Judée, Egypte, Grèce. Heredia—Cuba. Loti—Tahiti, Sénégal, Asie.' And he noted that in the period between 1894 and 1901, during which he had visited Africa six times, he had written *Les Chansons de Bilitis, Aphrodite, La Femme et le pantin, Les Aventures du roi Pausole*, and *L'Homme du pourpre*; whereas the years 1901 to 1911, during which he had not once returned to Africa, had been barren except for the publication of a few minor articles.[4]

While Louÿs made little progress with new literary projects during the first weeks of 1894, he could derive encouragement from the generally favourable reception accorded to the *Poésies de Méléagre* and to *Lêda*. Such criticism as was voiced of the former work was directed at the 'Vie de Méléagre', which constitutes the most original feature of the volume. Since scarcely anything is known about the poet, the 'Vie' is, in fact, little more than an agreeable product of Louÿs's imagination. 'Ce fut pour M. Louÿs l'occasion d'écrire un bien séduisant conte', A.-F. Hérold observed in the *Mercure de France* in February 1894; 'et d'ailleurs, la vie d'un poète, imaginée par un poète, n'est-elle pas plus vraie que reconstituée par le plus savant des érudits?' Not everyone shared this view. In an otherwise cordial article in *Le Temps* on 4 February, Gaston Deschamps expressed mild reservations concerning the final part of the 'Vie': 'La fin est charmante malgré plusieurs affirmations trop précises, qui ont réveillé en moi un archéologue assoupi.' Louÿs rashly challenged Deschamps, in an ironically worded note which the latter printed in *Le Temps* on 8 February, to identify the incorrect statements. Deschamps countered by quoting several scathing remarks communicated to him by Théodore Reinach, the well-known historian and editor of the *Revue des études grecques*. The 'Vie', Reinach declared, was 'un tissu d'erreurs', whilst the translation itself 'pullule de contresens'. Louÿs did not present a rejoinder in *Le Temps* ('où, contre un mandarin à bouton de cristal, un simple lettré ne prévaudrait point'[5]), but he drew up a spirited, detailed reply in which he refuted the charges, before counter-attacking by ridiculing a translation of *Hamlet* Reinach had published in his youth. The document was found among Louÿs's papers after his death and is reproduced in the complete edition of his works;[6] it does not appear to have been published.

If Louÿs's scholarship in the 'Vie' appeared suspect to some critics, there was unanimous praise for his prose style. One of the most enthusiastic reviewers was Philippe Gille who, in his article in *Le Figaro* on 27 December 1893, singled out the classical qualities of Louÿs's art, as displayed in the 'Vie': 'La clarté de l'idée, la netteté, la sobriété de l'expression, la simplicité de la forme m'ont saisi à la manière de la prose de Diderot dans sa préface de l'édition de La Fontaine ... La phrase est courte, le mot est choisi et ne laisse pas songer à un autre' (Louÿs was to write in *Poëtique*: 'Choisir le mot. Il n'en est qu'un.'[7]). And Gille concluded: 'Le morceau n'est pas long, mais il est fait de main d'écrivain.' Even Gide confided to Valéry that, despite the mixed feelings he entertained for Louÿs, he could not, after reading the 'Vie', be wholly angry with him, for 'je ne puis m'empêcher de trouver exquise sa prose'.[8]

Lêda likewise met with critical acclaim. Téodor de Wyzewa, in his review in the *Revue bleue* on 30 December 1893, perceptively recognized in its language and style some of the principal qualities of Heredia's sonnets, namely 'la richesse des images et leur simplicité, et la fermeté élégante du rythme, et puis ce bel art de noblesse pour ainsi dire antique'; in addition, he discerned in the narrative 'une singulière douceur un peu féminine, et des grâces attendries, que la scrupuleuse pureté de la forme fait paraître plus tendres encore'. In the March issue of the *Mercure de France* Mauclair, after praising the excellence of the style, drew attention to a further aspect: 'Une perversité secrète y transparaît parfois, la légende du cygne s'y altère en une corruption calculée où l'âme du moderne s'allie à celle du fervent néo-Grec'. *Lêda* thus contains, albeit it in a concentrated and still embryonic form, all the elements which ensured the outstanding success of *Aphrodite* and upon which Louÿs's fame rests to this day.

Louÿs himself had been uncertain of the literary merit of the story. 'Tu ne m'as toujours pas dit ce que tu pensais de *Lêda*', he reminded Georges on 21 January. 'J'ai hésité longtemps à publier ces trente pages parce que je ne savais pas ce que cela valait ... Tu sais que c'était fait quinze jours avant ton départ; si j'avais pensé que ce fût bien, je te les aurais montrées ... Régnier ne m'a fait que des compliments de politesse, et cela m'inquiète un peu, parce que je croyais avoir trouvé une voie et ce n'est pas toujours facile.'[9] A letter from Albert Besnard reassured him: 'Je crois que vous pouvez dormir sur les deux oreilles, comme disent les braves gens', the painter wrote on 24 February.[10] The favourable reviews helped to convince Louÿs that he had in truth found his way.

· · · · ·

With the advent of the milder weather, Louÿs regained his energy. 'Le printemps me donne beaucoup d'ardeur au travail,' he wrote to Georges on 6 April, 'je fais cinq ou six choses à la fois.'[11] Such a dispersal of efforts inevitably prevented significant progress with any one project. Eventually, the most fruitful one proved to be the series of *Chansons de Bilitis* which Louÿs began on 5 March and of which he completed several before his departure in the summer for Africa (where he was to receive further inspiration from Meriem ben Atala). In April *Scènes de la vie des courtisanes* was published by the Librairie de l'art indépendant, like the previous books at the author's own expense. This was not a new project, but a revised version of the translation he had made in Germany in 1892 of certain dialogues by Lucian.

A letter to Georges written in later April or early May offers a revealing glimpses of Louÿs's state of mind at this period:

Avant de te l'écrire [i.e. cette lettre] j'ai fait un examen de mes six mois de solitude. Il n'est pas brillant. Je crois que je suis vraiment incapable de vivre tout seul et de me diriger. Si je faisais le total de mes journées de travail depuis le mois d'octobre je crois que je n'en compterais pas quinze. D'autre part je continue à ne pas lire; je passe mes journées à faire des projets; j'ai treize contes 'commencés', trois romans 'ébauchés', un volume de vers 'presque achevé', trois traductions 'en train', un drame ... 'je n'ai plus qu'à l'écrire ...' Tu vois comme c'est déplorable ...

D'autre part je dépense beaucoup d'argent. J'avais acheté pour la rue Rembrandt un mobilier assez ridicule qui ne m'a jamais servi à rien puisque je ne m'amuse même pas. Je n'ai pas eu l'ombre d'une aventure ... Je vis seul ici, non seulement sur ton conseil mais parce que je redoute le collage comme la peste. En somme c'est une vie tout à fait terne. Appelle cela spleen ou neurasthénie, ce sera toujours aussi insupportable.[12]

He concluded that there was only one cure for this malady: marriage. But where was he to find a suitable bride? He intimated that there was a candidate wholly agreeable to himself and who would meet with Georges's approval. Moreover, he believed that he would himself be acceptable to her father—if only he possessed a moderate fortune. The girl he had in mind was the beautiful Marie de Heredia, to whom Louÿs felt increasingly attracted (a few months later he was to describe her as 'une perfection'[13]). Unfortunately, his financial assets and prospects were unlikely to satisfy a family like the Heredias who were themselves far from well-off. 'Je suis assez découragé', Louÿs confessed.

In early July Louÿs set out for Bayreuth, in the company of Ferdinand Hérold. They travelled by way of Champel, in the Swiss Jura, where André Gide was undergoing hydrotherapy. The reunion with Gide led to an abrupt change of their itinerary. 'Tu ne seras sans doute pas étonné que sur le chemin de Bayreuth j'ai fait une petite bifurcation', Louÿs wrote to Debussy from Geneva on 12 July. 'Je prends demain le train non de Bâle, mais de Lyon; et après-demain le train non de Fribourg, mais de Marseille, et dans trois jours le bateau non de Heidelberg, mais de Philippeville, et dans quatre jours, le train non de Nuremberg, mais de Biskra.'[14] Mainly responsible for this 'petite bifurcation' was a sixteen-year-old Arab beauty named Meriem ben Atala whom Gide had met during his stay at Biskra the previous winter. Meriem belonged to the Oulad Naïl tribe, whose young girls, by tradition, turned to prostitution for the purpose of accumulating their dowry The custom had enabled her to assist Gide in his pursuit of 'normalization'.

After his return to Europe Gide spent over two months in Rome and in Florence. He then travelled to Geneva to consult a well-known Swiss physician, Dr. Andreæ, about the recurrent attacks of pulmonary congestion he had suffered in Africa. Dr. Andreæ decided that Gide's poor health was due to nervous rather than physical causes and prescribed a cold-water cure at Champel. It was there that Louÿs visited him, because, Gide explains in his memoirs, 'il supportait mal de demeurer si long-temps sans me revoir'.[15]

The two friends had not lost contact during their long separation, but, for Gide at least, it does not appear to have been a case of absence making the heart grow fonder. He may have been touched by the solicitous letter which the news of his serious illness in Algeria elicited from Louÿs on 28 October 1893: 'On me dit que tu es malade. Écris-moi tout de suite ou fais-moi écrire par Laurens. Tu sais que plus que tout le monde je puis être inquiet . . .'[16] He may have been amused by the impetuous cabled message he received on 6 December: 'Crise amitié violente écrivons-nous toujours'.[17] He did not respond, however, to the spirit of these overtures, and in January Louÿs complained about the impersonal tone of his letters: 'Je ne sais plus rien de toi. Toujours des mots qui ne disent rien et de si vaines cachotteries.'[18] On 14 May Louÿs once more reproached Gide for the tone of indifference which had marked his correspondence during the past months. His own letter, on this occasion, was couched in extremely affectionate terms: 'Tu es un vilain, mais il n'y a tout de même que toi. Je n'en ai jamais douté. Si tu connaissais l'effet de ta seule écriture!'[19] The warmth of Louÿs's letters and the prospect of their imminent reunion at last reawakened in Gide deeper feelings of friendship, which found an unexpectedly emotional expression in two letters sent from Switzerland in late June or early July:

Ma seule passion à présent est de t'attendre ... Et il faut que tu t'arranges en sorte que nous n'ayons pas assez de jours ou d'heures, car nous aurons toujours assez d'esprit et de passions pour les remplir ... Tu jugeras ce que tu devras apporter de pensées, de projets et de manuscrits pour les lire, sous des ombrages que j'aurai par avance choisis ...

Mon ami de toutes les heures. T'attendre ici, m'apprit ce que c'est que d'attendre, de penser à toi maintenant m'apprend ce que c'est que de penser à quelqu'un. Nous avons l'un sur l'autre une préhension merveilleuse, plus vigoureuse et pathétique qu'avec nul autre, nous avons fait de notre amitié une expérience dangereuse et belle; nous nous sommes bien mérités ...[20]

At Champel, Louÿs was relieved to find Gide in far better health than he had expected. 'Je le crois tout à fait sauvé', he reported to Georges.[21] Indeed, he appeared 'saved' in more than one sense, for he gave every indication of having abjured the puritanical principles which had so irritated Louÿs. Not only did he give such an enthusiastic account of his relations with Meriem that Louÿs, fanatical Wagnerian though he was, did not hesitate to forsake the spiritual delights of Bayreuth for the physical pleasures of Biskra; he also read to his visitors 'La Ronde de la grenade', a poem celebrating in the most explicit terms the gratification of the senses. It was later printed in *Les Nourritures terrestres*, following its publication in *Le Centaure* in 1896. During the quarrel provoked by Gide's withdrawal from the editorial board of that review, Louÿs was to refer scathingly to the 'Ronde de la grenade', in a letter to its author, as 'votre écarlate priapée'.[22] He is, however, unlikely to have been dismayed by the frank sensuality of the poem when he first heard it in 1894, nor should it be thought that he was genuinely shocked by it two years later. On the contrary, the poem's intense voluptuousness may well have excited his interest in the country which had aroused such unexpected emotions in the formerly prim 'Gidouille'.[23]

Louÿs gave his brother various explanations for his change of travelling plans. 'Est-ce la nostalgie du soleil ou les récits de Besnard et de Gide, ou l'ennui d'aller à Bayreuth avec le compagnon que tu sais?' he wrote on 13 July. There was a further motive, arising from his feelings towards Gide: 'Enfin et surtout le désir d'aller d'*où Gide venait*, afin qu'il n'ait pas eu une émotion sans moi. Car tu ne peux savoir à quel point notre amitié dix-huit mois interrompue, s'est retrouvée unique et indispensable.'[24] The letter does not mention Meriem, but Gide, acknowledging that the 'capricious' and 'domineering' Louÿs 'avait des générosités exquises et je ne sais quelle fougue, quels élans qui rachetaient d'un coup tout le détail', mentions in his memoirs that Louÿs believed that he owed it to him as a friend to make Meriem his own mistress too.[25] As his remarks to Georges indicate, Louÿs would have preferred to undertake the journey without Hérold. Gide, having divined this, took a malicious pleasure in persuading Hérold to accompany Louÿs to his new destination. He succeeded easily in this purpose, and Louÿs left Champel with his all too faithful companion on 15 July for Marseille. They took with them a silk scarf given to Gide by Meriem, which was to establish their identity, and a musical box for Athman, the Arab boy who had been employed by Gide.

The travellers spent five days in Algiers before proceeding to Constantine and then to Biskra, where they lodged at the Maison des Pères Blancs. The heat was, however, so extreme—36° C. at midnight—that Louÿs fell ill with a high fever and grew delirious. They accordingly returned to the less torrid climate of Constantine and were joined there by Meriem at the beginning of August. Louÿs was enchanted with her. In view of Gide's statement that her presence can be felt in many of the *Chansons de Bilitis*,[26] it may be of interest to reproduce in full the portrait which Louÿs sketched of her in his letter to Gide on 10 August:

Méryem est l'être le plus joli, le plus gracieux, le plus délicat que j'aie encore vue. Elle est étonnamment petite javanaise. Elle a une façon qui est délicieuse de dire: 'Rienne di tout', en prenant entre ses lèvres un atome imaginaire et en ramenant en arrière la main ouverte et levée.—Mais elle est aussi Indienne d'Amérique, et par moments Vierge Marie, et encore courtisane tyrienne, sous ses bijoux qui sont les mêmes que ceux des tombeaux antiques: le diadème, la margoulette d'or et les périscelis d'argent.

Elle est tout cela; malheureusement il est aussi impossible de traîner ce petit animal dans une ville civilisée que de présenter une panthère dans un salon bien rangé. Elle est intenable. Hérold qui est la douceur même supporte et cède. Quant à moi, je t'en demande pardon, mais je la bats comme une petite chienne. Sois tranquille, je ne te l'abîme pas, mais je la bats, et non pas avec une fleur. Maintenant tu n'imagines pas que c'est qu'une 'Fille du Désert' sur qui on lève la main, d'autant qu'elle a une admirable mâchoire qui est toujours prête à mordre, et treize bracelets d'argent plein qui sont un terrible casse-tête.[27]

Many of the *Chansons de Bilitis*, as well as the prefatory 'Vie', were written at Constantine. It was appropriate that the volume should have been dedicated to Gide, with a special reference to 'M.b.A', that is to say, to Meriem ben Atala.

Louÿs returned to Paris at the end of August. 'Pierre Louÿs revient d'Algérie avec un burnous et des impressions qui ne dépassent pas ce même burnous', Debussy informed his friend Henri Lerolle somewhat enigmatically on 28 August.[28] Louÿs completed the manuscript of the *Chansons de Bilitis* on 8 September. However, even while the type was being set up, he was already revising the text. Over the next few weeks he modified and corrected, polished and rewrote one piece after another, line by line, at times word for word. Of some he composed up to five versions before feeling passably satisfied. Later he sent the proofs to Gide, imploring him to suggest further improvements: 'Je t'obéirai une fois sur trois, mais cette fois-là est nécessaire', he assured Gide on 10 October.[29] Not until mid-November did he feel sufficiently confident to return the proofs to the printers. He then faced a fresh problem. He was once again defraying the publication costs, but was by this time unable to provide the required one thousand francs out of the funds at his disposal. He was accordingly obliged to appeal to Georges for assistance. Presumably Georges responded with his customary generosity, for the *Chansons de Bilitis* were duly published by the Librairie de l'art indépendant in December (Edmond

Bailly also brought out two more of Louÿs's stories that year, *La Maison sur le Nil* and *Ariane*, the latter having previously appeared in the *Revue blanche*).

The journey to Africa constituted the only truly happy interlude in a year filled for Louÿs with steadily darkening shadows. His unhappiness, which drove him to the brink of suicide, had two main sources: ill health and penury. By the autumn of 1894, barely three years after receiving the considerable sum of money left to him by his father, he had spent it all. The reason for his financial recklessness has already been explained: believing himself condemned to an early death, he tried frantically to cram as many pleasurable experiences as he could into the brief period remaining to him: 'J'ai voulu faire en trois semaines ce qu'on fait en trente ans . . .'[30] On 21 October 1894 he complained: 'Je viens de passer un mois qui m'a fait l'effet d'un mois de misère: omnibus, dîners à prix fixe, mont-de-piété . . .'[31] Before long, even cheap lunches were beyond his means. A restaurant meal, he told Debussy, appeared as unattainable as a two-keyboard Mustel organ, but he would be happy to offer him a dish of figs and a glass of milk.[32] In November he lacked the necessary money to buy braces 'pour empêcher mon pantalon de me serrer où j'ai mal'.[33] And on 1 December he informed Georges that he was unable to purchase an undervest for the winter and, as he had only eleven sous left, could not even send him a cable to ask for more money.[34] There is hardly a letter to his brother during this period in which Louÿs does not acknowledge receipt of a cheque or beg him to send another. The constant need to appeal to Georges's generosity depressed him intensely, for it made him painfully aware of the dependence into which his recklessness had again forced him. 'Je sais tout ce qu'on peut dire contre moi,' he admitted, 'je te supplie de ne pas me le dire toi-même. Je suis assez malheureux et assez peiné de ma vie stupide.'[35] In November Georges offered to provide him with a regular allowance. 'Il est vraiment admirable', Louÿs wrote to Gide on 11 November. 'Mais je commence à être honteux, parce que j'aurais voulu retomber sur mes pieds, et non dans le filet de sûreté. Je sens que c'est mal d'accepter ce qu'il offre. Mais combien je l'en aime . . .'[36]

In his distress, he sought Georges's permission to join him in Cairo: 'Maintenant qu'après avoir tout perdu . . . et que je me trouve de nouveau à ta charge, je me défierais trop de moi si je restais à Paris. J'auris trop de tentations, trop d'occasions de dépenses, je suis sûr que je me conduirais mal. Et je n'en ai plus le droit.'[37] However, Georges refused his request.

The situation was aggravated by the fact that Louÿs was suffering from typhlitis, which caused him great discomfort. 'Je mène une vie insupportable', he wrote dolefully on 18 November. 'Je ne peux pas travailler parce que je ne suis pas en train. Je ne peux pas sortir comme je voudrais, parce que, sans aller mal, je sens toujours mon ventre . . .'[38] He longed to leave Paris, to travel to a warmer climate. His thoughts turned to Greece, to Spain, above all to Africa, for his stay there in the summer had left him with a strong desire to return as soon as possible: 'Quel admirable voyage! Je ne peux plus regarder une carte d'Afrique sans m'attendrir.'[39] He went as far as to rent an apartment at Biskra, in anticipation of a chance to escape from his gloomy existence in the rue Grétry. Different destinations were proposed to him, sometimes for unexpected reasons. Judith Gautier favoured Palermo, because Wagner had written *Parsifal* there; Heredia argued persuasively in favour of the Canary Islands, 'parce qu'il y a dans la mer des flotilles de nautiles roses avec des voiles de chair irisée'.[40] All these plans were, of course, dependent for their realization on Georges's financial assistance. In the end, Louÿs chose Seville. He departed for Spain and sunshine on 6 January.

Only two weeks earlier, however, his depression had become so acute that he had seriously contemplated suicide. There is already a strong hint of overpowering distress in his letter to Georges on 1 December, in which he expressed his sadness at his brother's refusal to invite him to Cairo. He then gave a pitiable account of his extreme poverty, and added: 'Je crois que ma journée se serait achevée autrement si je n'avais pas de frère.'[41] Louÿs came even closer to breaking-point on Christmas Eve. On that evening, he later told Debussy, 'je me suis vu ruiné, sans un sou de capital, sans un traité avec un éditeur ou directeur quelconque, j'ai eu tout de suite la main au revolver. Je m'en serais servi *certainement* sans mon frère . . .'[42] Although Louÿs did not mention it, he had also been deeply affected by a bitter quarrel with Gide.

On Dr. Andreæ's advice, Gide had spent the latter part of the autumn at La Brévine in the Jura mountains. While they did not meet during this period, since Gide was writing *Paludes* and did not wish to be disturbed in his work, he and Louÿs continued to correspond. In November Gide expressed his admiration for the *Chansons de Bilitis* which he was then reading in proof: 'Être unique. L'Épitaphe de Bilitis est une chose exquise comme elle-même et précieuse. Je ne cesserai de la relire que lorsque je pourrai sans cela me la dire . . . Je commence à comprendre ce que c'est que du Pierre Louÿs, et ce qu'est mon ami lui-même . . .'[43] Gide completed *Paludes* in early December and by the middle of the month he was back in Paris where he remained until 25 December.

Shortly after his arrival Louÿs learned that Gide proposed to dedicate *Paludes* to Eugène Rouart, the son of the well-known art-collector Henri Rouart, with whom he had been on intimate terms since the previous year. Louÿs had dedicated *Lêda* to Gide in 1893. He had, moreover, just dedicated the *Chansons de Bilitis* to him. He therefore expected that Gide, who had not dedicated any of his earlier books to him, would offer him *Paludes*. Gide later admitted to Paul Iseler that Louÿs's wish was not unreasonable ('Je reconnais avoir été peu . . . amical en la circonstance.') but he explained that he had refrained from dedicating *Paludes* to Louÿs because 'je désirais reconquérir ma liberté et sentais trop nettement, trop impérieusement, nos divergences'.[44] It is difficult to understand why in December 1894 Gide should still have needed a negative gesture of this kind in order to 'regain his freedom'. He had long ago established his independence.

Louÿs felt the unkindness of the slight so keenly that he resolved to break off relations with Gide. 'André, j'ai senti hier cruellement toute l'insécurité, le vague et le réel égoïsme de ton affection pour moi', he wrote on 20 December. 'A l'heure où il faut qu'une amitié se manifeste et fasse ses preuves, je sais maintenant qu'on ne peut pas compter sur la tienne. C'est pourquoi tu me feras le plaisir de considérer désormais nos relations comme terminées.' He proposed that they should meet in Hérold's apartment on the following Saturday in order to return the letters and documents each had received from the other. These included, in his own case, the manuscripts of the *Cahiers d'André Walter* and the *Traité du Narcisse*. 'Je n'excepterai pas une seule feuille de ton écriture et j'espère que tu seras assez loyal pour en faire autant envers moi.'[45] It is unlikely that the exchange took place, but for once Louÿs was not to be easily appeased, and Valéry's mediation was required before their differences were at least superficially patched up. Perhaps Louÿs would have reacted less forcefully, had the incident occurred at any other time. In December of that year, for reasons that have already been explained, he longed for reassurance and affection, and was particularly vulnerable emotionally to any hurtful action. Within a few days of the quarrel he was contemplating shooting himself.

His faith in Georges's love and generosity helped him to surmount the crisis. On 28 December he wrote to his brother: 'Depuis deux mois, depuis quinze jours surtout, j'étais tellement bouleversé par mes ennuis que je ne faisais plus rien. Je n'ai pas écrit dix pages pendant ce temps. Sans toi, je ne sais pas du tout ce que j'aurais fait. J'étais anéanti.' However, he was able to reassure Georges: 'Je suis sauvé maintenant.'[46]

Although the first edition of the *Chansons de Bilitis* bears the date '1895', it was, in fact, published on 12 December 1894. The title *Les Chansons de Bilitis, traduites du grec pour la premiere fois par P.L.* (the author's name did not appear in full in the first edition) was, of course, a hoax, as was the prefatory 'Vie de Bilitis'. The latter offers a purportedly factual account of the poetess's childhood in Pamphylia, of her life in Lesbos and her friendship with Sappho, and of her later years as a religious prostitute in the service of Aphrodite at Amathus in Cyprus. Mention is made of the recent discovery of her tomb—said to have contained the text of the songs—by a German scholar, Professor G. Heim, who, elsewhere in the volume, is identified as the first editor of her poems published at Leipzig in 1894 (Louÿs discarded an earlier plan to insert an 'Avertissement' signed by Heim). Needless to say, Bilitis is not a historical person of the sixth century B.C.: her creation was inspired by a brief passage in Philostratus's *Life of Appolonius* about a certain Damophyle, described as being of Pamphylian origin, an intimate of Sappho, and the author of hymns in honour of Artemis. Many readers were taken in by the hoax, even though, as Louÿs pointed out to a correspondent in 1896, anyone with a knowledge of German should have been put on his guard by the professor's name, since 'G/Heim = Geheim = Le mystérieux'.[47] One distinguished Hellenist who occupied a chair of Greek archaeology at a well-known French university and to whom Louÿs had sent the *Chansons de Bilitis* together with a copy of the *Poésies de Méléagre*, even declared that those two Greek poets 'n'étaient pas pour lui des inconnus' and that he had for many years regarded them 'comme des amis personnels'.[48] He did not hesitate, moreover, to suggest some alternative translations of the original songs.[49] Madame Jean Bertheroy, 'Lauréate de l'Académie', went one better and actually published in the *Revue des jeunes filles* on 5 January 1896 a *new* translation of six of the *chansons*.

Many reviewers were, however, doubtful of the authenticity of the *Chansons de Bilitis*, while others realized from the outset that they were merely a pastiche of a certain type of Greek poetry. Paul Ginisty, in the *Gil Blas* on 5 January 1895, kept an open mind on the matter: 'Si c'est un jeu littéraire, il est charmant. Si c'est une traduction véritable, ce doit être une traduction assez libre, car, tant que s'évoque là l'esprit grec, ces poèmes paraissent imprégnés aussi quelque peu d'esprit moderne.' In the *Echo de Paris* on 21 January Jean Lorrain, writing under the pseudonym 'Raitif de la Bretonne', spoke of reading aloud to himself the '*Chansons de Biblitis* [*sic*], ce délicieux pastiche du poète René Louys', thus paying the author a pleasing compliment which, at the same time, showed that Louÿs was scarcely known as yet outside the small circle of his acquaintances. His name was better known by 8 August 1896—following the triumph of *Aphrodite*—when Lorrain, who was to become a steadfast admirer of Louÿs, included the *Chansons de Bilitis* among the select books he considered 'des amis de chevet, déjà lus, archi-lus et que je relirai'. Inevitably, reference was made by reviewers to the erotic character of the poetry and to the underlying lesbianism. 'C'est peut-être, entre nous, un effort d'art assez pervers que cette illusion du naturel dans l'anormal', Ginisty observed. However, few readers were shocked by the subject-matter, and critical reaction was largely favourable. Camille Mauclair composed a eulogistic notice for the *Mercure de France* (April 1895) which included the following remarks:

L'érudition, le détail technique de reconstruction ne blessent jamais ici. Le côté bouquin, si odieux et presque inévitable, est évité. C'est avec une netteté de composition absolue, dans la langue la plus savoureuse, la plus concise, la plus transparente, sur des sensations aiguës que se déroule la vie, apparue par aspects familiers ou passionnelle, de la petite courtisane grecque ... Toute une psychologie troublante de l'inversion sexuelle se devine là ... M. Pierre Louÿs est tout à fait un poète ... Il a écrit là un des meilleurs livres d'art que cette génération ait donnés. Ce modeste recueil de chansons d'une petite morte est une œuvre.

The only harsh note was struck by the famous German classical scholar Ulrich von Wilamowitz-Moellendorff. In a singularly humourless and ponderous article published in the *Göttinger gelehrte Anzeigen* in 1896,[50] he severely criticized Louÿs for displaying an insufficient knowledge of the Greek language (as evidenced in periphrastic expressions and the formation of names), for introducing countless anachronisms into the poems (for instance, in the attitude towards nature), and, in general, for travestying the true spirit of the Hellenic civilization. These scholarly objections were coupled with a moralistic condemnation of the 'in part disgustingly obscene content' of the *chansons*. Not only was Louÿs acquainted with this extremely hostile article; it was, curiously enough, the only review he included in the bibliography printed in the enlarged edition of 1898.

1895

LOUŸS REACHED Seville on 10 January and took a room at the Grand Hôtel de Paris. Ferdinand Hérold accompanied him on the journey, but Louÿs's correspondence with Georges suggests that he did not remain in Spain long. Despite an attack of bronchitis, brought on by a period of rain, Louÿs was delighted with Seville. 'C'est un pays délicieux', he wrote enthusiastically to Georges on 18 January.[1] The weather soon improved and Louÿs felt his strength return.

As was his habit when travelling, he had brought a handsome library with him: no fewer than one hundred and twenty volumes, including nine dictionaries and four atlases, were transported from Paris to Seville.[2] As usual, he had drawn up an ambitious programme of literary activities, of which, also as usual, he failed to carry out more than a modest part. During the first month he proposed to undertake a complete revision of his 'roman de Saint-Énogat', in other words, of the early version of *Aphrodite* written at Le Pré des Oiseaux in July 1893. The second month was to be devoted to a new book provisionally entitled *Nichinette* (probably another novel, since the manuscript was to run to some three hundred pages).[3] Louÿs made little, if any, progress with the former project, whilst the latter appears to have been abandoned almost immediately. Nothing further is heard, either, of a curious story he had briefly worked on the previous autumn, which, under the title *Le Journal de Sigebert III*, was to present the diary of a mad king of France who believes his son to be God.[4] In fact, the only tangible literary results of Louÿs's stay in Seville were some poems intended for an enlarged edition of the *Chansons de Bilitis*. He at first proposed to increase the number from the original ninety-three to two or even three hundred, but by 25 February he had decided to limit the additions to forty, of which twenty-two were then already completed.[5] When the augmented edition appeared in 1898, it contained one hundred and forty-six 'translated' pieces.

Louÿs had originally planned to remain in Seville until May, but he was soon complaining about lack of funds and loneliness.

The warm Spanish sun improved his health; it did not cure his melancholy. On 10 February he wrote to Georges: 'Si je n'étais pas si seul, je serais content, mais je n'ai personne à qui parler; ou pis encore: des amis d'hôtel. Horreur! Je continue mes leçons d'espagnol ... Je crois qu'en littérature, ce sera le plus clair de mes bénéfices, car je ne fais pas grand'chose moi-même. Pas très en train ... je n'avais pas assez d'argent pour t'envoyer un télégramme.'[6] In his letter of 25 February he again referred to his financial situation: 'Je suis même resté huit jours sans un sou dans ma poche ... Enfin tu vois que cet hiver dans le Midi n'est pas tout rose pour moi: mauvaises connaissances, dèche, pluie et solitude'.[7] By early March he was already making preparations for his return to France. However, instead of going directly to Paris, he travelled back by way of North Africa. The purpose of this extended journey was to bring about a reconciliation with Gide.

For once, Gide had felt himself to have been at fault in their quarrel in December. Through Valéry, he made peace overtures. Louÿs would lose an admirable friend in him, he confided to Valéry in early January, manifestly hoping that the message would be passed on to Louÿs. 'Mon affection ne fut jamais plus vive; il s'est mépris étrangement sur mes possibles sentimentaux; mauvais psychologue. Je m'obsède à le regretter ... Je désire immodérément sa présence ... Je suis dispos pour le revoir. Je veux qu'il ne croie pas le contraire, et je lui écrirais s'il ne devait pas me renvoyer la lettre.'[8] On 17 January Gide set out from Montpellier on yet another journey to Africa. He landed in Algiers on 22 January and, after spending the following two weeks there and at Blidah, he arrived on 4 February at Biskra where he took up more permanent residence. On 27 January he begged Valéry to inform Louÿs that 'depuis que je ne peux plus l'y associer, ma vie ne m'intéresse plus du tout'. And he added: 'Dis-lui qu'il y a maldonne et recommençons la partie. Voilà assez de temps que nous jouons au whist.'[9]

Valéry's attempts at mediation were successful and direct contact was established between Seville and Biskra (characteristically, it was Louÿs who made the first move).[10] On 11 March Louÿs reported to Georges on his recent 'correspondence' with Gide: 'Séville–Biskra. (Télégr.). "Comment va Meryem?" Biskra–Séville. (Télégr.). "Elle t'attend."—Un silence, puis Biskra reprend: (Télégr.). "Moi aussi . . ."[11] Louÿs explained to Gide that his funds, which were in any case provided by his brother, would not permit him to travel as far as Biskra; if Gide wished to see him, he should come to Seville. When Gide persisted in his invitation, Louÿs proposed an alternative arrangement less costly to himself: he would return to Paris by way of Algiers: 'C'est là qu'aura lieu cette entrevue biskrie-andalouse dans un petit endroit que je connais à la Pointe-Pescade . . . dans la mer!'[12] They arranged to meet in Algiers on Saturday, 23 March.

The attempted reconciliation began auspiciously enough, with one of those spontaneous expressions of affection so typical of Louÿs. Rather than wait for Gide in Algiers which he had reached earlier that day, he travelled some distance towards Biskra and joined Gide's train several stations before the city. Despite this gesture, Gide's response was lukewarm. 'J'avais été surpris déjà du peu d'émotion que j'eus à le revoir,' he reported to Valéry; 'j'attendais une joie plus vive, plus naïve et subite . . .'[13] The reunion lasted three days. Gide wrote two accounts of it, one in a letter to Valéry, a day or two after the quarrel;[14] the other in *Si le grain ne meurt*, the memoirs published thirty years after the event.[15] Though largely complementary, the two versions do present certain common features, notably the bitter complaints about Louÿs's intransigence and capricious behaviour, as well as about his eagerness to do verbal battle at the slightest provocation (but in his memoirs Gide observes perceptively that Louÿs's pugnacity stemmed perhaps less from a desire to force his interlocutor into complete submission than from an innate delight in skirmishing).

To Valéry, Gide further mentioned the annoyance he had increasingly felt at Louÿs's offensive remarks about some of his friends, in particular André Walkenaer, Paul Laurens, and Eugène Rouart (the latter, it will be remembered, had been the cause of their dispute in December); moreover, Gide added, 'tu y passas aussi . . . quoique très, très légèrement . . .' According to this version of the quarrel, Gide's 'very calm' remark that he regarded Rouart as a friend and therefore did not wish to hear him thus attacked had caused Louÿs to break with him: 'et s'il a depuis gardé le silence, si nous ne nous rencontrons plus, c'est certes plutôt à cause de l'irritation qu'il a de voir que mes relations avec

Rouart ont continué à travers les scènes qu'il fit pour les rompre'.
The letter to Valéry also tells of Louÿs's desire to visit the Kasbah
'à la faveur des femmes' and how Gide, to make himself agreeable, accompanied him there, 'et nous partageâmes assez bien les
amoureuses besognes'. No suggestion is made that these expeditions were a source of vexation to Gide.

In *Si le grain ne meurt* there is no mention of Louÿs's attacks on
Gide's friends. On the other hand, pride of place is given to the
'amoureuses besognes' and especially to their tragicomic consequences—Gide believing himself to have been infected, and
Louÿs maliciously confirming his fears, while at the same time
comforting him by citing various famous men who without a
doubt owed their genius to the pox. According to this version of
the quarrel, it was evidently this episode which precipitated the
break, and this time the implication is that the decisive step was
taken by Gide: 'A mon dégoût et à ma crainte s'ajouta vite une
espèce de fureur contre Louis. Décidément nous ne pouvions
plus nous entendre, plus nous souffrir.'

The differences between the two versions of the quarrel are
significant, but not difficult to explain. Like so many persons,
Gide tailored his correspondence to the character of its recipient.
His letters to Valéry were very largely free of allusions to sexual
activities, conventional or otherwise. He may have felt that
indelicate discussions of such matters would have displeased the
fastidious Valéry, who had, of course, no inkling of the battles his
friend had been waging for years against his sexual demons. Perhaps Gide was also reluctant to reveal the somewhat ludicrous
figure he had cut in the incident. Moreover, Valéry was more
likely to approve of the stand Gide described himself as having
taken in the defence of his friends. The fact that Valéry himself
was said to have been criticized was certain to make him still more
sympathetic to Gide's attitude, and all the more ready to accept the
latter's claim that 'Louÿs a bien voulu cette fois se donner tous les
torts de sorte que je sors satisfait de cette inévitable brouille'. In
his memoirs Gide presented a more balanced judgement of their
respective responsibility for the quarrel, conceding that his
character at that time was none of the easiest and that the fault
may in part have been his own.

One enigmatic aspect of Gide's account of the dispute is the
absence of any reference to Oscar Wilde. Jean Delay has cate-

gorically stated that 'le procès de Wilde' constituted its principal cause, but unfortunately he offers no evidence to substantiate this statement and, in any case, he mistakenly places the Algiers meeting between Louÿs and Gide in April[16]—the month which saw the Marquess of Queensberry's trial and acquittal (3–5 April), Wilde's arrest (5 April), and his own first trial (26 April–1 May). In March there was no question as yet of Wilde's arraignment on criminal charges. Louÿs and Gide might very well, however, have discussed Wilde's morals and the possible consequences of his forthcoming prosecution of Queensberry for libel; if so, they were well placed to appreciate the hopelessness of his action and the risks he was taking. Both were, moreover, following the developments closely. 'Cela devait arriver,' Louÿs observed in a letter to Georges on 11 March, 'mais quelle terrible aventure.'[17] Gide, for his part, asked his mother on 17 March to send him 'tout ce que tu pourras de découpures à propos du scandaleux procès que le marquis de Queensberry intente à Wilde'[18] (in reality, the original action for libel had, of course, been launched by Wilde, not Queensberry).

If Louÿs and Gide did exchange views about the scandal, those views are almost certain to have clashed. Louÿs had broken with Wilde precisely because of his distaste for the latter's inverted instincts. He is not likely to have condoned them on this occasion. Gide, on the other hand, had two months earlier enjoyed a homosexual experience in Algiers, at Wilde's instigation, which had marked a further decisive stage in his emancipation. In addition, Wilde's open acknowledgement of his own homoerotic preferences and his uninhibited indulgence of his tastes had imparted to Gide's experience a liberating force which purged his sense of guilt. Consequently, he was becoming more indifferent to public opinion, as is shown by his changed attitude towards Lord Alfred Douglas.[19] It was ridiculous, he wrote to his mother on 2 February to attach too much importance to appearances: 'l'important c'est d' *Être* et *paraître* ne signifie rien qu'ensuite.'[20] Gide, with his newly acquired horror of hypocrisy, would probably have felt impelled to defend a man who was facing public disgrace as a result of actions similar to those he had himself recently performed and which he now regarded as a proper means of satisfying his sexual desires.

.   .   .   .   .   .

The quarrel in North Africa in March 1895 constituted the climactic episode in the 'contredanse mouvementée' to which Gide subsequently compared his friendship with Louÿs.[21] From Algiers he wrote to Valéry: 'Au reste, n'avoir,—car je n'en ai, presque, aucun ressentiment contre lui,—c'est impliquer qu'on le considère dorénavant comme un être sans *vraie valeur* personnelle, sans personnalité et quasi irresponsable, ou ne m'intéressant que peu . . .'[22] In the past their disputes had, sooner or later, been followed by a reconciliation. There was to be none on this occasion, even though a short time later Louÿs held out an olive branch. On 2 June, on learning of the death of Mme Gide, he sent off an affectionate letter of condolence: 'Je t'embrasse de tout cœur, mon cher André, et je suis avec toi plus que jamais . . .'[23] Two days later he received Gide's reply:

Non, Pierre;—ne revenons pas sur un irréparable passé. Ne cherche pas à me revoir; quand nous nous rencontrerons dans la vie, et ce sera, je pense, très souvent—car nous avons tous deux le vif amour des nobles choses—, lorsque nous nous rencontrerons, je serrerai ta main si tu la tends, ou te tendrai la mienne—car il est inutile et fâcheux de donner nos incompréhensions en spectacle—, mais ne parle plus d'amitié entre nous . . .

Pourtant je te remercie de ta lettre—je te remercie *cordialement*, te sachant *parfaitement sincère*, et je t'assure qu'il m'est *très dur* (je suis sincère aussi—et je le souligne) de me soustraire à ton étreinte, qui si longtemps me fut *la meilleure*—et de m'y soustraire précisément à une heure où mon pauvre cœur crie de douleur et de soif d'affection . . . Je m'imagine que nous nous abusons tous deux sur les motifs de notre déprise. Je la crois durable et venant du plus profond de nos divergentes natures. Je mets beaucoup de torts de mon côté . . . mais ce qui m'a définitivement peiné, ce fut de voir que tu me connaissais assez peu pour prendre ces torts pour autre chose que des maladresses. Peut-être après ton frère est-ce moi qui t'ai le plus aimé . . .

Adieu . . . j'ai voulu t'écrire aussitôt pour ceci: l'ensevelissement de ma mère a lieu demain mardi à midi; je compte sur ta délicatesse et sur ta dignité pour n'y pas venir.[24]

This letter formally marks the end of Louÿs's friendship with André Gide. The most surprising feature of their relationship is not that they quarrelled so frequently, but that the final break did not occur earlier, for they could not be regarded as kindred spirits except in a very superficial sense. Jacques-Émile Blanche, who knew them both well, was far closer to the truth in describing them as 'deux ennemis nés'.[25] Very dissimilar by background as well as by temperament, they held profoundly different views on morals and on literature. As a result, Gide increasingly found Louÿs superficial and dissipated, whilst Louÿs came to regard Gide more and more as representative of the puritanical Protestantism he so wholeheartedly detested. Some years after their final break he was to lampoon him in *Les Aventures du roi Pausole* in the person of Taxis, a Huguenot who serves his master in the important position of Chief Eunuch—for which office, the author tells us, he is particularly well qualified by temperament, since 'le Ciel lui avait épargné les concupiscences de la chair et les épargnait également, par un surcroît de miséricorde, à toutes les femmes qui l'approchaient'. Incapable of feeling or inspiring physical attraction, Taxis becomes neither the victim nor the source of sin. He possesses 'un sens de l'ordre et un respect du principe qui dépassaient de beaucoup la simple manie'.

Gide was, in retrospect at least, well aware of the impression Louÿs and other friends formed of his character. In a diary entry in 1931 he noted with regret that Valéry, whose affection for him was beyond doubt, had none the less never made any attempt to truly understand him, with the result that 'la représentation qu'il se fait de moi reste si sensiblement la même ... que pouvait se faire Pierre Louÿs au temps de nos pires désaccords. Je représentais pour lui, pour eux, le protestant, le moraliste, le puritain, le sacrificateur de la forme à l'idée, l'anti-artiste, l'ennemi.'[26]

In spite of his strong disapproval of Wilde's homosexual tendencies, Louÿs appears to have been among those French writers and artists who condemned his arrest, if one is to judge by a letter sent by Wilde from Holloway Prison to Robert Sherard in Paris on 13 April: 'I cannot tell you ... how glad I am that Sarah [Bernhardt], and Goncourt, and other artists are sympathising with me. Pray assure Louÿs, Stuart Merrill, Moréas, and all others how touched—touched beyond words—I am.'[27] However, it was not Wilde's predicament, but his own position which was to cause Louÿs most concern, for the legal proceedings brought him unwelcome notoriety. Among the most sensational documents cited at Lord Queensberry's trial was a love-letter sent by Wilde to Lord Alfred Douglas, probably in January 1893, and which had later been stolen and used in an attempt to blackmail Wilde. Its introduction by Wilde's counsel proved highly damaging to his case and was partly responsible for its collapse. This letter had, perhaps at Wilde's suggestion, been turned into a French sonnet by Louÿs during his second visit to London. The poem was printed on 4 May 1893, over Louÿs's name, in the Oxford undergraduate magazine the *Spirit Lamp*, whose editor was none other than Douglas. Reference was made in court to this poem, as well as to its author who was described by Wilde as 'a young French poet of great distinction' and 'a friend of mine'.[28]

Louÿs feared that his well-publicized association with Wilde and Douglas might provoke scurrilous gossip in Paris and cast suspicion on his own morals. Yet, as he pointed out to Georges on 12 April, 'tout ce que j'ai écrit, tous mes goûts démentent ce qu'on pourrait penser'. He spoke of the mental anguish he had suffered since his return to France: 'tu ne peux pas te figurer dans quel affolement je vis depuis quinze jours . . . je n'ai plus ni sommeil ni repos, et pourtant il faut que je sorte tous les jours, tous les soirs et que je voie tout le monde afin d'observer quelle mine on me fait.' So far, he noted with relief, all his acquaintances had been extremely kind and had treated the whole matter as a joke; and he added: 'Il faut bien que je rie aussi, mais jamais je n'en eus moins d'envie.' At a large reception attended by many prominent persons, including Heredia and Mallarmé, 'tous ont été charmants pour moi. Je n'ai pas vu un dos tourné.' He was none the less wondering what conclusions might be drawn by people not personally acquainted with him, and he prophesied gloomily: 'Je me vois poursuivi jusqu'à la fin de ma vie par cette histoire, c'est à devenir fou.'[29] His fear proved unfounded: despite his connection with Wilde and his circle, Louÿs never appears to have been regarded as anything but the ardent heterosexual he was.

In the same letter of 12 April Louÿs also furnished Georges with details of his financial situation. All that remained of his father's legacy, he explained, was one 5-franc coin, preserved by him 'comme souvenir'. A number of paintings, books, and other articles he owned might fetch about 7,000 francs at public auction. He now declared himself ready to accept a regular monthly allowance and asked Georges to fix its amount: 'Tu sais beaucoup mieux que moi ce que doit dépenser un jeune homme très invité.' On 17 May, in response to a request for further details, he told Georges that he had spent 12,000 francs during the past year, but might manage on 500 francs a month ('c'est le minimum qui permette la redingote sur mesure, c'est-à-dire la visite'[30]). Painfully aware of his habitual extravagance, he asked that the allowance be paid fortnightly. This letter by no means marks the end of the financial lament, which continues to provide a dark strand in the texture of the correspondence. On 7 June he wrote: 'Je ne peux pas te dire combien la vie est sombre autour de moi depuis l'hiver. Je me sens constamment au bord d'une catastrophe et je n'ai en moi aucune force pour lutter. J'ai absolument besoin de bonheur pour travailler. Les préoccupations m'abrutissent, je n'ai pas de force de caractère et j'en souffre plus que de tout . . . Je vis dans une incertitude et une détresse continuelles . . . Je crois qu'il est grand temps que tu reviennes et que tu me dictes la vie.'[31] And on 20 June: 'Que c'est insupportable, cette dèche perpétuelle! Surtout quand on n'en peut accuser que soi!'[32]

He was soon to know even greater unhappiness. At the beginning of July he left his *garçonnière* in the rue Grétry for a new one at 11 rue Chateaubriand, close to the rue Balzac where the Heredias lived with their three daughters. The proximity of their apartment was indeed his main reason for moving to the rue Chateaubriand, for he was by now deeply attached to Marie. His distress can therefore be imagined when, on 6 July, she announced her engagement to Henri de Régnier.

The circumstances leading to the betrothal have been related by Claude Farrère, first in the novel *L'Homme seul*, which is based on Louÿs's life, and subsequently in his book *Mon ami Pierre Louÿs*. According to Farrère, who claims to have heard the details from Marie herself, Louÿs and Régnier were both in love with her and well aware of each other's feelings, but they agreed, out of friendship, not to make a formal declaration of their love—or, at any rate, to wait a while before declaring it on the same day. Farrère accuses Régnier of taking advantage of Louÿs's temporary absence from Paris to break the pact. Marie would have preferred Louÿs, but, misinterpreting his silence as reluctance to commit himself, she accepted Régnier's proposal. When she later learned the truth, she was persuaded by her mother, who favoured the match, to go through with the arrangement.

Louÿs was heart-broken at the news of the engagement. 'Je l'adorais', he wrote to Georges on 15 July; 'en mille occasions nous nous sommes pressés [*sic*] les mains avec une passion que je n'ai jamais eue, pour personne.' His grief was all the more acute because he was convinced that she would have been happy to marry him:

Je suis *absolument* [twice underlined] sûr que si je l'avais demandée le le premier, si même elle avait pu penser que je la demanderais un jour, elle m'aurait accepté ou attendu. J'ai écrit aujourd'hui à son père la lettre suivante:—'Monsieur, j'adorais votre fille Marie. Je ne le lui ai jamais dit. Depuis trois ans je rêvais de l'épouser le jour où le succès m'aurait permis de lui offrir autre chose que la bourse d'un jeune homme pauvre et un nom inconnu. Je sais aujourd'hui que j'ai été devancé: je n'ai plus rien à espérer. Pardonnez-moi seulement si je n'ai plus le courage de revenir dans une maison où j'ai toujours été si affectueusement reçu et où je ne pourrais plus reparaître sans pleurer.'

And he added disconsolately to Georges: 'Je n'ai vraiment pas de chance dans la vie et je crois que je ferais mieux de m'en aller tout de suite . . . Je suis né sous une mauvaise étoile.'[33]

In the spring, on his return to Paris, Louÿs had somewhat fitfully resumed his literary activities. The first project to engage his attention was the completion of a *conte* he had begun the preceding autumn and which appeared in the *Mercure de France* in July under the title *Danaë ou le malheur*. He was also much occupied during several weeks with discussions concerning a spectacle to be presented at the Opéra-Comique at Christmas, for which he had been commissioned to write the libretto and Debussy to compose the music. Subjects considered by Louÿs included the Erl King, Psyche, and, especially, Cinderella. The story was called in turn *Geneviève, Kundrynette*—after the enchantress Kundry in *Parsifal*— and finally *Cendrelune*. Louÿs sketched out a scenario, but by mid-May he had become so dissatisfied with the changes made in the story at the suggestion of Debussy's publisher Georges Hartmann that he advised Debussy to write the libretto himself. Their published correspondence shows that over the next few years Debussy repeatedly tried to rekindle Louÿs's interest in the project, but without success.

For the remainder of the year Louÿs concentrated his efforts on producing a revised and expanded version of his 'roman de Saint-Enogat'. To the ten chapters completed at Judith Gautier's summer house in July 1893, which formed the first two parts of the novel, he had added in September 1893 the prologue to Part

III and in March 1894 the opening chapter of that section. In this incomplete form, he proposed the book to various editors— including Henri Simond of the *Écho de Paris* and Lucien Muhlfeld of the *Revue blanche*—for serialized publication under the title *Le Bien Aimé* (other titles considered were *Chrysis*; *Le Miroir, le peigne et le collier*; *L'Amour*; and *La Passion*). None of the editors he approached showed any interest in the manuscript. Louÿs thereupon submitted it, together with a plan for transforming the short work into a full-length novel of conventional size, to Alfred Vallette, who agreed to serialize the novel in the *Mercure de France*. It was printed in six successive numbers, from August 1895 to January 1896, under a new title: *L'Esclavage*. Louÿs clearly attached the greatest importance to finding the 'perfect' title. In 1901 he affirmed: 'Quand vous avez achevé un manuscrit vous tenez le sort de ces 400 pages entre vos mains. S'il est bon ... TOUT dépend du titre que vous lui donnerez.'[34] In due course the title *L'Esclavage* was also judged to be unsuitable, as the author explained in a note to the November instalment: 'Quelques lecteurs ayant jugé que *L'Esclavage* était un titre amphibologique qui paraissait annoncer un roman sur la servitude antique, et non pas, comme le souhaitait l'auteur, sur l'esclavage de la passion, cet ouvrage sera publié en volume sous le titre nouveau d'*Aphrodite*.'

Although Louÿs had intended to work on the revised version in Seville, it was not until June that he was able to record satisfactory progress. 'Depuis quinze jours je travaille à force ...', he wrote to Georges on 20 June.[35] In early August he went south to stay with Ferdinand Hérold's family at Lapras, a small village near Lamastre, in the Massif Central. At 'Hérold-House', as Debussy called it,[36] Louÿs worked furiously, in a frantic effort to meet the approaching deadlines. 'Je travaille comme un malheureux de minuit à 4 heures du matin toutes les nuits et souvent dans la journée,' he informed Debussy on 21 August, 'mais mon roman ne sera jamais fini à temps.'[37] At the same time, he had grave doubts about the quality of the novel. The opening chapters, he told Georges, 'étaient si faibles que je n'ai pas osé te montrer la livraison'.[38] When he read the proofs of the second instalment he was filled with dismay: 'Il y a de bons "couplets", et encore! Mais ce n'est pas avec des cavatines qu'on fait un opéra. Les transitions sont d'un gosse, et le tout est plein d'inexpérience. Je commence à croire que j'aurais mieux fait de jeter simplement au panier une chose qui est évidemment plus mauvaise que *Bilitis* et qui par conséquent ne peut me faire que du tort.'[39]

Louÿs had hoped to complete the text at Lapras; but when he left at the beginning of September, much still remained to be written. He later described to Camille Erlanger the conditions in which the final instalments were composed:

Tout en demeurant rue Chateaubriand, je passais ma vie entière au Quartier Latin qui est le seul endroit du monde où j'aie jamais entendu rire avec un peu de sincérité. Avec mon pauvre ami Jean de Tinan qui est mort depuis, et un groupe de jeunes gens aussi gais que nous deux, je vivais là trois semaines sur quatre et quand revenait le douzième jour du mois, je rentrais dans mon calme quartier de l'Étoile pour écrire sagement mes cinquante pages qui devaient être remises le 18 à la revue . . .[40]

In the meantime he was again plagued by money worries, and obliged to sell some of his books and etchings. His difficulties were aggravated by the irregularity with which Georges's fortnightly allowance reached him. On 4 November he complained that the last remittance was three weeks overdue, and added: 'Tu penses bien, d'ailleurs, que je n'écris plus une ligne de mon roman depuis ce temps-là. J'ai fait six pages en trois semaines. Quand j'ai à me demander tout le temps comment je déjeunerai le lendemain, je ne peux pas penser aux malheurs de Démétrios. Les miens passent avant . . .'[41] On 14 November he wrote: 'Quand tu n'est pas là, je me démonte pour rien. Je me sens tellement seul, tellement environné d'indifférents ou d'hostiles que même la confidence de mes ennuis n'intéresserait pas, et qui, à plus forte raison, ne feraient rien pour m'en tirer! . . . J'ai d'abord essayé de travailler, mais je n'ai pas pu écrire une ligne et sur les six chapitres que je dois remettre demain, il y en a deux de faits.'[42] But shortly afterwards he was able to announce: 'Chrysis est morte lundi à 4h. du matin, heure fatale.'[43] The Monday in question, which occupies a place of some interest in the annals of literary history, was either 25 November or, more probably, 2 December. By 9 December the manuscript of *L'Esclavage* was finished, only just in time, for the final instalment had to be delivered to the *Mercure de France* by mid-December.

The despondency which frequently assailed Louÿs that autumn was not due solely to his financial problems. On 17 October any hope he may still have entertained of marrying Marie de Heredia was dashed by her marriage, celebrated at the Church of Saint-Philippe-du-Roule, to Henri de Régnier. Francis Jammes recalled in his memoirs that the bride 'répandait un grand charme exotique, tout enveloppée d'une spirale de vieilles dentelles, dont on eût dit d'un flot se dressant sur la mer Caraïbe'.[44]

Two propositions considered by Louÿs during the final weeks of 1895 might have eased his financial difficulties. On 27 November he invited Debussy to compose the music for a short ballet based on the story of Daphnis and Chloe, for which he would himself devise the scenario.[45] Debussy was unenthusiastic, perhaps because the ballet had to be ready for performance at the Théâtre de la Bodinière on 15 December. Louÿs thereupon approached Jules Massenet, but without success. However, Debussy was vexed to learn that Louÿs had written to Massenet, and promptly displayed a belated interest in the subject.[46] In consequence, there was some further discussion of the project during the following months, but nothing came of it. On 20 March 1896 Debussy expressed his dissatisfaction with 'Daphnis qui ne va pas et Chloé qui l'imite'.[47] He was still working on the music towards the end of April. The published correspondence between Debussy and Louÿs contains no further reference to the proposed ballet. However, years later Louÿs reminded Debussy of his broken promise: 'En 1895, tu confisquas un génial scénario de ballet intitulé *Daphnis et Chloé* (à propos, où est-il?) et tu fis serment par les Prunes de le muer en harmonies avec une hâte égale à ton amitié.'[48] It is astonishing, in view of their close friendship and their frequent attempts at artistic collaboration, that the latter should ultimately have yielded no richer results than the setting of three of the *Chansons de Bilitis* and some incidental music for a dramatic presentation of the same work.

In another, equally abortive effort to achieve financial solvency, Louÿs tried to negotiate a contract under which he would have regularly contributed articles to a publication about to be launched, called *Le Grand Journal*. What made the proposition particularly attractive in his eyes was the fact that the articles were to take the form of letters sent from Athens. 'Je vais, encore un hiver, me mettre à l'abri des rhumes,' he wrote to Georges on 25 December, 'et cette fois dans le pays que j'aime le plus au monde et dont je parle depuis six ans sans l'avoir vu.'[49] Once more, his expectations were not fulfilled. Disappointed, Louÿs turned away from journalism. 'Non, décidément, l'épreuve est faite', he remarked to Henri Kistemaeckers, whose acquaintance he had recently made in connection with these negotiations. 'Je ne suis pas né pour ce métier-là.'[50] During his whole life he wrote no more than a handful of occasional articles for newspapers.

Years of Fame: 1896–1901

1896

WHEN THE negotiations with *Le Grand Journal* broke down, Louÿs toyed for a short while with the idea of visiting Greece at his own expense.[1] 'Louÿs part mardi pour Athènes en traversant l'Italie. Tu le verras chez d'Annunzio dans quelques jours', Valéry wrote on 11 January to Gide[2] who was then in Florence where he had recently been introduced to the Italian writer. By 15 January, however, Louÿs felt obliged to give up the idea because of lack of funds. He persuaded himself that it was all for the best, 'que j'aurais fait une folie en quittant Paris au moment où mon premier livre s'imprime . . . que c'était le point de départ de toute une carrière, et que, le laisser sans surveillance c'eût été purement insensé'.[3] For *Aphrodite* was finished and about to be sent to the printers.

No sooner had Louÿs delivered the final chapter of *L'Esclavage* to Alfred Vallette than he set about revising and polishing the story for its appearance in book form. Even before serialization commenced in the *Mercure de France*, Vallette had agreed to the subsequent publication of the novel as a separate volume. It had been his original intention to print each instalment simultaneously for the review and the book, using the same type which would then be immediately broken up, as it was needed for other purposes. Louÿs objected that since the complete text was not ready at the outset, the earlier sections might have to be modified to take account of later episodes. Vallette thereupon offered to set up the type anew for the book, even though this would entail additional expense. Louÿs, however, insisted on defraying the printing costs himself. It was to prove an inspired decision, for the more favourable royalty terms he obtained in consequence—750 instead of 300 francs for the first thousand copies sold, with higher amounts for the later editions[4]—were to provide a considerable income from the unexpectedly spectacular sales. In view of the encouraging response to the serialized version—'le bruit continue, surtout chez les femmes', Louÿs informed Georges on 26 February[5]—Vallette suggested an initial edition of 2,000 copies but Louÿs demurred: 'pour un livre de début, mille exemplaires achetés c'est déjà joli'.[6] At the same time, if his financial expectations remained modest, he was not entirely unprepared for the wordly success awaiting him. 'Le mois qui va s'achever est peut-être LE DERNIER de ma vie tranquille', he wrote prophetically. 'Malgré tout le plaisir que j'aurais à réussir, j'ai peur de tous les ennuis que donnent même les célébrités de jeunesse, et je commence à envier le nom bienheureux de Tartempion [i.e. 'nonentity'], le seul qui vous laisse la LIBERTÉ de la vie.'[7]

Louÿs at first proposed to dedicate *Aphrodite* to Heredia, for whom he continued to feel profound admiration and affection. But Heredia, although lavishing praise on the novel, declined the offer with the facetious explanation, in an obvious allusion to the sensational character of the story, that he still had two daughters to marry off.[8] Louÿs then approached Albert Besnard, who accepted the dedication of *Aphrodite*, declaring himself 'très touché (quoique un peu effrayé) de me sentir avec lui certaines affinités, littéraires et artistiques s'entend', a remark which did not greatly please the author.[9]

To Louÿs's dismay, the publication date, originally fixed for late February, was postponed more than once. On 29 January he was still confident that *Aphrodite* would appear on 25 February,[10] but on 11 February he complained that although the text had been at the printers' for three weeks, he had not yet received any proofs.[11] They did not reach him until the end of the month. On 11 March he announced that the book would not now be published before April, adding pessimistically, 'et encore ça n'est pas certain'.[12] The principal reason for his concern was, as always, lack of money; he was counting on his royalties to relieve the situation. In addition, he was troubled by the pulmonary infection which habitually assailed him in the Parisian winter climate. 'Toujours patraque. Je ne suis pas sorti depuis dix jours', he lamented on 9 March. 'Je passe presque toutes mes journées seul, sans pouvoir ni travailler, ni lire, ni fumer et dans un état d'esprit très démonté . . .'[13] Two days later he wrote: 'Je vais être sans un sou à la fin du mois . . . Je me sens bien ridicule de continuer ainsi de mois en mois mes demandes qui doivent toujours être chacune la dernière.'[14] No doubt Georges responded to this 'final' appeal, as he had to so many earlier ones.

Aphrodite was published by the Société du Mercure de France on 28 March 1896. Despite the *succès de scandale* which its intense sensuality and provocative moral licence had achieved upon its serialization in the *Mercure de France*, early sales were modest and failed to produce the rapid flow of royalties Louÿs so desperately needed. According to Thierry Sandre, Louÿs, in an attempt to raise money for his rent, tried to persuade the publisher Alphonse Lemerre to bring out a new, augmented edition of the *Chansons de Bilitis* and for this purpose offered to sell him the already completed manuscript for the sum of 500 francs. Lemerre declined the proposition, but two days later, on 16 April, he informed Louÿs by express letter that his refusal was not to be regarded as final: 'Vous savez, cher ami, je ne vous ai pas donné mon dernier mot. Revenez me voir, nous nous entendrons.' Lemerre's change of heart was clearly prompted by the appearance in *Le Journal* that morning of François Coppée's eulogistic review of the novel. Louÿs did not take up Lemerre's belated offer.[15]

Coppée's article, prominently displayed on the front page of the newspaper, was everything a young author could have desired.[16] Louÿs was naturally delighted with it. 'C'est une chance inconcevable . . . Je puis écrire maintenant où je veux.'[17] He felt, moreover, that Coppée had displayed rare artistic probity in so warmly recommending a book which championed moral ideals very different from his own. 'Il signale mon livre à tout un public familial qui l'eût excommunié sans sa recommandation', Louÿs wrote to Jean Lorrain. 'Je suis très frappé du désintéressement avec lequel il loue un roman qui combat l'idéal moral de toute sa vie et dont le succès ne peut que nuire à son influence personnelle.'[18] To another correspondent he affirmed: 'C'est le fait d'une âme singulièrement noble.'[19] The irony of the situation is that Louÿs and his friends had always detested Coppée's writings— 'le vieux concierge pour bonnes sœurs', Jean de Tinan derisively called him,[20] and Régnier had published a highly critical article, 'La tête de M. Coppée', in the *Revue blanche* the previous year.

A few days after the review had appeared, Louÿs presented himself at the rue Oudinot to thank his benefactor in person. Coppée explained that he had been particularly moved by the lament of

Myrtocleia and Rhodis over the death of Chrysis and by their pious actions during her burial: 'Sans elles, je crois bien que vous ne seriez pas venu m'apporter votre remerciement!'[21] It was the poet Albert Samain who had prevailed upon Coppée to set aside his initial scruples about praising so highly erotic a work.[22] When Louÿs learned of Samain's intercession on his behalf, he invited him to dinner, and subsequently maintained friendly relations with both him and Coppée, offering to both repeated tokens of his gratitude.

In his hour of triumph Louÿs did not forget the great debt he owed to Georges. 'J'aurais raté ma vie entière si tu ne m'avais pas permis de la diriger moi-même—et donné les moyens de le faire', he wrote to him on 20 April. And he added: 'Pas un des mes amis n'a un *père* qui soit pour lui comme tu es pour moi.'[23] The remark appears a particularly touching one in view of what is now sometimes believed to have been the true relationship between him and Georges.

The history of publishing offers few more striking demonstrations of the power of literary critics than the impact made by Coppée's article. The initial printing was quickly exhausted. Within two weeks 5,000 copies had been sold[24] and many more could have been disposed of, had supplies kept pace with demand. Each day the staircase leading to the offices of the Société du Mercure de France in the rue de l'Échaudé, off the boulevard Saint-Germain, was crowded with deliverymen impatiently awaiting the arrival of the day's consignment of fresh copies from the printer. Over a period of only a few days 14,000 copies were ordered by the Hachette bookshops alone.[25] By the end of the year some 50,000 copies of the book had been printed and the first illustrated edition of *Aphrodite* had been published by the Librairie Borel.

Even the occasional critical reviewer usually saw fit to praise some aspect of the novel. Thus Ferdinand Brunetière, who, in the *Revue des deux mondes* on 15 May, pronounced *Aphrodite* to be lacking in originality, none the less spoke of it as 'ce brillant début' and commended 'la souplesse, l'adresse et l'éclat' of the author's talent. Léon Barracaud, in the *Revue bleue* on 30 May, regretted the absence of intellectual content and the undue emphasis placed on 'ce qui est le produit et l'indice manifestes de la plus extrême décadence et de l'épuisement viril', but admired 'le goût parfait qui domine, et qui avait d'autant plus à se surveiller que le terrain se hérissait de pièges et de chausse-trapes tendus en tout sens'. Needless to say, the occasional denunciation of the 'scandalous' nature of the book merely served to whet the appetite of the general reading public. One noteworthy attack was launched in *Le Temps* on 7 June by Gaston Deschamps who maliciously credited Louÿs with having invented a new *mal du siècle*, namely 'le regret de ne pas être nu'. Deschamps condemned also the abundance of erotic passages which, he feared, were all too likely to receive 'l'approbation fâcheuse des vieux messieurs et des potaches', and he surmised gloomily that 'ces litanies de Vénus, psalmodiées par un enfant de chœur terrible, sont lues en cachette dans beaucoup de maisons bourgeoises et aussi, j'imagine, dans les coins sombres de nos lycées nationaux'.

However little one may approve of self-appointed guardians of public morality such as Gaston Deschamps or Louÿs's principal future adversary, the Senator René Bérenger, it must be recognized that the influence exercised by *Aphrodite* was far from negligible, at any rate on its younger readers. In his review of the play based on the novel, Alphonse Brisson recalled in *Le Temps* on 23 March 1914 that *Aphrodite* had indeed replaced the work of Longus and Boccaccio in the high-school student's desk. Colette acknowledged that she owed her first contact with the occult arts to a young woman 'que la vogue d'*Aphrodite* et des *Chansons de Bilitis* incitait à quelques indiscrétions de mœurs'.[26] And at Louÿs's funeral Anatole de Monzie, the Minister of Education, claimed that the preface to *Aphrodite* was even better known than Hugo's celebrated preface to *Cromwell*.[27] It was in this preface that Louÿs had declared: 'Il n'y a rien de plus sacré sous le soleil que l'amour physique, rien de plus beau que le corps humain'.

The success of *Aphrodite* naturally focused public interest on its author who became overnight the star attraction of Parisian society. 'Treize dîners en ville en treize jours, une quarantaine de visites, cent cinquante lettres et deux cents dédicaces,—voilà mon bilan de quinzaine', he reported to Georges on 29 April.[28] Everyone wished to meet the author of *Aphrodite*. Mme Geneviève Straus invited him to her famous salon, the illustrious Princesse Edmond de Polignac requested the pleasure of his company at a musical matinée, the distinguished politician Joseph Reinach offered him two of his books in friendly tribute, Anatole France sent a charming letter to congratulate his 'confrère' and assure him that 'les dieux vous aiment'.[29] Louÿs strove to keep his balance in the eddies of curiosity and admiration in which he found himself caught up. 'Je ne peux pas m'habituer à croire que je puisse avoir un intérêt pour les gens sérieux', he confessed. 'Il me semble toujours que j'ai 15 ans.'[30]

The month of May, in which Louÿs once again fell in love— with a young foreigner of mixed Romanian-Turkish parentage who 'naturally' bore a physical resemblance to Marie de Régnier[31] —also witnessed the last recorded contact of any significance between himself and Gide. It arose in connection with the publication of a new literary review, *Le Centaure*, which had been launched in February with a banquet given at the Café d'Harcourt for fifty-five persons by Régnier, Hérold, Tinan, Lebey, Valéry, Henri Albert, and Louÿs. The guests, Louÿs reported to Georges, included 'Mme H.G.V. (jeune femme d'un journaliste récent dont tu reconnaîtras peut-être les initiales)'.[32] Mme Henry Gauthier-Villars became better known later under the name of 'Colette'.

The review was to be edited by Albert, with the assistance of the other six friends. Subsequently, Gide was also associated with the venture. The first number, published in May, included Louÿs's story *Byblis ou l'enchantement des larmes* and Gide's poem 'La Ronde de la grenade' which he had read to Louÿs at Champel two years before. When Gide received his copy of *Le Centaure* at La Roque, he discovered to his dismay that several other contributions were hardly less erotic in content than his own. The over-all effect produced by the number, he complained to Valéry, was 'une assez plate invitation à la débauche et une succursale à la quatrième page de certains journaux du samedi'.[33] He therefore resolved to withdraw from the review and wrote to advise his co-editors of his decision. His resignation caused considerable irritation and, in particular, provoked a heavily ironical response from Louÿs, who professed surprise that Gide should have regarded the other items as excessively licentious, when his own poem far surpassed them in lewdness: 'nous pensons que vous avez rougi après coup d'avoir publié un poème dont la lubricité acquiert, par contraste avec nos littératures plus calmes, un ton quelque peu révoltant'.[34] In the end, Gide agreed to the insertion of his story *El Hadj* in the second, and final, number of *Le Centaure* which appeared towards the end of that year. The issue also contained Valéry's *La Soirée avec Monsieur Teste* and, from Louÿs's pen, three poems collectively entitled 'Les Hamadryades' and a *Vie de Marie Dupin*.

In both issues of *Le Centaure* Louÿs listed an imposing number of literary projects as being 'in preparation'. The most interesting because the only eventually fruitful one, is '*Le roi Pausole*, roman philosophique'. In February he had seen a revue sketch at the Moulin Rouge, depicting the visit to Paris of a number of kings, among them the roi d'Yvetot (the ruler of this small medieval principality sometimes assumed the title of 'King', since he owed neither homage nor tallage to the French Crown). This sketch, together with a story told to him by Ferdinand Hérold of a king who had proclaimed a decree declaring all vice to be virtue, gave Louÿs the idea for a novel. 'Je pense beaucoup à mon roi d'Yvetot', he wrote to Georges that same month. 'Il est même commencé (trois pages). Cela s'appelle le *Roi Pausole*.'[35] However, Louÿs did not develop these notes into a full-scale book until several years later. In the meantime he commenced work that autumn on another new novel.

On 26 August Louÿs left Paris for a month's stay in Seville. As on his previous visit, the city delighted him, even though he was troubled by the extreme heat: 'Mais quelle ville charmante, et libre, et gaie! Quelle belle langue, quel beau soleil et quelles belles femmes.'[36]

To Debussy he sent a succinct report on his activities: 'Dans la plus rose des Séville, je corromps des petites filles. Mais je travaille, aussi, bigre!'[37] In fact, on 1 September he began a novel set in Seville and to which he assigned the preliminary title *La Mozita*. Within six days he had written fifty-three pages, representing a quarter of the planned book, after which he succumbed to his habitual lethargy and wrote no more. Not until March 1898 did he take up the manuscript again and, in the space of two weeks, complete what was to be his finest novel, *La Femme et le pantin*.

The fame of *Aphrodite* had by this time spread beyond the frontiers of France and had even reached Seville, where the porter of Louÿs's hotel proudly pointed him out to the other guests, thereby causing him some embarrassment: 'c'est tout de même très désagréable de voir des gens qui regardent de quelle façon on prend son café et qui en tirent certainement des conclusions littéraires'.[38] Sales of *Aphrodite* continued to climb. By 23 September, shortly after his return to Paris, the fiftieth edition was sold out.[39] At the same time, he was distressed to find that his success gave rise to jealousy and ill will: 'J'en suis arrivé à faire bon marché des éloges d'avril pour ne plus penser qu'à ce débordement de rancunes qui ne cessent pas', he wrote to Georges on 23 September, adding that if he had an income of 20,000 francs, he would publish his future works once again in editions limited to a hundred copies 'et on ne verrait plus une ligne de moi, ni dans un journal ni sous une couverture jaune'; and he concluded: 'Je suis un peu dans l'état d'esprit d'un joueur qui voudrait prendre son chapeau après avoir fait sauter la banque'.[40]

The very extent of his triumph disconcerted and almost frightened him. 'Je continue à ne pas me représenter du tout les proportions et les conséquences de ce succès-là', he wrote on 15 October. 'Je ne *vois* pas ce public.'[41] And when Georges asked what more he desired to be happy, he replied on 4 November: 'Tu me demandes ce que je veux "de plus"; mais c'est "de moins en moins!" Les compliments ne me font plus de plaisir et les critiques me peinent. Je voudrais qu'on ne parle plus de moi.'[42] He increasingly regretted, moreover, the demands made on his time and energy by the multitudinous schemes aimed at cashing in on the popular success of *Aphrodite*: 'Depuis six mois ma vie se passe à empêcher qu'on ne fasse des bêtises autour de mon livre: illustrateurs, éditeurs, commissionnaires, traducteurs, journalistes, auteurs dramatiques, acteurs, c'est une armée! Et encore je ne réussis pas toujours . . .'[43] Proposals for translations into German, Hungarian, and other languages had to be considered, steps had to be taken to prevent the publication of an unauthorized Portuguese version. In November, in sheer exasperation, he refused permission for a translation into English, 'beaucoup parce que je ne veux plus entendre parler de ce livre-là'.[44] For the same reason he failed to attend a luncheon with Yvette Guilbert and Camille Saint-Saëns to discuss a proposal to turn the novel into an operetta.

Though not yet thirty, Yvette Guilbert was already well established as a star of the music-hall, but she had long desired to sing in an operetta and now believed that she had found the ideal subject in *Aphrodite*. Realizing that Louÿs might hesitate to entrust his heroine to a *café concert* performer, she resolved to strengthen her case by asking her friend Maurice Donnay, the well-known poet and playwright, to collaborate on the libretto, and by holding Camille Saint-Saëns to a long-standing promise that he would one day compose a full-length work for her. Thus forearmed against any objections Louÿs might raise, Yvette Guilbert presented herself at his apartment on 22 October. Louÿs described her visit to Georges that same evening: 'Une dame longue comme un parapluie enseigne, avec des cheveux très jaunes, articule: "Mr. Pierre Löüysssssse?"' She told him of her contempt for her *café concert* audiences ('Les soirs où j'ai des gants blancs i's n'applaudissent pas') and of her determination to end her career at the first opportunity ('Moi j'en ai assez d' me rayer l' gosier pour ces gens-là'). She had, however, so she assured Louÿs, set her heart on singing in an operetta before retiring from the world of entertainment; and she added: 'Je me suis toquée de Chrysis, je veux jouer Chrysis.'[45]

Louÿs's initial reaction was encouraging, although he did not minimize the difficulties likely to be encountered. As for the two proposed collaborators, he doubted that Donnay would accept, but thought that Saint-Saëns might. The latter's participation, he wrote to Yvette Guilbert the next day, was indeed essential, as 'le nom de ce musicien et le caractère que le public attribue à ses œuvres, sera pour beaucoup dans le succès qui vous attend'.[46] To his brother he put matters differently: although he felt no admiration for Saint-Saëns, he hoped that 'sa fausse réputation de musicien sérieux compenserait . . . le nez et la bouche d'Yvette'.[47] To Louÿs's surprise, not only Saint-Saëns but also Donnay quickly acceded to Yvette Guilbert's request. Since Louÿs had in the meantime become more uneasy about 'cette histoire un peu ridicule', as he termed the project in another letter to Georges on 27 October, he welcomed Donnay's unexpected and, to him, puzzling willingness to prepare the libretto, mainly because he would thus be able to place the entire responsibility for the text on Donnay's shoulders: 'S'il défigure le roman, c'est à lui qu'on s'en prendra et s'il en fait une jolie chose, c'est moi qui recevrai les saluts'.[48] He accordingly stipulated that his own name should not be mentioned in connection with the operetta, a condition that proved unacceptable to both Donnay and Saint-Saëns. In the face of Louÿs's adamant refusal to be publicly associated with the production, the project was abandoned.

Louÿs's disillusionment with his newly acquired fame was now complete. A letter he wrote to Georges on 6 November sheds much light on his state of mind during this period:

Je me sens dans un état d'esprit si avide d'imprévu, si anxieux de trouver quelque chose à quoi me raccrocher, si prêt à me donner tout entier, que je serais capable de tout si j'aimais en ce moment ... Voici onze ans que je sens en moi des tendresses s'amasser pour quelqu'un qui ne vient jamais ... D'autres diraient pourtant que je ne suis pas à plaindre; je n'ai jamais eu d'ennuis avec une maîtresse quelconque; jamais de scènes; pas un lâchage, je suis toujours parti le premier. Mais c'est de cela que je pleure, c'est d'être toujours parti! c'est de n'avoir jamais trouvé l'épaule avec la certitude qu'il n'y en a pas de meilleure ... Je ne sais pas ce qui fait le bonheur mais ce n'est sûrement pas le succès littéraire. Je suis furieux de la déception qu'il me donne. Quand je pense que je le rêvais comme une chose impossible, ce succès-là, et que je n'osais pas l'espérer, et qu'il est venu, et que le monde me l'envie, et que je le donnerais ce soir à une femme, comme un bijou, si je pouvais!—Je pourrais t'écrire quarante pages sur ce ton et les dater 'de tous les instants de ma vie'. Je ne crois pas que tu puisses très bien t'imaginer à quel point elles sont ma vie en effet, car avec toi et même avec d'autres, j'ai des accès d'animation nerveuse; mais dès que je me retrouve seul, l'abattement me reprend. J'ai un caractère à être malheureux de tout. Le bonheur glisse sur moi comme de l'eau sur des plumes; je n'en retiens rien que l'étonnement de l'avoir attendu ...[49]

This important letter helps to explain the strikingly contrasting impressions of Louÿs's character which the reader derives from the correspondence with Georges and from the recollections of so many of his friends. To the latter he appeared a delightful and stimulating companion, confident and gay, if somewhat wilful; to the former he almost consistently disclosed a gloomy and pessimistic outlook, marked by self-criticism and doubt. Even with Georges, it may be noted, he presented a different mood in his letters and even during their meetings, at which his 'accès d'animation nerveuse' imparted to his comportment a glossy veneer of high-spiritedness and insouciance.

At the approach of winter, Louÿs's thoughts turned as usual towards the south. This time, at least, he was not dependent on

Georges's generosity for his travelling expenses. On 15 December, after an extremely rough, thirty-hour-long sea-journey, he arrived in Algiers. Three days later he rented a villa at Fontaine-Bleue, in the southern suburb of Mustapha: 'J'ai des roses, des aloès, un platane, deux chiens, un chat et un Arabe. Tout cela (sauf l'Arabe) coûte 6 fr. 66 par jour . . .—et pour le même prix, j'ai mes deux terrasses d'où je vois tout Alger, tout Mustapha, le Djurdjura neigeux, la baie et toute la mer.'[50] In this delightful place Louÿs spent the following four months.

LOVE AND illness were the outstanding features of Louÿs's stay in Algiers. Viewed in this perspective, it can be said to have commenced badly and finished well, with a major crisis in between. On 19 January he informed Georges that he was afflicted with 'un petit ennui' which, although still unidentified by his doctor, obliged him to lead a more sober existence than he would have wished.[1] Another letter, dated 30 January, provided more specific details of the ailment. Its nature may be guessed from the following remarks which, at the same time, testify to the patient's remarkable sexual promiscuity: 'Je suis loin de Paris. Ça c'est une veine. Cela me permettra sans doute de tenir cet incident secret, si les conséquences n'en sont pas trop éclatantes . . . J'ignore absolument d'où me vient ce petit cadeau, s'il est parisien, marseillais ou algérois; et, en admettant que je l'aie reçu ici, je ne sais encore s'il est français, espagnol ou arabe . . .'[2] Obliged by his indisposition to abstain temporarily from his amorous pursuit of the local girls, Louÿs took to drawing them instead. The idea came to him after he had commenced sittings for the painter Louis-Édouard Brindeau who had travelled to Algiers for the express purpose of doing his portrait. Louÿs engaged several models and spent most of his mornings sketching them. He felt pleased with the results: 'Je n'ai mis ni les seins sous le bras, ni le nombril au milieu de la cuisse.'[3]

An attack of broncho-pneumonia, in February, was potentially more dangerous. For three days Louÿs lay very ill, with a high fever: "Vers la 70e heure de mes 40°, je me sentais tellement faible, tellement anéanti, que je me suis demandé très sérieusement si je n'allais pas "passer" avant ton arrivée. Et l'idée de faire cela sans toi m'était odieuse.'[4] Alarmed by the news of the fever, Georges had hurriedly arranged a trip from Cairo to Paris by way of Algiers, for the purpose of visiting his brother. Louÿs was deeply touched by this mark of affection which made him regret all the more their long separation. On 19 February, while awaiting Georges's arrival, Louÿs wrote to him: 'Je crois bien que nous sommes l'un pour l'autre ce que nous avons de plus cher et nous vivons à des mille lieues de distance. C'est absurde. Celui de nous deux qui aura le malheur de vivre longtemps ne se pardonnera jamais ces quatre années de séparation.'⁵ On 3 March, after Georges's departure: 'Soirée très triste hier. Je ne me sens jamais aussi seul que quand tu viens de me quitter . . . J'attends tout de ton affection et pourtant je suis toujours stupéfait quand je la mesure.'⁶ And on 20 April, shortly before leaving Fontaine-Bleue: 'Dans cette maison blanche, j'ai pensé beaucoup: là j'ai vécu seul, là j'ai cru mourir une semaine, là je t'ai vu venir de très loin et c'est un des endroits du monde où j'ai le plus senti ce que nous sommes l'un pour l'autre . . . Je t'ai dit vingt fois combien je souffrais d'être perpétuellement où tu n'es pas. Depuis ton départ je pense tous les jours que je pourrais être où tu es, et cela seul me retient de m'endormir ici.'⁷

Louÿs's convalescence was speeded up by a new love affair ('Il n'y a pas de quinquina qui vaille une bouche aimée').⁸ The object of his affections was a Moorish girl named Zohra ben Brahim who, having been educated by French nuns, spoke the language fluently with a Parisian accent. Though unable to read or write, she was not lacking in intelligence and Louÿs was delighted with her quick wit and sense of fun. He considered her pleasantly attractive rather than beautiful, and particularly admired her expressive eyes. He was probably recalling them in his description of Aracœli, one of the principal characters of the novel *Psyché*, who was partly modelled on Zohra: 'Ces yeux-là séduisirent Aimery dès qu'il eut croisé leur regard. Entre leurs paupières nuancées dont les bords étaient naturellement noirâtres, ils souriaient d'un sourire très tendre, humide, effilé en arc et si voluptueux qu'ils semblaient toujours murmurer le merci du plaisir suprême.'⁹

Within a month, Louÿs described himself as deeply in love, 'déplorablement pincé'.¹⁰ He acknowledged, however, that he was incapable of fathoming Zohra's thoughts, and wondered whether a relationship between two persons of such fundamentally different mentalities could bring true happiness. Several of his friends assured him that it could not, and tried to dissuade him from taking her back to France with him, as he was soon proposing to do. He heeded their advice to the extent of calling at the steamship office with the intention of purchasing only one ticket; but when he found the office closed, he accepted his fate: 'Alors j'ai été dans le magasin à côté lui acheter un costume de voyage, parce que j'ai bien compris que je n'aurais pas cette énergie deux fois de suite.'[11] They left Algiers together towards the end of April.

Zohra was not the only new figure to enter Louÿs's life during his stay in Algiers. In March he made the acquaintance of the Vicomte Auguste Gilbert de Voisins, who was to play an even more significant role in his life. The twenty-year-old Vicomte, a grandson of the famous dancer La Taglioni, was visiting relatives in Algeria when he learned of Louÿs's presence in Algiers. Eager to meet the author of *Aphrodite*, he introduced himself to Louÿs and Zohra one day in the restaurant of the Hôtel de l'Oasis. He subsequently spent a few days with them at Fontaine-Bleue. Thus began a friendship which endured for sixteen years. The course of their relationship has been charted by Robert Fleury in his exceptionally well-documented study *Pierre Louÿs et Gilbert de Voisins. Une Curieuse Amitié.*

The literary results of Louÿs's four months' stay in North Africa were extremely slight, being confined to several further *Chansons de Bilitis*, composed at Georges's suggestion and inspired by his love for Zohra. He made no effort to complete his Spanish novel, partly because of a certain reluctance to publish a story which was apparently to some extent based on the personal experiences of a close friend,[12] probably André Lebey. Louÿs was himself dismayed by the lack of any sustained creative activity since the completion of *Aphrodite*. 'Depuis seize mois je n'ai rien terminé', he lamented on 20 April. 'Il est temps que cela cesse et que l'air de Paris, l'odeur des journaux frais, les discussions littéraires me forcent au travail.'[13] He felt, however, increasingly inhibited by the popular acclaim bestowed on his first novel, for he feared that its fame would jeopardize the success of any future book he might write. As a result, he would have preferred not to publish anything for several years, but he was obliged to recognize that not even the royalties from *Aphrodite* would relieve him of the necessity of finding further sources of income before long. In the circumstances he concluded that he would be wise to adopt a philosophy of Oriental fatalism which would enable him to remain as undisturbed by future disappointments as he had been unaffected emotionally by the triumphs of the past year 'qui ont fait de moi, au dire de tout le monde, "un heureux jeune homme"'.[14]

·   ·   ·   ·   ·

On arrival in Paris, Louÿs installed Zohra in the new apartment he had rented, shortly before leaving for Africa, at 147 boulevard Malesherbes. Valéry visited them there, but came away unimpressed: 'P.L. est à Paris, avec sa Morisque pas jolie, mais fort énervante, parlant un bon français sucré. Installation catapultueuse, cabinet de travail à moitié atelier, baies vitrées, ciel ouvert, au fond, en caverne, les bibliothèques peintes en mauve. Je n'aime pas les couleurs y employées. Dans la chambre à coucher (si j'ose m'exprimer ainsi), lampes électriques de toutes parts et surtout à terre, comme des astres pour périnée.'[15] Zohra's exotic appearance naturally aroused curiosity and set tongues wagging, often maliciously. Aracœli in *Psyché* found herself exposed to similar gossip: 'L'apparition de cette curiosité anthropologique dans le quartier de la Ville-l'Évêque fit quelque bruit. On prétendit qu'Aimery Jouvelle avait acheté une maîtresse au Jardin d'Acclimatation; qu'elle avait un anneau dans le nez, un pagne de verroteries, et je ne sais quelles autres sottises.'[16] At the same time, Louÿs seems to have taken pleasure in ostentatiously displaying his mistress in the salons and theatres of Paris. At a performance of *Antigone* at the Comédie-Française she caused a sensation by wearing a bright red dress with a spectacularly daring *décolletage*.[17]

Several photographs taken by Louÿs of Zohra, in different states of dress and undress, have survived, including one showing her in the company of Claude Debussy. The two friends had resumed their intimate contact, and Louÿs continued to offer Debussy both material and moral support, encouraging him to persist with his composing ('Promets-moi seulement de travailler quatre heures par jour pendant une semaine')[18] and on occasion advancing him money. It was during this year that their artistic association produced its sole significant result. Having been invited to contribute a piece of music to the review *L'Image*—in which Louÿs had published the poem 'Les Petites Faunesses' in December 1896 —Debussy decided to set some of the *Chansons de Bilitis*. His first choice was 'La Flûte de Pan' (no. 20 of the original series),[19] but the poem printed in *L'Image* in October 1897, with Debussy's music and an illustration by Kees van Dongen, was in fact 'La Chevelure', one of the additional *Chansons de Bilitis* published by Louÿs in the *Mercure de France* in August 1897 and later included in the augmented edition of the *Chansons*. However, Debussy also set 'La

Flûte de Pan', as well as a third poem, 'Le Tombeau des naïades', which he completed early in 1898. Louÿs was delighted with the compositions: 'Ce que tu as fait sur mes *Bilitis* est adorablement bien; tu ne peux pas sentir le plaisir que j'en ai', he assured Debussy on 8 July, with reference to the first two.[20] The three songs did not receive a public performance until 1900.[21]

A further attempt at collaboration in November 1897 proved less successful. Louÿs asked Debussy to compose music for a ballet or pantomime based on *Aphrodite*, which was to be staged at the Olympia music-hall in Paris.[22] Debussy was, however reluctant to write for a variety theatre, so the project fell through. Four months later, in March 1898, a pantomime by Ch. Aubert entitled *Vénus Aphrodite* and apparently inspired by Louÿs's novel was performed at the Olympia, to music by Émile Bonnamy.[23] Debussy's refusal may have stemmed partly from the fact that he had more ambitious plans, for he had asked Louÿs in 1896 to grant him exclusive rights to the operatic treatment of *Aphrodite*. He later lost interest in the project.[24]

Except when Louÿs took her for a seaside vacation to Étretat in August, Zohra stayed on in the apartment in the boulevard Malesherbes, where she presided over the gatherings of his friends. Louÿs remained devoted to her. Zohra's unashamed sensuality and her freedom from sexual hypocrisy formed, moreover, a pleasing contrast with the puritanical and, in his opinion, perverse moral code which governed French society. Perhaps Zohra, like Aracœli 'ne se trouvait bien que nue'.[25] In any case, it is hardly pure coincidence that during his liaison with Zohra he should have published—in the *Mercure de France* in October 1897—a 'Plaidoyer pour la liberté morale' in which he attacked the prevailing view that 'la nudité et l'amour sont des objets de scandale'. In one sense, of course, this article constitutes no more than a logical development of earlier writings and, in particular, of the preface to *Aphrodite*. At the same time, his contact with Zohra is likely to have confirmed him in his standpoint by offering him a practical demonstration of the liberating effect produced by such a neo-pagan attitude.

The fictional Aracœli possesses two further estimable qualities: absolute faithfulness, and toleration of her lover's infidelity. If Zohra resembled Aracœli in this respect also, she had occasion to display the latter virtue that autumn, when Pierre Louÿs and Marie de Heredia, now Marie de Régnier, caught up with the happiness which had eluded them two years before. Marie had been angry with him—angry through jealousy—for bringing his Moorish mistress to Paris, and they remained estranged for several months. It was not until October that a reconciliation took place. On 17 October they met for the first time alone, in a rented furnished apartment in the avenue Carnot:

Le jour où l'on se réconcilie. Appartement quelconque. Chambre à deux fenêtres.—Lit.—Canapé.
Elle arrive à 5h. On s'embrasse. Canapé. Après quelques 'instants' (elle tout habillée, moi aussi, et chastement! je t'assure), je dis: 'Quelle heure?—6h 1/4'!
Et le lit était là. J'avais 27 ans, elle 22.—Est-ce beau?
Un tel jour, à un tel âge, pendant soixante-quinze minutes, elle et moi, seule à seul pour la première fois, nous n'avons pas pensé un instant à l'amour,—tant *l'affection* est plus *forte* que lui.
Thèse qui m'est chère,—depuis *Aphr[odite]*.—Mais avant tout, c'est un des plus chers souvenirs de ma vie.[26]

Before long, this exquisite chasteness was replaced by sensual fulfilment. The lovers met regularly in the apartment in the avenue Carnot and later in one in the avenue Mac-Mahon, frequently arranging their trysts through messages inserted in the *Echo de Paris* under the initials 'H.M.L.' (probably standing for the names of the three sisters Hélène–Marie–Louise). Marie received the name 'Mouche':

Je t'ai donné ce nom, ma Mouche, pour les ailes
De tes cheveux si noirs, si longs, si fins, si bleus
Et pour les reflets d'or qui cernent tes prunelles
Dans la grande ombre de tes innombrables yeux.[27]

Marie fully returned Louÿs's love, as is touchingly demonstrated by the following letter:

Tu vas croire en voyant ce pneu à quelque chose de très important et de très pressé. Eh bien c'est tout simplement pour te dire que je t'aime de tout mon cœur, que je t'embrasse de toutes mes lèvres et que c'est bien long les jours sans toi, dix sous de tendresse, quoi! Je crois bien, mon cher amour, t'aimer maintenant encore plus si cela est possible que je ne t'ai jamais aimé . . . Aime-moi longtemps, longtemps, moi j'ai de l'amour pour toi pour plusieurs jeunesses; si tu veux, nous en remplirons notre pauvre petite, seule et unique vie qu'on nous a si chichement accordée, et je voudrais être si jolie toujours pour toi . . . Mouche.[28]

Their love affair which, with some interruptions, continued for four years, was the most profound emotional experience of Louÿs's life. It inspired the beautiful 'Pervigilium Mortis'.

His emotional involvement with Marie did not prevent Louÿs from realizing his long-standing desire to spend an extensive period with Georges in Egypt. 'J'ai grand-hâte d'avoir de mal de mer le plus tôt possible, pour ne plus y penser', he wrote to Jean de Tinan on 5 December.[29] In the same letter he announced his plans for the following years. They provided for a long journey to South America ('Rastaland') which, he hoped, would be partly financed by a newspaper such as *Le Journal*:

Janvier–Avril . . . au Caire. Mai–Juin . . . Paris. Juillet–Août . . . Une mer. Septembre . . . Paris. Octobre 98 à Juin 99 . . . Rastaland . . . J'aurai (exaucez-moi, Seigneur!) 25.000 balles d'un Xau, Yau ou Zau extrêmement aimable,[30] aux yeux duquel je ferai miroiter un *Outre-mer* un peu moins rasant; et j'explorerai la Guadeloupe, . . . Pointe-à-Pitre, Quito, Lima, Cuzco, Chuquisaca, Valparaiso, San Juan, Rosario, Duchos-Ayres et la Terre de Feu . . . En Juin 99, j'apparais, porteur de diverses castagnettes sud-américaines. Et je disparais à nouveau, tel un songe, vers plusieurs Extrêmes-Orients, jusques à l'aurore de ma vingt-neuvième année, qui verra la fin du siècle . . .

Louÿs's expectations of obtaining financial support from a newspaper for a journey to South America received encouragement from the fact that Xau was advancing him 3,000 francs in December 1897, on the understanding that he would finish his Spanish novel, now retitled *La Sévillane*, during his stay in Cairo and authorize its serialization in *Le Journal* prior to publication in book form.

A harrowing experience still lay in store for Louÿs before he could leave France: his separation from Zohra. He described the grief which their parting caused him in two separate—but, to judge from the published extracts, partly identical—accounts written on 29 December, the day on which she sailed to Algeria from Marseille where he had accompanied her. The first, headed 'Ma pauvre petite Zo!', opens with a touchingly precise calculation of the length of their shared happiness: 'Ainsi, c'est bien fini, éternellement fini. Pendant deux cent quatre-vingt-dix jours, du 15 mars au 29 décembre, d'une année de ma vie, je t'aurai eue à tous les instants de chacune de mes journées.'[31] The other account is contained in a letter to Georges. In it Louÿs related the story of their last hours together and the farewell scene on the steamship *Maréchal Bugeaud*:

C'est dans la voiture qui m'emmenait [from the boulevard Malesherbes] que j'ai commencé à pleurer. Mais sur le quai la voici qui me sourit, en un long manteau beige à col de castor, toque de loutre et voilette noire . . .

Dois-je jouir le plus possible de sa présence pendant que je l'ai encore, dois-je ne plus la regarder pour la regretter moins? Depuis le matin je vais de l'une à l'autre de ces deux alternatives et je ne sais pas, et je ne sais rien . . . sauf que les larmes m'étouffent . . .

Nous voici revenus au paquebot, négociations d'une heure pour obtenir une cabine seule. Enfin nous y voici. Je ferme la porte. Etreinte désespérée. Ah! comme je l'ai connue une dernière fois, comme je l'ai embrassée, sur la bouche, sur les yeux, sur les joues et dans les cheveux. Tout ce que je pouvais atteindre de nu sous sa robe épaisse et lourde, je l'ai caressé comme si j'allais la mettre en bière . . .

Comme j'ai pleuré depuis ce matin, je pleurais en pleine rue, j'étais comme je n'ai jamais été, sauf peut-être pendant les fiançailles de Mouche. Et encore non, ce n'était pas la même chose, je n'avais jamais senti cela, quelque chose d'étouffant qui ne voulait pas descendre gonflait le haut de ma poitrine, mes yeux me piquaient à force de larmes, on ne sait pas pleurer quand on est enfant, c'est un don qui s'obtient![32]

It was ironically appropriate, as if to mark more insistently the closing of a chapter of Louÿs's life, that his parting from Zohra should have coincided with the publication of the augmented edition of the *Chansons de Bilitis*, some of which owed their inspiration to her. But, appearances notwithstanding, the chapter was not yet finally closed: he was to see Zohra again.

1898

LOUŸS LEFT for Egypt at the beginning of January. He was delighted to be spending yet another winter far from cold, gloomy, hypocritical Europe, and above all, to be spending it with Georges. Ugo Ojetti, who made the two brothers' acquaintance during this period, recalls in his book *Cose Viste* that their house was cool and silent, 'with that vibrant silence of oriental houses in which servants in white tunics move around in slippered feet on plush carpets, in the half-light, and one does not even hear their breathing'. Ojetti also mentions that Georges treated Pierre, who appeared to be in indifferent health, with 'motherly kindliness'.[1]

Louÿs remained in Egypt until late April, staying mostly in Cairo, except for sightseeing excursions to such places as Philae and Luxor. It was probably during this period that he began to translate those passages from the classics which, under the title 'Lectures antiques', appeared in the *Mercure de France* from June onwards. In Cairo also, under prodding from Xau who was impatiently awaiting the arrival of the manuscript, he completed *La Sévillane* in the two weeks between 23 March and 6 April. The novel was serialized in *Le Journal* from 19 May to 8 June under a new title, *La Femme et le pantin*, and published in book form by the Société du Mercure de France in June.

Two days after his return to Paris on 3 May, Louÿs terminated his liaison with Marie de Régnier. On his calendar he noted on 5 May: 'Déjeuné avec Hérold.—Dîner avec Robert [the painter Paul Robert].—Envoyé lettre de rupture M.' To Georges he wrote on the same day: 'Ma lettre à M. est mise à la poste. C'est une grosse décision et pas gaie!'[2] Robert Fleury implies that there was a direct connection between Louÿs's decision to break with Marie and the fact of her having informed him in January that she was expecting a child. Perhaps so. There may, however, have been a further important reason: during his absence Marie had become the mistress of Jean de Tinan. If Louÿs had learned of their affair on his arrival in Paris, he would certainly have regarded it as a betrayal of his trust in both of them. Under these circumstances he may have preferred not to see Marie again.

His feelings for Tinan had lost much of their warmth already before this incident. A letter written by Louÿs on 21 November 1898, two days after Tinan's death, contains the following passage, prompted by a reference to the funeral held that morning at the Père Lachaise cemetery:

Comme je revenais de là, tout à l'heure, je pensais avec une sorte de soulagement heureux, que Jean n'aura jamais connu l'aversion que j'avais pour lui. Après avoir cru en son serrement de main comme en une affection sûre et presque tendre, je m'étais senti séparé de lui peu à peu mais pour toujours par des traits de caractère et d'âme que je ne vous dirai pas, vous le pensez bien, mais si froids et si trompeurs qu'il n'était même plus pour moi ce que je peux appeler un camarade. Plus tard, d'ineffaçables choses auxquelles je ne pense pas encore ce soir sans frisson . . .
Je ne lui avais jamais fait de reproches ni de scènes. A quoi bon? Il était ainsi. Et plus tard, il avait fait cela, par plaisir, sachant tout et se disant mon frère. On ne changerait rien, ni à lui, ni aux faits. Je comptais lui parler, un jour; mais il fallait choisir ce jour. Je n'attendais qu'une occasion. Et voici que tout à coup j'ai appris qu'il était mourant. Il a bien fallu oublier . . .[3]

The letter was addressed to Augustine Bulteau, one of the most appealing figures of Parisian society at the turn of the century. A woman of rare distinction and refinement, she received on Sunday afternoons, at her house at 149 avenue de Wagram, a select company of politicians, scientists, and especially artists and writers. Endowed with considerable compassion, psychological insight and, not least, discretion, she was an ideal confidante and counsellor to her younger friends. Throughout the final months of his illness Tinan carried on a regular, sometimes daily, correspondence with her.[4]

Tinan had for some time been suffering from chronic nephritis, and his already weakened constitution had been further debilitated by his intemperate manner of living. In the summer of 1898, while staying with an aunt at Jumièges, near Rouen, he was struck down by a serious attack of the ailment. His legs swelled up painfully and his general condition rapidly deteriorated. A brief improvement was followed by a relapse: 'Je suis de nouveau enflé jusqu'a la taille', he informed Paul-Jean Toulet on 11 August, 'et . . . j'ai la respiration un peu courte.'[5] In the same letter he mentioned that Louÿs, accompanied by their mutual friend, the painter Maxime Dethomas (who had collaborated on the first number of *Le Centaure*), had arrived on a short visit. On 14 August Louÿs reported to Dethomas who had left Jumièges before him: 'Consultation du médecin une demi-heure avant mon départ. L'albuminurie est à un degré qui ne peut plus être enrayé. Cela durera huit jours, quinze ou vingt jours et le médecin dit déjà que l'agonie sera affreuse. C'est épouvantable.'[6]

It was presumably to this conversation with Tinan's doctor that Louÿs was referring in the aforementioned letter to Mme Bulteau. From that moment on he tried to suppress the strong dislike he had conceived for Tinan:

Ce jour-là ... j'ai été pris d'une pitié si profonde que le reste s'y est perdu, sa jeunesse, son ardeur de vivre, sa gloire avortée, sa fin au moment où il allait réaliser tant d'ambitions et de joies futures, c'était une telle misère que tout cela! J'en ai eu la même secousse que j'aurais eue pour tout autre, pour n'importe qui, un indifférent. Je me suis promis d'oublier, tant qu'il serait vivant, un passé dont je ne voulais pas qu'il eût même le repentir, et, comme il se sentait très seul, j'ai pris auprès de lui une grande place, que j'aurais volontiers cédée, sans qu'il s'en soit jamais douté.

Ainsi Jean aura conservé jusqu'à la fin l'illusion d'avoir un ami. En somme, ces illusions-là valent bien des réalités. Mais il aura fait que je les ai perdues.[7]

Tinan, indeed, did not suspect that Louÿs's feelings towards him had undergone such a profound transformation, any more than he realized that he was dying. In early September Louÿs returned to Jumièges in order to assist in his transportation to the Maison Dubois, a municipal hospital located at 200 rue du Faubourg Saint-Denis in Paris. The specialist treating him, Dr. Fernand Widal, declared his case to be hopeless, but thought he might linger on for a while. Louÿs visited him regularly at the hospital.

For Louÿs, the autumn of 1898 was a period of considerable emotional turmoil. Its most significant events were a birth, two deaths, and some moments of great happiness.

In the early hours of 8 September Marie de Régnier gave birth to a son. Unexpectedly, Louÿs was present in her apartment at the time, as he explained in 1918 to Pierre de Régnier:

Jeune Pierre, comme disait Heredia, la nuit où tu es né, je suis allé faire à ton grand-père une visite inexplicable, vers dix heures du soir. Il ne recevait pas, il ne m'avait pas invité au spectacle de ta naissance et moi qui me demandais depuis un quart d'heure dans une balançoire hippomobile pourquoi j'allais si tard chez Heredia sans avoir rien à lui dire, je n'ai pas été surpris de le rencontrer sur son palier, ni surtout de lui entendre dire: 'C'est vous? Bien, venez avec nous.'[8]

Though it was unexpected, Louÿs's presence was none the less highly appropriate; for Marie later assured him that Pierre-Marie-Joseph-Henri de Régnier, called 'Tigre' by his family, was his son.[9] At Marie's suggestion, Louÿs became Tigre's godfather, and, in that capacity, he took part in the baptismal ceremony on 27 September.

On 9 September, in his villa at Valvins, Mallarmé suffocated while trying to demonstrate to his doctor how he had suffered a laryngal spasm the day before. Louÿs was informed of his death on 10 September by Valéry, whom Mallarmé's daughter Geneviève had at once notified. 'Je suis bouleversé et démoli,' Valéry wrote to Louÿs, 'Mallarmé est mort hier matin . . .'[10]

Despite his increasingly frequent and lengthy absences from Paris, Louÿs had by no means lost contact with Mallarmé. On occasion he even sent messages from abroad to express his continued admiration. Thus, on 27 January 1897, at a time when Mallarmé was being criticized in some quarters for excessive obscurity and his friends rallied round him, Louÿs wrote from Algiers to state his conviction that Mallarmé's poetry would eventually triumph over public incomprehension. He compared Mallarmé's position to that of Heraclitus, 'parce que, après vingt-cinq siècles et 25 millions de Systèmes du Monde, c'est au sien que les savants modernes se rallient . . .' Louÿs then referred to Mallarmé's recently published book *Divagations*: 'Il me semble que dans un futur que nous ne pouvons même imaginer, *c'est à lui qu'on se reportera pour fixer les limites de la rêverie humaine, et, mieux encore, ses lois éternelles.*' And he ended his letter with a declaration of solidarity: 'Je ne puis dire à quel point, Monsieur Mallarmé, je suis votre admirateur honteux, et, tandis que de braves gens sans malice s'efforcent avec tant de conscience contre vous dans une ou deux jeunes Revues, je n'ai, moi, qu'un regret, c'est d'être votre partisan le plus convaincu, sans avoir vraiment le droit de me dire votre disciple.'[11] Mallarmé, for his part, did not fail to pronounce Louÿs's name among those of his absent friends, in the toast he offered at the banquet which was held in his honour at the Restaurant Lathuile on 2 February 1897.[12] Louÿs at first intended to accompany Valéry, Régnier, Heredia, and numerous other mourners to the funeral which took place at Valvins on Sunday, 11 September, but decided, at the last moment, not to make the journey. Perhaps the reason was the reappearance of Zohra in the apartment on the boulevard Malesherbes the previous day. Louÿs paid his formal tribute to Mallarmé in October, when the *Mercure de France* printed his 'Sonnet adressé à M. Mallarmé le jour où il eut cinquante ans,' a poem originally presented to its subject in March 1892.

The birth of 'Tigre' led to renewed personal contact between Louÿs and Marie de Régnier. At the end of October he spent two days in Amsterdam with Marie and her husband. The journey was undertaken at Marie's suggestion, ostensibly for the purpose of visiting a Rembrandt exhibition, in reality in order to create conditions propitious to the re-establishment of a more intimate relationship with Louÿs. Considered from this point of view, the expedition appears to have been a success.

On 4 November Jean de Tinan was transported from the Maison Dubois to his parents' apartment at 88 rue de l'Université. His days in the hospital had been filled with pain which he faced with admirable courage and in a spirit of detached irony, if his letters to Mme Bulteau can be regarded as offering a fair reflection of his state of mind. He was even making plans—or was he only pretending?—to join her in Venice, where he hoped to finish his novel *Aimienne*. Only very rarely did he complain or yield to self-pity. The following letter to Louÿs is therefore all the more moving: 'Si on te cite comme désagréable, le supplice de la crucifixion dont on parle dans l'Évangile et dans *Aphrodite*, hausse les épaules, ami, avec un désolé sourire et réponds: Tinan depuis le 22 courant souffre quelque chose de bien pire ... Il ne peut, expliqueras-tu, ni marcher, ni se coucher, ni respirer, ni penser, ni sourire, ni écrire lisiblement, ni fixer cinq minutes

ses pensées sur quelque chose; il a envie de hurler sans en avoir
la force!'[13]

Tinan's condition continued to deteriorate after his transfer
from the hospital. During more than a week, the oedema in his
hands made it impossible for him to write. But on 15 November
he was able to send a short pencilled message to Mme Bulteau:
'Ai bien l'honneur de vous apprendre que la faiblesse diminue un
peu, d'où cet autographe. Quelle vie!!!'[14] On the evening of
17 November Marie de Régnier and Pierre Louÿs spent some
time with him. They were his last visitors, for he died in the early
hours of the next day. 'A aucun moment de son agonie, il n'a
compris que sa fin était certaine,' Louÿs assured Mme Bulteau,
'et comme il n'était pas catholique on a eu la charité de ne pas le lui
dire.'[15]

In a note added in 1918 to the diary he had kept in his youth,
Louÿs recalled 'la saveur de la mort en ta vingt-septième année, au
premier jour des ving-sept mois incomparables'.[16] The 'taste of
death' evidently refers to the grave illness which almost carried
him off in February 1897, during his stay in Algiers. Twenty-
seven months from that date takes one to May–June 1899, the
time of his engagement and marriage to Louise de Heredia. In
describing the intervening months as 'incomparable', Louÿs was
doubtless thinking, in part, of his travels in Algeria and Egypt.
Above all, however, the period was distinguished by the great
happiness he derived from his love affair with Marie de Régnier.
One of the most memorable incidents in their relationship occurred
on 29 November 1898.

The novel *Psyché*, which was left incomplete by Louÿs, contains
a chapter entitled 'L'Apogée' (II, 7), of which the following sentence is evidently inspired by this experience: 'S'il est dans la vie
de quelques amants un sommet, une apogée, un instant incomparable où tout à coup le bonheur se pose, Aimery et Psyché
connurent ce miracle en cet instant de ce jour-là, et rien que la
mort ne put le leur faire oublier.' That same evening Psyché finds
the following poem on her writing-table:

Psyché, ma sœur, écoute immobile, et frissonne . . .
Le bonheur vient, nous touche et nous parle à genoux.
Pressons nos mains. Sois grave. Ecoute encor . . . Personne
N'est plus heureux ce soir, n'est plus divin que nous.

Une immense tendresse attire à travers l'ombre
Nos yeux presque fermés. Que reste-t-il encor
Du baiser qui s'apaise et du soupir qui sombre?
La vie a retourné notre sablier d'or.

C'est notre heure éternelle, éternellement grande,
L'heure qui va survivre à ce fragile amour
Comme un voile embaumé de rose et de lavande
Conserve après cent ans la jeunesse d'un jour.

Plus tard, ô ma Psyché, quand des nuits étrangères
Auront passé sur vous qui ne m'attendrez plus,
Quand d'autres, s'il se peut, amie aux mains légères,
Jaloux de mon prénom, toucheront vos pieds nus,

Rappelez-vous qu'un soir nous vécûmes ensemble
L'heure unique, où les Dieux accordent un instant
A la tête qui penche, à l'épaule qui tremble
L'esprit pur de la vie en fuite avec le temps,

Rappelez-vous qu'un soir, couchés sur notre couche,
En caressant nos doigts frémissants de s'unir
Nous avons échangé de la bouche à la bouche
La perle impérissable où dort le Souvenir.[17]

This poem was first printed on 15 May 1907 in the review
Les Lettres, under the title 'L'Apogée'. It forms the fourth part of
the 'Pervigilium Mortis'—the other sections were not published
during Louÿs's lifetime—which Yves-Gérard Le Dantec has rightly
called 'non seulement . . . le sommet de l'art de Pierre Louÿs,
mais . . . l'une des merveilles du lyrisme français'.[18] In view of the
outstanding importance, both from a personal and a literary point
of view, of that 'heure unique', it appears of interest to reproduce
here in its entirety the explanatory note headed 'Pour l'historique
de PSYCHÉ' which Louÿs wrote on 29 November 1918, exactly
twenty years after the event:

LE 29 NOVEMBRE 1898.

Ce qui s'est dit en prose était prononcé tout bas, sans intonation ni
accent. Je l'ai écrit le soir même, textuellement, puis en vers, ne
comprenant pas bien ce qui s'était passé ni pourquoi cette heure-là . . .
L'heure éternelle . . .
était venue tout à coup entre deux amants qui en avaient connu tant

d'autres; mais comprenant que jamais plus ce miracle:—éprouver au delà du désir—ne se réaliserait; que c'était

> *L'heure unique où les dieux accordent un instant*
> *A la tete qui penche, à l'épaule qui tremble*
> *L'esprit pur de la vie en fuite avec le temps.*

J'avais 27 ans, j'avais fait trois séjours en Algérie, deux à Séville et un en Egypte,—j'avais écrit *Bilitis, Aphrodite* et *Concha Perez* [i.e. *La Femme et le pantin*] (etc.). Je croyais vraiment tout savoir sur l'inaccessibilité du désir par son objet.—Et tout à coup: la plénitude.

Les véritables paroles échangées sont singulières. Elles montrent que cette heure-là fut pour tous deux un phénomène extraordinaire. Phrases courtes, lentes, monotones, tranquilles et toutes *alternées*: distiques. 'Nous sommes heureux.—Nous nous adorons.—Tous les deux.—Tous les deux.—Nous sommes jeunes.—Nous sommes . . . etc.' Au milieu, ce mot capital: '*Nous de désirons rien.*'—J'en passe. Voici les dernières: 'Personne n'est plus heureux que nous ce soir.—Personne.'

Les voix restaient lentes et basses. Les certitudes sont calmes. Et ces paroles vraies, si simples qu'elles soient, prouvent mieux que les vers ce que disent les vers. J'ai remarqué ce soir que pas une seule ne dit: 'je' ni 'tu'. Invariablement: Nous.—Donc, cette quadrature impossible— l'union—s'était faite.

J'avais trouvé depuis cinq ans . . . (et c'est même une des plus belles découvertes de la pensée) . . . que fort au-dessus de 'Je t'aime' et combien plus riche de puissance et d'attraction, il y a: 'Tu m'aimes.' Mais '*Nous* nous adorons' est invraisemblable. C'est là qu'est l'apogée, mais aussi c'est là qu'est la fin.[19]

The meaning of the final sentence becomes clear when one bears in mind a remark made by Louÿs in a letter to Georges on 13 December 1916, at a time when he was revising the text of 'Pervigilium Mortis': 'Si l'on coupe une scène d'amour en trois actes: Avant, Pendant, Après, les vers à Psyché sont le troisième acte. J'en suis sûr, puisque c'est une heure que j'ai vécue . . .'[20]

In May 1896, when he had fallen in love yet again, Louÿs wrote to Georges: 'Je ne sais pas ce que vaudront les romans que je ferai, mais ceux que je vis sont d'un intérêt! Il n'y manque pas une péripétie, pas une fin de chapitre.'[21] Few novels could have convincingly presented a love interest as intriguingly complex as the situation in which Louÿs found himself in the autumn of 1898. There was, in the first place, Maxime Dethomas's sister

Germaine whom he had met in July. Within a very short time there had been talk of a possible engagement, but before the acquaintance could reach a decisive stage, Germaine left Paris in early August for Saint-Médard-en-Jalles near Bordeaux, from where she was not expected to return until the following spring. 'J'aime votre sœur. Elle le sait', Louÿs wrote to Maxime after her departure. 'Je lui ai parlé trois semaines avant son départ, espérant trouver sans peine des occasions de causeries qui lui auraient permis de me connaître davantage et de décider librement si ma vie lui semble faite pour se confondre avec la sienne. Ces rapprochements ne sont pas venus avec la simplicité que j'attendais et vous me dites aujourd'hui qu'ils seront peut-être impossibles pendant huit ou neuf mois encore.'[22] For a man of Louÿs's temperament, such delay spelt danger for any incipient romance, as he explained to Georges in a letter dated 16 September 1898:

Tu me demandes si j'y tiens encore vraiment à ce mariage? Non, mais cela ne veut rien dire; c'est un défaut de mon caractère, je ne peux rien désirer longtemps. Ce que je n'ai pas eu tout de suite ne me tente plus un mois après. Cela ne prouve pas que je n'aie pas eu raison de le désirer au début.—Tu me présenteras cet hiver à toutes les petites Levantines qui cherchent un époux honnête; je reverrai Diane [i.e. Germaine] au printemps et après toutes sortes de comparaisons réfléchies, il est probable que je l'épouserai. Probable seulement . . .[23]

While Germaine was being courted by Louÿs, her friend Louise de Heredia was falling in love with him. Louise, three years younger than Marie, was now an attractive and high-spirited girl of twenty. Louÿs had, of course, known her for several years, but in the past he had treated her rather like a younger sister, teasing her without taking serious notice of her. He was now being made increasingly aware of her feelings, for 'Loulouse' did not attempt to dissemble them: 'Autant que les yeux peuvent exprimer un reproche spécial et complexe (ils le peuvent), elle me répète à satiété avec son regard: "Pourquoi m'avez-vous embrassée sur la bouche, si vous ne vouliez ni m'épouser, ni recommencer? Croyez-vous qu'une soirée pareille ne soit pas un événement dans la vie d'une jeune fille comme moi? Je suis prête à ce que vous voudrez. Pourquoi ne me proposez-vous rien?"'[24] The letter to Georges (written on 25 November) from which this passage is taken indicates that Louÿs was evidently disconcerted by Louise's passionate response to his innocent kiss, and uneasy about the possible consequences, for Louise's behaviour was often unpredictable. Needless to say, the resumption of his intimate relations with her sister—even though Louise was, most probably, unaware of them—complicated the situation still further. Finally, it must not be forgotten that throughout this period Zohra remained installed in Louÿs's apartment. If credence can be attached to the explanation he offered Maxime Dethomas for her presence, he had summoned Zohra back solely in order to protect Germaine from any unwelcome gossip that might have resulted from the premature reports already circulating about her possible engagement to him. Zohra's return, he pointed out, had effectively scotched those rumours. One may wonder what Dethomas and his sister thought of this original method of saving them possible embarrassment. Louÿs took care to paint an exceedingly drab picture of life at 147 boulevard Malesherbes for Dethomas's benefit:

Maintenant est-ce à vous que j'ai besoin d'expliquer comment cette vie commune n'est pas un océan de plaisirs? Vous savez que les vieilles dames s'abusent sur les voluptés infernales des ménages irréguliers. Ce n'est pas ohé! ohé! du tout; mais pas du tout, cher Ami. Si vous voulez des détails, Zo dort de neuf heures et demie à sept heures et moi de trois à onze; nous nous succédons. L'après-midi, chacun sort de son côté. On se voit aux heures des repas comme à Venise. Et encore, je dîne en ville.[25]

Louÿs obviously hoped that this bleak account of his life with Zohra would silence any reproach Dethomas might have been inclined to voice at the arrangement. Zohra left Paris on 10 December. Dethomas must have been surprised to learn a few weeks later that, notwithstanding their supposed indifference towards one another, Louÿs was about to join her in Algeria.

The year 1898 closed on an agreeable note which testified to the growth of Louÿs's literary reputation abroad. Already on 29 October Gilbert de Voisins, whose acquaintance with Louÿs had by now developed into a very close friendship, had published an article in the *Saturday Review* in London, entitled 'In Praise of Pierre Louÿs' (the originally proposed title 'A Master of Life and Lust' having, fortunately, been discarded). Now, in December, the prominent English critic Edmund Gosse wrote a eulogistic review of *La Femme et le pantin* in the influential *Contemporary*

Review. Gosse hailed the novel as 'the most remarkable production of French fiction for many months', while admitting that it was 'not suited for family use'. The heroine he regarded as a unique creation, 'a variety of the she-devil never before revealed to science; at all events, in so magnificently consistent a specimen'. Gosse concluded his review by asserting that 'it would be an idle bigotry to deny that his [Louÿs's] marvellous power over language, his lucidity and gaiety, his originality of approach, his palpitating and sparkling vitality, make him beyond question the most interesting of the young writers of France to-day'.

1899

LOUŸS APPEARS to have given no further thought to his earlier
plans for an extensive trip through South America. Instead, when
he was once more looking for a place in the sun in January he
again chose North Africa. No doubt Zohra's presence there influenced his decision. On 29 January he informed Debussy of his
imminent departure: 'Je dîne ce soir chez Mme Judith Gautier,
30, rue Washington; demain chez Mme P. C[harpentier], ma
cousine, 58, rue de Vaugirard; après-demain dans le wagon-
restaurant du train de 5 h 40; le jour suivant à Nice, puis dans
divers pays inexplorés de l'Afrique du Nord . . .'[1] He spent
February with Zohra at M'sila, at the foot of the Hodna mountains—'la délicieuse M'sila, oasis adorable', he had called it two
years before, after briefly staying there with Zohra.[2]

By the beginning of March he had returned to Paris where he
was promptly caught up again in the complexities of the matri-
monial puzzle: should he marry Germaine Dethomas, or Louise
de Heredia—or neither? Despite the doubts he had expressed to
Georges about the likelihood of his love for Germaine surviving
several months' separation, he still appears at this stage to have
seriously considered marrying her. However, a remark she made
about his relations with Louise offended him so greatly that,
following a stormy meeting on 24 April, he renounced all interest
in an engagement with Germaine.[3]

Louise was thus rid of her most serious rival. However, she was
not yet certain of victory, for Louŷs, who was not in love with her
though he may well have found her attractive, could not bring
himself to take the decisive step of proposing. The dilemma was
finally resolved by an incident which fatally propelled Louÿs into
matrimony. One day, while visiting him in his apartment, Louise
revealed that owing to the considerable debts incurred by her
father—Heredia had a well-founded reputation of being an
inveterate gambler—her family was reduced to an impoverished
condition, which ruled out any possibility of a substantial dowry
being offered to a prospective suitor. Since she was, in consequence, unlikely to find a husband, she was anxious to be at least

in a position to provide for her own needs. Could Pierre not employ her as his secretary? Moved by compassion for the beautiful Loulouse, Pierre yielded instead to an impulse of momentary desire . . . On the evening of that same day, 4 May, he wrote to her: 'Vous vous êtes donnée à moi aujourd'hui, très simplement, avec toute la confiance et l'abandon d'une affection dont je ne doute plus . . . Et dans l'avenir, je vous en prie, rendons-nous heureux: nous le pouvons. Vous verrez bientôt qu'avec moi, pourvu que vous m'aimiez un peu, vous ferez tout ce qu'il vous plaira . . . Je vous promets le bonheur si je puis vous le donner et je vous serre dans mes bras.'[4]

Louÿs's reservations about the marriage are clearly reflected in the tone of this letter, which deserves to be described as one of 'cautious optimism' rather than of 'passionate enthusiasm'. In 1913, bitterly hurt by Louise's decision to obtain a divorce, he assured Georges that he had married her 'par charité'.[5] Three years later, he declared: 'En mai 1899 j'ai fait la dernière des sottises pour quelqu'un à qui—sois tranquille!—je ne dédierai jamais deux alexandrins.'[6] Of course, this latter statement was likewise dictated by the lasting hostility he felt on account of the divorce. It is nevertheless a significant fact that, as far as is known, he never addressed a single poem to her throughout the fourteen years of their married life.

Louÿs's engagement to Louise was announced on 15 May. Debussy was asked to compose a wedding march for the ceremony which was due to take place the following month:

Par un amour de la rime riche qui lui vient sans doute de son père Mlle Louise de Heredia échange son nom contre celui de Louise Louÿs qui est plus symétrique et plus équilibré . . .

Le mariage aura lieu à Saint-Philippe dans six semaines. Connais-tu l'organiste de ce curieux monument? J'ai l'intention de lui suggérer un petit programme sébastienbachique auquel on pourrait donner pour introduction la célèbre et inédite *Hochzeit*[s]*marsch* de Debussy. Es-tu disposé à calligraphier deux cents mesures pour deux claviers et pédale, dans le rythme bizarre de la marche à quatre temps,— morceau d'un caractère pompeux, lascif et jaculatoire comme il sied aux cortèges nuptiaux? Ce sont de ces petits chefs-d'œuvre comme on en écrit tous les jours sur un coin de table, au restaurant, entre le scotch et le grand Valle. Tu ne peux refuser cela à un vieux camarade, dis?[7]

To Mme de Bonnières, Louÿs conveyed the news of his engagement in a more enigmatic message: 'J'épouse Louise de Heredia dans un mois. Il paraît qu'on le sait depuis un an; moi, je ne l'ai appris qu'hier soir et je suis un peu honteux d'être si mal informé . . .'[8] The die was cast. Nothing was allowed to interfere with the preparations for the wedding, not even Zohra's unexpected and doubtless unwelcome reappearance. Although she was now, clearly, *persona non grata* in the apartment on the boulevard Malesherbes, she remained in Paris and was taken on as a model—perhaps at Louÿs's suggestion—by the painter Louis-Édouard Brindeau.

The civil marriage took place at the Mairie of the eighth *arondissement* on Thursday, 22 June. It was, however, the religious ceremony held at the fashionable church of Saint-Philippe-du-Roule on the afternoon of Saturday, 24 June, which attracted the attention of Parisian society. Among the numerous guests were many luminaries from the world of literature, including Sully-Prudhomme, Marcel Prévost, Ferdinand Brunetière, Catulle Mendès, Léon Dierx, Fernand Gregh, Alfred Vallette and his wife (the novelist Rachilde), Anna de Noailles, Robert de Bonnières, Abel Hermant, Auguste Dorchain, Paul Hervieu, the publisher Alphonse Lemerre, and Jean Lorrain, the ironic chronicler of the Parisian scene, who wrote a witty account of the event in his 'Pall-Mall Semaine' in *Le Journal*.[9] The aristocracy was represented by the Princesse de Caraman-Chimay, the Duchesse de Mecklembourg, the Comtesse Récopé, and the Baronne Deslande. As befitted the occasion, there was a profusion of elegant attire. 'Madame Henri de Régnier', Lorrain reported, 'a une bien jolie robe d'un cerise mourant, couleur robe dite *singe malade*, c'est elle qui veut bien m'en informer', whilst the Princesse de Caraman-Chimay wore 'une robe si ajustée qu'on la dirait peinte sur elle-même'. The cynosure of all eyes was, however, Pierre Louÿs himself, who owed this distinction not only to the leading role assigned to him in the ceremony but still more to his superb sartorial chic: 'La redingote à collet de velours de M. Pierre Louÿs, sa cravate mauve et son pantalon gris perle réunissent tous les suffrages', Lorrain noted admiringly. 'On ne se mariera plus que comme ça . . .'

The witnesses for the bride were Henri de Régnier and Dr.

Samuel Pozzi, the well-known surgeon and Senator for the Dordogne; those for the bridegroom Dr. Félix Mougeot and François Coppée. That same evening Louÿs expressed his gratitude to the latter for participating in the ceremony:

Laissez-moi vous remercier encore d'avoir bien voulu être mon témoin aujourd'hui. Je sais combien vos heures sont précieuses, et que vous avez, depuis cet hiver surtout, des préoccupations et des devoirs qui auraient mille fois excusé votre absence. Vous êtes venu néanmoins. Vous avez compris que je tenais à publier, dans une grave circonstance de ma vie, l'affection reconnaissante que je vous ai vouée. J'en suis touché profondément.[10]

Louÿs's choice of Coppée as a witness constituted more than just a public acknowledgement of his indebtedness. It also signified, to a certain extent, an affirmation of political solidarity. Coppée had assumed an active role in the anti-Dreyfus and anti-revisionist campaigns. Among other functions, he had accepted the honorary presidency of the Ligue de la patrie française, the nationalist movement founded in December 1898 for the purpose of defending the country against the 'stateless' Dreyfusard intellectuals—the term 'stateless' being used in this context to designate the French Jews. In 1899 the 'Affair' had reached a critical stage. On 3 June the High Court of Appeal, announcing its verdict on Dreyfus's petition for a new trial, declared null and void the sentence passed at the court-martial in December 1894 and ordered that a further court-martial be held at Rennes. Zola returned from his eleven months' exile in England and, on 5 June, published his article 'Justice' in *L'Aurore* (the newspaper which had printed his celebrated protest 'J'accuse!' on 13 January 1898). On 12 June, Prime Minister Dupuy's cabinet resigned. The weight of public opinion was at last swinging round in favour of Dreyfus's rehabilitation. Coppée's active association with the extreme nationalist and anti-Semitic circles exposed him, in consequence, to increasingly violent attacks from the liberal Press. This explains Lorrain's remark that Louÿs's invitation to Coppée 'est très crâne et a une belle allure indépendante par ces temps de dreyfusisis intellectuel'. In fact, Louÿs had always been a confirmed anti-Dreyfusard, and his correspondence shows marked traces of anti-Semitism. He was, moreover, among the signatories of the first manifesto issued by the Ligue de la patrie française. Furthermore, when the violently anti-Semitic newspaper *La Libre Parole*, edited by the notorious Édouard Drumont, opened a much-publicized subscription to enable the widow of Lieutenant-Colonel Henry to sue Joseph Reinach for publishing 'libellous' attacks on her husband's integrity in *Le Siècle*, Louÿs contributed the sum of 20 francs (as, incidentally, did Jean Lorrain).

Another participant in the wedding-service deserves to be mentioned: Gilbert de Voisins, Louÿs's close friend—and his eventual successor as husband to the bride—took the collection.

After the ceremony a reception and luncheon were held in Heredia's apartment in the rue Balzac, on which occasion the guests could also offer their congratulations to Hélène de Heredia on her engagement to Maurice Maindron (they were married on 29 July). Louÿs and his wife stayed during the following ten days at the Hôtel Voltaire, before leaving on their honeymoon— slightly delayed by Louÿs's indisposition—which took them first to Monte Carlo and then to Pallanza Verbania, on the west shore of the Lago Maggiore. There they remained until the end of August. On their return to Paris they lived for several weeks with Louise's parents, while the apartment on the boulevard Malesherbes was being renovated. They moved into it at the beginning of November.

On 19 October Louÿs was himself a witness, together with Éric Satie and Lucien Fontaine, at a far more modest wedding, that of Claude Debussy and Rosalie Texier, a mannequin employed by the Sœurs Callot store in the rue Taitbout. They were married in a civil ceremony, because the cost of a religious one was beyond their means.[11] In fact, on the morning of his marriage, Debussy was obliged to give a piano lesson to pay for the wedding breakfast.

In the autumn of 1899 Louÿs interceded on Gilbert de Voisins's behalf, when the latter's novel *La Petite Angoisse* was rejected by the *Mercure de France*. After Louÿs had used his influence to have the decision reversed, Voisins expressed his gratitude: 'Tu sais, Pierre, je ne veux pas te faire des phrases, mais tout de même ta bonté à mon égard, je ne l'oublierai pas de longtemps. Je te serre la main, tu es un brave garçon et un bon ami.'[12]

The year 1899 was a meagre one as far as Louÿs's literary output was concerned. The most important new publication was the story *Une Volupté nouvelle*, which appeared in the *Mercure de France* in February and was later that year issued in an illustrated edition by the Librairie Borel. The 'volupté' referred to in the title is smoking, the only new pleasure, the author declared, which had been discovered by man since classical times: 'L'important est d'avoir toujours une cigarette à la main; il faut envelopper les objets d'une nuée céleste et fine qui baigne les lumières et les ombres, efface les angles matériels, et, par un sortilège parfumé, impose à l'esprit qui s'agite un équilibre variable d'où il puisse tomber dans le songe.'[13] This passage is of particular significance in any biography of Pierre Louÿs, for, as André Lebey recalled, 'autour de lui, sans fin, éternellement, l'encens des cigarettes. Il ne cessait de fumer. Environ deux ou trois paquets par jour.'[14] And Fernand Gregh speculated on the effect which so much nicotine must have had on Louÿs's health: 'Balzac disait: Je meurs de dix milles tasses de café. Louÿs eût pu dire: Je meurs de sept cent mille cigarettes (60 par jour, l'aveu est de sa main, depuis 35 ans).'[15]

1900

UNLIKE THE preceding year, which was notable primarily for the fundamental changes in Louÿs's private life, the first year of the new century produced a further landmark in his literary career: his third novel, the last to be published during his lifetime. He had conceived the idea of writing a novel about the 'roi Pausole' after seeing a review at the Moulin Rouge in February 1896.[1] The book was announced as being 'in preparation' in the early editions of *Aphrodite* as well as in both numbers of *Le Centaure*. The project then lay dormant for several years before Louÿs took it up in earnest. When *Le Journal*, whose literary editor was none other than José-Maria de Heredia, acquired the publication rights, only the early chapters were ready, and even when its serialization began on 20 March 1900, the novel was still far from completion. Louÿs always found it very difficult to write under pressure, but he soon had to work under conditions which could hardly have been worse for a person of his artistic temperament. He described them in a letter to Debussy:

Si tu avais assisté aux tragédies qui se sont passées 147, boulevard Malesherbes entre M. Henri Letellier, directeur intérimaire du *Journal* et M. Pierre Louÿs depuis dimanche dernier jusques et y compris aujourd'hui jeudi, tu saurais pourquoi j'interromps nos correspondances.

Ça se résume en un mot:
Mr H. L.—Ayez la gracieuseté de m'envoyer 210 lignes de feuilleton.
Mr P. L.—Ayez la courtoisie d'en accepter désormais 190.
Mr H. L.—Pardon; j'aimerais mieux 210.
Mr P. L.—Désolé. 190.
Mr H. L.—Trente [*sic*] lignes de plus.—Non.—Si.—Non.—Si.—
      Non.—Si.—Non.—Si.—M . . .
Lettres, bleus, télégrammes, cartes, dépêches, pneumatiques, billets, commis, employés, gérants, secrétaires . . . mon cher, c'était à se suicider. J'en ai été *malade* de *fureur* hier soir. C'est le gosse qui vous dit: 'Je veux de la confiture.—Je n'en ai pas.—J'en veux.—Je n'en ai pas.— J'en veux tout de même.—Mais puisqu *'il n'y en a pas*.—Donne-m'en un peu, dis, si t'es gentil.'[2]

At seven o'clock each evening a messenger arrived from *Le Journal* to fetch the next instalment. He was frequently obliged to wait for Louÿs to finish the day's assignment.

The *roman-feuilleton*, that is to say a novel published in serialized form in a daily newspaper, used to be a popular feature of the European Press. Clearly, certain types of novels lend themselves better to such a presentation than others: an episodic structure, for instance, is more suitable than a closely knit narrative which, in its later stages, frequently depends, for full comprehension, on the recollection of earlier incidents. There is, moreover, a significant difference between the piecemeal printing of a completed manuscript which is simply divided into a number of sections in accordance with the allotted space, and the publication of a novel still largely unfinished when printing begins. In the latter case, it is obviously impossible to alter earlier passages in the light of what may subsequently be considered desirable improvements in the plot, nor is there adequate time for stylistically refining the text through several versions.

Owing to his usual dilatoriness where literary composition was concerned, Louÿs had had to complete *La Femme et le pantin* under some pressure (rendered less acute by the fact that he was then in Cairo, 2,000 miles from Fernand Xau and *Le Journal*) but he did complete it before publication began, and, furthermore, insisted on having the proofs submitted to him for possible correction. The major part of *Les Aventures du roi Pausole* was written under conditions which precluded any careful general planning or polishing of details. On a writer who attached overriding importance to *le mot juste*, to rhythm and euphony, in short to stylistic perfection, such a situation imposed an intolerable burden. Unfortunately, this galley-slave existence not only resulted in an inevitable unevenness of quality, but it also seriously damaged Louÿs's health. Debussy vainly sought to calm his friend's strained nerves. 'Pour toi, je ne comprends pas très bien l'état exaspéré où tu mènes ta pauvre vie. Sapristi, n'oublie donc jamais que tu es Pierre Louÿs . . .', he wrote on 25 April. 'Maintenant, si tu voulais être un peu plus calme et ne pas te croire obligé de servir de phare aux passants attardés du boulevard Malesherbes, ça vaudrait mieux . . .'[3] Louÿs's ordeal came to an end on 7 May, with the appearance of the final instalment. By that time he was in a state of physical and nervous exhaustion. *Les Aventures du roi*

Pausole constituted a significant event in Louÿs's literary career as well as in his life, for the physical and mental effort its composition necessitated permanently affected both his health and his capacity for sustained creative activity.

In March 1900 the three *Chansons de Bilitis* set to music by Debussy at last received a public performance. On 24 March 1898 the composer had informed Pierre de Bréville, in reference to a possible performance at the Société nationale: 'Il n'y a personne pour chanter les *Bilitis*.' On 14 March 1889 he indicated that Mme Jeanne Raunay had refused to sing them, because 'la morale de Bilitis lui semble incompatible avec son haut talent'.[4] Happily, Blanche Marot, a member of the Opéra-Comique company, had no such scruples. She interpreted the songs at a concert given at the Société nationale on 17 March 1900.

Henri and Marie de Régnier spent three months in the early part of that year touring the United States where Régnier delivered lectures on French poetry at several leading universities. Louÿs met them on their return at Le Havre on 10 May. His marriage had not led to the immediate termination of his liaison with Marie, and even during her absence in America they were able to exchange personal messages with the aid of a prearranged code. The affair continued, with various interruptions, for another eighteen months.

In July Louÿs was afflicted with a severe bout of asthma, as a result of the pulmonary emphysema from which he chronically suffered. The strain which his constitution had recently undergone probably helped to bring on the attacks. In order to obtain relief from them, he took the cure in August at La Bourboule, a spa in the Auvergne famous for the treatment of asthma.

His first impressions were none too favourable: 'La Bourboule est un hameau sale, ni pavé, ni arrosé, ni tenu d'aucune façon', he wrote to Georges on 14 August.[5] The early effects of the cure were equally discouraging, for it gave rise to fever and nausea. From Paris, Debussy sent a message of encouragement and counselled patience: 'Il faut que tu suives ton régime avec une minutie stupide, tu en as besoin.'[6] Despite his wife's presence, Louÿs found time heavy on his hands. In the afternoons he applied himself diligently to the revision of the text of the *Aventures du roi Pausole*, but he did so with no great enthusiasm, and with little success. In the evenings he regularly tried his luck at the casino, and on 21 August was able to report that he had, over nine days, won the magnificent sum of 17 francs, adding ironically: 'voilà de quoi payer mes dettes . . .'[7] For his life was once more burdened with debts.

Having completed his cure, Louÿs turned southwards towards Spain. Early in September he arrived with his wife in Barcelona. 'La ville est très vivante, avec plus d'animation que de bruit et plus d'entrain que de gaîté. On n'y rit pas mais on n'y bâille jamais', he wrote on 10 September to his new sister-in-law,[8] for Georges had married Paz Ortega Morejon in Paris on 26 June. Louÿs was still in a state of nervous tension, and a murder committed directly beneath his hotel-room threw him into considerable agitation, especially since Louise was also greatly upset by the incident. 'Sa femme a pensé en mourir d'émoi et lui paraît très affecté de l'état où elle a été', Valéry informed Gide. He then referred to the note of depression which had marked Louÿs's letter: 'Puis un dégoût et une tristesse énormes semblent le tenir, une détestation de la littérature et de sa littérature, ou de la voie prise. Cela m'a frappé . . . Il y a un accent nouveau et positivement noir chez P.L.'[9] Gide was strangely moved by Valéry's remarks: 'Il m'est impossible d'obtenir de moi *l'indifférence* à son égard, et, sans plus de haine ni d'amour, je m'intéresserai toujours avec une certaine passion à tous les passages étroits de sa route. Il est certain que ce que tu m'en dis, cette lettre qu'il t'écrit, etc., éveillent en moi un sentiment très vif, qui ressemble terriblement à de l'affection . . .'[10]

An even more distressing experience lay in store for Louÿs. On 23 September his wife was taken gravely ill. The next day he sent Georges an account of what had happened:

Je crois que je n'ai jamais souffert comme depuis vingt-quatre heures. Une fausse couche se préparait . . . Hier soir, à partir de 7 h., hémorragies effrayantes, une mer de sang . . . Jamais je n'ai vu quelqu'un de vivant avec le visage qu'elle avait à cette heure-là. Elle était glacée des pieds à la tête, trempée de sueur, plus de pouls—et pas une plainte, avec des souffrances atroces. Quand elle me parlait, c'était pour me dire: 'Voyons, ne t'inquiète pas, mon petit, ce n'est rien.' Et pendant tout ce temps-là, je la sentais mourir . . .—Arrivée des médecins, opération complète.—Les médecins disent qu'ils sont contents et que tout va bien.—J'ai passé la nuit dernière à me passer la main sur le front et à ne

pouvoir enlever de mon esprit l'imagination que tout était déjà fini.
Elle ne remuait pas … Jamais je n'ai eu mal comme cette nuit-là …
—Ce matin, consultation, bon résultat … Et alors j'ai eu une crise de
larmes qui a duré trois heures … Je sanglotais au pied de son lit en lui
'expliquant' que c'était de joie. Et la pauvre petite me consolait …
—Les Heredia arrivent demain soir …[11]

Two days later, Louise's condition was still extremely serious.
Louÿs continued to marvel at the courage she displayed in keeping
up the pretence that there was no reason for concern; yet she was
well aware of the gravity of her illness, as is clear from her deli-
cately worded request: 'Si je te quittais, je ne dis pas maintenant,
mais pendant que tu es jeune tout de même, promets-moi de ne
pas me regretter longtemps.'[12] On 2 October he was able to assure
Georges—whose own wife had just suffered a miscarriage—that
Louise, though still losing blood, 'est moins pâle, dort et se
nourrit'.[13] The cause of her illness was finally diagnosed as metritis
by one of the attending doctors, who declared that no pregnancy
had occurred. By this time Louise was pronounced out of danger,
but her recovery proceeded slowly.

No sooner was Louÿs's concern about his wife's health relieved
by the reassuring medical report than his peace of mind was disturbed by news calculated to increase still further his distaste for
literature. To his considerable annoyance, he learned of the
publication of unauthorized German translations of several of his
stories and books, including the *Aventures du roi Pausole*—the
version of that novel being inevitably based on the text printed in
Le Journal, with which he was far from satisfied. In addition, he
became involved in a violent dispute with his old friend Ferdinand
Hérold about the proposed staging of the latter's dramatic adaptation of *Aphrodite*. Hérold commenced and perhaps completed the
first version of his play even before the publication of the novel in
book form, for Valéry referred to it in a letter to Gide in early
February 1896.[14] It was listed among works 'in preparation' in
both issues of *Le Centaure*, in the first under the title *Chrysis*, in the
second under that of *Aphrodite*. On 21 September 1897, in one of
his 'Pall-Mall' articles in *Le Journal*, Jean Lorrain inquired what
had become of the 'cinq actes de mise en scène aphrodisiaque et
luxueuse'. According to Lorrain, Hérold and Louÿs had unsuccessfully tried to interest Sarah Bernhardt, and later Réjane, in the
play. Thereafter Louÿs's enthusiasm for arranging a performance

appears to have cooled, while Hérold still waited hopefully for a suitable opportunity. This finally occurred in October 1900 when Abel Deval considered producing the play at the Théâtre de l'Athénée, of which he had recently been appointed director. Hérold's request for Louÿs's permission could not have been more unfortunately timed: 'Je pense bien à la littérature!', Louÿs, still preoccupied with his wife's health, commented in a letter to Georges on 7 October.[15] He was, in any case, probably reluctant to authorize a production he could not himself supervise. Accordingly, he refused his permission. When he learned that Hérold was none the less proceeding with the arrangements, he dispatched furious letters to Hérold as well as to Deval, threatening to seek a court injunction prohibiting the presentation of the play. 'Hérold a beau être mon ami de dix ans,' Louÿs wrote to Georges on 23 October, 'je n'ai pas hésité une minute à me brouiller avec lui à la suite de cela. Pourquoi conserver un ami qui est capable de me traiter en mineur et de négliger ma signature pour piller mes pauvres livres! Je lui ai écrit une page 1/2 assez tapée . . .'[16] In a letter to Debussy two days later Louÿs referred tartly to 'mon ex-ami Hérold'.[17] In the face of his determined opposition, the project was dropped.

By the end of October Louise had sufficiently recovered to leave Barcelona and return to Paris. In order to ensure that her convalescence would not be impeded by domestic duties, Louÿs engaged two servants to assist in the running of the household.

During his stay in La Bourboule and Barcelona, Louÿs had not lost contact with his Parisian friends. Among his most regular correspondents was Gilbert de Voisins, several of whose letters, remarkable for both their warmth and their confidential nature, have been printed in their entirety by Robert Fleury. He also cites an interesting passage from a note written in December 1900, which indicates that Voisins had fallen into the habit of visiting Louise in Pierre's absence. Already in February of that year Voisins had, on more than one occasion, expressed his appreciation of Louise's charm and hospitality in letters to Pierre: 'J'ai eu tant de fois le plaisir de causer avec ta femme que c'est une vraie joie que tu m'offres en m'invitant.'—'Vraiment je n'ai jamais vu personne recevoir les amis de son mari d'une façon aussi exquise . . .'[18] Now, on 29 December, he wrote: 'J'ai passé une partie de l'après-midi avec ta femme, *j'aimerais être sûr que ça ne l'embête pas que j'aille la voir si souvent,* tu es trop mon ami pour ne pas me le dire, n'est-ce pas? Tu comprends, je ne suis pas très gai, je n'ai pas grand-chose à lui raconter, mais c'est si bon de rester près d'une jeune femme comme elle qu'on sait être bonne et belle.'[19] Voisins's relationship with Louise was moving—however innocently—towards a greater intimacy.

Before the year was out Louÿs fired off another broadside in his long-standing battle for greater sexual freedom. Three articles published by him in *Le Journal* on 24 November, 9 December, and 18 December under the general title 'Liberté pour l'amour et le mariage' attracted much attention. They were prompted by recently announced figures showing that the declining French birth rate was now only half as great at that of Germany, a fact which had led Alphonse Bertillon, the well-known demographer and head of the statistical institute of the city of Paris, to calculate that within seven years every French soldier would be faced by two 'enemies'.

Louÿs argued that if the French Government really wished to encourage a rise in the birth rate, it ought to set itself two main objectives: firstly, the development of a more enlightened attitude towards unmarried mothers, backed up by a legislative programme which would provide servants and factory-workers with protection against arbitrary dismissal during pregnancy and the three months following confinement, and would offer poor women the possibility of placing their children in public-assistance nurseries for the first two years after birth; and, secondly, the removal of the numerous irksome obstacles placed in the path of those wishing to marry, notably the considerable expense involved, the insistence on the presentation of many, largely irrelevant, documents, and the law forbidding any man under the age of twenty-five and any woman under that of eighteen to marry without their parents' consent.[20]

As a result of the articles Louÿs received many letters, including one from an established dramatist offering to turn the second article ('Histoire d'un fiancé') into a one-act play to be called *Gai! Gai! Marions-nous!*[21] Louÿs was amused, but not enough to respond favourably.

1901

THE BEGINNING of 1901 found Louÿs, as usual, eager to spend the winter months in a warmer climate. Before leaving Paris he was, however, expected to deliver the already long-overdue revised manuscript of *Les Aventures du roi Pausole* to Eugène Fasquelle, for the forthcoming publication of the volume by the Librairie Charpentier et Fasquelle. If anything, he was more dilatory than ever, and even more prone than in the past to react with exasperation to any unexpected turn of events. 'Ma vie d'affaires littéraires continue aussi déplaisante,' he complained on 9 January. 'Tous les deux ou trois jours, il m'en tombe une nouvelle et comme la plupart des anciennes durent encore, je me sens à bout . . .'[1] On 23 January he still felt confident about completing the revision by the end of the month.[2] In fact, Fasquelle did not receive the manuscript until several weeks later. Yet, despite the long delay, the changes made in the text originally printed in *Le Journal* were few and of relatively minor importance.

Louÿs derived greater satisfaction from another venture. On Thursday, 7 February, a special private performance was given in the Salle des fêtes of *Le Journal* of ten *Chansons de Bilitis*. The poems were recited by Mlle Milton and mimed by a group of statuesque young ladies. At Louÿs's request, Debussy composed a short score (for two harps, two flutes, and celesta) to accompany the spectacle. Louÿs himself supervised the rehearsals, with care and not without pleasure. 'Je passe cette semaine toutes mes après-midi avec des femmes nues', he informed Georges on 23 January. 'C'est du joli. Il s'agit des modèles qui vont représenter onze *chansons de Bilitis* sur la scène du *Journal*, tantôt avec des voiles drapés, tantôt en robes de kôs, tantôt sans rien du tout que leurs deux mains ou leur position de 3/4 en arrière.'[3] News of this brazen display of unveiled or, at best, barely veiled pulchritude reached Senator René Bérenger who threatened the editor of the newspaper with prosecution if he went ahead with the planned spectacle.

A distinguished legislator and politician who had played an important part in the establishment of the Third Republic,

Bérenger was also one of the most prominent champions of the puritanical attitudes Louÿs so bitterly opposed. His violent and uncompromising opposition to any activity he deemed a danger to moral rectitude frequently led him to censure essentially harmless incidents and earned him the nickname 'Père-la-Pudeur'.

On this occasion, Bérenger's warning went unheeded and *Le Journal* proudly claimed on 8 February that the select audience had witnessed 'un des spectacles les plus artistiques qu'il ait été donné de voir'. Although Louÿs had told Georges that eleven *chansons* were to be performed, only ten are mentioned in the newspaper account: 'Chant Pastoral', 'Les Comparaisons', 'Les Contes', 'La Partie d'osselets', 'Bilitis', 'Le Tombeau sans nom', 'L'Eau pure du bassin', 'Les Courtisanes égyptiennes', 'La Danseuse aux crotales,' 'La Pluie au matin'. The beautiful girls, the reporter added, had greatly contributed to the realization of the ideal envisaged by the poet: 'A contempler ces merveilleuses académies, tantôt grêles, tantôt puissantes, toujours pures et drapées avec art, les spectateurs purent se croire transportés aux grandes époques de la nudité pure.' Louÿs had reason to be well pleased with the success of the evening; the composer less so, notwithstanding the reference to his 'musique gracieuse, ingénieusement archaïque', for the consistent mis-spelling of his name as 'M. de Bussy' underlined his obscurity, in contrast to the fame enjoyed by the author who, the report asserted, 'n'est plus de ceux qu'on présente au monde littéraire'.

Nothing more was heard of a suggestion contained in a letter from Louÿs on 25 October 1900 that further performances of the *Chansons de Bilitis* should be presented at the Théâtre des Variétés.[4] In 1914 Debussy arranged six of the pieces for piano duet and piano solo under the title *Six épigraphes antiques*. Many years later Ernest Ansermet made a full orchestral version of them.

On 8 February, the day following the soirée organized by *Le Journal*, Louÿs and his wife left Paris. Gilbert de Voisins came to the station to bid them good-bye. On 9 February they embarked at Marseille for Egypt, on what was to be Louÿs's last journey to Africa. His funds were so low by this time that, in order to pay for it, he was obliged to borrow 2,000 francs from Georges and 1,500 francs from his father-in-law. A year later the loans had not been repaid.[5]

After spending some six weeks in Egypt as the guests of Georges and Paz, Louÿs and his wife travelled back to Europe at the end of March. They visited Italy before returning to France, and it was during their stay in Naples that Louÿs experienced the first signs of the eye-disease which, ten years later, would lead to temporary blindness. He attributed the trouble to the severe headaches from which he had lately suffered. A local ophthalmologist prescribed a treatment which restored his normal vision. In Paris, where he arrived on 20 April, he consulted a specialist, whose reassuring diagnosis set his mind at rest.

To find a cure for his financial sickness proved more difficult. In fact, he never succeeded in obtaining more than passing relief from it throughout the rest of his life. 'On a 16 francs en caisse et 7 ou 8.000 fr. de dettes, comme la France elle-même, proportions gardées', he wrote to Georges on 21 May.[6] His situation was somewhat improved by the royalties he received for *Les Aventures du roi Pausole* which achieved satisfactory early sales, 11,500 copies being purchased in the four days following the publication of the novel in book form on 20 June.[7] The story *L'Homme de pourpre*, written during his visit to Egypt, was, moreover, serialized in *Le Journal* between 27 June and 1 July and published almost simultaneously in an illustrated edition by the Librairie Borel. Louÿs also commenced negotiations for yet another contract for a series of newspaper articles—this time with *Le Figaro*, at a proposed initial rate of 250 francs apiece, with complete freedom of choice as to subject, 'exception faite pour la tribadie'.[8] Needless to say, this last project proved as barren as similar ones had before. Louÿs did continue to contribute occasional articles to different newspapers or magazines (three appeared in *Le Journal* during the course of that year) but the prospect of having to write 'to order' to meet datelines quickly inspired in him a distaste which exceeded in intensity even the perennial desire to replenish the constantly emptying family coffers.

In the autumn Louÿs resumed work on a historical project which had already briefly occupied him in 1895: the story of Louise O'Murphy, an Irish girl commonly known as 'La Morphie' or 'La Morphise' who became the mistress of Louis XV in 1750, when she was thirteen. She had been discovered by Casanova who arranged to have her painted in the nude. The portrait was shown to the King, who promptly resolved to verify its likeness by having the girl brought to court for his inspection. She became the most famous occupant of the celebrated Parc aux Cerfs, the small villa in the town of Versailles which was the residence of the select troupe of Louis's courtesans. La Morphise remained the King's mistress for three years, an unusually long period for the house-guests at the Parc aux Cerfs. She was painted at least twice by François Boucher in the same delightfully provocative pose (one of these pictures now hangs in the Louvre, the other in the Alte Pinakothek in Munich). Louÿs first mentions his renewed interest in La Morphise to Georges on 10 September.[9] A letter written on 26 December testifies to his continuing preoccupation with the 'petite souillon':

J'ai mon livre à finir et à peine le temps de le faire. Tu me demandes ce que c'est et si je l'écris à la louange de Louise Morphy. Non: pas du tout à sa louange, mais pas non plus pour l'attaquer. J'ai trouvé simplement 'libre de tout historien' une personne qui a été tour à tour: pauvresse irlandaise à Rouen, fille de savetier à Paris, sœur de filles et d'actrices vagues, maîtresse de Louis XV pendant trois ans, femme d'officer (1er mari), femme de fonctionnaire des finances (2e mari), femme de conventionnel (3e mari) et qui est morte enfin, en 1814, après avoir mené la vie la plus romanesque et la plus variée qu'on puisse inventer.[10]

Gradually, however, Louÿs's progress grew more halting and eventually petered out altogether. Yet the subject never lost its fascination for him. Cardinne-Petit relates that in 1917 Louÿs talked incessantly of Louise O'Murphy, and in so vivid a fashion that his words brought her most convincingly to life: 'A chaque fois, je me laissais prendre au piège qu'il me tendait innocemment et me persuadais qu'elle allait surgir d'une pièce voisine: "Murphy, ma beauté, il est l'heure de se mettre à table!"'[11]

According to Robert Fleury, Louÿs's liaison with Marie de Régnier came to an end in November 1901.[12] In this connection, he believes that the separation imposed on the lovers by the Régniers' lengthy visit to America in 1900 contributed even more than Louÿs's marriage to the breakup of their relationship.[13] It is, of course, difficult to assess the plausibility of this theory. What can be said with some confidence is that Louÿs himself regarded his union with Louise as the principal cause of the estrangement. In December 1916 he wrote to Georges:

Un poète ne doit faire en vers aucun reproche à une ancienne maîtresse; pas même pour ajouter qu'il la plaint ou qu'il lui pardonne. D'ailleurs, ce serait à moi de me faire pardonner, car je n'ai malheureusement plus de doute. C'est moi qui ai eu tous les torts, ici. En mai 1899 j'ai fait la dernière des sottises pour quelqu'un à qui—sois tranquille!—je ne dédierai jamais deux alexandrins.—Mais si je n'en avais que le regret, ce ne serait rien. J'en ai le remords.[14]

Louÿs continued to worship Marie long after their liaison had ceased. In 1917, Cardinne-Petit recalled, he still spoke of her 'comme on parle d'une idole, comme le croyant parle de sa religion'.[15]

The loss of Marie's love was not the sole reason for Louÿs's unhappiness that autumn. As happened so frequently, the final months of the year constituted a period of illness and general wretchedness. 'Depuis six semaines, je vais de rhumes en bronchites . . .', he complained on 27 November. 'Je perds deux mois de vie, c'est insupportable.'[16] To Debussy he wrote shortly afterwards: 'De la fin d'octobre au commencement de décembre j'ai passé plus de jours au lit qu'à la chambre, et pas quatre au dehors.'[17] To add to his despondency, he was again desperately short of cash. In December he had to borrow 2,000 francs from Gilbert de Voisins, thus adding a further private debt to those he had already incurred towards Heredia and towards Georges (to the latter he then owed no less than 30,000 francs).[18] Louÿs was, moreover, greatly saddened by several deaths in his family that year, including that of Georges's five-month-old son. His dejection was made complete by the death in December of his last surviving uncle, to whom he was greatly attached. From Épernay, where he had attended his uncle's funeral, he addressed these sombre reflections to Georges on 18 December: 'Je comptais ce soir tous ceux que j'avais connus là . . . Dix ou douze ans d'absence, on revient et il n'y a plus personne de tous ceux qu'on a trouvés autour d'une table. Ainsi tous les dix ans, il faut refaire sa vie, son milieu, ses affections, ses amitiés. Comment est-ce que c'est possible? . . . Je me sens déjà tout près des vieillards, j'ai comme eux du ventre et des rides et je ne sais quelle incuriosité des choses qui me passionnaient jadis . . .'[19] This letter was written one week after Louÿs's thirty-first birthday. Five days later his tone had become still more desperate:

Je suis revenu [to Paris] dans un état moral dont je suis réellement malade, avec des angoisses à la gorge et des frissons dans la poitrine, tout le long du jour ... C'est un accablement général, un décourage-ment absolu devant l'existence ... Je me sens les bras cassés devant l'inutilité, la vanité de tout.—Hier soir, je travaillais ... je n'ai pas l'ombre d'une ambition, pas une envie, pas un désir. Si quelqu'un me veut du mal, il pourrait me faire ce soir tout ce qui lui plairait. Je ne me défendrais contre rien ... Je suis dans une disposition d'esprit à n'attendre et à ne chercher aucune espèce de bonheur ...[20]

In a letter to his sister-in-law Paz, that same day, he attributed his despondency mainly to the fact that Georges, who had spent a part of the summer in France, was once again far away.[21] His love for Georges was, indeed, as profound as it had ever been. Neither the frequency nor the tone of his letters was in any way affected by his own or his brother's marriage: 'Nous sommes tellement unis que chacun de nous est une part de l'autre', he assured Georges on 24 June 1903.[22]

At the end of December Louÿs and his wife were living on the 100 francs she had received from her mother as a Christmas present. When he caught a chill and the coal-merchant refused to deliver any more fuel unless paid in cash—a condition which, needless to say, Louÿs was unable to fulfil—he was obliged to accept the hospitality offered to them by his parents-in-law in their apartment at the Arsenal Library, of which Heredia had been appointed Director the previous February. It was on this inauspi-cious note that the year 1902 opened.

Twilight Years: 1902–1919

IT APPEARS appropriate to conclude the detailed biography of
Pierre Louÿs with the year 1901, since from the literary as well as
the personal point of view it constitutes the end of the most
interesting period of his life. During 1901 he undertook his last
major journey abroad and published his last important work of
fiction, the two events being intimately linked in his own mind
inasmuch as he regarded the impressions derived from foreign
travel as an essential stimulus for his imagination, and was repeatedly to cite his inability to visit warmer and more colourful
countries as one of the main causes of the decline in his creative
faculty. From this time onwards, moreover, Louÿs withdrew
increasingly from the numerous social contacts and activities
which had formed such a significant aspect of his life during the
preceding decade. He began, to use his own expression, to live 'on
tiptoe'.[1]

During the eighteen years covered by this chapter, Louÿs published only very few new works. The following merit special
mention: *Sanguines* (1903), a volume of stories, most of them not
previously printed; *Archipel* (1906), a collection of articles originally written for newspapers, particularly *Le Journal*; the poems
'Svbscriptvm Tvmvlo Ioannis Secvndi' and 'L'Apogée' which
appeared in the review *Les Lettres* in 1906 and 1907 respectively
(although composed several years earlier); the poem 'Isthi',
privately printed and distributed in 1916; and, finally, *Poëtique*,
published in the *Mercure de France* in 1916 before being issued
separately, in a limited edition, the following year. In addition,
Louÿs made several scholarly contributions to the elucidation of
problems of bibliography and literary history (including *L'Auteur
des 'XV Joyes de mariage'* (1903), a privately printed essay in
detection). Such fame as he continued to enjoy among the general
cultured public derived almost entirely from reissues of his three
novels and the *Chansons de Bilitis*, as well as by various adaptations
of *Aphrodite* and *La Femme et le pantin* for the dramatic and operatic stage. In 1919, however, his controversial theories on the
Corneille–Molière partnership brought him briefly back into the

limelight. This was to be the last occasion during Louÿs's life when public interest focused on him.

The despondency reflected in Louÿs's letters to his brother in the latter part of 1901 long maintained its hold over him. He himself found it difficult to account satisfactorily for this profound disspiritedness, even to Georges:

Disons que c'est la maladie de la trentaine. On appelait cela le spleen en 1830. Je me sens tout à fait sans désirs; sans plaisir; sans ambition. Voilà.—Cela ne veut pas dire que je m'ennuie; et la preuve c'est que je continue à me coucher tard, c'est-à-dire à reculer la fin de la journée à son extrême limite: signe qu'elle ne m'ennuie pas; mais rien ne m'attire au dehors, ni les gens, ni les choses. Je ne fais de visites ni aux dames, ni aux amis, ni aux musées. Je ne vais jamais au théâtre et, ce qui t'étonnera davantage: jamais au concert ... Je ne fais rien non plus pour 'soigner' ma situation littéraire. Tu vas me dire que tout cela n'est pas nouveau chez moi. Si; je me sens très changé, depuis trois mois surtout, ou plutôt depuis trois mois j'ai pris conscience du sentiment qui me change depuis quelques années ...[2]

Louÿs longed to get away from Paris, but could not leave because he had promised a publisher to finish the book on Louise O'Murphy, had undertaken to write a *conte*, had offered to contribute a preface ... As usual, his progress was painfully slow. On 9 April 1902 he wrote to Georges: 'Le retard que je mets à faire tout ce que j'ai promis d'écrire, arrive à mécontenter tout le monde. C'est à cause de cela que je refuse tout, que je ne peux ni m'absenter, ni mettre aucun ordre dans ma vie. Quelle triste et incurable maladie morale.—Et on vous dit: ayez de l'énergie, de la volonté. C'est comme si on disait à un phtisique: ayez du muscle. Cela ne se trouve ni chez les pharmaciens ni chez les conseilleurs.'[3] The thought of depending on his writing for his livelihood exercised a paralysing effect on Louÿs's creative ability. 'Depuis 95 je n'ai guère travaillé ...—du moins je n'ai guère "composé",— parce que j'ai ma vie à gagner et que cette seule idée me rend ma plume odieuse', he wrote on 29 April 1902. 'L'idée que cette ligne vaut vingt sous m'empêche absolument de l'écrire pour la vendre. Le plaisir que j'ai à t'écrire à toi est un vrai plaisir parce que je n'irai pas ensuite chez le caissier du *Journal* dire: "Monsieur, c'est 225 fr."'[4] He had, in any case, always felt ill at ease when writing for a newspaper with a large circulation. In November 1896 he had withdrawn from an agreement to contribute regular fort-nightly articles to *Le Journal* because he could not bear the thought that they would be printed in 200,000 copies.[5] Until the end of his life he was haunted by his early ambition to be appre-ciated only by the charmed circle of the 'happy few'.

At the same time, Louÿs was tormented, over the years, by the knowledge that he could easily earn a comfortable income if only he succeeded in surmounting the psychological obstacle which made it impossible for him to work under such conditions:

Si j'avais un peu plus de fécondité je gagnerais largement mes dépenses de chaque année. Aux prix qu'on me donne maintenant je gagnerais même le double. Mais tout ce que j'essaie d'écrire par devoir est exé-crable et je me vois sans cesse dans l'alternative, ou de produire à la ligne et de ruiner ma réputation en un an, ou de continuer comme par le passé, entraînant un cortège de dettes qui devient la seule pensée de mes soirées. La littérature est le plus libre et le plus délicieux de tous les métiers pour ceux qui ne l'ont pas pour unique ressource. Pour les autres, même quand ils font des envieux, c'est l'incertitude et le tracas perpétuel.[6]

Of course, his financial situation did not allow him to travel widely. Yet he had come to regard these journeys, especially those to warmer countries, as necessary stimuli for his literary produc-tion. Accordingly, he found himself caught up in an insoluble dilemma: he could not write because he did not travel; he could not travel because he did not write. 'Les voyages me sont indis-pensables à tous les points de vue . . .', he told Georges in a letter on 22 January 1905. 'Depuis notre voyage au Caire (février 1901) voici quatre ans que nous renonçons à tous les voyages—et quatre ans que je ne publie rien . . . Quatre ans sans les vacances étran-gères dont j'ai moralement besoin, tu ne peux pas t'imaginer comme c'est long pour moi . . . Je suis bien ennuyé et découragé.'[7] And several years later he wrote: 'De 1901 à 1911, pendant plus de dix ans je ne suis pas allé en Afrique. Je n'ai plus rien publié, que de vagues articles.'[8]

Louÿs spent most of his holidays either at Biarritz where Georges, following his return to France from Egypt in 1902, had acquired a villa, or at Tamaris-sur-Mer, on the Mediterranean coast near Toulon. He is known to have stayed in Biarritz in May 1902, from mid-February to mid-April 1903, in October 1903, and again from late July until late September 1906; in Tamaris from

August until early October 1905, from July to October 1907, and from March to November 1910. In 1911 he was in Arcachon from late July until the end of September. Only rarely did he travel abroad after 1901 and then only on short visits to nearby countries such as Spain (a week in Seville in April 1903) or Holland (a brief stay in Rotterdam in April 1908).

Louÿs's first impressions of Tamaris, in the summer of 1905, were highly favourable:

L'endroit es délicieux. L'horizon ressemble à celui de Saint-Sébastien: une rade avec une presqu'île très élevée au fond, reliée à la terre par un petit isthme bas; mais entre elle et nous, il y a ton azur, ô Méditerranée . . . Les petits palmiers ridicules de cette côte-ci qui me faisaient rire il y a dix ans sont devenus de très beaux arbres, il y a des buissons de lauriers-roses partout: je ne peux pas choisir un meilleur coin de terre pour écrire des choses de Grèce, à moins d'aller à Corinthe même . . . Et puis c'est l'air d'ici qui me ravit. Dès que j'ai passé Valence en France ou Cordoue en Espagne, ou en Italie, la mi-chemin entre Rome et Naples . . . on trouve un air léger, heureux, où on a l'impression que tout est bien . . . Je me sens chez moi dans ces pays-là. Rien ne peut t'exprimer à quel point je revis quand j'ai passé Valence . . .[9]

In the long run, however, not even Tamaris could adequately replace other, more exotic places.

In the late autumn of 1902 Louÿs moved to a rented house at 29 rue de Boulainvilliers where he lived for the rest of his life. The rue de Boulainvilliers, which lies within the Hameau de Boulainvilliers created by a certain M. de Maupeou in 1832 in the grounds of the former Château de Passy, was more remote from the centre of the social and cultural life of the capital than any of his previous residences. Its tranquil, almost rural setting fitted in well with his increasing desire for seclusion.

Louÿs remained a charming host for his invited guests, but disapproved of unexpected visitors. Ernest Gaubert relates that if any presented themselves at the door, the maid was instructed to inform them that the master was out; during that time silence was imposed on all those present, and conversation was not resumed until the unwelcome caller had departed.[10] His closest friends included Gilbert de Voisins with whom he maintained excellent relations until the divorce proceedings in 1913 and Voisins's subsequent marriage with Louise. With Paul Valéry he remained on good terms until his death. Another person whom he saw frequently and with whom he corresponded assiduously was the journalist, author, and future 'Prince des Gastronomes', Maurice Sailland, better known as 'Curnonsky'. In his memoirs, a chapter of which is affectionately devoted to 'Pierre Louÿs et l'art épistolaire', Curnonsky states that between 1898 and 1920 he received more than two hundred and twenty letters from Louÿs.[11] Like others with whom Louÿs associated during these so often unhappy years, Curnonsky recalls above all the wit, the charm, and the gaiety of his conversation and correspondence.

Louÿs's friendship with Claude Debussy endured until 1904. He had, over the years, offered constant encouragement to the composer, for whose music he felt a genuine admiration. On 5 May 1898, in reply to a despairing letter in which Debussy had expressed grave doubts about his talent, he wrote:

Toi, mon vieux, tu n'as pas l'ombre d'une excuse pour avoir de ces cauchemars;—parce que TU ES UN GRAND HOMME, comprends-tu ce que cela veut dire? On te l'a laissé entendre; moi, je te le dis. Et tu me croirais peut-être si j'ajoute que je n'ai jamais dit cela à personne. Quels que soient les ennuis que tu as, cette pensée-là doit tout dominer. Il faut que tu continues ton œuvre et que tu la fasses connaître ... Si tu crois que je puisse t'être utile, dis-moi comment. Je ferai de mon côté ce que je pourrai sans t'en parler ...[12]

Louÿs continued to lend moral support. According to Cardinne-Petit, who claims to have heard the story from Louÿs himself, he prevented Debussy from destroying the completed score of *Pelléas et Mélisande* in a fit of depression.[13] Naturally, Louÿs was present at the dress rehearsal of the work at the Opéra-Comique on the afternoon of 28 April 1902: 'Compte sur moi, Claude, j'invite cinq personnes pour emplir la baignoire d'applaudissements.'[14] He also attended the first performance two days later, and in May offered his services once more for the first matinée: 'On me dit ... qu'il y a encore intérêt à intimider les idiots de ce nouveau public. Si tu as deux places, n'oublie pas que j'ai des mains retentissantes.'[15]

For his part, Debussy frequently stressed the deep affection in which he held Louÿs. Thus he wrote on 27 March 1898, while Louÿs was in Egypt: 'J'aimerais à t'avoir près de moi, car tu es le seul en qui mon amitié ait confiance'.[16] And on 17 June 1903:

'Tu es celui de mes amis que j'ai certainement le plus aimé . . .'[17] Yet the same letter indicates that the two friends had then not seen each other for more than a year. The published correspondence reveals, indeed, that their meetings became much rarer after their respective marriages in 1899.

Their contacts ceased altogether after Debussy had left his wife Lilly for Emma Bardac in June 1904. Like many others of Debussy's friends, Louÿs strongly condemned his action. Lilly's fate evoked even greater sympathy from him following her attempted suicide in October. 'Ma sortie d'hier a été pour aller voir la pauvre Mme Debussy qui s'est tiré un coup de revolver dans la poitrine le 13 octobre après avoir été abandonné par son mari', Louÿs wrote to Georges. 'La balle a traversé deux fois l'estomac . . . l'opération a pourtant bien réussi et la malheureuse paraît hors d'affaire; mais elle reste sans un sou et sans un gîte . . . Le mari est parti avec une juive de quarante et quelques années, Mme S. B. [Sigismond Bardac] . . .'[18] The letter is remarkable for the cold reference to 'le mari', who was by no means unknown to Georges; the fact that Debussy had gone off with a Jewess probably made the desertion even more contemptible in Louÿs's eyes. At the same time, he appears to have felt genuine compassion for Lilly, for he mentions in the same letter having suggested to Louise that they invite her to stay with them for several weeks. He also contributed to the subscription opened for her benefit, on condition that his name was not divulged.[19]

A reconciliation between the two men took place later, although no details are available. In his book *Catherine et ses amis*, Sylvain Bonmariage (the nom de plume assumed by the Comte Sylvain Bonmariage de Cercy) describes a meeting between Louÿs and Debussy at the house of the Marquise Catherine de Givré in the avenue Mozart.[20] It can with some probability be ascribed to May 1912. If Bonmariage's recollection is correct, Debussy was aware that Louÿs would be present when he accepted the invitation. Neither in their conversation, as reconstructed at length by Bonmariage, nor in the latter's remarks about Debussy and Louÿs, is there the slightest hint of any strained feelings. Thus they are likely to have resumed their contacts, at least on a superficial basis, prior to that date. A remark reported by Cardinne-Petit suggests that Debussy continued to hope for the re-establishment of closer relations. When *Poëtique* was published in 1917,

Louÿs observed maliciously: 'Je ne lui enverrai pas ma *Poëtique*, car dans son désir de m'être agréable, il ne manquerait pas de la mettre en musique!'[21]

Above all, Louÿs was fortunate, with regard to his friends, in being able to count, during the latter part of his life, on the unfailing affection of three persons who did their utmost to make his often wretched existence as agreeable as possible and who, in particular, strove to protect him, during the years immediately following the end of the war, from the often unpleasant consequences of his debilitating habits.

One was the poet Fernand Gregh, a close neighbour in the Hameau de Boulainvilliers. Another was André Lebey, the confidant of his youth and, with Jean de Tinan, his constant companion during the many happy days and nights spent in the Latin Quarter in the mid-1890s. Their friendship withstood triumphantly the test of time. When Lebey published his article 'D'*Astarté* au *Roi Pausole*' in *L'Eclair* on 21 January 1922, Louÿs, who was ill at the time, wrote to him: 'Viens m'embrasser. J'ai besoin de te revoir. Je t'aime avec trente ans de ma vie.'[22]

The third friend was Charles Bargone who, at Louÿs's suggestion, adopted the pseudonym 'Claude Farrère'. To him Louÿs confided on 31 December 1917: 'Il n'y a pas de jour où je ne pense au bonheur que j'ai d'être votre ami.'[23] No one could have been more devoted or faithful, even beyond the grave. Where others, at the most, composed a handful of commemorative tributes, Farrère wrote two entire books about Louÿs, first a fictionalized biography, *L'Homme seul* (Paris, 1942), and twelve years later *Mon ami Pierre Louÿs*. A large section of his *Souvenirs* (Paris, 1953) is likewise taken up with memories of Louÿs.

The circumstances which led to his first meeting with Bargone show Louÿs in a highly favourable light: generous, unconceited, genuinely eager to encourage a promising young writer, willing to take considerable trouble to assist a friend, even a very recent one. In November 1901 *Le Journal* announced a short-story competition. Louÿs was asked by Heredia, who as literary editor presided over the selection committee, to read some of the entries. One story entitled *Fumée d'opium*, which was eventually awarded the fourth prize, especially caught his attention. On 9 March 1902 its author, a young naval officer cadet by the name of Charles Bargone, received the following letter from Louÿs: 'Monsieur, Vous avez envoyé au Concours du *Journal* une nouvelle qui est absolument remarquable et que je préfère à toutes ses concurrentes. Voulez-vous me permettre de vous demander si vous avez déjs écrit, ou publié, d'autres pages. Il me semble que j'aurai désormaià un plaisir très rare et très nouveau, à lire tout ce qui paraîtra sous votre signature . . .'[24] Bargone admitted in reply that he had indeed written a very bad novel, and, at Louÿs's insistence, sent him the manuscript. Shortly afterwards Gilbert de Voisins was asked by Louÿs to travel to Toulon, where Bargone was stationed, in order to make his acquaintance. Bargone met Louÿs for the first time on Sunday, 15 June, when he was invited to lunch at the boulevard de Malesherbes. He was assured that a warm welcome awaited him: 'Dites-vous seulement que vous serez reçu en ami, et pas du tout en disciple quoique votre extrême modestie vous fasse prendre ce titre. Quand on a votre talent on n'est l'élève de personne.'[25]

Louÿs provided Farrère, as Bargone soon called himself for literary purposes, with much sound advice—offered hesitantly and with great tact—and when Farrère was subsequently posted to Constantinople, Louÿs contacted editors and negotiated contracts on his behalf. He again exerted himself on Farrère's behalf in 1905, when, having persuaded him to enter the by now published novel for the Prix Goncourt, he led an active and successful campaign for its selection. It is an ironic reflection on the worth of such awards that Lucien Descaves voted for *Les Civilisés* because he mistakenly regarded it as a strongly anti-militaristic novel, while Rachilde's support stemmed from her belief that 'Claude' Farrère was a woman.

Louÿs evidently derived very little income from his literary production after 1901, even though *Sanguines* sold 4,200 copies on the first day,[26] a very respectable figure for a volume of stories. The sales of *Sanguines* provide, indeed, a clear indication of the considerable income he could have earned, if only he had been more productive. As it was, he had to rely mainly, for whatever sums he could obtain from publishers, on his earlier books. Fortunately, *Les Chansons de Bilitis* and, still more, the three novels, continued to enjoy a steady popularity. They possessed, moreover, the great advantage of featuring exotic scenes and spectacular incidents which were well suited to presentation in illustrated editions. Louÿs was accordingly able to negotiate numerous contracts with various publishers for new editions of these works The years between 1902 and 1925 saw the appearance of at least six further editions of *Les Chansons de Bilitis*, nine of *Aphrodite*, five of *La Femme et le pantin*, and seven of *Les Aventures du roi Pausole*. In addition to the money received under these contracts, Louÿs was granted several advances for the publication rights to his future works—which, however, were never delivered. In July 1907, he summed up his situation with lucidity in a letter to Georges: '*Pausole* a été achevé (et mal achevé) en avril 1900. Depuis sept ans et trois mois, je n'ai pas terminé un livre. J'ai vécu de remoutures, de rééditions, de publications de luxe et de quatre avances sur quatre livres dont aucun n'est écrit. Les conditions dans lesquelles je puis écrire sont tellement délicates et tellement fugitives qu'évidemment je ne puis faire aucun fonds sur ma production.'[27] He concluded that 'la littérature n'est pas pour moi un moyen d'existence et il faut que je cherche autre chose'. Not for the first time, therefore, he spoke of the possibility of a post in the government service; not for the first time, nothing came of these vague plans. Yet that very summer provided still further disconcerting proof of his incapacity for undertaking any concentrated creative activity.

A certain mystery surrounds the composition of the novel *Psyché* which was found in an incomplete state after Louÿs's death. Farrère, in his notes to the posthumous edition, reports a statement by Louÿs that he conceived the idea of *Psyché* in 1900 or 1901, but did not commence the novel until 1906.[28] Robert Fleury, on the other hand, affirms—though without citing any supporting evidence—that the opening chapters were written as early as 1903 at Biarritz.[29] Louÿs is, in any case, known to have worked on *Psyché* at Biarritz in the summer of 1906, and he was hoping to complete the book during his stay at Tamaris the following year. However, the mental exertion brought him once again close to a nervous breakdown, as he explained in a long letter to Georges:

Je suis absolument éreinté. Chaque nuit, je dors huit heures comme une masse; il faut ensuite à Louise trois quarts d'heure d'efforts pour me réveiller; et tout le reste du jour je suis dans l'état de quelqu'un qui aurait passé deux nuits blanches!

Depuis sept ans, le travail d'imagination ne m'est plus possible. Quand je m'y mets je ne dis pas que 'je crois prendre une rame à la main' mais le bateau tout entier avec ses douze galériens. Cela m'épuise cérébralement et physiquement. Je veux continuer, quoique depuis huit jours, plus je me fatigue et moins cela avance; et je sens très bien ce que je me réserve: c'est une nouvelle période de neurasthénie comme celle qui a suivi l'effort de *Pausole* et qui m'a duré des années. Seulement celle-là sera plus sérieuse. On m'a prévenu médicalement. De cela on se guérit une fois mais pas deux.

Dès maintenant, je me sens la tête trouble et instable comme aux plus mauvais jours de mon roman précédent. Terminerai-je celui-là? Je n'en sais plus rien. En tout cas, ce sera bien le dernier. Je t'en prie, quand tu seras de retour, fais ce que tu pourras pour que j'obtienne une autre direction de vie. Je voudrais te faire comprendre combien c'est sérieux. Je sens que je me fais le plus grand mal en forçant mon cerveau à ce qu'il ne peut pas accomplir. Et dans six mois il sera peut-être trop tard pour prendre une résolution. Si je redeviens après *Psyché* dans l'état où j'ai été après *Pausole*, en 1902–1903, je ne pourrai exercer alors aucune profession, pas même celle de copiste.[30]

Louÿs did not finish *Psyché* at Tamaris that summer, but on 8 May 1908 he informed Farrère that he had 'at last' delivered the first two parts of the novel to *Le Journal*, although the third was still incomplete.[31] Presumably, the newspaper proposed to serialize the novel, as it had done *La Femme et le pantin* and *Les Aventures du roi Pausole*. In the end, however, *Psyché* did not appear in *Le Journal* after all. Perhaps Louÿs withdrew the text, or the editor may have been reluctant to accept an unfinished manuscript, especially in view of the difficulties that had attended the composition of *Les Aventures du roi Pausole* in 1900. Three years later, in July 1911, the editor of *Le Journal* provided Louÿs with rail tickets to Arcachon for himself and his wife, on the understanding 'que vous emportez la fin de *Psyché* pour nous la rendre absolument complète à votre retour'.[32] According to Farrère, Louÿs showed him the final chapters describing the death of Psyché Vannetty 'vers 1912'. He furthermore states that Louÿs told Thierry Sandre in 1913 that he had completed the book 'exactement, le 13 juillet de cette année'.[33] Finally, Cardinne-Petit believes that the manuscript he saw in 1917 lacked only Chapters 2 and 3 of the third section. Louÿs assured him that no more than seventeen pages remained to be added, which could easily be written in two weeks, 'mais que ces pages-là, il sentait bien qu'il ne les écrirait jamais'.[34]

Farrère surmises that Louÿs himself destroyed most of what he had written of Part III because of its too personal nature. The novel is, in fact, strongly autobiographical, for it owes its inspiration to Louÿs's love for Marie de Régnier. This fact is emphasized by the insertion of the poem 'L'Apogée' at a crucial point in the story.[35] Louÿs was still troubled by the intimate character of the book many years later, for in October 1924, after authorizing Jean Thorhauer to negotiate a contract with *Le Journal* and certain publishers for the first two sections—which, he suggested, could be presented as a story complete in itself—he withdrew his permission on the grounds that *Psyché* should not yet be published.[36] The first edition finally appeared posthumously in 1927, with a summary of the concluding chapters supplied by Farrère from his recollections of the text which Louÿs had read to him in 1912.

Dramatic adaptations of the novels constituted, from time to time, an additional source of income for Louÿs. Attention centred, in particular, on the best-selling *Aphrodite* which attracted many operatic composers. Louÿs, however, turned down all proposals for two years, in compliance with Debussy's request for the exclusive rights to the subject. Only after Debussy had lost interest did Louÿs begin to accept offers in 1898, granting non-exclusive rights to all applicants. By the year 1900 they included Albeniz, Leoncavallo, Ernest Moret, André Pollonais, and Arturo Berutti.[37] Of this first group, only Berutti seems to have availed himself of the authorization. His four-act opera *Khrysé*, performed at the Teatro Politeama Argentino in Buenos Aires in 1902, represents the earliest known setting of the novel. The leading roles were sung by Emma Carelli and Amadeo Bassi. Among other composers attracted by the operatic possibilities of *Aphrodite* was Giacomo Puccini, who considered it briefly when he was casting around for a new subject after the completion of *Tosca* in 1899.[38] His choice finally settled on David Belasco's play *Madame Butterfly*.

By far the best-known musical setting of *Aphrodite* is the opera of that name by Camille Erlanger, based on a libretto by Louis de Gramont. At the première, which took place at the Opéra-Comique on 27 March 1906, the principal role was sung by Mary Garden, Debussy's first Mélisande. Like the novel itself, this opera owed much of its appeal to its erotic subject, for as Mary Garden herself later conceded, 'everyone wanted to see it for reasons other than art'.[39] No efforts were spared to make the spectacle as colourful and exciting as possible. The audience was nevertheless denied the ultimate thrill of seeing an apparently naked Chrysis visiting her lover's studio in one of the key scenes of the opera: 'M. Carré [the Director of the Opéra-Comique] tried every light that he had in his possession to get me through a veil. I wore just that veil over my body, and he wanted the people to think that I was naked. But we never could arrive at that illusion . . .'[40] Despite this disappointment, the public acclaimed *Aphrodite* and its interpreters. In addition to Mary Garden, these included Léon Beyle as Démétrios (the part had been offered to Jean de Reske, but he was reluctant to break his retirement) and, in the dancing rôle of Théano, the young Régina Badet. Erlanger's opera maintained its popularity for many years. It reached its hundredth performance on 15 October 1913.

Other composers followed suit. On 16 March 1912 a one-act opera, *Aphrodite*, with libretto by Hans Liebstöckl and music by Max Oberleithner, was produced in Austria, apparently without Louÿs's authorization. Its chief historical interest is that at its première Maria Jeritza (still known as Mitzi Jeritza), who was destined to become one of the leading sopranos of the Vienna Opera in the period between the two world wars, made her début at that theatre in the leading role. On that occasion she delighted the audience not only with her beautiful voice, but, in addition, by appearing 'in a nakedness never before seen on the stage of a Court opera house'.[41] Another full-length opera inspired by Louÿs's novel, *Afrodita*, by Arturo Luzzati, was given at the Teatro Colon in Buenos Aires on 5 August 1928, with Nena Juarez as Chrysis and Pedro Mirassou as Démétrios.

In the same year which saw the first production of Erlanger's *Aphrodite* at the Opéra-Comique, Louÿs was engaged in negotiations with Puccini for an opera to be based on *La Femme et le pantin*. Puccini, who was once again in search of a promising operatic subject, had asked his publisher Giulio Ricordi on 18 February 1906 to inquire about the availability of Louÿs's novel. On 22 June he informed his English friend Sybil Seligman that he had signed an agreement for the composition of the opera[42] (this must have been as a preliminary to the conclusion of the formal contract with Ricordi on 1 October[43]). The libretto was prepared by Maurice Vaucaire in French and subsequently translated into Italian and adapted by Luigi Illica. Vaucaire sent portions of it to

Puccini in Italy and joined the composer at Boscolungo Abetone in August to work on the text with him. In July Puccini had visited Paris and met Louÿs on whom he had made a most favourable impression: 'C'est ... un homme de 48 ans, silencieux, sérieux, sans pose ...', Louÿs wrote to Georges.[44]

Discussions seemed to be progressing well, but before long Puccini was overcome by his customary vacillation and began to have doubts about the suitability of the plot and especially the heroine's character for the operatic stage. He also felt exasperated by the cumbersome procedure which had to be followed in the preparation of the libretto, necessitating consultations between collaborators residing in two different countries. He accordingly took advantage of a lengthy visit to Paris in November and December 1906, in connection with the first French production of *Madame Butterfly* on 28 December, to hold further discussions with Louÿs, to whom, in his correspondence he usually referred ironically as 'Épatant' or 'Inouï', presumably because of Louÿs's predilection for these two words. However, Puccini still felt displeased with the libretto. Ricordi sent messages designed to rekindle his enthusiasm, but the flame burned unsteadily, if at all.

Although Puccini continued, over the following months, to attribute his hesitation to his dissatisfaction with certain dramatic and psychological aspects of the libretto, his uneasiness was doubtless increased by the hostile reception accorded to Richard Strauss's *Salome* in New York, where that opera had to be hastily withdrawn because of the 'scandalous' nature of its subject. Puccini happened to be present at the one and only performance at the Metropolitan Opera House on 22 January 1907, having gone to New York to attend the American première of *Madame Butterfly*. In an interview printed in the *New York Times* on 28 February he stated: 'I haven't a new score started—at least, not on any definite idea. I have not found the subject which appeals to me. I haven't even commenced to work on *La Femme et le Pantin*. I have doubts if the American public would accept that after the treatment *Salome* recently received.' During the same stay in New York he saw David Belasco's play *The Girl of the Golden West* which he was eventually to choose as the subject of his next opera. By the time he returned to Europe, he was resolved to wash his hands of the 'Spanish slut'. His decision provoked several long letters from Ricordi entreating him to change his mind, and, from

'Inouï', some 'furious', 'ridiculous' and 'idiotic' demands for damages, which he appears to have shrugged off nonchalantly. This was the end of the collaboration between Puccini and Pierre Louÿs. Mosco Carner has, however, made the interesting suggestion that something of Conchita may have flowed into the character of Puccini's cruel Chinese princess Turandot.[45]

Maurice Vaucaire's libretto (in an Italian version prepared by Carlo Zangarine) was eventually set to music by Ricardo Zandonai. At the first performance of *Conchita* at the Teatro del Verme in Milan on 14 October 1911 the title role was sung by Tarquinia Tarquini (who was to become Zandonai's wife in 1917). The opera was the first major success of the twenty-eight-year-old Zandonai and received fourteen performances before sold-out houses. It is regarded as one of the last important examples of 'verismo'. The realism of the music seems to have been paralleled by that of the production, for Tarquinia Tarquini had to keep to her bed on the day following the première, having been struck black and blue by her Mateo, Piero Schiavazzi.[46]

Conchita was presented at Covent Garden on 3 July 1912, with the same two singers in the leading roles. The soprano was highly praised, but the tenor was disappointing. The opera itself did not make a good impression. 'Is there no end to the permutations and combinations of the sordid in modern operatic Italy?' inquired the *Daily Telegraph* sadly. *Conchita* disappeared from Covent Garden after the second performance, but it was subsequently given in many cities including Rio de Janeiro, San Francisco, New York, and, on 11 March 1929, at the Opéra-Comique in Paris.

Louÿs's third novel had to wait much longer for a musical adaptation. It was not until 12 December 1930 that the operetta *Le Roi Pausole*, with music by Arthur Honegger to a libretto by Albert Willemetz, was staged at the Théâtre des Bouffes Parisiens. The principal parts were taken on that occasion by Dorville (Pausole), René Koval (Taxis), Pasquali (Giglio), and Jacqueline Francell (La Blanche Aline). Four minor roles were entrusted to a quartet of budding actresses who were to become famous: Suzy Delair, Pauline Dubost, Simone Simon, Edwige Feuillère. The operetta was an enormous success and ran for close on five hundred performances.

.   .   .   .   .

Régina Badet, who had participated as a dancer in the opera *Aphrodite*, starred in 1910, opposite Firmin Gémier, in the play *La Femme et le pantin*. Although this was announced as the joint work of Pierre Louÿs and Pierre Frondaie, the following statement by Louÿs suggests that his share in the collaboration was largely a nominal one: 'Une seule fois, et pendant vingt minutes à peine, j'ai vu répéter, sans costumes, un acte de *la Femme et le Pantin*. Après cela j'ai quitté le théâtre pour n'y plus retourner, et je décline ici toute responsabilité sur le texte [Louÿs had crossed out the original words 'sur les naïvetés du texte'] qu'on ne me permet pas de corriger et sur les détails de la mise en scène qui, par suite, ne m'intéressent plus.'[47] The casting of the principal feminine role presented a certain difficulty, for Concha Perez is a flamenco dancer and some of the most striking passages of the novel describe her executing these dances. It was therefore necessary, in the interests of verisimilitude, to find an actress who was also an accomplished dancer. After Polaire, who had been the authors' first choice, had withdrawn because of delays in production, the part was accordingly offered to Régina Badet, who was then a leading ballerina at the Opéra-Comique. She achieved a considerable success in both aspects of her role: 'cette ravissante grande danseuse est une petite comédienne ravissante', Gaston Sorbets wrote in *L'Illustration théâtrale* on 11 February 1911.

The première took place at the Théâtre Antoine on 8 December 1910. While the critics were divided in their reactions to the play itself—many considered it only a feeble adaptation of the novel—they were almost unanimous in their praise for the actors. Public response was very favourable. 'C'est le triomphe', affirmed a note in *Le Figaro* on 18 December. 'Les recettes ne descendent pas au-dessous de 4,500 francs. Jamais pareils chiffres n'avaient été constatés au Théâtre Antoine.' To meet the demand, several matinées were announced for the remainder of the month. As a result, *La Femme et le pantin* reached its thirtieth performance on 31 December. 'Cette mauvaise pièce pour laquelle la presse a été si justement désagréable a un succès scandaleux', Louÿs observed in a letter to Mme de Heredia.[48] The curiosity of the public had been aroused by Senator Bérenger's vociferous censure of Régina Badet for appearing in a highly revealing costume. 'Régina Badet ... avait un sein nu. C'était la première fois qu'une actrice connue se décolletait ainsi. Scandale. Protestations', Louÿs later recalled with a pleasure which was heightened by the knowledge that the courts had refused to act upon Bérenger's denunciation.[49] To a correspondent Louÿs pointed out at the time that he was in no way responsible for the actress's dress, adding that had he been consulted, he would have arranged for Mlle Badet to dance completely naked, 'sans aucun égard pour les trois morales du méthodisme, du calvinisme et du presbytérianisme'.[50] *La Femme et le pantin* ran until the following April and achieved altogether the very respectable total of one hundred and fifty-six performances.

Pierre Frondaie was also the author of the play *Aphrodite* which received its first performance at the Théâtre de la Renaissance on 17 March 1914. The cast included Cora Laparcerie as Chrysis, Jean Worms as Démétrios, Alice de Tender as Théano, and Paule Andras as Bacchys. The famous dress designer Paul Poiret contributed splendid costumes to the production which, however, at the same time, relied for an important part of its appeal on the lack of apparel, for 'une douzaine d'actrices ont les deux seins nus, et une danseuse paraît sans aucun costume'.[51] The spectacle featured, furthermore, a statue of the Goddess of Love commissioned from Rodin and incidental music composed by Henri Février. Despite these various attractions, the play pleased neither the critics nor the public. While the fault undoubtedly lay primarily with Frondaie's insipid verse text, the acting also drew unfavourable comments, particularly that of Cora Laparcerie who was criticized for giving a wooden performance. 'Mme Cora Laparcerie n'a pas manqué à ce qu'elle a considéré comme un devoir', a reviewer remarked drily in *Le Temps* on 19 March. The play ran until 18 May.

Finally, Louÿs's books have inspired several films. Most of them were made after his death, but at least one appeared in his lifetime and Louÿs must have benefited financially from it: *The Woman and the Puppet*, with Geraldine Farrar in the leading part, reached the silent screen in 1920. Fifteen years later Joseph von Sternberg directed another American version of the same novel, entitled *The Devil is a Woman*, with Marlene Dietrich as the devilish heroine. Brigitte Bardot starred in *La Femme et le pantin*, made by Julien Duvivier in 1958. The Russian-born director Alexis Granowski was responsible for the French film *Les Aventures du roi Pausole* which appeared in 1933.

. . . . . .

The income from royalties proved quite inadequate to meet Louÿs's financial needs, and he was accordingly forced to borrow from friends and money-lenders on several occasions. Gilbert de Voisins, from whom he had already obtained 2,000 francs in 1901, advanced him a further 2,000 in 1904, and, three years later, no less then 25,000 francs[52] (with Farrère's help, Louÿs was able to repay Voisins at the time of the divorce). In 1910 he accepted another 30,000 francs from a friend of Voisins's.[53] Despite these loans, Louÿs's life became one of chronic penury, for any money received was at once swallowed up in desperate efforts to stem the constantly rising tide of his debts. In his letters to Georges he continued to complain about his financial problems. The following three extracts are typical examples: 'Je n'ai pas de chaussures; depuis septembre je marche avec la même vieille paire éculée. Et je n'ai pas de pantoufles, les miennes sont en loques. Et je ne peux pas recevoir autrement qu'habillé parce que mes chemises de nuit de flanelle, à force d'etre rétrécies, ont les manches au coude et le col grand ouvert' (1 January 1903);[54] 'Je me suis arrangé comme j'ai pu; j'ai eu un peu d'argent [i.e. royalties] ... mais tout cela n'était pas gros et tout était absorbé d'avance par les créanciers. Et alors, depuis quatre mois, nous nous sommes trouvés plus de dix fois, n'ayant que 4 ou 5 fr. en poche et ne sachant pas du tout où en trouver d'autres ...' (late 1903?);[55] 'lettres incessantes de fournisseurs ... Je n'en puis plus, et je ne pense qu'à cela ...' (30 July 1905).[56]

If ever any money remained after the most pressing debts had been settled—and sometimes, one suspects, even before—it was promptly spent to satisfy Louÿs's literary or artistic tastes. In this connection, a letter addressed by Louÿs to Georges on 28 January 1902 reveals a situation which recurred with alarming frequency. After complaining, as usual, about his lack of funds—he and Louise were, at that time, still staying with the Heredias, because they did not possess enough money to pay their tradesmen's bills—he remarked in reference to a recent communication from his brother: '[La lettre] est arrivée juste au moment où je venais de dépenser à l'Hôtel des Ventes les quelques francs qui me restaient ... La vente était d'estampes japonaises'.[57]

Above all, Louÿs had, by the early years of the century, become an ardent bibliophile. In 1916 he justified his addiction to book-collecting with the following argument: 'La bibliophilie est une des rares passions qui sachent donner plus qu'on n'espérait d'elles. Le jeu, la gloire, la chasse, déçoivent. Les amours, et celles des livres, accordent, exceptionnellement, plus de bonheur qu'il ne fallait pour qu'elles fussent délicieuses.'[58] Already in 1902 he was himself surprised by the size of his private library which had to be transported from the boulevard Malesherbes to the rue de Boulain-villiers: 'Un libraire est venu prendre ce matin le métrage de mes rayons de livres pour leur déménagement', he wrote to Georges on 3 October 1902. 'Il y en a 140 m. Si l'on mettait cela en pile, cela ferait plus de deux fois les tours de Notre-Dame. A force de revenir souvent chez soi un bouquin dans son pardessus, voilà où on en arrive!'[59] A week later he reported further on the packing of the books: 'On a empli jusqu'au bord 34 paniers et il en reste une douzaine à faire pour demain ... Je dois avoir 3.000 volumes.'[60]

Over the following years Louÿs, far from reducing the volume of his purchases, vastly increased it. He extended their range, moreover, to include rare early books. His interest focused especially on certain aspects of seventeenth-century literature, to an extent which later led Frédéric Lachèvre to affirm that by 1907 'Pierre Louÿs possédait (sans être encore complète) la collection la plus riche, existant en France et à l'Étranger, des florilèges libres et satiriques qui ont vu le jour dans le premier quart du XVIIe siècle'.[61] Lachèvre also paid eloquent tribute to the generosity shown to him by Louÿs who not only willingly opened his library to him, but also freely placed his time at his disposal, spending many hours in correcting and adding information to the proofs of Lachèvre's *Bibliographie des recueils collectifs de poésies libres et satiriques publiés depuis 1600 jusqu'à ... 1626* (published in 1914), while firmly refusing the suggestion that he be cited as co-author. Lachèvre recalled: 'L'accueil de Pierre Louÿs était inoubliable. Aucun homme n'a réuni à un si haut degré le don de conquérir son auditeur. Rien chez lui ne trahissait son écrasante supériorité. Le charme qui se dégageait de sa personne, sa cour-toisie, sa délicatesse vous mettaient à l'aise, jamais un de ces mots susceptibles de faire sentir la distance qui vous séparait de son merveilleux esprit.'[62] Louÿs himself indicated that he acquired the bulk of his rare book collection between 1900 and 1914.[63] By then his library comprised some 20,000 volumes.

·   ·   ·   ·   ·

During the last twenty-five years of his life, Louÿs was frequently plagued by ill health. In addition to his chronic pulmonary weakness and the constant risk of a recurrence of the neurasthenia from which he had suffered after the composition of *Les Aventures du roi Pausole*, his failing eyesight caused him much concern. The effects of this disability were particularly serious for him, since his life increasingly revolved around his books and he concentrated more and more on bibliography and critical textual analysis. The first warning signs, which had appeared in the spring of 1901, had quickly subsided, but during the autumn of the following year he began to experience severe pains in his left eye. 'Je n'ai pas de tête du tout en ce moment, je ne vais pas bien . . .', he wrote to Georges on 16 November 1902, from his new quarters in the Hameau de Boulainvilliers. 'Pendant la moitié de la journée, j'ai la tête électrisée avec des courants nerveux qui viennent tout à coup, me traversent la cervelle, tournent autour de l'œil, tremblent entre les deux sourcils.'[64] And on 2 December: 'Maintenant je vais me coucher; c'est le mauvais moment; dès que j'ai la tête horizontale, il s'y passe des choses étranges.'[65] When the inflammation of the iris and the choroid grew more pronounced, it was feared that this might indicate the presence of glaucoma. Once again the trouble cleared up, after a long vacation in Biarritz during the early months of 1903 which enabled Louÿs to regain some of his physical and intellectual vigour.

As the following years passed by without a recurrence of these grave ocular disorders, there were good grounds for hoping that the improvement would be permanent. However, in the late autumn of 1911, on returning from a long and pleasant holiday at Arcachon, Louÿs experienced for the first time a spell of total blindness. Careful treatment provided partial relief and restored some of the vision, but his eyesight was permanently affected, although the extent of the affliction tended to vary at different periods. Louÿs was also, henceforth, frequently plagued by migraine.

At the same time, Louÿs steadfastly ignored his wife's pleas to install electricity in the house, preferring to rely, for his own needs, on a petroleum lamp, on a gas chandelier that was only rarely lit, and, especially, on a *lampe Pigeon*, a small portable lamp which shed a relatively feeble light. He would, moreover, never allow any sunlight to penetrate into his study for fear that it might fade the expensively bound books, and never kept open a window long to let in fresh air but preferred to spend his days and, increasingly, his nights, in an atmosphere heavy with stale tobacco smoke. Farrère was therefore probably right in suggesting that Louÿs's eccentricities contributed in no small measure to the progressive decline of his eyesight.[66] After the first spell of blindness he always used a magnifying glass.

To help him with his bibliographical research and his correspondence, Louÿs engaged the services of Charles Moulié who had previously been the secretary of Gilbert de Voisins. Moulié, who became a good personal friend, later made a name for himself as a writer (in 1924 he was awarded the Prix Goncourt for his novel *La Chèvrefeuille* and other books published under the pseudonym 'Thierry Sandre').

The limited literary output between 1902 and 1919 might be taken as an indication of intellectual stagnation. Nothing could be farther from the truth. Throughout most of these years Louÿs devoted innumerable hours to reading and studying, to literary analysis and bibliographical research, as his many letters to Frédéric Lachèvre amply demonstrate. 'Je ne cesse pas de travailler, je ne sors point, je ne vois personne', Louÿs told Émile Henriot several years before his death. 'J'emploie tout mon temps à écrire: j'écris quarante-huit heures par jour . . .'[67] Lachèvre, himself a well-known scholar, acknowledged Louÿs's pre-eminence by referring to him as 'le bibliophile le plus savant et le plus spirituel de notre époque',[68] Others have written with admiration of his immense curiosity and vast general culture. Farrère called him 'une encyclopédie vivante';[69] Fernand Gregh considered him 'un des hommes les plus cultivés que j'aie connus dans ma longue vie littéraire' and remarked that Louÿs, during his later years, 'ne vivait plus guère que pour comprendre'.[70] Louÿs himself on one occasion humorously surveyed the wide range of his interests:

J'ai eu dans ma vie cent curiosités, j'ai voulu avoir 'des clartés de tout', j'ai fait de la chimie, de la pointe sèche, des vers, de l'équitation, du pastel, du roman, du fleuret, de la peinture à l'huile, des traductions grecques, du violon, de l'alto, du saxophone, de la clarinette basse, du piano, de l'harmonium, de l'orgue, de la bicyclette, de l'entomologie, du conte en prose, du fusain, du tennis, de l'harmonie, de l'érotologie, de la grammaire comparée, du vernis mou, de la bibliophilie, de la botanique, des castagnettes, un peu de paléographie, de l'aquarelle, du sanscrit, de la sculpture, du footing, de l'archéologie, des châteaux de

cartes, du crayon noir, du latin, du cerf-volant, des ballades, de l'ana-
tomie, de la photographie, de l'allemand, du bilboquet, de la poétique,
de l'histoire littéraire, de l'anthropologie, de la sanguine, du tir à cible,
et de la critique et de l'arabe et de la théologie morale, et de la décalco-
manie quand j'avais sept ans . . .[71]

In the silence of his library Louÿs filled sheet upon sheet with
notes. Among the manuscripts sold after his death were four
volumes containing lists of Alexandrines taken from the works of
many poets, classified in accordance with different rhythmic
patterns.[72] In 1974 the Librairie C. Coulet et A. Faure offered for
sale a 300-page manuscript about 'L'Affaire Corneille–Molière'.[73]
These are merely two samples of the numerous studies undertaken
by Louÿs who once declared that his accumulated manuscript
notes, stored in several boxes, weighed no less than 420 kilo-
grammes.[74] Some of these notes have been published by Frédéric
Lachèvre, a few were reproduced in the collected edition of
Louÿs's work, but the majority were dispersed after his death.

Among the literary problems attracting Louÿs's attention was
an intriguing one posed by a set of forty-five handsomely bound
volumes in manuscript, which he bought from the antiquarian
bookseller Louis Dorbon on 2 January 1907. They contained the
memoirs of the nineteenth-century architect Henry Alexandre
Legrand, who had composed them in a highly intricate code
which had until then defied all attempts at decipherment. After
many vain efforts Louÿs claimed to have cracked the code which
he found to be based on two ciphers derived from the Arabic and
Sanskrit alphabets. To render detection still more difficult, the
author had used no fewer than five different European languages
and had frequently changed the alignment of his text so that it
pointed at times upward, at others downward, or towards the
right or the left. On occasion, the words had to be read in one
direction while the individual letters followed the contrary order.
Louÿs then discovered from the sample pages he laboriously
deciphered that the memoirs, which covered the period from 1835
to 1865, presented highly indiscreet accounts, illustrated by letters
and other original documents, not only of Legrand's own love
affairs, but also of the amours of many highly placed members of
the French aristocracy. Certain volumes offered a similarly spicy
chronicle of the Spanish court.

Louÿs calculated that the transcription of the complete series, assuming a rate of decipherment of ten pages a day, would take over seven years. There was no way of knowing, of course, what the exact contents might reveal. It was clear, however, that they were likely to be of considerable historical interest. Louÿs outlined his discoveries in an article, 'Le Manuscrit mystérieux', published in *L'Éclair* on 28 February 1907 and again in the *Mercure de France* the following month. He next proposed to present specimen extracts in *L'Illustration*. At that point the literary critic of that magazine, Eugène Ledrain, who had several years earlier engaged in a somewhat ludicrous debate with Louÿs about certain supposed 'improbabilities' in *Aphrodite*, warned the editorial board that they were in danger of becoming the victims of a new hoax by the author of the *Chansons de Bilitis*—whereupon they prudently refused to print the passages in question. Discouraged by this reaction, Louÿs then appears to have dropped the idea of deciphering further portions of the text. A similar fear of a new 'mystification' was to prevent any objective discussions of Louÿs's theory concerning Corneille's collaboration with Molière.

Louÿs's interest in early books led him to found a review, together with Louis Loviot, called *Revue des livres anciens*, which appeared in March 1913. The first three fascicules contained several articles by Louÿs. Publication was suspended after the fifth issue because of the outbreak of the war, but resumed in April 1916. The review closed down permanently after the January 1917 number, following a quarrel between Louÿs and Loviot the previous May. The dispute was provoked by their research on a seventeenth-century satirical work, *Le Zombi du Pérou ou la Comtesse de Cocagne* by Corneille Blessebois (1697). Its cause was, however, of a personal rather than a literary nature, and Lachèvre later concluded that Loviot had been in the wrong, having acted in an unethical manner by deliberately failing to respect Louÿs's prior claim to certain discoveries.[75]

To the various factors compounding Louÿs's unhappiness, the year 1913 added yet another, devastating one. The breakup of his marriage not only left him with a sense of betrayal and caused him great sorrow, despite the fact that he was not in love with Louise and probably never had been; it also increased his isolation, by obliging him to break off relations with several friends and intimates of long standing—in particular, Gilbert de Voisins and the Régniers—as well as with at least one member of his own family, his cousin and godmother Élisabeth Charpentier (*née* Mougeot).

For Louise, marriage had turned out to be a distressing experience. The grave illness or miscarriage which had brought her close to death in Barcelona in 1900 was followed by a series of other ailments which left her health in a permanently weakened state. The life of poverty imposed upon her by Louÿs's inability to earn a steady income and by his reckless expenditure of any available money on his library undermined her failing strength still further. The faithful Farrère quotes approvingly a remark by Marie de Régnier: 'Si on tient à payer les notes d'épicier au jour le jour, il ne faut pas épouser un artiste. Il faut épouser l'épicier.'[76] Louise must often have wished that she *had* married the grocer. At least she would have been saved many embarrassing experiences, such as being forced to remain at the Grand Hôtel at Tamaris in 1910 as a pledge for the eventual settlement of the bill, while her husband returned to Paris to attend to professional matters. Finally, she must have been exasperated by Louÿs's tendency to pursue every pretty woman who crossed his path or the threshold of his house. One day she remarked somewhat resignedly to Polaire, who was repeatedly summoned to the rue de Boulainvilliers to provide Louÿs with the necessary 'inspiration' for the dramatic adaptation of *La Femme et le pantin* in which she was to star: 'Que voulez-vous, il ne peut pas travailler quand vous n'êtes pas auprès de lui . . . Seulement, quand vous y êtes il ne travaille plus!'[77] Fernand Gregh, despite the admiration and affection he felt for Louÿs, judged his conduct with greater objectiveness than Farrère: 'La vie de Loulouse', he recalled in his memoirs, 'a été un long martyre, jusqu'au jour où, sur le point de mourir de tristesse et d'inanition, elle eut un sursaut, quitta son mari et divorça.'[78]

In December 1912, Louise was suddenly stricken with severe haemoptysis. Tuberculosis developed, accompanied by a high fever. 'Pendant plus de quinze jours je n'ai pas eu d'autre pensée que mon inquiétude,' Louÿs wrote to Frédéric Lachèvre on 27 December, 'mais les médecins parlent enfin de convalescence . . .'[79] Élisabeth Charpentier, who was very fond of Louise, moved to the rue de Boulainvilliers to look after her. Soon she was reproaching Louÿs for the insensitive and unloving manner in which he

treated his wife. By February Louise was well enough to travel.
'J'espère . . . que tu feras pour ta femme qui a si besoin de ton
affection, le sacrifice de tes préférences pour essayer de la sauver
de la crise qu'elle traverse, en lui donnant le soleil et le calme qui
lui sont indispensables', Mme Charpentier admonished Louÿs.[80]
Louise chose Arcachon for her convalescence, against the wishes
of Pierre who would have preferred Grasse. He was, moreover,
vexed by her insistence on leaving without him, with Mme
Charpentier as her sole companion. Angry and hurt, he refused
to see them off at the station, and although he demanded daily
reports on Louise's health from Mme Charpentier, he did not
write directly to his wife during the several weeks she spent at
Arcachon, nor she to him. Their relations were rapidly approaching breaking-point, as Mme Charpentier perceived very clearly:

Depuis que je suis ici je découvre beaucoup de choses dont je ne me
doutais pas et qui me font tellement de peine que j'ai peur d'en tomber
malade. D'abord mon grand étonnement de ne voir arriver aucune
lettre de toi à Louise et son refus de t'écrire et de ne rien trouver
d'aimable pour elle dans tes lettres! Beaucoup d'autres détails me font
voir chaque jour des dissentiments que je ne prévoyais pas si graves.
Mais comme tu m'as accusée de vouloir brouiller ton ménage, je veux
te dire que mon seul désir était au contraire d'empêcher une rupture
que je ne croyais pas du tout aussi menaçante.[81]

On her return to Paris in late April, Louise did not stay in the
rue de Boulainvilliers, but, instead, in Élisabeth Charpentier's
apartment in the rue de Vaugirard. From this point on, events
took their inevitable course, and did so, moreover, with surprising
speed. On 2 May 1913 Louÿs dispatched what amounted to an
ultimatum, and, characteristically, he sent it to Mme Charpentier
for transmission to Louise:

Cette situation ne peut se prolonger. Louise a voulu partir sans moi.
Je lui ai télégraphié trois dépêches, elle a trois fois refusé de répondre
et depuis qu'elle est dans ta maison je n'ai pas reçu une ligne de sa main.
Comme je sais qu'elle écrit à mes amis, son attitude à mon égard ne peut
avoir qu'un sens, c'est qu'elle a l'intention de ne plus revenir ici.
Après avoir subi plusieurs mois de silence, je lui demande maintenant
une déclaration catégorique, dans le sens qu'il lui plaira de choisir . . .
Mais je n'attendrai pas plus longtemps.[82]

On 15 May, Louÿs informed Farrère of the impending divorce and
briefly described his feelings:

Je viens de vous dire que j'en étais très troublé, mais je n'en suis pas très ému; autrement dit, j'en ai plus d'agitation que de peine. Autant j'avais souffert pendant les inquiétudes de la maladie, autant je me suis senti la force de supporter la rupture, dont je n'ai pas pris d'ailleurs (vous en êtes certain d'avance) l'initiative.

C'est que je suis incapable d'aimer qui ne m'aime pas. L'affection non partagée est un sentiment si étranger à mon esprit qu'il me paraît en dehors des lois de la nature . . . C'est pour cela que j'ai traité de Pantin celui de mes héros qui supplie . . .

Il me reste les pensées les plus tristes, sinon sur l'avenir, du moins sur le passé . . . On me quitte pour un sort plus heureux.[83]

The final sentence refers to Gilbert de Voisins—for even before the divorce proceedings were completed, it was understood that he would marry Louise as soon as she was free. In his *Souvenirs*, Farrère accused Mme de Heredia of cunningly master-minding the whole affair. More specifically, he held her responsible not only for the breakup of the marriage, but also for cleverly convincing 'le pauvre Gilbert de Voisins . . . *qu'il avait compromis sa fille, et que l'honneur exigeait qu'il l'épousât*'.[84] Mme de Heredia may well have assumed a leading role in the drama, but can she really be blamed for wishing to rescue her daughter from what even Fernand Gregh described as a 'long martyrdom', and for helping her to find tranquillity and happiness with a husband devoted to her and capable of offering her complete financial security? Moreover, Gilbert de Voisins was far from being a reluctant suitor who had to be manipulated, through stratagems and plots, into matrimony with Louise. It is true that even Louÿs himself considered Voisins to have been more sinned against than sinning: 'Voisins, irresponsable. . . . Grandes qualités de cœur. A été circonvenu. S'est trompé de devoir . . .'[85] Farrère relates, however, that Voisins had confided to him several years before—the conversation can be ascribed to 1909 or early 1910—that he was 'amoureux fou de Louise Louÿs'.[86] Voisins was far too honourable a man to betray a friend, and it may be assumed that he did not reveal his feelings to Louise until she had decided to leave Pierre. It is clear, though, that if there is any truth in the depiction of Mme de Heredia as a puppet-master craftily pulling the appropriate strings, then Voisins was a most willing puppet. On 1 August 1913 he wrote to Marie de Régnier: 'Ah! oui, je suis heureux! Je ne m'y habitue pas. Cela me semble étrange, incompréhensible, ce bel allègement!

... je ne puis vous promettre qu'une chose, c'est que je me donnerai tout entier à cette œuvre: rendre Louise heureuse, lui réapprendre ce que c'est que la paix et lui faire oublier si possible, tout ce qu'elle a souffert, tout ce qu'elle a enduré si vaillamment!'[87] On 5 August Voisins joined Louise at Arcachon. The divorce had been officially pronounced on 29 July, both parties being held equally responsible for the collapse of the marriage. Nothing, therefore, stood in the way of an early wedding. Nevertheless, Gilbert de Voisins was not married to Louise until 19 June 1915 and then only by proxy, since he was serving in the army at the time.

Of all the persons Louÿs himself held responsible for the break-up of his marriage, for which he appears to have been unwilling to accept any serious blame himself, it was Élisabeth Charpentier who provoked his most violent anger and bitter enmity. 'Élisabeth, absolument sans excuse', he wrote to Georges. 'Elle est catholique. Elle avait juré à mon baptême d'être ma marraine, c. à d. de remplacer ma mère si ma mère mourait.' Instead of considering his interests she had, he alleged, deliberately acted against him, 'par sottise, par égoïsme et par agressivité—et aussi par snobisme'.[88]

It may appear strange that Louÿs should have been so greatly affected by his divorce from a woman he professed not to have loved. Perhaps it was the injury to his pride which offended him most deeply. In any case, it is certain that Louise's departure from the Hameau de Boulainvilliers intensified his sense of loneliness and hastened his physical decline, for her disappearance removed the last restraint on his indulgence in a mode of life which, in the long run, was bound to have serious consequences. Even before the divorce, Louÿs had begun to invert occasionally the tradi-tional pattern of day and night. Before long he was to yield entirely to his noctiphilia.

Unexpectedly, during the year following his divorce Louÿs briefly found greater happiness than he had experienced for many years. In 1916 he was to confess to Georges: 'Depuis bien long-temps pour moi, depuis quinze ans, avec un seul intervalle (printemps de 1914) je ne crains plus la mort. Je ne crains que la vie.'[89] If Louÿs temporarily regained his zest for life in the spring of 1914, it was as a result of his liaison with Jeanne Montaud (stage-name: Jane Moriane or simply Moriane) who was playing the small role of the Alexandrian courtesan Ioessa—and later the more important one of Bacchys—in the dramatic adaptation of *Aphrodite* at the Théâtre de la renaissance. Louÿs fell head over heels in love with her. He described the exhilarating effect of this experience in a letter to Georges on 3 April:

Ma vie est toute bouleversée . . . Ce n'est pas la seule aventure mais c'est certainement la seule passion que j'aie eue depuis quinze ans . . . C'est une aventure extraordinaire. Cette femme, la plus simple et la plus normale qui soit, m'a rendu toute me jeunesse. J'ai vingt-cinq ans depuis quinze jours. Il me semble que la machine à explorer le temps m'a ramené tout à coup au fond de mon passé et que ma vie recommence comme si tant d'années n'avaient pas tristement coulé derrière moi. Hier et aujourd'hui, nous sommes restés ensemble, non pas de 5 à 7h. du soir mais de 5h. du soir à 7h. du matin, sans autre interruption que les heures de théâtre et c'est ainsi presque tous les jours . . .[90]

The affair was short lived, for in the middle of May Moriane went on tour to North Africa with a company headed by Réjane. Louÿs sent a long farewell letter to Marseille where Moriane was due to embark on the liner *Moïse* for Tunis:

Vous n'êtes pas encore partie et pour moi vous êtes déjà aussi loin que le paquebot africain où cette triste lettre ira vous attendre. Votre bonne amitié m'était devenue très chère et si vous croyez un peu à l'affection que j'ai voulu vous témoigner, vous ne pouvez douter que votre départ ne laisse un grand vide dans mon existence.

Je crois que je regretterai longtemps de ne pas vous avoir accompagnée. Tout me le conseillait . . .

Faites bon voyage . . . Je me rappelle certaines traversées où la Méditerranée était si calme que je jouais aux échecs dans le salon du bateau. Puissiez-vous en avoir une semblable : la seconde, la meilleure, celle qui vous ramènera.[91]

In June he wrote:

Trois semaines d'absence! cela n'a pas le sens commun. Je serai mort ou marié quand vous reviendrez. Boulainvilliers sera détruit. Vous trouverez à la place une maison de cinq étages habitée par mes arrière-petits-enfants qui vous diront avec respect : 'Vous l'avez connu, grand'-mère?' . . . Votre beau-frère [the actor J. Périer] . . . m'a demandé quel nouveau livre je préparais. J'ai failli lui répondre : 'J'écris un volume de trois cents pages qui est intitulé: *Lettres à Mademoiselle Moriane*, et pour peu que sa tournée dure encore six mois je commencerai bientôt le tome II' . . . Je relis cette lettre où j'avais voulu vous écrire mille reproches et il me semble que malgré moi je n'y ai mis que des tendresses . . .[92]

Despite this affectionate correspondence the affair did not survive the lovers' separation. The memory of Moriane remained, however, long present in Louÿs's mind.

Louÿs was a passionate patriot. Accordingly, when war broke out in August 1914, he tried to enlist, but was rejected as unfit for military service. Throughout the following years he grieved over his inability to contribute actively to the defence of his country. 'Je vous écris dans une journée de désespoir', he wrote to Farrère on 25 August. 'C'est hier par téléphone et ce matin par la presse que j'ai appris la défaite de Charleroi. Presque tous les miens sont là-bas, peut-être morts, et pas même un peu de gloire pour couvrir ces fosses! Et moi qui reste ici à la fois aveugle et paralytique, incapable de prendre une part quelconque à cette levée en masse de toute la nation. Je suis triste à mourir.'[93] He avidly collected every scrap of information about the progress of the campaigns. During the early months of the war he was well placed to pick up all the latest news and rumours, for he spent them at Bordeaux where the French Government and the newspapers had moved.[94] His letters to Georges, who was then at Biarritz, were full of gossip about military and political matters, spiced with such titillating phrases as 'Je sais enfin le secret qui nous a tous intrigués . . .', 'suite des renseignements recueillis aujourd'hui et qui ne sont pas dans les journaux . . .', 'on dit que . . .' However, the sense of excitement occasioned by his proximity to the official and unofficial sources of red-hot information could not in the long run compensate for the discomfort of living in a hotel room, nor for the intellectual inactivity resulting from the remoteness of his personal library. By the beginning of December he was complaining about the uselessness and emptiness of the life he was leading at Bordeaux.[95] A few weeks later he returned to Paris.

In the claustrophobic and feverish atmosphere of Bordeaux where many of the exiled Parisians had little else to do but while away long hours in discussing the latest reports from the front, many old acquaintances were renewed. In particular, Louÿs frequently met a friend of Jean de Tinan's, Paul Leclercq, whom he had briefly known twenty years earlier. He fell into the habit of spending his nights with Leclercq and a few other companions.

'Quand le petit jour commençait à poindre et que l'on faisait mine, après une longue conversation, de vouloir le quitter enfin,' Leclercq recalled in *Paradis perdus*, 'il n'y a pas de subterfuges, de ruses qu'il n'inventât (tel que cacher une canne ou un chapeau) pour vous retenir plus longtemps auprès de lui.'[96] In many ways, Louÿs led a far more intensive social life in Bordeaux than he had done in Paris, and the pleasure he derived from it influenced his behaviour even after his return to the capital. A notebook kept by him during 1915 records numerous social activities in the town, in addition to the many amorous adventures which were being enacted mainly in the house in the rue de Boulainvilliers.[97] The year 1915 was perhaps the last relatively happy one of Louÿs's life.

For a short time that year he stayed at the Hôtel Vouillemont in the rue Boissy d'Anglas, near the place de la Concorde. During this period he continued to see a great deal of Paul Leclercq who lived in the rue Marbœuf, a few steps from the Champs Élysées. He was affectionately christened 'Le Matou' ('Tom-cat') by Leclercq's friends who took good care, however, knowing his extreme touchiness, not to reveal the nickname to him:

Il restait souvent, tout en bavardant et fumant cigarettes sur cigarettes, de longues heures à errer, comme un gros chat familier, parmi mes bibelots et mes livres ... Tant que je restais seul avec lui ou que nous n'étions que deux ou trois amis réunis autour du Matou, il se montrait plein de la plus folle fantaisie et l'on se sentait pénétré par la douceur de son charme intime et très particulier. Mais aussitôt que la réunion devenait plus nombreuse, le Matou paraissait effarouché, il devenait nerveux, et comme un chat dérangé dans sa quiétude il manifestait des signes d'impatience et ne prononçait plus un mot.[98]

At night he roamed the streets in search of cafés or bars still open, in defiance of the official decree requiring public establishments to close at 11 o'clock—he discovered several in the Saint Lazare district—or he would visit the bar located in the basement of the Hôtel Meurice in the rue de Rivoli, which, like himself, kept late hours.

Louÿs owed much of whatever happiness he knew that year to a young dancer whom, Paul Leclercq recalled, 'le Tout-Montmartre connaissait sous le nom de Claudine ou même de la Môme Claudine'.[99] Her full name was Claudine Rolland. She was twenty-two years old and of Belgian extraction. Louÿs had met her in June 1914, shortly after Moriane's departure; according to Cardinne-

Petit, he was introduced to her in a restaurant by Curnonsky.[100] Soon after his return from Bordeaux he met Claudine again, and from then on he saw her almost every day. In late March she became his mistress. Their liaison lasted, intermittently, until 1920. Louÿs appreciated Claudine's good looks, gaiety, and ready wit. She was, moreover, affectionate and undemanding. Above all, she brought youth and laughter into his life, and he found her company at once delightful and stimulating. Cardinne-Petit described her thus: 'Claudine était agréablement tournée. Son visage spirituel accusait la franchise et un certain étonnement de vivre. Elle était gentille, incapable de méchanceté, et très simple.'[101] And Farrère declared: 'Certes, Claudine, toujours de belle humeur, toujours drôle, et ne se fâchant jamais de rien, était bien la compagne qu'il fallait à Pierre Louÿs pour égayer sa mortelle mélancolie.'[102] Claudine's half-sister Aline Steenackers, whom she had introduced to Louÿs in August 1914, also visited the rue de Boulainvilliers.[103] From October 1915 onwards her name recurs regularly in Louÿs's notebook, though with less frequency than Claudine's.

The year 1916, in marked contrast to the preceding one, brought Louÿs much distress. His quarrel with Loviot, though vexing and upsetting,[104] was of relatively slight significance compared with the grave material problems which were taking a heavy toll of his physical and moral reserves that summer. In the draft of a letter to André Lebey, in late June, he wrote:

Ici, tout est de plus en plus triste. Si je viens souvent le mardi soir, et si j'attends au matin pour te prévenir quand je ne viens pas, c'est que je ne suis pas encore absolument 'lassé de tout, même de l'espérance'. Cela viendra . . .

J'ai toujours eu des ennuis; mais rien de comparable à mon existence depuis cent jours. Mieux vaut pour moi ne reparaître que 'victorieux ou mort' de ce qui m'ensevelit.[105]

Yet, in another respect, the year 1916 stands out as an unusually fruitful one in this period. In the spring Louÿs worked on *Poëtique*, which appeared in the *Mercure de France* in June, before being published separately, in a revised version, in 1917. The poem 'Isthi' was written in June or early July. Three hundred and fifty copies were printed by 22 July, 'pour les amis de l'auteur et pour ceux de la Librairie Crès'.[106] Louÿs distributed them in the course of the following weeks. Finally, while looking through some of his unpublished poems later that year, Louÿs came across one entitled 'Pervigilium Mortis', which opened with the words 'Ouvre sur moi tes yeux si tristes et si tendres'. While he had forgotten the poem, that first line had remained tantalizingly fixed in his memory and he had, in fact, been trying to trace its author for several years. Like 'L'Apogée', the poem had been inspired by Louÿs's love for Marie de Régnier. Within the space of a few days he now entirely revised the rediscovered poem, into which he inserted 'L'Apogée'. The new version of 'Pervigilium Mortis' was published posthumously in the *Œuvres complètes*.

Louÿs was particularly pleased with *Poëtique*:

De toutes mes pages, les quatre qui me déplaisent le moins sont celles qui viennent de paraître. Je flanquerais *Aphrodite* dans le ruisseau plutôt que cette *Poëtique*. Pour le fond et pour la forme, j'en suis à peu près content et jamais je ne me suis dit cela pour quoi que ce fût d'aujourd 'hui.—Le *Mercure de France* a triplé ses droits d'auteur à cette occasion. Je n'ai pas le sou, mais j'ai tout refusé ... Tout ce qui m'émeut le plus est là-dedans. Je ne passe pas à la caisse après avoir dit *Credo*.[107]

The following year he assured Cardinne-Petit that *Poëtique* 'est mon œuvre capitale. Elle m'a coûté plus de nuits de travail que n'importe lequel de mes romans'.[108]

While Louÿs was preparing *Poëtique*, Valéry was engaged in the composition of 'La Jeune Parque'. Louÿs took a lively interest in the progress of Valéry's poem which, even before it was finished, he praised as 'une des plus belles choses qu'on ait faites en français depuis cinquante ans'.[109] The fifteen letters from Valéry to Louÿs covering the period 1915–17, which were published in 1926, afford a fascinating insight into their frequent discussions of poetry in general and of the text of 'La Jeune Parque' in particular.[110] Upon learning that Valéry would have called the poem 'Psyché', if he had not himself chosen that name for his still unpublished novel, he promptly offered the title to Valéry. However, the latter declined the gift as too generous.

Louÿs made his offer after receiving a letter from Valéry intimating his intention of abandoning the composition of 'La Jeune Parque', because he lacked the necessary tranquillity and solitude. The purpose of the offer was evidently to stimulate Valéry's desire to continue working on the poem. At the same time, Louÿs also endeavoured to find a more practical way of easing Valéry's situation. Valéry was then earning his living as private secretary to Édouard Lebey, the Director of the Agence Havas and the uncle of André Lebey. Louÿs therefore thought of asking the latter to persuade his uncle to grant Valéry an immediate leave of two months. The request is contained in the previously mentioned draft of a letter dating from June 1916, in which Louÿs described his own wretched existence.[111] Together with the offer of the title 'Psyché', it provides touching proof of the deep affection and admiration Louÿs felt for Valéry. These gestures of friendship are all the more remarkable for having been made at a time when he was himself so preoccupied with serious personal problems. 'Pour moi, je lui donnerais mon titre', he intended to write to Lebey. 'C'est tout ce que mon propriétaire n'ait pas encore saisi.'[112] It is not known whether, or in what form, the letter was finally sent.

A few months later Louÿs experienced the profoundest grief of his life. Since his retirement from the diplomatic service, following his recall by President Poincaré from his post of Ambassador to Russia in 1913, Georges Louis had been living at Biarritz and, latterly, in the rue de Tournon in Paris. He was approaching his seventieth birthday and had been ill for some time when, early in 1917, his condition worsened. In order to be nearer to his brother, Louÿs took a room at the Hôtel Vouillemont in the rue Boissy d'Anglas, where he had already stayed in 1915. Georges Louis died on 17 April 1917. By his death, as he told Cardinne-Petit later that year, Louÿs lost 'l'être que j'aimais le plus au monde'.[113] Sufficient evidence has been presented in this book to attest the truth of that statement.

Perhaps, if Georges had lived longer, Louÿs's final decline would have been less rapid and some of the most painful incidents of his last years might have been avoided. As it was, Georges's death speeded the collapse, for in his despair Louÿs resorted to drugs, especially cocaine. In 1901, he had written to Paz Louis: 'Georges sait depuis plusieurs années que mon existence se partage en saisons régulières blanches et noires, celles où je le vois et celles où je ne le vois pas.'[114] The seasons remaining to him were almost entirely black . . .

The drugs which Louÿs was taking provoked a serious deterioration in his already weak eyesight during the summer of 1917. As a result, he once more needed the services of a secretary. At the suggestion of Paul Fort, he engaged the eighteen-year-old Robert Cardinne-Petit who, with some friends, had recently founded a small *avant-garde* poetry review. Since Louÿs was by this time living almost entirely by night, Cardinne-Petit usually reported to the rue de Boulainvilliers towards the end of the afternoon, in time to read aloud the latest government communiqués and military reports while his employer was 'breakfasting' between six and seven o'clock. His other duties consisted mainly in writing letters at Louÿs's dictation and, perhaps most important of all, in keeping him company for a few hours. When his secretary had left for the evening, Louÿs settled down, magnifying-glass in hand, to hours of painfully slow reading and note-taking. Cardinne-Petit's description of the laborious method to which Louÿs was obliged to resort on the rare occasions when he wished to reply himself to a friend, shows how very poor his eyesight had become: 'Penché sur sa loupe qu'il maintenait au-dessus du papier de la main gauche, il fallait qu'une main amie guidât sa main droite et maintînt convenablement le porte-plume entre ses doigts, les deux becs bien d'aplomb sur la feuille. Il traçait ses caractères lettre à lettre, s'interrompait à chaque instant, et pour éviter que les caractères ne se chevauchassent, on devait veiller pour lui sur leur alignement.'[115] A short letter to Farrère on 20 February 1918 concludes: 'Même à la loupe je relis mal ce que j'écris sans y voir et avec tant de peine. Je vois si peu le bec de ma plume que je manque presque toutes les lettres de chaque mot et je repasse au hasard. J'ai honte de vous offrir cette écriture lamentable.'[116]

During the six months Cardinne-Petit worked for him, Louÿs left the house on only two occasions, the purpose of one of these expeditions being to call on Valéry. Among Louÿs's regular visitors was Paz Louis who was soon to try, unsuccessfully, to persuade him to marry her. Claudine still came frequently. Her presence cheered him and, at the same time, prompted him to match her high spirits, however temporarily, by making up stories and poems for her amusement.

On the last day of 1917, Louÿs sent the following note to Claude Farrère:

Claude, je n'écris à personne, ma vue est trop faible, mais je suis moins seul que cet été.

On me lit mes lettres. Écrivez-moi quelques lignes. J'ai fait prendre de vos nouvelles chez vous et je n'osais pas vous donner signe de vie parce que j'y vois de moins en moins et que ma compagnie est trop triste. L'année meurt ce soir. Il n'y a pas de jour où je ne pense au bonheur que j'ai d'être votre ami.[117]

It was clearly only a question of time before Louÿs would be forced to part with some of his books which constituted the only marketable commodity he still possessed. A sale had, in fact, been planned for November 1914,[118] but the moratorium declared by the French Government on debts after the outbreak of the war had saved Louÿs from that painful solution. It was not until four years later, by which time his situation was, if anything, even more desperate, that a sale took place. In late 1918 a catalogue was published listing 707 of Louÿs's most valuable books which were to be sold by the Librairie Henri Leclerc between 25 and 28 November. A few days before the auction was due to be held, a wealthy collector, Émile Mayen, arranged—through André Doderet, the well-known translator of Gabriele d'Annunzio and a friend of Louÿs's—to buy all the books for the considerable sum of 300,000 francs. Louÿs received 150,000 francs immediately; the balance was due to be paid in three equal instalments the following year. As a letter from Louÿs to Doderet on 30 September 1919 makes clear, no formal contract was drawn up: 'Je n'ai pas demandé à M. Mayen un contrat par devant notaire. Votre amitié pour lui et sa parole valaient mieux qu'un acte de vente'.[119] It is characteristic of Louÿs's financial situation that the money due from the final two instalments should have been assigned in advance: 'Vous savez que cette somme de cent mille francs représente un peu plus que mon capital', he informed Doderet in the afore-mentioned letter. 'Mon propriétaire a droit sur elle.' Émile Mayen undertook to maintain the collection intact. The major part of it was eventually sold at auction and dispersed in November 1930.

Louÿs later pointed out to Frédéric Lachèvre that he had obtained an excellent return on his investment: 'Les sept cents volumes m'avaient coûté au plus 50,000 francs. Voilà comment "je me ruinais". A 600 pour 100. Outre les 700, il me reste chez moi 1,500 livres aussi précieux et 18,000 bouquins presque tous en bel état et parmi lesquels on pourrait "faire un sort" à quinze cents autres.'[120] Evidently a 500 per cent yield on investment represents a very handsome profit. Louÿs's self-congratulatory statement overlooks, however, the fact that he could ill afford to pay out 50,000 francs in the first place, with the result that the purchase of these seven hundred volumes, together with the acquisition of the other twenty thousand books he mentions, contributed materially to his financial ruin which had such unhappy consequences for his marriage and for his health.

In 1919 Louÿs emerged for the last time from the twilight in which so much of his life was lived during this period. The Corneille–Molière debate was launched by him with an article in the August 1919 number of the *Intermédiaire des chercheurs et des curieux*, provocatively entitled 'Corneille est-il l'auteur d'*Amphytrion?*' Over the following months the *Intermédiaire* printed six replies, all equally hostile. It was, however, the publication of a series of articles by Louÿs during October and November in *Le Temps* and *Comœdia*, with their much larger circulation and wider range of readers, which sparked off the most violent polemic. Very briefly stated, Louÿs's theory was that Corneille had collaborated in several plays bearing Molière's name (*L'École des Femmes, Dom Juan, Le Misanthrope, Tartuffe, Les Femmes savantes*), contributing in each case the passages of the greatest literary merit, and that he had been solely responsible for at least one play, *Amphytrion*. Numerous replies appeared in *Le Temps*, in which the attackers far outnumbered the defenders. The criticism frequently assumed a vituperative or derisive tone; very rarely was any attempt made to subject Louÿs's arguments to a dispassionate, scholarly examination. Furious protests were received from outraged Moliéristes, determined to protect the reputation of Jean-Baptiste Poquelin and thirsting for the blood of his detractor. A group of actors from the Comédie-Française went so far as to demand that Louÿs be prosecuted for libelling their patron saint.

Louÿs had, of course, expected his theory to provoke much initial opposition, and he had intended to counter this reaction by placing before the public all the evidence he had so carefully assembled over several years. He had not anticipated, however, that his articles would call forth such hysterical hostility and such ridicule. The truth is that his literary past had once more caught up with him. Louÿs himself, on one occasion, somewhat ruefully referred to the *Chansons de Bilitis* as 'à la fois mon succès et ma perte'.[121] The very skill of the pastiche which had persuaded many readers and critics to accept the poems as translations of authentic Greek texts had stamped Louÿs once and for all as a clever hoaxer, and thereby gravely weakened his credibility as a serious literary critic. The enduring popularity of the *Chansons de Bilitis*—since the appearance of the augmented version in 1898, there had been further editions in 1900, 1906, 1912, and 1914—had, moreover, helped to keep the memory of the deception alive.

Louÿs felt hurt by the insults and exasperated by the gibes of his adversaries who refused to give serious consideration to his theory and instead chose the easier course of dismissing it as the latest leg-pull of an inveterate 'mystificateur'. In the face of this, to him highly offensive, attitude, he preferred to withdraw from the debate and refrained from publishing any further supporting material. It is interesting to note, however, that his theory was not entirely forgotten: forty years later it found a notable champion in Henry Poulaille who dedicated his most important book on the subject, *Corneille sous le masque de Molière*,[122] 'à la mémoire de Pierre Louÿs qui posa la question Molière'.

The numerous detailed textual analyses which Louÿs undertook in connection with his research on the seventeenth-century theatre imposed a further strain on his eyes, especially as, in his enthusiasm, he in no way spared himself (on one occasion he told Farrère that he had not been to bed more than twice in twenty-four days[123]). In a letter to Farrère on 21 December 1919 he complained: 'Mes yeux, toujours, mes yeux qui se voilent si vite et se fatiguent d'une loupe à la 10ᵉ ligne,—et qui sont *très* fatigués depuis deux mois parce qu'à propos de Corneille et de Molière j'ai un travail et une correspondance au-dessus de mes forces visuelles . . .'[124] On the following day he was present as a witness at the civil ceremony of Farrère's marriage to Hélène Roggers. Sadly, Farrère watched him leave the Mairie, leaning heavily on the arm of his secretary and cautiously tapping his stick against the steps descending towards the avenue Henri-Martin. Louÿs apologized for not feeling strong enough to attend the church wedding. From this time on, he went out still more rarely. In the rue de Boulainvilliers Claudine Rolland had in the meantime been displaced by her half-sister Aline Steenackers.

Last Years: 1920–1925

HAVING SOLVED the problem of the Corneille–Molière partnership to his satisfaction, Louÿs turned his attention to other aspects of literary history. For a time he studied Greek drama, but he continued to concentrate his research on the seventeenth century, and especially on Corneille, to whom he attributed several works normally labelled 'anonymous', as well as some usually credited to other authors, such as *La Vraye Histoire comique de Francion* which is generally considered to have been written by Charles Sorel. The spring of 1921 proved an exceptionally stimulating period for Louÿs, as is evident from the content and tone of his letters to Frédéric Lachèvre. 'J'ai trouvé la semaine dernière un problème historique dont je ne puis garder le secret pour mes notes silencieuses . . .', he wrote on 6 April. 'C'est énorme . . . J'aurais grand plaisir à vous en parler, si vous étiez libre de venir causer avec moi quelque jour.'[1] On 15 April: 'Puisque vous voulez bien garder pour vous seul les détails de mes travaux, je vous dois la confidence de ce que j'ai trouvé hier . . .'[2] On 6 May: 'Depuis votre visite le "déchiffrement" de Corneille anonyme continue de s'accroître avec une facilité chaque jour plus féconde.'[3] And on the next day: 'Vous avez bien voulu m'envoyer un nouvel exemplaire des *Satyres commentées* [by Boileau]—et mon travail m'absorbe si passionnément que j'oubliais hier de vous remercier.'[4]

Louÿs's renewed intellectual vigour coincided with a marked improvement in his eyesight, strikingly reflected in the reappearance of his clear, firm, and smoothly flowing handwriting. This was, however, to be the final period of such activity in his life. In the autumn of 1921 he fell gravely ill and was confined to bed for several months. In January 1922 he underwent an operation, after which he was given up for lost. That same month he expressed the view that, very likely, 'les dates 1870–1922 limiteront ma biographie dans les dictionnaires'.[5] He faced the prospect of impending death with composure, but in spite of his weakened condition he led a more extravagant existence than ever, taking morphine and cocaine, and consuming vast quantities of alcohol, at the rate of two bottles of champagne, three bottles of wine, and one bottle of Vin Mariani, a tonic wine, each day.[6] Not surprisingly, his physical health as well as his mental equilibrium deteriorated rapidly. On 21 May, escorted by Farrère, his nephew Robert Louis and his secretary Jean Cassou, he was transported to a nursing-home at Rueil-Malmaison, on the western outskirts of Paris. He insisted that Aline Steenackers, by whom he had had a son in 1920,[7] should occupy a room next to his own. To humour him and persuade him to agree to the move, she accompanied him to Malmaison, but once he had been admitted, she returned to the rue de Boulainvilliers.[8]

Claudine, who had been ailing for several years, died that spring. The circumstances surrounding her last illness gave rise to an estrangement between Louÿs and Farrère. Replaced in the rue de Boulainvilliers by her own half-sister and abandoned by her former lover, the 'gentle and charming Claudine',[9] dying in a hospital at Versailles, had appealed to Farrère for help. Farrère thereupon arranged for her to spend her last days in a less forbidding and sordid setting. Louÿs apparently took offence at Farrère's action which he regarded as an interference in his personal affairs. Notwithstanding Farrère's prompt apology, Louÿs asked him not to call for some time.[10]

Louÿs's condition had not improved by the end of the year. Paul Léautaud noted in his diary on 7 December 1922: 'Quant à la santé de Pierre Louÿs, pas meilleure. Cassou dit qu'il continue à déménager. Il passe son temps à demander l'heure, oublie la réponse, et demande de nouveau. Son intelligence ne se retrouve que lorsqu'on lui parle de Mallarmé ou de Heredia. Il redit alors tout ce qu'il a dit cent fois, clairement, puis sorti de là, est complètement gâteux. Cassou dit que c'est la cocaïne qui l'a amené à cet état,'[11] At that time Louÿs was staying with Paz Louis in Neuilly, for shortly after leaving the nursing-home at Rueil-Malmaison he had been temporarily evicted by the proprietor of the house in the rue de Boulainvilliers, presumably for non-payment of the rent (yet in June he had received 50,000 francs from Albin Michel who was preparing a new edition of *Aphrodite*).

Two important events occurred in 1923. On 26 January a second child, Suzanne, was born; and on 6 October, at Anglet near Biarritz, where they had spent the preceding weeks, Louÿs was married to Aline Steenackers.

Only scant information is available about the final period of Louÿs's life. A series of poems written in March 1924 contain references to the seizure and sale of his property, including some of his books, as well as to other misfortunes. A few characteristic extracts from these poems, which plumb the depths of despair, are quoted below:

Je mourrai sans autre raison
Que d'avoir revu ma maison
Eventrée ainsi qu'une femme,
Tous mes biens volés ou perdus,
Souillés, dispersés ou vendus,
A la fin d'une histoire infâme!

*

Entre ces tristes murs poudreux
Je fus heureux ou malheureux,
Je fus autrefois quelque chose.
Mais ils ne m'ont plus rien laissé.
Tout ce que j'avais amassé,
L'or a péri comme la rose.

*

Je le répète? Ils m'ont tout pris . . .
Ils me prendront même ces vers
Envers et contre tout, envers
Le rhythme saint de ma pensée,
Je m'attends à n'importe quoi
Et ne sais pas encor pourquoi
Autant d'amour s'est dépensée.

*

Ils ont coupé l'herbe sur pied,
Ils ont tout pris, tout épié,
Tout volé! quel manège infâme!
Rien ne me resterait-il plus
De ces nobles jours révolus?
Pas un désir? Pas une femme?

*

Les tristesses de la saison
Vont pleuvant sur cette maison
Qui suinte ou pleure goutte à goutte.
Ce que j'y heurte m'y déplaît.
Tout y est moisi, tout est laid,
Tout m'y écœure et m'en dégoûte.[12]

Perhaps it was at this time that Louÿs wrote the note later found among his papers: 'S'il m'arrivait un bonheur, c'est-à-dire si je mourais . . .'[13]

It is generally believed that certain erotic and even obscene poems and other writings which were published after his death date from this same period. The assumption is probably correct, although it must be pointed out that not all such poems attributed to Louÿs are authentic. In any case, there can be no doubt that he never envisaged the publication of these works.

Louÿs's health improved a little in the spring of 1924 and he even went out on several occasions. Yet in September he had once more to undergo treatment in a nursing-home, this time at Saint-Mandé. While there, he frequently rebelled against the hospital atmosphere and flew into violent rages, creating so much disturbance that the doctors finally lost patience and sent him back to the rue de Boulainvilliers.

Conflicting statements have been made concerning Louÿs's physical condition during the last months of his life. Farrère mentions that he was completely blind towards the end,[14] while Cardinne-Petit declares that during the final fifteen months Louÿs 'demeure "enfermé" avec lui-même, dans son silence à lui, à demi immobile sur son lit d'agonie et de libération'.[15] Neither Farrère nor Cardinne-Petit, however, saw Louÿs during this period. On the other hand, Jean Thorhauer, who visited him regularly twice weekly for business discussions and talked with him for the last time six days before his death, gave a less distressing account of his condition. The final conversation, Thorhauer recalled, had turned mainly on the forthcoming publication, in a photographic reproduction, of the original manuscript of *La Femme et le pantin*, a project which Louÿs viewed with much pleasure.[16] Since it had been decided that the edition should carry a photograph taken during the late 1890s, Louÿs amused himself with choosing a suitable one: 'Celle-ci est bien médiocre . . . et cette autre. Suis-je niais . . .'[17] Louÿs was thus still enjoying partial eyesight. Moreover, Jean Cassou who, though he had been replaced as secretary by Georges Serrières, remained in contact with Louÿs, has indicated that he seemed in better spirits during the two or three months preceding his death and even invited guests to dinner.[18]

Louÿs, who had for so long been reconciled to the prospect of an early death, who had even frequently longed for it, suddenly felt reluctant to loose his hold on life. 'Ah! c'est que je veux vivre', he was heard to murmur on 3 June 1925, filled with a momentary hope that all was not yet lost. And listening to music by Bach and Mozart on the phonograph, he wept for a long time.[19] Yet the next morning he is reported to have told his secretary: 'Aujourd'hui sera mon dernier jour.' He repeated the remark to the maid, and said to the doctor who had come to examine him: 'Docteur, ce n'est plus un vivant que vous auscultez, mais un mort.'[20] He died later that day, peacefully, without pain—according to one story, a few moments after his wife had lit a cigarette for him.

Louÿs's death gave rise to a bizarre incident. He had always refused to authorize the commercial sale of his photograph, and since the turn of the century had gone to great lengths to prevent any reproduction of his portrait. Thus, when the review *L'Illustration théâtrale* was preparing a special issue (published on 11 February 1911) on the play *La Femme et le pantin*, he particularly requested the editor, Gaston Sorbets, to respect his wishes in this matter: 'Depuis quinze ans j'ai fait ce qu'il fallait faire pour ne pas avoir une "tête connue". J'y ai parfaitement réussi.' Sorbets printed Louÿs's letter, together with one Louÿs had previously written to R. H. Sherard and in which he had stated with evident satisfaction: 'Je n'ai pas fait faire ma photographie depuis le siècle dernier, et je ne laisse même pas vendre celle de jadis chez les marchands. Personne ne connaît mon visage.' There was doubtless a link, initially, between this attitude and Louÿs's conception of the 'true' artist, his preference for limited editions, his distaste for publicity and popular success. As he grew older, however, this idealistic attitude became increasingly rigid under the influence of more complex psychological factors stemming from his nervous and physical disorders. Cardinne-Petit noticed in 1917 that Louÿs suffered physically if recognized in public.[21]

This obsessive desire for physical anonymity is responsible for the absence of photographs showing Louÿs during the last twenty years of his life; if any were taken privately, they have not yet been published. Only after his death was a photographer allowed into the house in the rue de Boulainvilliers. Even that permission turned out to have been misguided, for the picture taken was grotesquely touched up afterwards so as to depict the subject in an upright position, with one eye open. This photograph was then published as a portrait supposedly taken during the author's lifetime. Literary commercialism had triumphed after all.

Louÿs's body was placed in a coffin at five o'clock on Friday afternoon, 5 June, in the presence of Paz Louis, Claude Farrère, Henriette Roggers, Fernand Gregh, André Lebey, Jean Cassou, and Georges Serrières. The funeral took place on Sunday, 7 June. The religious service was celebrated at the Church of Notre-Dame de la Miséricorde, in the nearby rue de l'Assomption. Afterwards, the eulogy was pronounced in front of the church by the Minister of Education, Anatole de Monzie. Pierre Louÿs would have appreciated his tribute: 'Il a honoré la beauté d'une dévotion sans bassesse, honoré la langue française d'un culte sans défaillance.' He would, moreover, have been delighted with Monzie's concluding remark: 'Je salue sa dépouille du même homage dont j'eusse salué un filleul de Ronsard.'[22]

Some twenty friends, led by Claude Farrère, André Lebey, and Fernand Gregh, escorted the coffin on its long journey to the Montparnasse cemetery. Among them were Paul Fort, Jacques-Émile Blanche, André Messager, Pierre Lalo, Thierry Sandre, Charles Maurras, Henry Bordeaux, and Pierre Frondaie.

Three days after the funeral, Aline Louÿs gave birth to her third child, Claudine.

Postscript

ALINE LOUŸS married Georges Serrières, Louÿs's last secretary, on 14 December 1927. Five children were born of this marriage. Georges and Aline Serrières were divorced in 1954.

On 19 June 1925 the wedding was performed at the Church of Saint-Philippe-du-Roule, in Paris, of the Count and Countess Augusto Gilbert de Voisins, who had been married in a civil ceremony (Voisins by proxy) at Arcachon exactly ten years earlier. It was at this same church that Louise de Heredia had married Pierre Louÿs in 1899. Louise de Voisins died on 10 December 1930, Gilbert de Voisins on 8 December 1939.

Marie de Régnier died on 6 February 1963, at the age of eighty-eight. She had survived both her husband, Henri de Régnier (died 23 May 1935), and her son Pierre-Marie-Joseph-Henri de Régnier (died 1 December 1943) who may also have been the son of Pierre Louÿs.

An 'Association des amis de Pierre Louÿs' was formed in 1977 under the presidency of Dr Robert Fleury.

Appendix: F. Coppée's Review of Aphrodite

(*Le Journal,* 16 April 1896)

DEPUIS QUINZE jours, je suis pareil au bonhomme La Fontaine courant par les rues et demandant à tous ceux qu'il rencontrait: 'Avez-vous lu Baruch?'; et je vais à travers la ville, interrogeant les amis et les camarades qu'un bon hasard met sur mon chemin, et leur disant: 'Avez-vous lu l'*Aphrodite*, de Pierre Louÿs?'

Ceux qui lisent, ceux qui sont 'au courant', me répondent tout de suite: 'Si j'ai lu *Aphrodite?* . . . Cela va sans dire . . . C'est un chef d'œuvre, et Pierre Louÿs est un prosateur de premier ordre.'

Mais d'autres, moins littéraires, me questionnent, et je laisse alors éclater mon enthousiasme:

'Vous n'avez pas lu *Aphrodite!* Alors qu'est-ce que vous faites entre vos repas? Sachez qu'on n'a rien écrit de plus parfait en prose française depuis le *Roman de la Momie* et depuis *Salammbô*. Soyez sûrs que les cendres de Gautier ont frémi de joie, à l'apparition de ce livre, et que, dans le paradis des lettrés, l'ombre de Flaubert hurle, à l'heure qu'il est, des phrases de Pierre Louÿs, les soumet à l'infaillible épreuve de son gueuloir, et qu'elles la subissent victorieusement. Mais laissons les morts tranquilles, et allons trouver un bon juge, l'auteur de *Thaïs*, par exemple, qui est vivant, celui-là, et essaie peut-être, en ce moment, son habit d'académicien. Allons trouver Anatole France, un maître, n'est-ce pas? en matière de style souple et pur et d'évocation du monde antique. Je gage qu'il est amoureux, comme moi, de la Galiléenne Chrysis, de la belle courtisane d'Alexandrie, de qui Pierre Louÿs vient de nous conter les débauches, les amours et la mort. Enfin, voilà donc un jeune, un vrai jeune,—Pierre Louÿs n'a pas vingt-six ans,— qui nous donne un beau livre; un livre écrit dans une langue impeccable avec les formules classiques et les mots de tout le monde, mais rénovés et rajeunis à force de goût et d'art; un livre très savant et où se révèle, à chaque page, une connaissance approfondie de l'antiquité et de la littérature grecque, mais sans pédantisme aucun et ne sentant jamais l'huile et l'effort; un livre dont la fable contient sans doute un symbole ingénieux et poétique, mais un symbole parfaitement clair; un livre enfin qui est vraiment issu de notre tradition et animé de notre génie, et dans lequel la beauté, la force et la grâce se montrent toujours en plein soleil et inondées d'éclatante lumière! . . . Vous n'avez pas lu l'*Aphrodite* de Pierre Louÿs? . . . Alors, courez rue de l'Échaudé, à la librairie du *Mercure de France*, allez ensuite vous enfermer avec le volume et dégustez-moi ça. Vous m'en direz des nouvelles. C'est du nanan !'

Telle est, à peu près, la harangue que j'ai improvisée une vingtaine de fois, ces jours derniers. C'est si doux d'avoir fait la découverte soudaine d'un jeune talent et de le dire à tout le monde. C'est si doux et c'est si rare !

Chaque soir, j'ouvre un livre et, je vous assure, toujours avec bonne volonté. Mais, la plupart du temps, je suis pris de découragement après avoir lu quelques pages. Non que le talent manque dans tous ces poèmes, dans tous ces romans. Au contraire, grand Dieu ! il court les rues, le talent. Mais, la plupart du temps, je ne rencontre que des qualités acquises, que le résultat—très appréciable, à coup sûr, mais sans puissance et surtout sans charme—du travail et de la volonté. Il manque, dans presque tous les ouvrages nouveaux, ce je ne sais quoi qui peut être l'esprit, ou la grâce, et l'émotion,—et, pour les œuvres supérieures, la beauté,—mais qui jaillit directement de la nature et du tempérament de l'écrivain et qui, sur-le-champ, domine le lecteur ou le séduit. Cet attrait mystérieux m'a entraîné, dès le début d'*Aphrodite*. Je me suis écrié: 'A la bonne heure ! Cela, c'est du vrai talent !' et, depuis quinze jours, je ne cesse de le répéter à tous les échos.

Pourquoi faut-il, après m'être donné cette grande joie de dire publiquement à M. Pierre Louÿs la sincère admiration que m'inspire son œuvre, pourquoi faut-il que je sois forcé—et cela par un ordre impérieux de ma conscience—de faire une réserve, une très grosse réserve, et d'ajouter que je recommande la lecture d'*Aphrodite* à tous les artistes, mais seulement aux artistes ? Car *Aphrodite* est un beau livre, mais un livre très impur; et je crois faire mon devoir en jouant, à présent, le rôle du gardien qui ne permet pas à tout le monde de pénétrer dans le 'musée secret', du bibliothécaire qui n'accorde pas au premier venu la communication d'un volume classé dans 'l'enfer'.

Attention ! Je ne voudrais pas que mon reproche se convertît en réclame aux yeux des libertins, et je m'empresse de les prévenir que la lecture d'*Aphrodite* sera pour eux une déception. Il leur faut pire que cela, et dans l'atmosphère de sensualité qui enveloppe toute l'histoire de la belle Chrysis on ne peut pourtant voir une seule image trop 'découverte', comme disent les catalogues spéciaux. Mais, si elle n'offre rien qui soit de nature à satisfaire les clients des librairies secrètes de Bruxelles, *Aphrodite* n'en reste pas moins—à mon humble avis—un livre à interdire à beaucoup de lecteurs.

N'allez pas croire non plus, que je m'affilie, en ce moment, à la ligue de M. le sénateur Bérenger, homme fort estimable, d'ailleurs, qui eut l'honneur d'attacher son nom à une loi très sage et très humaine, et qui, malgré les blagues des journaux et des cafés-concerts, ne me paraît pas si ridicule, quand il exprime son dégoût devant la pornographie triomphante. Je ne suis pas si pudibond; et, dans le cas particulier de M. Pierre Louÿs, je m'explique très bien que cet helléniste, nourri d'Aristophane et des *Dialogues* de Lucien, et qui nous conte les aventures d'une courtisane de l'Égypte décadente, n'ait pas reculé devant les scènes les plus vives et soit allé jusqu'à l'extrême limite de la hardiesse, s'arrêtant toujours, avec un tact exquis—je me hâte de le dire—au point où la licence devient de l'obscénité.

Après tout, j'en ai lu bien d'autres, et *Aphrodite* n'est pas destinée aux écoles primaires.

Non, ce qui me chiffonne, c'est la préface. Que M. Pierre Louÿs me pardonne ma franchise, mais il me semble qu'il nous y a développé— toujours dans un style délicieux, c'est entendu—un paradoxe qui a déjà beaucoup servi, tranchons le mot, une rengaine. L'exaltation du culte d'Aphrodite, l'amour sensuel considéré comme divin, le regret du temps où la nudité humaine se montrait sans voile et où la 'majestueuse tolérance du peuple qui a bâti l'Acropole' ne se scandalisait pas qu'un homme et une femme, sans être engagés par aucun lien, d'ailleurs, s'unissent, fût-ce en public, tout cela n'est point nouveau, et nous connaissons, depuis longtemps, cette rhétorique. Les jeunes savants de l'école d'Athènes ont eux-mêmes renoncé à ces lieux communs, qui furent chers à leurs devanciers, et ils se souviennent, à ce sujet, du terrible sonnet de Louis Veuillot.

Je ne crois pas être un janséniste ni un mômier de Genève, et je n'ai jamais mis de feuille de vigne sur aucune statue. Mais mon esprit ne peut se résigner à admettre que l'habitude de se vêtir des pieds à la tête soit un signe manifeste de décadence et un retour à la barbarie. J'ai, dans le sang, dix-neuf siècles de civilisation occidentale et chrétienne, et je n'arrive pas à me convaincre—moi, très impur, hélas!— que la pudeur soit une si funeste invention.

Du reste, je suis bien tranquille. Nous ne nous aviserons jamais d'aller tout nus; car, au point de vue esthétique, ce serait pitoyable. Nos nudités sont, en général, fort laides; et notre expérience des conseils de revision et des bains sur la rivière ne nous permet aucune illusion à cet égard. Pour dire toute ma pensée, j'imagine que la parfaite beauté a dû toujours être—oui, dans tous les temps et dans tous les pays—assez rare, sinon exceptionnelle. Oui, même dans la divine Hellas, puisque, seuls, ces horribles sauvages de Lacédémoniens jetaient leurs enfants mal venus dans le barathre. Tous mes préjugés classiques en souffrent, mais je suppose que, sur l'Agora des cités antiques, on rencontrait tout de même des gens difformes et hideux, se promenant *in naturalibus*, et qui eussent été beaucoup plus présentables en jaquette et en pantalon.

Je sais bien, Phidias? . . . Mais il choisissait ses modèles; et il devait y avoir des Athéniens dignes de poser pour Daumier.

Que Pierre Louÿs me pardonne ces blasphèmes! Malgré ma réserve sur le caractère beaucoup trop licencieux de son premier ouvrage, malgré mon léger accès d'humeur contre sa préface, décidément bien tapageuse et un peu jeunette, je salue en lui un artiste accompli, un écrivain de race, à qui nous devons déjà un livre charmant et sur qui les lettres françaises ont le droit de fonder de magnifiques espérances.

Notes

Preface

1 F. Gregh, *L'Age de Fer,* Paris, 1956, p. 36.

Prelude: 1870 –1889

1 b. 7 Aug. 1812, d. 14 Apr. 1889.
2 b. 11 Sept. 1822, d. 4 Feb. 1852.
3 b. 31 Jan. 1844, d. 10 Jan. 1920; m. Edmond Chardon 20 Dec. 1864.
4 b. 21 Mar. 1847, d. 7 Apr. 1917; m. Paz Ortega Morejon 26 June 1900.
5 b. 26 Dec. 1832, d. 29 May 1879.
6 b. 4 July 1857, d. 22 Oct. 1884.
7 The details of their voyage are taken from R. Fleury, 'La Naissance de Pierre Louÿs', *Bulletin des Amis de Pierre Louÿs,* March 1977, and 'Erratum', ibid., June 1977.
8 Ibid.
9 See R. Fleury, 'Junot, Duc d'Abrantès, et Pierre Louÿs. Leur parenté', *Bulletin du bibliophile et du bibliothécaire,* 1962.
10 *OC* ix, 91–2.
11 Ibid. 88–9.
12 Paris, 1920. See also E. Judet, *Georges Louis,* Paris, 1925.
13 *OC* ix. 145–50.
14 Ibid. 145 n. 1.
15 Draft of letter reproduced, without addressee's name, in 'Quelques lettres de Pierre Louÿs à A. G.', *Nouvelle Revue française,* Nov.–Dec. 1929.
16 *OC* ix. 102.
17 Ibid. 36.
18 Ibid. 150.
19 *Correspondance de Claude Debussy et de Pierre Louÿs (1893–1904),* ed. H. Borgeaud, Paris, 1945, p. 30.
20 R. Cardinne-Petit, *Pierre Louÿs inconnu,* Paris, 1948, p. 26.
21 *OC* ix. 261.
22 Ibid. 179.
23 P. Iseler, *Les Débuts d'André Gide vus par Pierre Louÿs,* Paris, 1937, p. 19.
24 *Les Poëmes de Pierre Louÿs 1887–1924,* ed. Y.-G. Le Dantec, 2 vols., Paris, 1945, ii. 695–6.
25 'Quelques lettres de Pierre Louÿs à A.G.' (the letter, although ascribed to late 1889, was in fact written in mid-August, probably on the thirteenth).
26 A. Gide, *Journal 1889–1939,* Paris, 1965, p. 13.
27 Iseler, p. 91.
28 *Journal 1889–1939,* p. 347.
29 In draft of letter to L. Blum (see n. 15 above).
30 Ibid.
31 J. Delay, *La Jeunesse d'André Gide,* 2 vols., Paris, 1956–7, ii. 164.
32 Ibid. 65.

Years of Promise: 1890–1895

1890

[1] Bibliothèque Jacques Doucet γ.1.26.

[2] *Journal 1889–1939*, p. 15.

[3] *OC* ix. 300–2.

[4] A copy of the Statutes in Louÿs's handwriting and dated 26 January 1890 is photographically reproduced in J.-M. Place and A. Vasseur, *Bibliographie des revues et journaux littéraires des XIXe et XXe siècles*, Paris, 1973, ii. 180–1.

[5] Iseler, *Débuts*, p. 18.

[6] *OC* ix. 175.

[7] Delay, *La Jeunesse d'André Gide*, i. 429.

[8] Iseler, pp. 23–5.

[9] Bibl. Doucet γ.1.33 (letter of 26 Feb. 1890).

[10] P. Louÿs, *Journal intime 1882–1891*, Éditions Montaigne, Paris, 1929, p. 292 (entry omitted in *OC* ix).

[11] *OC* ix. 290.

[12] Iseler, pp. 121–2, except first sentence (Bibl. Doucet γ.1.39).

[13] F. Lefèvre, *Entretiens avec Paul Valéry*, Paris, 1926, pp. 30–1.

[14] Iseler, p. 122 (letter of 4 June 1890).

[15] Ibid., p. 123 (26 June 1890). 'Allain' is the title of André Walter's novel.

[16] Ibid., pp. 127–8 (19 July 1890).

[17] Ibid.

[18] Librairie A. Blaizot et Fils, *Catalogue: Vente du 25 juin 1937*, no. 120, Paris, 1937.

[19] Valéry so described himself in his first letter to Mallarmé (*Lettres à quelques-uns*, p. 28).

[20] Blaizot, no. 127 (letter of 3 July 1890).

[21] Thus Valéry refers to Mallarmé in his letter of 2 June 1890 (ibid., no. 121).

[22] Ibid., no. 129. Valéry was then half-way through a year's military service, during which he was stationed at the Minimes Depot at Montpellier.

[23] Ibid., no. 121.

[24] Ibid., no. 123.

[25] P. Valéry, 'Pierre Louÿs (1870–1925)', *Les Nouvelles littéraires*, 13 June 1925.

[26] Blaizot, no. 125 (17 (?) June 1890).

[27] Ibid., no. 124 (16 June 1890).

[28] Ibid., no. 130 (16 July 1890).

[29] Ibid., no. 146 (28 Sept. 1890).

[30] Ibid., no. 147 (2 Oct. 1890).

[31] Ibid., no. 153 (24 Oct. 1890).

[32] Ibid., no. 143 (24 Sept. 1890).

[33] Ibid., no. 134 (31 July (?) 1890).

[34] Ibid., no. 141 (letter from Valéry dated 22 Sept. 1890) and no. 142 (undated letter from Louÿs).

[35] Valéry, *Lettres à quelques-uns*, pp. 25–6 (letter of 26 Sept. 1890).

[36] Ibid., p. 24.

[37] P. Léautaud, *Journal littéraire*, 19 vols., Paris, 1956–66, v. 343.

[38] See pp. 206–7 below.

[39] *OC* ix. 279.

[40] C. Mauclair, *Servitude et grandeur littéraires*, Paris, 1922, p. 46.

[41] Ibid., p. 48.

[42] *OC* ix. 276, 278.

[43] Ibid. 299–300.

[44] A. Fontainas, *Confession d'un poète*, Paris, 1936, p. 104.

[45] A. Gide, 'In Memoriam Stéphane Mallarmé', *Prétextes*, Paris, 1943, p. 120.

[46] Fontainas, p. 105.

[47] Ibid., p. 108.

[48] Gide, 'In Memoriam'.

[49] P. Fort, *Mes mémoires*, Paris, 1944, p. 58.

[50] A. Gide, 'Saint Mallarmé l'ésotérique', *Interviews imaginaires*, New York, 1943, p. 174.

[51] Mauclair, p. 51.

[52] Iseler, pp. 67–8 (18 June 1890).

[53] Ibid., p. 124.

[54] *OC* ix. 293.

[55] Blaizot, no. 130.

[56] Valéry, *Lettres à quelques-uns*, p. 19.

[57] H. Mondor, *Vie de Mallarmé*, Paris, 1941, p. 577 (letter of 22 Sept. 1890).

[58] *OC* ix. 294.

[59] Blaizot, no. 126 (22 June 1890).

[60] *OC* ix. 296.

[61] Bibl. Doucet γ.1.55.

[62] *OC* ix. 294 n. 1.

[63] Ibid. 299.

[64] Ibid. 300.

[65] Blaizot, no. 134.

[66] Bibl. Doucet γ.913. Like Gide himself, the fictional André Walter is greatly fascinated by the Grande Chartreuse—and deliberately forgoes the opportunity of a visit (*Les Cahiers et les poésies d'André Walter*, Paris, 1952, p. 110).

[67] Bibl. Doucet γ.1.40.

[68] *OC* ix. 306–7.

[69] M. Barrès, *Un Homme libre*, Paris, 1922, pp. xx, 157.

[70] Blaizot, no. 138 (9 Sept. 1890).

[71] Louÿs's diary contains a lengthy account of his retreat at the Grande Chartreuse, including a detailed discussion of these projects (*OC* ix. 303–30 and *Journal intime*, Paris, 1929, pp. 309–37).

[72] Blaizot, no. 138.

[73] Reproduced in the *Journal intime*, Paris, 1929, but not in *OC* ix.

[74] Delay, i. 457 n. 2.

[75] Iseler, pp. 132–3.

[76] Blaizot, no. 138 (9 Sept. 1890).

[77] Ibid.

[78] In 'Pierre Louÿs (1870–1925)'.

[79] *OC* ix. 322–3.

[80] Iseler, pp. 131–2.

[81] Ibid., pp. 96–7.

[82] *Si le grain ne meurt*, in *Journal 1939–1949. Souvenirs*, Paris, 1966, p. 523.

[83] Delay, i. 469, 470.

[84] *OC* ix. 341–3.

[85] Ibid., 349–51.

[86] M. Martin du Gard, *Les Mémorables*, 2 vols., Paris, 1957–60, i. 336.

[87] L. Pierre-Quint, *André Gide*, Paris, 1952, p. 486.

[88] *OC* ix. 352–3.

[89] Delay, i. 472.

[90] See p. 18 above.

[91] *Si le grain ne meurt*, p. 523.

[92] Bibl. Doucet γ.1.54.

[93] *OC* ix. 350.
[94] Bibl. Doucet γ.1.56.
[95] *OC* ix. 332.
[96] Ibid. 339.
[97] See *OC* xii. 99–102.
[98] Blaizot, no. 161 (5 Dec. 1890).
[99] *La Mêlée symboliste, 1ère partie: 1870–1890*, Paris, 1918, pp. 137–47.
[100] *OC* ix. 334.
[101] S. Mallarmé, *Correspondance IV (1890–1891)*, ed. H. Mondor and L. J. Austin, Paris, 1973, p. 146.
[102] *OC* ix. 334.
[103] H. Mondor, 'Le Premier Entretien Mallarmé–Valéry', in *Paul Valéry vivant*, Marseille, 1946, p. 59.
[104] Mondor, *Vie de Mallarmé*, p. 645.
[105] Ibid., p. 672.
[106] Cardinne-Petit, *Pierre Louÿs inconnu*, p. 86.
[107] *OC* ix. 355.
[108] *Si le grain ne meurt*, p. 535.
[109] *OC* ix. 293.
[110] P. Reboux, *Mes Mémoires*, Paris, 1956, p. 292.
[111] *Si le grain ne meurt*, p. 535.
[112] *OC* ix. 354 (28 Dec. 1890).
[113] See p. 45 above.
[114] *OC* ix. 353 (25 Nov. 1890).
[115] Ibid., 354. The date '9 décembre' has been omitted by mistake from the diary.
[116] C. Coulet and A. Faure, Paris, *Catalogue no. 138*, no. 725. See also A. Godoy, 'Pierre Louÿs et José-Maria de Heredia', *Mercure de Flandre*, Mar. 1928.
[117] Coulet and Faure, *Catalogue no. 138*, no. 125.
[118] Blaizot, no. 163. One of these three sonnets actually employs the rhyme 'dompteé/Thermondontée'.
[119] *Les Poëmes de Pierre Louÿs*, i. 343.
[120] F. Gregh, *L'Age d'or,* Paris, 1947, pp. 226–7.
[121] H. de Régnier, *Nos rencontres*, Paris, 1931, pp. 29–30.
[122] *Si le grain ne meurt*, pp. 532–3.
[123] Fontainas, p. 104.
[124] Bibl. Doucet γ.1.65 (letter to Gide of 21 Dec. 1890).
[125] Gregh, p. 231.
[126] Ibid., p. 232.
[127] Ibid., p. 231.
[128] Ibid., p. 232.
[129] *Biblis B* 35 (27 July 1892).
[130] H. Mondor, *Les Premiers Temps d'une amitié: André Gide et Paul Valéry*, Monaco, 1947, p. 93.
[131] Ibid., pp. 93–4.
[132] Ibid., p. 9.
[133] Ibid., p. 16.
[134] Ibid., p. 143.
[135] In his diary, Gide wrote in 1893: 'J'ai vécu jusqu'à vingt-trois ans complètement vierge et dépravé . . .' (*Journal 1889–1939*, p. 33).
[136] *OC* ix. 269–75 (14 Apr. 1890).
[137] Ibid., 272.
[138] Blaizot, no. 163 (12 Dec. 1890). In his diary he had written: 'Qu'importe ce que fait le corps, si l'âme n'y consent pas' (*OC* ix. 273–4).

[139] *Lettres à quelques-uns*, p. 41 (21 Dec. 1890).

1891

[1] *Si le grain ne meurt*, p. 532.
[2] Ibid.
[3] *André Gide–Paul Valéry. Correspondance 1890–1942*, ed. R. Mallet, Paris, 1955, p. 64 (7 Mar. 1891).
[4] *Si le grain ne meurt*, p. 533.
[5] *Gide–Valéry Corresp.*, p. 64.
[6] Iseler, *Débuts*, p. 75.
[7] See H. P. Clive, 'Oscar Wilde's first meeting with Mallarmé', *French Studies*, Apr. 1970.
[8] *Gide–Valéry Corresp.*, pp. 46–7.
[9] Mondor, *Vie de Mallarmé*, p. 595.
[10] J. Canqueteau, '*La Conque* et *le Centaure*', *Les Nouvelles littéraires*, 13 June 1925.
[11] Bibl. Doucet γ.1.31.
[12] R. H. Sherard, *The Real Oscar Wilde* [London], 1915, pp. 38–9.
[13] For further details of *La Conque* see Place and Vasseur, *Bibliographie des revues et journaux littéraires* ii. 179–93; A. Vasseur, *Collection André Vasseur*, Paris, 1974, p. 30; H. P. Clive, 'Notes on *La Conque* and on the Early Friendship of Pierre Louÿs and Paul Valéry', *Studi Francesi*, Jan.–Apr. 1974; and the documents preserved under call number Rés.m.Ye.608 at the Bibliothèque nationale.
[14] P. Valéry, 'Sur les *Narcisse*', *Paul Valéry vivant*, p. 289.
[15] Mondor, *Les Premiers Temps d'une amitié*, pp. 125–6.
[16] *OC* ix. 47.
[17] Ibid., 149.
[18] Ibid., 363. This is the final entry in Louÿs's diary, at any rate of the published version.
[19] *Biblis B* 68. (7 Nov. 1894).
[20] *Biblis A* 81.
[21] *Gide–Valéry Corresp.*, p. 96.
[22] Iseler, pp. 72–3.
[23] *Gide–Valéry Corresp.*, p. 97.
[24] Ibid., pp. 97–8.
[25] Ibid., p. 98.
[26] Ibid.
[27] Ibid., p. 102.
[28] Gide, *Journal 1889–1939*, p. 22.
[29] *Gide–Valéry Corresp.*, p. 106.
[30] Gide, *Journal 1889–1939*, p. 22.
[31] *Gide–Valéry Corresp.*, p. 99 (cf. also pp. 42–3).
[32] Iseler, p. 27 (for Gide's reply to 'Emmanuèle', see ibid., pp. 27–8).
[33] Ibid., pp. 30–1.
[34] *Biblis A* 6.
[35] Ibid. 7.
[36] *Si le grain ne meurt*, p. 540.
[37] *Biblis B* 16.
[38] Ibid. 18 (6 Aug. 1891), *Biblis A* 8 (7 Aug. 1891).
[39] *Pierre Louÿs inconnu*, pp. 227–8.
[40] *Biblis A* 11 (7 Aug. 1891).
[41] Ibid. 9 ([13] Aug. 1891).
[42] Iseler, p. 29.

[43] Delay, *La Jeunesse d'André Gide*, ii. 59.
[44] Bibl. Doucet γ.913.
[45] Ibid.
[46] Ibid.
[47] Ibid. γ.1.107.
[48] Delay, ii. 68.
[49] Bibl. Doucet γ.913.
[50] See p. 62 above.
[51] *Gide–Valéry Corresp.*, p. 134.
[52] *Si le grain ne meurt*, p. 531. For a further discussion of this ambiguous language see pp. 82–4 below.
[53] On 16 September Louÿs had attended a performance of *Lohengrin* at the Opéra ('Triomphe! ... Ah! quelle soirée!—on va donc pouvoir enfin entendre de la musique sans payer mille francs pour aller en Bavière ...'—*Biblis A* 20, 17 Sept. 1891).
[54] Mallarmé, *Correspondance IV*, p. 318 n.1.
[55] Title of book published by Henri Mondor in Lausanne in 1947.
[56] Lausanne, 1947, pp. 25–6. See also J.-R. Lawler, 'Saint Mallarmé', *Yale French Studies*, 1970.
[57] *Gide–Valéry Corresp.*, p. 137.
[58] Ibid., p. 134.
[59] Librairie L. Carteret, *Manuscrits de Pierre Louÿs et de divers auteurs contemporains*, Paris, 1926, No. 4.
[60] *OC* ix. 102.
[61] Ibid. 129.
[62] Ibid. 239.
[63] See *Les Poëmes de Pierre Louÿs*, ii. 704–9, 844–7.
[64] *OC* ix. 128 n.3.
[65] Ibid. 237 n.1.
[66] According to the *Écho de Paris* of 19 Dec. 1891. Mallarmé, in a letter to Whistler on 23 December, refers somewhat maliciously to the 'réclame prodigieuse autour d'O.W'. (*Mallarmé–Whistler: Correspondance*, ed. C. P. Barbier, Paris, 1964, p. 104).
[67] *The Letters of Oscar Wilde*, ed. R. Hart-Davis, London, 1962, pp. 298–9.
[68] 'In Memoriam Oscar Wilde', *Prétextes*, p. 126.
[69] *Letters of Oscar Wilde*, p. 299 n.1.
[70] See F. J. L. Mouret, 'La Première Rencontre d'André Gide et d'Oscar Wilde', *French Studies*, Jan. 1968.
[71] Delay, ii. 132–3.
[72] *Gide–Valéry Corresp.*, pp. 141–2.
[73] Ibid., p. 139.
[74] Delay, ii, Ch. 7.
[75] *Si le grain ne meurt*, p. 588.
[76] E. Lockspeiser, *Debussy. His Life and Mind*, 2 vols., London, 1962–5, i. 177.
[77] *Letters of Oscar Wilde*, pp. 305–6.
[78] E. Raynaud, *La Mêlée symboliste. 2e partie: 1890–1900*, Paris, 1920, p. 135.

1892

[1] *Les Poëmes de Pierre Louÿs*, ii. 856.
[2] In 1924 Besnard became the first painter to be elected to the French Academy.
[3] *OC* ix. 51.
[4] Ibid. 189.

5 Ibid. 219.

6 *Les Poëmes de Pierre Loüÿs*, ii. 621, 790.

7 Ibid. 604–7.

8 Ibid. i. 307.

9 Blaizot, no. 120.

10 *Les Poëmes de Pierre Loüÿs*, ii. 615, 699.

11 Ibid. i. 206–7.

12 *Corresp. Debussy–Loüÿs*, p. 76. Debussy's interest in Rossetti's poetry had previously led him to compose the cantata *La Demoiselle élue*, inspired by 'The Blessed Damozel'.

13 Ibid.

14 Coulet and Faure, *Catalogue 138*, no. 577.

15 *OC* ix. 363.

16 Concerning this planned special number, see *Gide–Valéry Corresp.*, p. 154; also H. P. Clive, 'Notes on *La Conque*'.

17 Bibl. Doucet γ.1.127.

18 Ibid. 128.

19 H. de Régnier, *Lettres à André Gide (1891–1911)*, ed. D. J. Niederauer, Geneva, 1972, p. 29 n.1.

20 Ibid., p. 28.

21 *Gide–Valéry Corresp.*, p. 165.

22 *Biblis A* 24 [21 June 1892].

23 Ibid. 31.

24 *Letters of Oscar Wilde*, p. 337.

25 Fleury, *Pierre Loüÿs et Gilbert de Voisins*, Paris, 1973, p. 200.

26 *Letters of Oscar Wilde*, p. 315, and *Biblis A* 23 (14 June 1892).

27 *Biblis A* 27 (28 June 1892).

28 Ibid. 26 [23 or 30 June 1892].

29 Ibid. 28 (1 July 1892).

30 Ibid. 29.

31 Ibid. 31 [8 July 1892].

32 *Si le grain ne meurt*, p. 583.

33 See R. Lhombreaud, 'Une Amitié anglaise de Pierre Louÿs. Onze lettres inédites à John Gray', *Revue de littérature comparée*, July–Sept. 1953.

34 *Letters of Oscar Wilde*, p. 316.

35 *OC* ix. 153.

36 Ibid. 163.

37 *Pierre Loüÿs inconnu*, p. 68.

38 See pp. 67–8 above.

39 Delay. *La Jeunesse d'André Gide*, ii. 175.

40 *Gide–Valéry Corresp.*, p. 167 (25 July 1892).

41 Delay, ii. 175.

42 Bibl. Doucet γ.913 (only the first and last sentences are quoted in Delay, ii. 175).

43 Bibl. Doucet γ.1. 136.

44 Bibl. Doucet γ.913 (25 July 1892).

45 Delay, ii. 175 n. 6.

46 C. Farrère, *Mon ami Pierre Loüÿs*, Paris, 1954, p. 46.

47 *Biblis A* 30 (July 1892).

48 Ibid. 31.

49 *Biblis B* 36 (end July 1892).

50 Ibid. 37.

51 *Biblis A* 37.

52 *Biblis B* 29 (1 Sept. 1892: not 1891, as stated in the catalogue).

[53] *Biblis A* 39.

[54] Ibid. 33.

[55] Iseler, *Débuts*, p. 34.

[56] Ibid., p. 35.

[57] Delay, ii. 180. When, in 1928, Gide reread Louÿs's letters, he judged them to be almost totally lacking in interest: 'Ressorti la correspondance de Louÿs pour la faire "taper". Consterné par sa niaiserie, sa puérilité, sa scurrilité, son insignifiance . . . Parmi ce terrible fatras, intéressant tout au plus pour marquer les continuelles sautes de son humeur, à grand'peine je trouve quelques pages qui me paraissent mériter d'etre sauvées. (Je suis convaincu, du reste, que mes lettres à Pierre sont tout aussi décevantes)', (*Journal 1889–1939*, p. 882). Nevertheless, Gide published several of Louÿs's letters in the *Nouvelle Revue française* in Nov.–Dec. 1929.

[58] Iseler, p. 38.

[59] Delay, ii. 180–1.

[60] Bibl. Doucet γ.1. 155 (15 Oct. 1892).

[61] Delay, ii, 54 n. 2.

[62] 'Pierre Louÿs (1870–1925)'.

[63] J.-É. Blanche, 'La Jeunesse de Pierre Louÿs. Gide et Louÿs à l'École alsacienne. Louÿs et Claude Debussy', *Les Nouvelles littéraires*, 13 June 1925.

[64] Lockspeiser, *Debussy. His Life and Mind*, i. 160–1.

[65] According to Gide's letter to Jeanne Rondeaux of 23 Nov. 1892 (Delay, ii. 190).

1893

[1] Delay, *Le Jeunesse d'André Gide*, ii. 219.

[2] Ibid.

[3] Bibl. Doucet γ.913 (Delay, ii. 220 gives all but the first sentence).

[4] *Letters of Oscar Wilde*, p. 325.

[5] Ibid., pp. 334–5. The text of Louÿs's telegram is not known.

[6] *Biblis A* 32 [*c.* 20–1 Apr. 1893].

[7] *Biblis B* 33.

[8] In actual fact Wilde had only two sons.

[9] E. and J. de Goncourt, *Journal. Mémoires de la vie littéraire*, 4 vols., Paris, 1956, iv. 395. The hotel referred to by Régnier was probably not the Savoy, but the Albemarle.

[10] Sherard, *The Real Oscar Wilde*, pp. 41–2.

[11] *Si le grain ne meurt*, p. 583.

[12] Ibid., p. 589.

[13] *Letters of Oscar Wilde*, p. 410.

[14] G. de Saix, 'Oscar Wilde et Pierre Louÿs d'après des documents nouveaux', *Vendémiaire*, 18 Aug. 1937.

[15] *Mon ami Pierre Louÿs*, p. 44.

[16] This letter, formerly the property of the late Henri Mondor, can now be consulted in the Bibliothèque Doucet (MNR.α.635). It confirms the suggestion I made, on the basis of other evidence, in an article published in 1969 that the quarrel probably took place during the period around 25 May 1893 ('Pierre Louÿs and Oscar Wilde. A Chronicle of their Friendship', *Revue de littérature comparée*, July–Sept. 1969).

[17] Lhombreaud, 'Une Amitié anglaise de Pierre Louÿs' (concerning the date of this letter, see the article cited in the preceding note).

[18] Carteret, *Manuscrits de Pierre Louÿs*, no. 12.
[19] M. D. Camacho, *Judith Gautier. Sa vie et son œuvre*, Paris, 1939, pp. 108-9.
[20] *Biblis A* 57.
[21] See *Gide-Valéry Corresp.*, p. 185.
[22] *Disques et pellicules*, p. 219.
[23] *Gide-Valéry Corresp.*, p. 188.
[24] Ibid.
[25] Ibid., p. 189.
[26] 'Claude Debussy. Lettres inédites à Ernest Chausson', *La Revue musicale*, 1 Dec. 1925.
[27] *Corresp. Debussy-Louÿs*, p. 30 n. 1 (letter to Georges of 20 Apr. 1914).
[28] *Biblis A* 58 bis.
[29] According to Farrère's preface to *Les Chansons de Bilitis*, Paris, 1934.
[30] *Biblis A* 58 bis.
[31] A. Lebey, 'Quelques paroles sur l'auteur d'*Aphrodite*', *Comœdia*, 6 June 1925.
[32] Lebey, *Jean de Tinan. Souvenirs et Correspondance*, p. 8.
[33] Lebey was also for many years a socialist deputy, dubbed 'le citoyen Brummel' by Jaurès because of his sartorial elegance (Martin du Gard, *Les Mémorables* i.51).
[34] Lebey, *Jean de Tinan*, p. 8.
[35] Rachilde, *Portraits d'hommes*, Paris, 1930, pp. 121-33 (section on Tinan).
[36] Mauclair, *Servitude et grandeur littéraires*, p. 42.
[37] Rachilde, loc. cit.
[38] Mauclair, loc. cit.
[39] F. Jammes, *Les Caprices du poète*, Paris, 1923, pp. 16-17.
[40] Printed in *OC* iii.

1894

[1] *Disques et pellicules*, p. 222.
[2] *Biblis A* 64.
[3] *Biblis B* 61 (14 Mar. 1894).
[4] *OC* x (frontispiece).
[5] *OC* i. 171.
[6] Ibid. 169-74.
[7] *OC* xii. 18.
[8] *Gide-Valéry Corresp.*, p. 189.
[9] *Biblis B* 59.
[10] Ibid. 60.
[11] *Biblis A* 66.
[12] Autograph reproduced in Fleury, *Pierre Louÿs et Gilbert de Voisins*.
[13] *Biblis A* 74 (5 Jan. 1895).
[14] *Corresp. Debussy-Louÿs*, p. 35.
[15] *Si le grain ne meurt*, p. 573.
[16] Iseler, *Débuts*, pp. 22-3.
[17] Ibid., p. 58.
[18] Bibl. Doucet γ.1.191 (20 Jan. 1894).
[19] Iseler, p. 21.
[20] Librairie Charavay, Paris, *Catalogue 736*, no. 33576.
[21] *Biblis B* 63 (13 July 1894).
[22] Iseler, p. 116.

[23] This nickname is mentioned in L. Pierre-Quint, *André Gide*, p. 486.

[24] Delay, *La Jeunesse d'André Gide*, ii. 344–5.

[25] *Si le grain ne meurt*, p. 573.

[26] Ibid., p. 574. Gide spells her name 'Mériem', Louÿs 'Méryem'.

[27] Iseler, pp. 109–10.

[28] *Corresp. Debussy–Louÿs*, p. 40 n.1.

[29] Bibl. Doucet γ.1.221.

[30] See pp. 59–61 above.

[31] Biblis A 69 (not 23 Oct. as stated in the catalogue).

[32] *Corresp. Debussy–Louÿs*, p. 33.

[33] *Biblis B* 66 (4 Nov. 1894).

[34] Ibid. 72.

[35] Ibid.

[36] Bibl. Doucet γ.1.225.

[37] *Biblis B* 70 (12 Nov. 1894).

[38] *Biblis A* 70.

[39] Ibid.

[40] Ibid. 73 (28 Dec. 1894).

[41] *Biblis B* 72.

[42] Letter of 5 May 1898 (E. Lockspeiser, 'Neuf lettres de Pierre Louÿs à Debussy (1894–1898)', *Revue de musicologie*, July–Dec. 1962).

[43] Librairie Charavay, *Catalogue 736*, no. 33576.

[44] Iseler, p. 11.

[45] Bibl. Doucet γ.1.236.

[46] *Biblis A* 73.

[47] Coulet and Faure, *Catalogue 138*, no. 729.

[48] *OC* ii. 199.

[49] Coulet and Faure, loc. cit.

[50] Reprinted in the same author's *Sappho und Simonides. Untersuchungen über griechische Lyriker*, Berlin, 1913.

1895

[1] *Biblis A* 75.

[2] Ibid.

[3] Ibid.

[4] See *OC* xii: 'Projets et fragments'.

[5] *Biblis A* 77.

[6] Ibid. 76.

[7] Ibid. 77.

[8] *Gide–Valéry Corresp.*, pp. 230–1.

[9] Ibid., p. 231.

[10] Ibid., p. 234.

[11] *Biblis A* 78.

[12] Iseler, *Débuts*, p. 112 (12 Mar. 1895).

[13] *Gide–Valéry Corresp.*, p. 234.

[14] Ibid., pp. 233–6.

[15] Pp. 604–6.

[16] Delay, *La Jeunesse d'André Gide*, ii. 480–1.

[17] *Biblis A* 78.

[18] Delay, ii. 477.

[19] See ibid. 458–9.

20 Ibid. It is significant that one of the faults Gide singled out for condemnation in Louÿs, after their quarrel in Algiers, should have been 'la peur de paraître ce qu'il est ou ce qu'il n'est pas' (*Gide–Valéry Corresp.*, p. 234).

21 *Journal 1889–1939*, p. 882.

22 *Gide–Valéry Corresp.*, p. 235.

23 Bibl. Doucet γ.1.244.

24 'La Fin d'une amitié. La Dernière Lettre d'André Gide à Pierre Louÿs', *Bulletin des amis d'André Gide*, Apr. 1973.

25 Blanche, 'La Jeunesse de Pierre Louÿs . . .'

26 *Journal 1889–1939*, p. 1034.

27 *Letters of Oscar Wilde*, pp. 390–1.

28 H. M. Hyde, *The Trials of Oscar Wilde*, London, 1948, p. 118. See also Clive, 'Pierre Louÿs and Oscar Wilde'.

29 Coulet and Faure, *Catalogue 103*, no. 318.

30 *Biblis A* 80.

31 Ibid. 81.

32 Ibid. 82.

33 Bibl. Doucet MNR.a.603.

34 F. Lachèvre, *Pierre Louÿs et l'histoire littéraire* [Paris], 1928, p. 144.

35 *Biblis A* 82.

36 *Corresp. Debussy–Louÿs*, p. 59.

37 Ibid.

38 *Biblis A* 84 (6 Aug. 1895).

39 Ibid. 86 (21 Aug. 1895).

40 *Corresp. Debussy–Louÿs*, p. 62 n.1.

41 *Biblis A* 89.

42 *Biblis B* 84.

43 Librairie Andrieux, Paris, *Catalogue 16–17 December 1963*, no. 115.

44 F. Jammes, *L'Amour, les muses et la chasse*, Paris, 1922, pp. 186–7.

45 *Corresp. Debussy–Louÿs*, pp. 64–5.

46 Ibid., pp. 68–9.

47 Ibid., p. 72.

48 Ibid., p. 122.

49 *Biblis B* 86.

50 Quoted by Henri Kistemaeckers in the special number of *Le Capitole* devoted to Louÿs in 1925.

Years of Fame: 1896–1901

1896

1 *Biblis A* 93 (12 Jan. 1896).

2 *Gide–Valéry Corresp.*, p. 257.

3 *Biblis A* 94.

4 Ibid. 91 (4 Dec. 1895).

5 Librairie Andrieux, *Catalogue 15 June 1964*, no. 44.

6 Ibid.

7 Ibid.

8 *Biblis A* 90 (12 Nov. 1895).

9 Ibid 95 (29 Jan. 1895).

10 Ibid.

11 Ibid. 96.

12 Ibid. 99.

13 Ibid. 98.

[14] Ibid. 99.

[15] T. Sandre, in 'Hommage à Pierre Louÿs', *Le Journal littéraire*, 13 June 1925.

[16] See Appendix.

[17] Librairie Andrieux, *Catalogue 15 June 1964*, no. 45 (letter to Georges Louis, 20 Apr. 1896).

[18] *Catalogue Bibliothèque Sforza*, 1933, no. 486.

[19] *OC* xii, p. lxvi.

[20] Lebey, *Jean de Tinan. Souvenirs et Correspondance*, p. 48.

[21] Cardinne-Petit, *Pierre Louÿs inconnu*, p. 77.

[22] A. Samain, *Des lettres 1887–1900*, ed. J. Monval, Paris, 1933, p. 92, n. 1.

[23] Librairie Andrieux, *Catalogue 15 June 1964*, no. 45.

[24] *Biblis A* 100 (29 Apr. 1896).

[25] A. Vallette, in 'Hommage à Pierre Louÿs', *Comœdia*, 6 June 1925.

[26] Colette, *L'Étoile Vesper. Souvenirs*, Paris, 1946, p. 131.

[27] The text of A. de Monzie's speech was printed in *Le Tombeau de Pierre Louÿs*, Paris, 1925, pp. 11–16.

[28] *Biblis A* 100.

[29] 'Lettres inédites d'Anatole France', *Revue de Paris*, May 1945.

[30] *Biblis A* 100.

[31] Ibid. 101.

[32] Librairie Andrieux, *Catalogue 15 June 1964*, no. 44.

[33] *Gide–Valéry Corresp.*, p. 265.

[34] Iseler, *Débuts*, p. 116.

[35] Librairie Andrieux, *Catalogue 16–17 December 1963*, no. 116.

[36] *Biblis A* 105 (2 Sept. 1896).

[37] *Corresp. Debussy–Louÿs*, p. 82.

[38] *Biblis A* 107 (14 Sept. 1896).

[39] *Biblis B* 88 (24 Sept. 1896).

[40] Coulet and Faure, *Catalogue 103*, no. 319.

[41] Librairie Andrieux, *Catalogue 16–17 December 1963*, no. 115.

[42] *Biblis A* 112.

[43] Ibid.

[44] *Biblis B* 92 (15 Nov. 1896).

[45] Librairie Andrieux, *Catalogue 16–17 December 1963*, no. 117.

[46] Y. Guilbert, *Mes lettres d'amour*, Paris, 1933, pp. 179–80.

[47] Librairie Andrieux, *Catalogue 16–17 December 1963*, no. 117.

[48] *Biblis A* 111.

[49] Ibid. 113.

[50] Ibid. 114 (18 Dec. 1896).

1897

[1] *Biblis A* 117.

[2] Librairie B. Loliée, Paris, *Catalogue 1967*, no. 25.

[3] *Biblis A* 116 (11 Jan. 1897).

[4] Ibid. 121 (19 Feb. 1897).

[5] Ibid.

[6] Ibid. 122.

[7] Ibid. 128.

[8] Ibid. 124 (20 Mar. 1897).

[9] *OC* viii. 42. See also *Biblis A* 125 (22 Mar. 1897).

[10] *Biblis A* 127 (19 Apr. 1897).

[11] Ibid.

[12] *Biblis B* 95.

[13] *Biblis A* 128.

[14] Ibid.

[15] *Gide–Valéry Corresp.*, p. 294.

[16] *OC* viii. 44.

[17] Fleury, *Pierre Louÿs et Gilbert de Voisins*, p. 25.

[18] *Corresp. Debussy–Louÿs*, p. 95.

[19] Ibid., p. 94.

[20] Ibid., p. 97.

[21] See p. 165 below.

[22] *Corresp. Debussy–Louÿs*, pp. 100–2.

[23] Ibid., p. 102 n.1.

[24] Ibid., p. 122 n.2.

[25] *OC* viii. 45.

[26] Draft of letter to Georges Louis, quoted in *Les Poëmes de Pierre Louÿs*, ii. 822.

[27] From MS. reproduced in Fleury, op. cit.

[28] Ibid., p. 29.

[29] 'Quatre lettres inédites de Pierre Louÿs', *Mercure de Flandre*, Mar. 1928.

[30] Fernand Xau was the editor of *Le Journal*.

[31] *Corresp. Debussy–Louÿs*, p. 107 n.1.

[32] Fleury, pp. 30–1.

1898

[1] U. Ojetti, *Cose Viste*, Florence, 1960, pp. 637–8.

[2] Fleury, *Pierre Louÿs et Gilbert de Voisins*, p. 31.

[3] Quoted in C. Sicard, 'Jean de Tinan. Lettres à Madame Bulteau', unpublished doctoral dissertation, Univ. of Toulouse, 1968, pp. 411–12.

[4] Mme Bulteau was herself an author and journalist (she published frequent articles in *Le Figaro* under the pseudonym 'Fœmina').

[5] H. Martineau, *P.-J. Toulet, Jean de Tinan, et Mme Bulteau*, Paris, 1958, p. 28.

[6] Fleury, pp. 33–4.

[7] Sicard, pp. 412–13.

[8] Fleury, p. 35.

[9] Ibid., p. 39.

[10] Mondor, *Vie de Mallarmé*, p. 802.

[11] *Les Poëmes de Pierre Louÿs*, i. 334.

[12] Mondor, *Vie de Mallarmé*, p. 754.

[13] Fleury, p. 53 n.10.

[14] Martineau, p. 37.

[15] Sicard, p. 411.

[16] *OC* ix. 38 n.4.

[17] *OC* viii. 165–6.

[18] *Les Poëmes de Pierre Louÿs*, i. 374. For the complete text of the 'Pervigilium Mortis' see ibid. 125–30.

[19] Ibid. 377–8.

[20] Ibid. 375.

[21] *Biblis A* 101.

[22] Fleury, p. 43.

[23] *Biblis A* 133.
[24] Fleury, p. 49.
[25] Ibid., pp. 45–6.

1899

[1] *Corresp. Debussy–Louÿs*, pp. 126–7.
[2] *Biblis A* 126 (9 Apr. 1897).
[3] Fleury, *Pierre Louÿs et Gilbert de Voisins*, pp. 58–9.
[4] Ibid., p. 64 n.9.
[5] Ibid., p. 181.
[6] *Les Poëmes de Pierre Louÿs*, i. 428.
[7] *Corresp. Debussy–Louÿs*, p. 129.
[8] Coulet and Faure, *Catalogue 138*, no. 691.
[9] It was reprinted in his *Poussières de Paris*, Paris, 1902.
[10] J. Monval, 'Pierre Louÿs et François Coppée', *Mercure de Flandre*, Mar. 1928.
[11] This frequently cited reason for the absence of a religious ceremony was apparently confirmed by Lilly herself (L. Vallas, *Claude Debussy et son temps*, Paris, 1958, pp. 200–1).
[12] Fleury, p. 70.
[13] *OC* vii. 65–6.
[14] *Disques et pellicules*, p. 216.
[15] F. Gregh, 'Solitude . . . Fierté . . .', *Le Tombeau de Pierre Louÿs*, Paris, 1925, p. 72.

1900

[1] See p. 133 above.
[2] *Corresp. Debussy–Louÿs*, pp. 142–3.
[3] Ibid., p. 144.
[4] Vallas, *Debussy et son temps*, pp. 192–3.
[5] *Biblis A* 139.
[6] *Corresp. Debussy–Louÿs*, p. 149.
[7] *Biblis A* 140.
[8] Ibid. 142.
[9] *Gide–Valéry Corresp.*, p. 376 (this letter must have been written in September 1900, not October, as stated by Gide).
[10] Ibid., p. 375.
[11] *Biblis A* 143 (24 [not 22, as stated in the catalogue] Sept. 1900).
[12] *Biblis B* 96 ([26] (post-mark 28) Sept. 1900).
[13] *Biblis A* 144.
[14] *Gide–Valéry Corresp.*, p. 259.
[15] *Biblis B* 97.
[16] Ibid. 99.
[17] *Corresp. Debussy–Louÿs*, p. 150.
[18] Fleury, *Pierre Louÿs et Gilbert de Voisins*, p. 74. (letters of 2 and 8 Feb. 1900).
[19] Fleury, p. 84.
[20] The three articles are reprinted in *OC* xi. 99–137.
[21] *Biblis A* 146 (11 Dec. 1900).

1901

1 *Biblis B* 100.
2 *Biblis A* 147.
3 Ibid.
4 *Corresp. Debussy–Louÿs*, pp. 150–1.
5 Fleury, *Pierre Louÿs et Gilbert de Voisins*, p. 102 and *Biblis A* 166 (12 Jan. 1902).
6 *Biblis B* 105.
7 *Biblis A* 156.
8 Ibid. 158.
9 Ibid. 162.
10 *Biblis B* 121.
11 *Pierre Louÿs inconnu*, p. 166.
12 Fleury, p. 213.
13 Ibid., p. 72 n.13.
14 *Les Poëmes de Pierre Louÿs*, i, 428.
15 Cardinne-Petit, p. 102.
16 *Biblis A* 165.
17 *Corresp. Debussy–Louÿs*, p. 168.
18 *Biblis B* 116 (11 Dec. 1901).
19 Ibid. 118.
20 Ibid. 119 (23 Dec. 1901).
21 Ibid. 120.
22 *Biblis A* 187.

Twilight Years: 1902–1919

1 Cardinne-Petit, *Pierre Louÿs inconnu*, p. 252.
2 *Biblis A* 170 (30 Mar. 1902).
3 Ibid. 171.
4 Ibid. 173 (post-mark 30 Apr. 1902).
5 Ibid. 112 (4 Nov. 1896).
6 *Biblis B* 180 [1905?].
7 *Biblis A* 200.
8 *OC* x, frontispiece.
9 *Biblis A* 207 (15 Aug. 1905).
10 E. Gaubert, in 'Le Souvenir de Pierre Louÿs', *Le Figaro. Supplément littéraire*, 13 June 1925.
11 *Souvenirs littéraires et gastronomiques*, Paris, 1958, pp. 89–90.
12 Lockspeiser, 'Neuf lettres de Pierre Louÿs à Debussy'.
13 Cardinne-Petit, p. 176.
14 *Corresp. Debussy–Louÿs*, p. 170.
15 Ibid.
16 Ibid., p. 110.
17 Ibid., p. 173.
18 Librairies Charavay and Cornuau, Paris, *Catalogue Alfred Dupont. Autographes, 1ᵉ partie, 11–12 December 1956*, no. 224.
19 R. Peter, 'Claude Debussy. Vues prises de son intimité', *Les Œuvres libres*, 1931.
20 Gap, 1949, pp. 165–75.
21 Cardinne-Petit, p. 177.

[22] A. Lebey, 'Le Captif immortel . . .', *Le Tombeau de Pierre Louÿs*, pp. 56–7.

[23] Farrère, *Mon ami Pierre Louÿs*, p. 183.

[24] Cardinne-Petit, photocopy facing p. 17.

[25] Farrère, *Mon ami Pierre Louÿs*, p. 146.

[26] *Biblis A* 186 (18 June 1903).

[27] Coulet and Faure, *Catalogue 138*, no. 744.

[28] *OC* viii. 190.

[29] Fleury, *Pierre Louÿs et Gilbert de Voisins*, p. 108.

[30] *OC* viii. 203–4.

[31] Farrère, *Mon ami Pierre Louÿs*, p. 170.

[32] Fleury, p. 162.

[33] *OC* viii. 175–6.

[34] Cardinne-Petit, pp. 171–3.

[35] See pp. 151–2 above.

[36] J. Thorhauer, in 'Le Souvenir de Pierre Louÿs', *Le Figaro. Supplément Littéraire*, 13 June 1925.

[37] *Corresp. Debussy–Louÿs*, p. 122 n.2. Cf. also *OC* iv. 6.

[38] M. Carner, *Puccini. A Critical Biography*, London, 1958, p. 114.

[39] M. Garden and L. Biancolli, *Mary Garden's Story*, London, 1952, p. 95.

[40] Ibid.

[41] M. Prawy, *Die Wiener Oper*, Vienna, 1969, p. 96.

[42] V. Seligman, *Puccini among Friends*, London, 1938, p. 66.

[43] G. R. Marek, *Puccini*, London, 1952, p. 66.

[44] *Biblis A* 218 (12 July 1906).

[45] Op. cit., p. 144.

[46] T. Zandonai Tarquini, *Da 'Via del Paradiso al No 1'*, Rovereto, 1955, p. 131.

[47] *OC* v. 6.

[48] Fleury, p. 160 n.20.

[49] *Biblis A* 231 (18 Mar. 1914).

[50] *OC* v. 181.

[51] *Biblis A* 231.

[52] Fleury, pp. 122, 144.

[53] Ibid., p. 158.

[54] Ibid., p. 103.

[55] *Biblis B* 157.

[56] *Biblis A* 206.

[57] Ibid. 167.

[58] Lachèvre, *Pierre Louÿs et l'histoire littéraire*, p. 70.

[59] *Biblis B* 129 (post-mark 4 Oct. 1902).

[60] Ibid. 130 (12 Oct. 1902).

[61] F. Lachèvre, *Pierre Louÿs et l'histoire littéraire. Lettres à Frédéric Lachèvre (1907–1921)* [Paris], 1925, p. vi.

[62] Ibid., p. v. Lachèvre dedicated the bibliography to Louÿs.

[63] F. Lachèvre, *Nouvelles glanes bibliographiques et littéraires*, Paris, 1933, p. 264.

[64] *Biblis A* 178.

[65] Ibid. 180 (post-mark 3 Dec. 1902).

[66] Farrère, *Mon ami Pierre Louÿs*, pp. 101–3.

[67] É. Henriot, 'Quand il parlait de ses livres . . .', *Le Tombeau de Pierre Louÿs*, p. 312.

[68] *Lettres à F. Lachèvre*, p. v.

[69] Farrère, *Mon ami Pierre Louÿs*, p. 39.

[70] F. Gregh, *L'Age de fer*, Paris, 1956, pp. 39, 41.

[71] F. Lachèvre, 'Lettres et Notes inédites de Pierre Louÿs', *Mercure de France*, 15 Oct. 1932.

[72] Carteret, *Manuscrits de Pierre Louÿs*, no. 32.

[73] Coulet and Faure, *Catalogue 138*, no. 686. For details of that 'affair' see pp. 210–1 below.

[74] Henriot, 'Quand il parlait de ses livres . . .'.

[75] Lachèvre, *Pierre Louÿs et l'histoire littéraire*, pp. 57–79.

[76] Farrère, *Mon ami Pierre Louÿs*, p. 98.

[77] Polaire, *Polaire par elle-même*, Paris, 1933, p. 174.

[78] Gregh, *L'Age d'or*, p. 232.

[79] *Lettres à F. Lachèvre*, p. 75.

[80] Fleury, p. 173.

[81] Ibid., p. 176.

[82] Librairies Charavay and Cornuau, *Catalogue A. Dupont. Autographes, 3e partie, 3–4 December 1958*, no 201.

[83] Farrère, *Mon ami Pierre Louÿs*, p. 176.

[84] Farrère, *Souvenirs*, Paris, 1953, p. 75.

[85] Fleury, p. 181.

[86] Farrère, *Souvenirs*, p. 73.

[87] Fleury, p. 180.

[88] Ibid., pp. 181–2.

[89] *Les Poëmes de Pierre Louÿs*, ii. 825.

[90] *Biblis A* 235.

[91] From copy, in Louÿs's handwriting, of his letter to Moriane of 13 May 1914 (in the author's possession).

[92] Librairies Charavay and Cornuau, *Catalogue A. Dupont. Autographes, 3e partie*, no. 202.

[93] Farrère, *Mon ami Pierre Louÿs*, p. 179.

[94] Louÿs left Paris for Bordeaux on 27 August. In Bordeaux he resided at the Hôtel Montré, 10 rue Montesquieu.

[95] *Biblis A* 260.

[96] P. Leclercq, *Paradis perdus*, Paris, 1931, pp. 89–90.

[97] Coulet and Faure, *Catalogue 138*, no. 692.

[98] Leclercq, pp. 93–4.

[99] Ibid., p. 97.

[100] Cardinne-Petit, p. 116.

[101] Ibid.

[102] Farrère, *Mon ami Pierre Louÿs*, p. 107.

[103] Aline was three years younger than Claudine (she had been born on 25 Nov. 1895, Claudine on 19 June 1892).

[104] Cf. p. 197 above.

[105] Lachèvre, 'Lettres et notes inédites de Pierre Louÿs'. It is not known whether Louÿs actually sent the letter to Lebey.

[106] Note on the final page.

[107] *Les Poëmes de Pierre Louÿs*, i. 282.

[108] *Pierre Louÿs inconnu.* p. 175.

[109] Lachèvre, 'Lettres et notes inédites de Pierre Louÿs'.

[110] *XV lettres de Paul Valéry à Pierre Louÿs (1915–1917)*, Paris, 1926.

[111] See p. 205 above.

[112] Lachèvre, 'Lettres et notes inédites de Pierre Louÿs'.

[113] Cardinne-Petit, p. 184.

[114] *Biblis B* 120.

[115] Cardinne-Petit, p. 43.

[116] Farrère, *Mon ami Pierre Louÿs*, p. 185.

[117] Ibid., p. 183.

[118] *Biblis B* 192 (17 July 1914).
[119] G. Mirandola, *Pierre Louÿs*, Milan, 1974, p. 66.
[120] Lachèvre, *Nouvelles glanes bibliographiques et littéraires*, p. 264.
[121] Cardinne-Petit, p. 217.
[122] Paris, 1957.
[123] *OC* xii, p. xiii.
[124] Farrère, *Mon ami Pierre Louÿs*, p. 186.

Last Years: 1920–1925

[1] *Lettres à F. Lachèvre*, p. 112.
[2] Ibid.
[3] Ibid., p. 113.
[4] Ibid., p. 114.
[5] Lachèvre, *Pierre Louÿs et l'histoire littéraire*, p. 147.
[6] Léautaud, *Journal littéraire*, iv. 37.
[7] Gilles, b. 6 Jan. 1920.
[8] Léautaud, loc. cit.
[9] Cardinne-Petit, *Pierre Louÿs inconnu*, p. 243.
[10] Farrère, *Souvenirs*, p. 79.
[11] Léautaud, iv. 95.
[12] *Les Poëmes de Pierre Louÿs*, i. 159, 149, 151, 163, 162.
[13] Gregh, 'Solitude . . . Fierté . . .', p. 73.
[14] Farrère, *Mon ami Pierre Louÿs*, p. 126.
[15] Cardinne-Petit, p. 248.
[16] The manuscript was published later that year by the Éditions d'art Briant Robert.
[17] Thorhauer, in 'Le Souvenir de Pierre Louÿs'.
[18] J. Cassou, in 'Hommage à Pierre Louÿs', *Comœdia*, 6 June 1925.
[19] Gregh, 'Solitude . . . Fierté . . .', p. 73.
[20] 'Les Obsèques', in 'Hommage à Pierre Louÿs', *Comœdia*, 6 June 1925.
[21] Cardinne-Petit, p. 239.
[22] A. de Monzie, 'D'un filleul de Ronsard . . .', *Le Tombeau de Pierre Louÿs*, p. 16.

Bibliography

WORKS BY PIERRE LOUŸS

BOOKS

Only the first edition of each work is listed. Mention of posthumous volumes is limited to those presenting previously unpublished material.

Astarté, Librairie de l'art indépendant, Paris, 1891 [1892].

Chrysis ou la cérémonie matinale, Librairie de l'art indépendant, Paris, 1893.

Lêda ou la louange des bienheureuses ténèbres, Librairie de l'art indépendant, Paris, 1893.

Les Poésies de Méléagre, Librairie de l'art indépendant, Paris, 1893.

Ariane ou le chemin de la paix éternelle, Librairie de l'art indépendant, Paris, 1894.

La Maison sur le Nil ou les apparences de la vertu, Librairie de l'art indépendant, Paris, 1894.

Scènes de la vie des courtisanes, Librairie de l'art indépendant, Paris, 1894.

Danaë ou le malheur, Mercure de France [Paris], 1895 (off-print of story published in the review, with same pagination but separate cover).

Les Chansons de Bilitis, Librairie de l'art indépendant, Paris, 1895 [1894].

Aphrodite. Mœurs antiques, Société du Mercure de France, Paris, 1896.

Les Chansons de Bilitis, Société du Mercure de France, Paris, 1898 (augmented edition).

Byblis changée en fontaine, Librairie Borel, Paris, 1898.

La Femme et le pantin. Roman espagnol, Société du Mercure de France, Paris, 1898.

Une Volupté nouvelle, Librairie Borel, Paris, 1899.

L'Homme de pourpre, Librairie Borel, Paris, 1901.

Sanguines, Bibliothèque Charpentier, Eugène Fasquelle, Éditeur, Paris, 1903.

Une Enigme littéraire. L'Auteur des 'XV Joyes de Mariage', Paris, 1903 (published privately and anonymously).

Archipel, Bibliothèque Charpentier, Eugène Fasquelle, Éditeur, Paris, 1906.

Les Trois Roses de Marie-Anne, Librairie des Amateurs, Paris, 1909.

Contes choisis, Arthème Fayard, Paris [1911].

Isthi [Éditions Georges Crès et Cie., Paris], 1916 (published anonymously).

Poëtique, Éditions Georges Crès et Cie., Paris, 1917.

Le Crépuscule des nymphes, Éditions Montaigne, Paris, 1925 (contains *Lêda, Ariane, La Maison sur le Nil, Byblis, Danaë*).

Journal inédit, Éditions Excelsior, Paris, 1926 (covers only the period 24 June 1887–16 May 1888).

Poésies, Éditions Georges Crès et Cie., Paris, 1926.

Psyché, suivi de la Fin de Psyché par Claude Farrère, Albin Michel, Paris, 1927.

Poésies nouvelles, Éditions Montaigne, Paris, 1928.

Contes antiques, Éditions du Bois Sacré, Paris, 1929.

Contes choisis, Éditions Georges Crès et Cie., Paris, 1929.

Les Chansons de Bilitis inédites, Mytilène, 1929 (published anonymously).

Journal intime 1882–1891, Éditions Montaigne, Paris, 1929.

Œuvres complètes de Pierre Louÿs, Éditions Montaigne, Paris, 1929–31. 13 vols.: i *Poésies de Méléagre, Mimes des courtisanes*; ii *Les Chansons de Bilitis, Chansons modernes*; iii *Le Crépuscule des nymphes, Lectures antiques*; iv *Aphrodite*; v *La Femme et le pantin, Voyage en Espagne*; vi *Les Aventures du roi Pausole*; vii *Contes, Les Trois Roses de Marie-Anne*; viii *Psyché*; ix *Journal intime 1882–1891*; x *Littérature, Livres anciens, Inscriptions et belles lettres*; xi *Archipel, Dialogue sur la danse*; xii *Poëtique, Théâtre, Projets et fragments, Suite à Poëtique*; xiii *Poésies* (*Premiers vers*; *Astarté*; *Chrysis*; *Stances et poésies diverses*; *Derniers vers*).

Les Chansons secrètes de Bilitis, Marcel Lubineau, Paris [1931] (published anonymously).

Pibrac. Quatrains érotiques, Aux dépens d'un amateur [Paris], 1932 (published anonymously).

La Femme. Trente-neuf poèmes érotiques inédits, A l'enseigne de Bilitis, Mytilène, 1937 [1938].

Broutilles, recueillies par Frédéric Lachèvre, Paris [1938].

Les Poëmes de Pierre Louÿs 1887–1924, ed. Yves-Gérard Le Dantec, 2 vols., A. Michel, Paris, 1945.

(The most comprehensive selection of Louÿs's works in an English translation was the volume brought out in 1932 by the Liveright Publishing Corporation of New York under the title *The Collected Works of Pierre Louÿs*. It contained *Aphrodite, Woman and Puppet, The Songs of Bilitis, The Adventures of King Pausole, The Twilight of the Nymphs, Sanguines,* and *Psyche*. The translations were by Mitchell S. Buck, except that of *Sanguines* which was by James Cleugh.)

CONTRIBUTIONS TO PERIODICALS AND ANTHOLOGIES

(a) *Poetry*

'Présentation au lecteur', *Potache-revue*, 3 Feb. 1889.

'Sérail bleu', *Potache-Revue*, 3 Mar. 1889 (signed: Sully Prudhomme).

'Froissures', *Potache-Revue*, 15 Mar. 1889 (signed: Verlaine).

'L'Effloraison', *Revue d'aujourd'hui*, 25 July 1890.

'Émaux sur or et sur argent. Triptyque': i 'D'or et de sinople'; ii 'De gueules sur argent'; iii 'D'azur sur or', *La Wallonie*, Dec. 1890–Jan. 1891.

'Dernier sonnet pour *L'Idole* d'Albert Mérat' *La Plume*, 15 Dec. 1890 (published anonymously).

'La Vierge: La Nuit sur l'idole', *La Conque*, Mar. 1891 (reprinted in *Astarté* with title 'La Nuit').

'Le Boucoliaste', *La Conque*, Apr. 1891 (signed: Claude Moreau); (reprinted in *Astarté*).

'Les Fleurs sur l'eau qui gyre . . .', *La Conque*, Apr. 1891 (reprinted in *Astarté* with title 'Le Crépuscule de l'eau').

'La Femme qui danse', *La Conque*, May 1891 (reprinted in *Astarté* with title 'La Danseuse').

'Pégase', *La Conque*, May 1891 (signed: Claude Moreau); (reprinted in *Astarté*).

'Le Réveil', *La Conque*, June 1891 (signed: Claude Moreau); (reprinted in *Astarté* with title 'Heure morose').

'Piédestal', *La Conque*, June 1891 (reprinted in *Astarté* with title 'Le Symbole').

'Trouée', *La Wallonie*, June 1891 (reprinted in *Astarté* with title 'Chute de jour').

'Le Stigmate', *La Conque*, July 1891 (reprinted in *Astarté* with title 'Les Stigmates').

'De fleurs', *La Conque*, Sept. 1891 (signed: Claude Moreau); (reprinted in *Astarté* with title 'Les Filles du dieu').

'D'étoiles', *La Conque*, Sept. 1891 (reprinted in *Astarté* with title 'Funérailles').

'A Téodor de W.', *La Conque*, Oct. 1891 (reprinted in *Astarté* with title 'Le Geste de la lance').

'Un Port', *La Conque*, Nov. 1891 (signed: Claude Moreau); (reprinted in *Astarté*).

'La Femme aux paons', *La Conque*, Nov. 1891 (reprinted in *Astarté*).

'Glaucé', *La Conque*, Dec. 1891 (reprinted in *Astarté*).

'Astarté', *La Wallonie*, Jan.–Feb. 1892 (reprinted in *Astarté*).

'Sonnets', *La Conque*, no. 11 [1892] (signed: Claude Moreau); (reprinted in *Astarté* with titles 'Le Retour des nefs' and 'Vers les yeux des sirènes').

'Au Prince Taciturne', *La Conque*, no. 11 [1892] (reprinted in *Astarté*).

'Chrysis', *L'Ermitage*, 31 Jan. 1892.

'Les Aigles', *Floréal*, Mar. 1892 (reprinted in *Astarté*).

'A Paul Ambroise Valéry', *La Syrinx*, May 1892 (also printed in *Astarté*).

'Le Passant'; 'Sonnet pour un éventail'; 'Cléopâtre'; 'L'Iris'; 'La Prairie', *La Wallonie*, July 1892.

'Voix funèbre', *L'Ermitage*, Aug. 1892.

'Hyacinthe! . . .', *Spirit Lamp*, Oxford, 4 May 1893.

'Mise au tombeau', *La Plume*, 15 July 1893.

'Scènes dans la forêt des nymphes'; 'Le Matin' (subsequently retitled 'La Flèche'); 'Le Soir'; 'La Nuit', *La Revue blanche*, Mar. 1894.

'Aquarelles passionnées': i 'La Danse'; ii 'L'Amadzone'; iii 'Le Retour d'Adonis', *Mercure de France*, Apr. 1894.

'L'Aube de la lune', *Mercure de France*, Oct. 1894.

'Hivernales': 'L'Ombre'; 'Les Pêcheurs'; 'Sirène mourante'; 'Jour d'hiver'; 'Envoi'; 'Pour le tombeau de Baudelaire'; 'Pour la stèle de Leconte de Lisle', *La Revue blanche*, Jan. 1895.

'Aphrodite Ouriana', *Arte*, Coimbra, 1895.

'Fleur du mal' ('Pour le tombeau de Baudelaire'), *La Plume*, commemorative number on Baudelaire, 1896.

'Les Hamadryades', *Le Centaure*, ii, 1896.

'Les Petites Faunesses', *L'Image*, Dec. 1896.

'Chansons de Bilitis', *Mercure de France*, Aug. 1897.

'La Chevelure', *L'Image*, Oct. 1897.

'Sonnet adressé à M. Mallarmé le jour où il eut cinquante ans', *Mercure de France*, Oct. 1898.

'A la nymphe de Sumène', *La Vogue*, 15 Oct. 1899.

'Au Prince Taciturne'; 'Pégase'; 'Le Boucoliaste'; 'Chute de jour'; 'Sonnet adressé à M. Mallarmé . . .'; 'Tombeau de Baudelaire'; 'Hamadryade et satyre' ('Hamadryades', II), in A. van Bever and P. Léautaud, *Poètes d'aujourd'hui*, 3 vols., Paris, 1900, i.

'La Nasarde', *La Plume*, 15 Mar. 1902.

'Pégase'; 'Le Boucoliaste'; 'L'Ombre'; 'Sonnet adressé à M. Mallarmé . . .'; 'Pour la stèle de Leconte de Lisle', in G. Walch, *Anthologie des poètes français contemporains*, 3 vols., Paris, 1903, iii.

'Subscriptum tumulo Joannis Secundi', *Les Lettres*, 6 June 1906.

'L'Apogée', *Les Lettres*, 15 May 1907.

'L'Apogée'; 'Au Prince Taciturne'; 'Pégase'; 'Le Boucoliaste'; 'Chute de jour'; 'Sonnet adressé à M. Mallarmé . . .'; 'Tombeau de Baudelaire'; 'Hamadryade et satyre', in A. van Bever and P. Léautaud, *Poètes d'aujourd'hui*, 3 vols., Paris, 1908, ii.

'Prière de l'adolescente', in E. Gaubert, 'Pierre Louÿs', *Mercure de France*, 1 Jan. 1911.

'La Forêt des nymphes', *Vers et prose*, Jan.–Mar. 1912.

'Auprès d'Alger, dans la banlieue . . .'; 'Chrysis à André Walter', *Les Nouvelles littéraires*, 13 June 1925.

'Quelques vers inédits de Pierre Louÿs', *Le Supplément littéraire de*

Paris-Théâtre, 27 June 1925 ('Le Sermon dans la plaine'; 'Dans la forêt où j'ai coutume . . .'; [Le Soir à la campagne]).

'Ambition'; 'Aphrodite'; 'Damon, ce frais début . . .'; 'Le Bruit court sous la cathédrale . . .'; ['Sur une comédienne'], *Le Capitole*, Aug. 1925.

'Gibier divin', in *Le Tombeau de Pierre Louÿs*, Paris, 1925.

'La Mort de Sappho', *Les Nouvelles littéraires*, 27 Feb. 1926.

'Εὐχαρίστως', *Le Manuscrit autographe*, Mar.–Apr. 1926.

'Cher ami . . .', in *Le Souvenir de Pierre Louÿs*, special number of *Mercure de Flandre*, Mar. 1928.

'Lettre à un ami', *Le Rouge et le noir*, May–June 1926 (subsequently reprinted with title 'A Claude Debussy').

'A mon Ami Claude D . . .', *L'Esprit français*, 10 May 1931.

'La Saulaie', *L'Esprit français*, 10 Aug. 1931.

'L'Horizon rouge . . .', in Y.-G. Le Dantec, 'Pierre Louÿs et la genèse du *Pervigilium Mortis*', *Mercure de France*, 15 Dec. 1934.

'Tout rit qui vous approche . . .', *Marianne*, 31 Jan. 1940.

'Elles avaient eu peur . . .', *Heures perdues*, Jan. 1940.

'Perséphone ou Byblis . . .'; 'Tout rit qui vous approche . . .'; 'Thulé verra tes yeux . . .'; 'J'ai la mémoire sûre . . .'; 'Anathème', *Poésie*, Oct. 1941.

'Poèmes inédits', *Les Nouvelles littéraires*, 28 Mar. 1946.

'Un Poème inédit', *Arts et lettres*, Nov. 1946.

(b) Prose

'Le Naturalisme survivant', *Art et critique*, 1 Nov. 1890 (signed: Claude Moreau).

'Notes sur l'Exposition des Indépendants', *La Revue blanche*, Apr. 1892.

'Chrysis' ('Extrait de *La Tragique Histoire de Chrysis, courtisane d'Alexandrie*'), *La Wallonie*, Dec. 1892.

'Chrysis. Acte premier (Fragment)', *La Revue blanche*, July–Aug. 1893.

'Vive de Méléagre'; 'Dix épigrammes choisies', *Mercure de France*, Sept. 1893.

'Apologue qui servira de préface', *La Revue blanche*, May 1894.

'Ariane', *La Revue blanche*, July 1894.

'Les 36 situations dramatiques', *Mercure de France*, Jan. 1895.

'Danaë ou le malheur', *Mercure de France*, July 1895.

'L'Esclavage', *Mercure de France*, Aug. 1895–Jan. 1896.

'Alexandre Dumas fils et les écrivains nouveaux. Enquête'. Reply by Pierre Louÿs, *Mercure de France*, Jan. 1896.

'Préface à *Aphrodite*', *La Revue blanche*, May 1896.

'Byblis ou l'enchantement des larmes', *Le Centaure*, i, 1896.

'Paul Fort', *La Revue blanche*, June 1896.

'Vie de Marie Dupin, maîtresse de Ronsard', *Le Centaure*, ii, 1896.

'Plaidoyer pour la liberté morale', *Mercure de France*, Oct. 1897.

'L'Alsace-Lorraine et l'état actuel des esprits. Enquête'. Reply by Pierre Louÿs, *Mercure de France*, Dec. 1897.

'Enquête sur le roman illustré par la photographie'. Reply by Pierre Louÿs, *Mercure de France*, Jan. 1898.

'La Femme et le pantin', *Le Journal*, 19 May–8 June 1898.

'Lectures antiques', *Mercure de France*, June, July, Aug., Oct. 1898, Jan. 1899 (translations of Aristophanes, Nossis, Pindar, Procopius).

'Chansons des rois mages. Paroles de Henri Heine, musique de Pierre Louÿs', *Mercure de France*, Sept. 1898.

'*Aimienne, ou le détournement de mineure*' (by Jean de Tinan). Preface by Pierre Louÿs, *Mercure de France*, Feb. 1899.

'Une Volupté nouvelle', *Mercure de France*, Feb. 1899.

'Préface aux Mimes des courtisanes', *Mercure de France*, Nov. 1899.

'Les Jeux olympiques', *L'Auto*, 25 Apr. 1900.

'Les Aventures du roi Pausole', *Le Journal*, 20 Mar.–7 May 1900.

'Liberté pour l'amour et le mariage':
   i: *Le Journal*, 24 Nov. 1900;
   ii: 'Histoire d'un fiancé', *Le Journal*, 9 Dec. 1900;
   iii: 'Plaidoyer pour Roméo et Juliette', *Le Journal*, 18 Dec. 1900.

'Les Chercheurs de trésors', *Le Journal*, Jan. 1901.

'L'Homme de pourpre', *Le Journal*, 27 June–1 July 1901.

'L'Isle mystérieuse', *Le Journal*, Oct. 1901.

'Lesbos d'aujourd'hui', *Le Journal*, 5 Nov. 1901.

'Balzac péremptoire ou la fausse Esther', *La Renaissance latine*, 15 May 1902.

'La Ville plus belle que les monuments', *Le Journal*, 19 July 1902.

'La Poésie est une fleur d'Orient . . .', in G. Walch, *Anthologie des poètes français contemporains*, 3 vols., Paris, 1903, iii.

'Les Poèmes de Joannès Meursius', *Revue biblio-iconographique*, Dec. 1903.

'La Statue de la vérité', *Le Journal*, 5 Jan. 1904.

'Le Boulevard', *Le Figaro*, 11 July 1904.

'Un Fragment inédit d'*Aphrodite*', *Vers et prose*, 25 Apr. 1906.

'Benoit de Maillet, romancier', *L'Intermédiaire des chercheurs et des curieux*, Feb. 1907.

'Le Manuscrit mystérieux', *L'Éclair*, 28 Feb. 1907.

'Le Manuscrit mystérieux', *Mercure de France*, 15 Mar. 1907.

'Le Poète Sygognes', *Antée*, 1 May 1907.

'Stérilisation de l'eau chez les anciens Grecs', *Chronique médicale*, 1 Apr. 1908.

'Les Courtisanes de Corinthe', *Le Journal*, 8 Apr. 1908.

'Le Nu au théâtre', *Le Journal*, 27 Apr. 1908.

'Les Courtisanes de Corinthe', *Mercure de France*, 1 May 1908.

'Spondilles, espondilles et ospopondrilles', *Revue des études rabelaisiennes*, vii, 1909.

'Paroles de Verlaine', *Vers et prose*, Sept. 1910.

'Dialogue sur la danse', *Fémina*, Dec. 1910.

'Le Boulevard', *Le Gaulois du dimanche*, 10–11 Dec. 1910.

'Sous la musique que faut-il mettre: de beaux vers, de mauvais, des vers libres, de la prose? Enquête'. Reply by Pierre Louÿs, *Musica*, Mar. 1911.

'Le Poète Antoine du Saix'; 'Un Roman inédit de Restif'; '*Mensa philosophica*, 1509 (Exemplaire de La Monnoye)'; 'La Phisionomie d'Adamant, 1556'; 'Le Comte de Plélo et le régiment de la Calotte', *Revue des livres anciens*, Mar. 1913.

'Raphaël du Petit-Val, imprimeur de Rabelais'; '*Antiperistase, ou contraires différences d'amour* (1603)'; '*Discours prodigieux et véritable d'une fille de chambre, laquelle a produit un monstre après avoir eu la compagnie d'un singe en la ville de Messine*, s.d.'; 'Un Document sur le duc de la Vallière bibliophile'; 'Mesdemoiselles les chevalières de la Tabatière', *Revue des livres anciens*, July 1913.

'La Phrase inoubliable'; 'Une Annotation de Philippe Béroalde sur l'*Hymne* d'Apulée: *Tu quidem sancta*', *Revue des livres anciens*, Dec. 1913.

'Poëtique', *Mercure de France*, 1 June 1916.

'Corneille est-il l'auteur d'Amphitryon?' *L'Intermédiaire des chercheurs et des curieux*, Aug. 1919.

'L'Auteur d'*Amphitryon*', *Le Temps*, 16 Oct. 1919.

'Corneille le grand', *Comœdia*, 24 Oct. 1919.

'Avant de parler', *Comœdia*, 26 Oct. 1919.

'*Les Femmes savantes*', *Comœdia*, 27 Oct. 1919.

'Alceste qui fut Alceste', *Comœdia*, 28 Oct. 1919.

'*L'Imposteur* de Corneille et le *Tartuffe* de Molière', *Comœdia*, 7 Nov. 1919.

'Les Deux Textes de *Psyché*', *Comœdia*, 10 Nov. 1919.

'Un Inédit de Pierre Louÿs: La Maladie de Ronsard', *L'Art et la vie*, winter 1934.

(It is worth pointing out that several of the reviews in which Louÿs published his poems and prose works can today be readily consulted in reprints. Thus Slatkine Reprints of Geneva have brought out reprints of, among others, *Le Centaure, La Conque, L'Ermitage, Revue blanche, Revue d'aujourd'hui*, and *La Wallonie*. The *Mercure de France* is likewise available in reprint.)

DRAMATIC ADAPTATIONS

Marcillat, Paul de, *Aphrodite, conte dramatique en vers tiré du roman de Pierre Louÿs*, Cambrai, 1908.

Louÿs, Pierre and Frondaie, Pierre, 'La Femme et le pantin, pièce en 4 actes et 5 tableaux', *L'Illustration théâtrale*, 11 Feb. 1911.
Louÿs, Pierre and Frondaie, Pierre, *La Femme et le pantin, pièce en quatre actes et cinq tableaux*, Paris, 1911.
Louÿs, Pierre and Noel, Édouard, *Sonnet à une brune, comédie en un acte en prose*, Paris, 1912.
Frondaie, Pierre, *Aphrodite, drame en cinq actes et huit tableaux en vers, d'après le roman de Pierre Louÿs*, Paris, 1914.

PREFACES

Fort, Paul, *Ballades françaises*, Paris, 1897.
Tinan, Jean de, *Aimienne, ou le détournement de mineure*, Paris, 1899.
Peter, René, *La Tragédie de la mort*, Paris, 1900.
Martino, Ferdinand de and Sarwat, Abd. Al-Khálik, *Anthologie de l'amour arabe*, Paris, 1902.
Farrère, Claude, *Fumée d'opium*, Paris, 1904.
Voisins, Gilbert de, *Pour l'amour du laurier*, Paris, 1904.
Gaubert, Ernest, *Les Roses latines*, Paris, 1908.
Merlet, Jean-Louis, *Au seuil des temples*, Paris, 1908.
Quillot, Maurice, *La Fille de l'homme*, Paris, 1914.
Bouchor, Jean, *L'Ironie sentimentale*, Paris, 1924.

GENERAL

Adami, Giuseppe, *Puccini*, Milan, 1935.
Albalat, Antoine, *Souvenirs de la vie littéraire*, Paris, 1920.
—— *Trente ans de Quartier Latin. Nouveaux souvenirs littéraires*, Paris, 1930.
Ambrière, Francis, 'Grandes ventes. Les Livres de Pierre Louÿs', *Les Nouvelles littéraires*, 22 Nov. 1930.
Arthénice, *Le Salon bleu d'Arthénice par son ombre*, Paris, 1912.
Auriant, 'Chrysis et les archéologues', *Mercure de France*, 15 Jan. 1928.
—— 'L'Inspiratrice d'*Aphrodite*', *Mercure de France*, 1 Apr. 1937.
—— 'Les Métamorphoses de Chrysis', *La Guiterne*, July 1937.
—— 'Les Chansons d'*Aphrodite*', *Mercure de France*, 1 Dec. 1937.
—— 'La Tragique Histoire de Chrysis', *Mercure de France*, 1 Jan. 1938.
—— 'Petite histoire littéraire et anecdotes', *Mercure de France*, 15 June 1939.

Barney, Natalie C., *Aventures de l'esprit*, Paris, 1929.
Barre, André, *Le Symbolisme*, Paris, 1912.
Bauër, Gérard, 'Les Délices de Pierre Louÿs', *Écho de Paris*, 13 May 1926.
Baumal, Francis, 'Les Fautes d'orthographe de Molière', *Mercure de France*, 15 Jan. 1920.

Bernard, Suzanne, *Le Poème en prose de Baudelaire jusqu'à nos jours*, Paris, 1959.

Billy, André, *L'Époque 1900*, Paris, 1951.

—— 'Un Intermède dans le purgatoire de Pierre Louÿs', *Le Figaro*, 16 Dec. 1953.

Bonmariage, Sylvain, *Catherine et ses amis*, Gap, 1949.

—— *Mémoires fermés*, Paris, 1951.

Borel, Pierre, 'Pierre Louÿs et Paul Valéry', *Une Semaine dans le monde*, 4 Sept. 1948.

Buenzod, Emmanuel, *Une Époque littéraire: 1890–1900*, Neuchâtel, 1941.

Camacho, M. Dita, *Judith Gautier. Sa vie et son œuvre*, Paris, 1939.

Cardinne-Petit, Robert, *Pierre Louÿs intime. 'Le Solitaire du Hameau'*, Paris, 1942.

—— *Pierre Louÿs inconnu*, Paris, 1948.

—— 'On commémore le 25e anniversaire de la mort de Pierre Louÿs', *Paroles françaises*, 5–11 June 1950.

Carner, Mosco, *Puccini. A Critical Biography*, London, 1958.

Catalogues:

—— *Catalogue de livres anciens, rares et curieux . . . provenant de la bibliothèque de M. Pierre L*****, Librairie H. Leclerc, Paris, 1918.

—— *Manuscrits de Pierre Louÿs et de divers auteurs contemporains*, Librairie L. Carteret, Paris, 1926.

—— *Catalogue de la vente volontaire pour cause de départ au château d'Écrouves près Toul (M.–et–M.), M. et Mme Serrières–Pierre Louÿs, propriétaires*, 30 June 1934.

—— *Importante correspondance autographe inédite de Pierre Louÿs à son frère (1890–1915)*, Librairie Biblis, Paris, 1936.

—— *Importante correspondance autographe inédite de Pierre Louÿs à son frère (1890–1915). Seconde et dernière partie*, Librairie Biblis, Paris, 1937.

—— *Éditions originales romantiques et modernes, importants autographes de Georges Courteline, Gustave Flaubert, Guy de Maupassant, Alfred de Musset, Pierre Louÿs, Paul Valéry, Émile Zola, provenant des collections de M. Victor Sanson. Vente du 25 Juin 1937*, Librairie A. Blaizot et Fils, Paris, 1937.

—— *Livres anciens et modernes. Lettres et manuscrits de Pierre Louÿs*, Librairie C. Coulet et A. Faure, Paris, Catalogue 138, 1974.

Chabanel, F., 'M. Pierre Louÿs intime', *Madame et monsieur*, 29 Apr. 1906.

Champion, Édouard (ed.), *Le Tombeau de Louis Ménard*, Paris, 1902.

Clerc, Charly, *Le Génie du paganisme*, Paris, 1926.

Clive, H. Peter, 'Pierre Louÿs and Oscar Wilde. A Chronicle of their Friendship', *Revue de littérature comparée*, July–Sept. 1969.

—— 'Notes on *La Conque* and on the Early Friendship of Pierre Louÿs and Paul Valéry', *Studi Francesi*, Jan.–Apr. 1974.

Clouard, Henri, *Histoire de la littérature française du symbolisme à nos jours*, 2 vols., Paris, 1947, 1949.

Colette, *Mes apprentissages*, Paris, 1936.

—— *L'Étoile Vesper. Souvenirs*. Paris, 1946.

Cornell, Kenneth, *The Post-Symbolist Period*, New Haven, 1958.

Courtial, Marie-Thérèse, 'L'Érotisme symbolique de Pierre Louÿs. Étude d'*Aphrodite*', unpublished doctoral dissertation, Univ. of Toulouse, 1973.

Crepet, Jacques, 'Miettes baudelairiennes: *Les Œuvres posthumes de Baudelaire*, annotées par Pierre Louÿs', *Mercure de France*, 15 Feb. 1936.

Daudet, Léon, *Souvenirs littéraires*, Paris, 1968.

Debussy, Claude, *Correspondance de Claude Debussy et Pierre Louÿs (1893–1904)*, ed. H. Borgeaud, Paris, 1945.

Décaudin, Michel, *La Crise des valeurs symbolistes*, Toulouse, 1960.

Deffoux, Léon, 'Pierre Louÿs écolier. Sur un exemplaire des *Femmes savantes*', *L'Ami du lettré*, 1929.

—— 'Une Lettre de Pierre Louÿs', *Œuvre*, 2 June 1931.

—— *Le Pastiche littéraire des origines à nos jours*, Paris, 1932.

Delannoy, Marcel, *Honegger*, Paris, 1953.

Delay, Jean, *La Jeunesse d'André Gide*, 2 vols., Paris, 1956–7.

Dérieux, Henry, *La Poésie française contemporaine, 1885–1935*, Paris, 1935.

Descaves, Lucien, *Souvenirs d'un ours*, Paris, 1946.

Desonay, Fernand, *Le Rêve hellénique chez les poètes parnassiens*, Louvain, 1928.

Dietschy, Marcel, *La Passion de Claude Debussy*, Neuchâtel, 1962.

Di Maio, D., 'Pierre Louÿs, Leopardi e il mito di Saffo', in *Letteratura e Critica. Studi in onore di Natalino Sapergno*, Rome, 1975, pp. 803–26.

—— 'Pierre Louÿs in Italia', *Micromégas*, Jan.–Apr. 1975.

Doderet, André, 'Dixième anniversaire: Pierre Louÿs', *Candide*, 6 June 1935.

Doyon, René-Louis, 'Pierre Louÿs ou l'Éloge de la jeunesse', *Livrets du mandarin*, June 1933.

—— *Mémoire d'homme. Souvenirs irréguliers*, Paris, 1953.

Farrère, Claude, 'Pierre Louÿs', *Conferencia*, 5 and 20 Apr. 1928.

—— 'Pierre Louÿs', *Manuscrit autographe*, July–Sept. 1932.

—— *L'Homme seul*, Paris, 1942.

—— *Souvenirs*, Paris, 1953.

—— *Mon ami Pierre Louÿs*, Paris, 1954.

Flers, Robert de, 'Aphrodite est en deuil: Pierre Louÿs est mort hier', *Le Figaro*, 5 June 1925.

Fleury, Robert, 'Junot, Duc d'Abrantès, et Pierre Louÿs. Leur parenté', *Bulletin du bibliophile et du bibliothécaire*, 1962.

—— *Pierre Louÿs et Gilbert de Voisins. Une Curieuse Amitié*, Paris, 1973.

—— 'La Naissance de Pierre Louÿs, *Bulletin des Amis de Pierre Louÿs*, March 1977; 'Erratum', ibid., June 1977.

Fontainas, André, *Mes souvenirs du symbolisme*, Paris, 1928.

Franke, Karl, *Pierre Louÿs*, Bonn, 1937.

Garden, Mary and Biancolli, Louis, *Mary Garden's Story*, London, 1952.

Gaubert, Ernest, *Pierre Louÿs*, Paris, 1904.

—— 'Pierre Louÿs', *Mercure de France*, 1 Jan. 1911.

Germain, André, *Les Fous de 1900*, Paris, 1954.

Gide, André, 'Lettres inédites à Pierre Louÿs', *L'Art et la vie*, autumn 1933.

—— *Prétextes*, Paris, 1943.

—— *André Gide–Paul Valéry. Correspondance 1890–1942*, ed. R. Mallet, Paris, 1955.

—— *Journal 1889–1939*, Bibliothèque de la Pléiade, Paris, 1965.

—— *Si le grain ne meurt*, in *Journal 1939–1949. Souvenirs*, Bibliothèque de la Pléiade, Paris, 1966.

—— 'La Fin d'une amitié. La Dernière Lettre d'André Gide à Pierre Louÿs', *Bulletin des amis d'André Gide*, Apr. 1973.

Gosse, Edmund, 'Some Recent Literature in France', *Contemporary Review*, Dec. 1898.

Goujon, Jean-Paul, *L'Amitié de Pierre Louÿs et de Jean de Tinan*, Reims, 1977.

Gouttenoire de Toury, F., *Poincaré a-t-il voulu la guerre? Poincaré— avec Iswolsky—contre Georges Louis*, Paris, 1920.

Gramont, Elisabeth de, *Les Marroniers en fleurs*, Paris, 1929.

Gregh, Fernand, *L'Age d'or*, Paris, 1947.

—— *L'Age de fer*, Paris, 1956.

Guilbert, Yvette, *Mes lettres d'amour*, Paris, 1933.

Hart-Davis, Rupert (ed.), *The Letters of Oscar Wilde*, London, 1962.

Henriot, Émile, 'Quand Pierre Louÿs parlait de ses livres', *Le Temps*, 16 June 1925.

—— 'Ronsard, Nicandre et Pierre Louÿs', *Le Temps*, 2 March 1926.

—— 'Les Manuscrits de Pierre Louÿs', *Le Temps*, 4 May 1926.

—— *Livres et portraits. Courrier littéraire. Troisième série*, Paris, 1927.

—— 'L'Affaire Corneille et P. Louÿs', *Le Temps*, 21 Nov. 1933.

—— 'Louÿs et Valéry à vingt ans', *Le Temps*, 15 June 1937.

—— *Poètes français de Lamartine à Valéry*, Paris, 1946.

Hérold, A.-Ferdinand, *Portraits du prochain siècle*, Paris, 1894.

Houville, Gérard d', *Poésies*, Paris, 1931.

Hyde, H. Montgomery, *The Trials of Oscar Wilde*, London, 1948.

—— *Famous Trials, Seventh Series: Oscar Wilde*, London, 1962.

Ibrovac, Miodrag, *José-Maria de Heredia*, 2 vols., Paris, 1923.

Iseler, Paul, *Les Débuts d'André Gide vus par Pierre Louÿs*, Paris, 1937.

Jäckel, Kurt, *Richard Wagner in der französischen Literatur*, 2 vols., Breslau, 1931–2.

Jaloux, Edmond, *Souvenirs sur Henri de Régnier*, Paris, 1941.

Jammes, Francis, *Mémoires*, 3 vols., Paris, 1921–3.

Judet, Ernest, *Georges Louis*, Paris, 1925.

Lachèvre, Frédéric, *Pierre Louÿs et l'histoire littéraire. Lettres à Frédéric Lachèvre (1907–1921)* [Paris], 1925; *Supplément (1919–1921)* [Paris], 1928.

—— *Pierre Louÿs et l'histoire littéraire* [Paris], 1928.

—— 'Lettres inédites de Pierre Louÿs', *Manuscrit autographe*, Sept.–Oct. 1929.

—— 'Lettres et notes inédites de Pierre Louÿs', *Mercure de France*, 15 Oct. 1932.

—— *Poésies de Héliette de Vivonne . . . suivies de douze lettres inédites de Pierre Louÿs non envoyées à leurs destinataires*, Paris, 1932.

—— *Nouvelles glanes bibliographiques et littéraires*, Paris, 1933.

Léautaud, Paul, *Journal littéraire*, 19 vols., Paris, 1956–66.

Lebey, André, *Jean L. de Tinan*, Paris, 1921.

—— *Jean de Tinan. Souvenirs et correspondance*, Paris, 1922.

—— 'D'*Astarté* au *Roi Pausole*', *L'Éclair*, 21 Jan. 1922.

Le Cardonnel, Georges and Vellay, Charles, *La Littérature contemporaine (1905)*, Paris, 1905.

Leclercq, Paul, *Paradis perdus*, Paris, 1931.

Le Dantec, Yves-Gérard, 'Pierre Louÿs poète', *Les Nouvelles littéraires*, 28 Mar. 1946.

—— 'Les Premières Éditions de l'*Aphrodite* de Pierre Louÿs', *Le Courrier des arts graphiques*, xxxii, 1947.

Lefèvre, Frédéric, *Entretiens avec Paul Valéry*, Paris, 1926.

Lhombreaud, Roger, 'Une Amitié anglaise de Pierre Louÿs. Onze lettres inédites à John Gray', *Revue de littérature comparée*, July–Sept. 1953.

—— 'The Poetical Friendship of John Gray and Pierre Louÿs', in *Two Friends: John Gray and André Raffalovich: Essays biographical and critical*, ed. Brocard Sewell, Aylesford, 1963.

Lockspeiser, Edward, 'Neuf Lettres de Pierre Louÿs à Debussy (1894–1898)', *Revue de musicologie*, July–Dec. 1962.
—— *Debussy. His Life and Mind*, 2 vols., London, 1962–5.
Lorrain, Jean, *Poussières de Paris*, Paris, 1902.
—— *La Ville empoisonnée. Pall-Mall Paris*, Paris, 1936.
Louis, Georges, *Carnets*, 2 vols., Paris, 1926.
Louÿs, Pierre, 'Quelques Lettres à A[ndré] G [ide] ', *La Nouvelle Revue française*, Nov.–Dec. 1929.
—— 'Une Lettre inédite de P. Louÿs', *L'Art et la vie*, winter 1934.

Mallarmé, Stéphane, *Correspondance*, ed. H. Mondor and L. J. Austin, Paris, 1959 ff. (in progress).
Marek, Georges R., *Puccini*, London, 1952.
Martin-Mamy, *Les Nouveaux Païens*, Paris, 1914.
Mauclair, Camille, *Le Soleil des morts*, Paris, 1898.
—— *Servitude et grandeur littéraires*, Paris, 1922.
Maurras, Charles ['Criton'], 'Ce qu'il importe de distinguer: Pierre Louÿs et la Légion d'Honneur', *Action française*, 4 Jan. 1910.
Mazel, Henri, *Aux beaux temps du symbolisme, 1890–1895*, Paris, 1943.
Merrill, Stuart, 'Souvenirs sur le symbolisme', *La Plume*, 1 Feb. 1904.
—— *Prose et vers. Œuvres posthumes*, Paris, 1925.
Mirandola, Giorgio, 'André Gide e Pierre Louÿs: fasti e miseri di un' amicizia sbagliata', *Studi Francesi*, Sept.–Dec. 1971.
—— *Pierre Louÿs*, Milan, 1974.
—— 'Pierre Louÿs e André Doderet (con lettere inedite)', *Studi Francesi*, Sept.–Dec. 1975.
Mondor, Henri, *Vie de Mallarmé*, Paris, 1941.
—— *Les Premiers Temps d'une amitié: André Gide et Paul Valéry*, Monaco, 1947.
—— 'Le Premier Entretien Mallarmé–Valéry', *Paul Valéry vivant*, Marseille, 1946.
—— 'Paul Valéry, Pierre Louÿs et André Gide', *Les Nouvelles littéraires*, 4 Apr. 1946.
—— 'Les Premiers Vers d'André Gide', *Le Figaro littéraire*, 11 Sept. 1954.
—— *Précocité de Valéry*, Paris, 1957.
Monod, Julien-Pierre, *Regard sur Valéry*, Lausanne, 1947.

Niederauer, David J., 'The Life and Works of Pierre Louÿs', unpublished Ph.D. dissertation, Univ. of California, 1960.

Ojetti, Ugo, 'Souvenirs sur Pierre Louÿs', *Les Nouvelles littéraires*, 28 Jan. 1928.
—— *Cose Viste*, Florence, 1960.

Peter, René, *Claude Debussy*, Paris, 1944.

Pitollet, Camille, 'Pierre Louÿs et l'Espagne', *Moniteur universel*, Nov. 1931.

Place, Jean-Michel and Vasseur, André, *Bibliographie des revues et journaux littéraires des XIXe et XXe siècles*, Paris, 1973 ff. (in progress).

Polaire [Émilie-Marie Bouchard], *Polaire par elle-même*, Paris, 1933.

Psichari, Jean, 'Le Vers français aujourd'hui et les poètes décadents', *Revue bleue*, 6 June 1891.

Puccini, Giacomo, *Epistolario*, ed. G. Adami, Milan, 1928.

—— *Letters of Giacomo Puccini*, ed. G. Adami, trans. Ena Malin, London, 1931.

Raynaud, Ernest, *La Mêlée symboliste. 1ère partie: 1870–1890*, Paris, 1918.

—— *La Mêlée symboliste. 2e partie: 1890–1900*, Paris, 1920.

—— *En marge de la mêlée symboliste*, Paris, 1936.

Régnier, Henri de, *Lettres à André Gide (1891–1911)*, ed. D. J. Niederauer, Geneva, 1972.

Retté, Adolphe, *Le Symbolisme. Anecdotes et souvenirs*, Paris, 1903.

Rougemont, E. de, 'Portraits graphologiques. Pierre Louÿs', *Mercure de France*, Dec. 1912.

Royère, Jean, 'La Lettre de Pierre Louÿs à Paul Valéry', *Manuscrit autographe*, May–June 1931.

—— 'Glose sur les manuscrits importants inédits de Pierre Louÿs', *Manuscrit autographe*, Nov.–Dec. 1931.

—— 'Glose sur les versions inédites de *Les Chansons de Bilitis*', *Manuscript autographe*, Apr.–June 1932.

—— *Le Point de vue de Sirius*, Paris, 1935.

Ryals, Clyde de L., 'Oscar Wilde's *Salome*', *Notes and Queries*, Feb. 1959.

Samain, Albert, *Des lettres 1887–1900*, ed. J. Monval, Paris, 1933.

Schenouda, Horus W., 'Essai sur la vie et l'œuvre de Pierre Louÿs' unpublished doctoral dissertation, Univ. of Paris, 1947.

Schwab, Raymond, 'Hugo annoté par Pierre Louÿs', *Marges*, 10 July 1935.

Segard, Achille, *Les Voluptueux et les hommes d'action*, Paris, 1900.

Seligman, Vincent, *Puccini among Friends*, London, 1938.

Sherard, Robert H., *The Real Oscar Wilde* [London], 1915.

Sicard, Claude, 'Jean de Tinan. Lettres à Madame Bulteau', unpublished doctoral dissertation, Un. of Toulouse, 1968.

Swinburne, Algernon C., *Letters*, ed. Cecil Y. Lang, 6 vols., New Haven, 1959–62.

Tarquini, Tarquinia Zandonai, *Da 'Via del Paradiso al No 1'*, Rovereto, 1955.

Tarquini, Vittoria B., *Riccardo Zandonai*, Milan, 1951.

Valéry, Paul, *XV lettres de Paul Valéry a Pierre Louÿs (1915–1917)*, Paris, 1926.

—— 'Lettres de jeunesse à Pierre Louÿs', *L'Art et la vie*, winter 1934.

—— *Lettres à quelques-uns*, Paris, 1952.

Varrin, René, *Anthologie de l'érotisme. De Pierre Louÿs à Jean-Paul Sartre*, Paris, 1948.

Vasseur, André, *Collection André Vasseur*, Paris, 1974.

Virard, Jean ,'L'*Aphrodite* de Pierre Louÿs devant les tribunaux turcs', *Ordre*, 15 Jan. 1940.

Voisins, Gilbert de, 'In Praise of Pierre Louÿs, *Saturday Review*, 29 Oct. 1898.

—— *Sentiments*, Paris, 1905.

Wilamowitz-Moellendorff, Ulrich von, *Sappho und Simonides. Untersuchungen über griechische Lyriker*, Berlin, 1913.

COMMEMORATIVE VOLUMES AND REVIEW NUMBERS

'Pierre Louÿs. L'Homme et l'œuvre', *Le Figaro, Supplément littéraire*, 13 June 1925:
Fernand Gregh, 'Pierre Louÿs'; François Montel, 'Pierre Louÿs, bibliophile'.—'Le Souvenir de Pierre Louÿs': Jean Cassou, Elisabeth de Clermont-Tonnerre, Claude Farrère, Ernest Gaubert, Harlette Fernand Gregh, A.-Ferdinand Hérold, André Lebey, Rachilde, Jean Thorhauer, Alfred Vallette.

'Hommage à Pierre Louÿs', *Les Nouvelles littéraires*, 13 June 1925:
Jacques-Émile Blanche, 'La Jeunesse de Pierre Louÿs. Gide et Louÿs à l'École alsacienne. Louÿs et Claude Debussy'; J. Canqueteau, '*La Conque* et *le Centaure*'; Jean Cassou, 'Les Derniers Travaux'; Pierre Frondaie, 'La première et la dernière entrevue'; Fernand Gregh, 'Pierre Louÿs. Œuvre classique, vie romantique'; Edmond Jaloux, 'L'Esprit des livres. Pierre Louÿs'; Paul Léautaud, 'Mes souvenirs de Pierre Louÿs'; André Lebey, 'Tel qu'en lui-même enfin . . .'; Paul Leclercq, 'Les Deux Pierre Louÿs'; Maurice Martin du Gard, 'Mais pour ceux-là qui respectent les nuits . . .'; Paul Valéry, 'Pierre Louÿs (1870–1925)'.

'Pierre Louÿs. L'Écrivain, le poète, l'homme', *Le Capitole*, 1925:
Anne Armandie, 'L'Œuvre de Pierre Louÿs'; Aurel, 'Pierre Louÿs

et la femme'; Robert Cardinne-Petit, 'Auprès de Pierre Louÿs`; André Doderet, 'Pierre Louÿs'; Claude Farrère, 'Pierre Louÿs'; Fernand Gregh, 'Pierre Louÿs mystique de l'art'; Frédéric Lachèvre, 'Pierre Louÿs bibliophile et bibliographe'; André Lebey, 'Pierre Louÿs et le Quartier Latin'; Georges Lecomte, 'Le Poète Pierre Louÿs'; Guillot de Saix, 'Pierre Louÿs et Pierre Corneille'; Thierry Sandre, 'Quelques anecdotes et souvenirs'; Jean Thorhauer, 'Un Matin . . .';—'Des souvenirs . . . des témoignages': Elisabeth de Clermont–Tonnerre, Curnonsky, Lucie Delarue-Mardrus, Franc-Nohain, Henry Kistemaeckers, Camille Mauclair, Francis de Miomandre, Georges Montorgueil, Anna de Noailles, François Porché, Marcel Prévost, Louis Thomas.

Le Tombeau de Pierre Louÿs, Éditions du Monde Moderne, Paris, 1925: Jacques-Émile Blanche, 'Au-dessus de son temps'; Kh. Nizam El Moulk, 'De lourdes lueurs asiatiques . . .'; Claude Farrère, 'Il est mort . . .'; Fernand Gregh, 'Solitude . . . Fierté . . .'; Émile Henriot, 'Quand il parlait de ses livres . . .'; André Lebey, 'Le Captif immortel . . .'; Maurice Martin du Gard, 'Ce grand faune endormi . . .'; Anatole de Monzie, 'D'un filleul de Ronsard . . .'; Thierry Sandre, 'Le Plus Pur Silence . . .'; Franz Toussaint, 'Et advolvit lapidem adostium sepulchri . . .'; Paul Valéry, 'Que voulez-vous que je dise . . .'.

'Le Souvenir de Pierre Louÿs', *Mercure de Flandre*, Mar. 1928: Maurice Beaubourg, 'Souvenirs sur Pierre Louÿs'; Sylvain Bonmariage, 'La Leçon de Pierre Louÿs'; Nicolas Bourgeois, 'Pierre Louÿs—Post scriptum aux "Souvenirs"'; Jean Cassou, 'La Querelle Corneille–Molière'; René Derville, 'Autour d'*Astarté*'; Fagus, 'Le Huguenot Taxis grand eunuque du roi'; André Fontainas, 'Pierre Louÿs—un peu de sa figure'; Gaston Gérardot, 'Pour le tombeau de Pierre Louÿs'; Armand Godoy, 'Pierre Louÿs et J.-M. de Heredia'; Fernand Gregh, 'Sur Pierre Louÿs'; A.-Ferdinand Hérold, '*Aphrodite*'; André Jeanroy, 'La Poésie de Pierre Louÿs'; André Lebey, 'Le Mythe d'Orphée'; Fernand Mazade, 'A Pierre Louÿs'; Camille Mauclair, 'Hommage'; Jean Monval, 'Pierre Louÿs et François Coppée'; Jules Mouquet, 'Les Traductions de Pierre Louÿs'; Georges Normandy, 'Pierre Louÿs et Jean Lorrain'; Jean Royère, 'Pierre Louÿs homme de lettres'; Franz Toussaint, 'Lettre à Pierre Louÿs'; Théo Varlet, 'Hommage à Pierre Louÿs'.

NOTE
The 'Association des Amis de Pierre Louÿs' founded in 1977 has begun publication of a quarterly *Bulletin* and an annual *Cahier*.

Index

DATE DUE